TYRANNY OF THE WEAK

Studies of the Weatherhead East Asian Institute, Columbia University

The Weatherhead East Asian Institute is Columbia University's center for research, publication, and teaching on modern and contemporary East Asia regions. The Studies of the Weatherhead East Asian Institute were inaugurated in 1962 to bring to a wider public the results of significant new research on modern and contemporary East Asia.

TYRANNY OF THE WEAK

North Korea and the World, 1950–1992

Charles K. Armstrong

CORNELL UNIVERSITY PRESS   ITHACA AND LONDON

First published 2013 by Cornell University Press

Printed in the United States of America

Library of Congress Cataloging-in-Publication Data

Armstrong, Charles K., author.
    Tyranny of the weak : North Korea and the world, 1950–1992 / Charles K. Armstrong.
        pages cm. — (Studies of the Weatherhead East Asian Institute, Columbia University)
    Includes bibliographical references and index.
    ISBN 978-0-8014-5082-2 (cloth : alk. paper)
    1. Korea (North)—Foreign relations. 2. Korea (North)—Politics and government. I. Title. II. Series: Studies of the Weatherhead East Asian Institute, Columbia University.
    DS935.65.A76   2013
    951.9304'3—dc23   2013000079

Cornell University Press strives to use environmentally responsible suppliers and materials to the fullest extent possible in the publishing of its books. Such materials include vegetable-based, low-VOC inks and acid-free papers that are recycled, totally chlorine-free, or partly composed of nonwood fibers. For further information, visit our website at www.cornellpress.cornell.edu.

Cloth printing   10 9 8 7 6 5 4 3 2 1

Contents

Acknowledgments

Many individuals and institutions helped in the research and writing of this book. Roger Haydon proved himself once again to be a fine and patient editor, shepherding the project through from beginning to end. A Smith-Richardson Junior Faculty Research Grant funded the initial research, and I would like to thank the Smith-Richardson Foundation and especially Allan Song for their generous support. A German Academic Exchange Service (DAAD) grant supported my visit to the German Foreign Ministry Archives in Berlin. A subsequent trip to Berlin for research in the Federal Archives, as well as research visits to Washington, DC; Seoul; Beijing; Budapest; Vienna; Addis Ababa; St. Petersburg; and Pyongyang, were made possible by faculty research grants from Columbia University's Weatherhead East Asian Institute. Resident scholars in all of these cities were extremely helpful and accommodating hosts. My Columbia colleague Mahmood Mamdani gave me invaluable advice for my visit to Ethiopia. In Vienna, Professor Ruediger Frank of Vienna University coorganized a fascinating, two-day discussion with former diplomats and Korea specialists from various East European countries. Dr. Frank was also my guide during my first research trip to Berlin, and I deeply appreciate his sharing with me his contacts in Europe and his many profound insights into North Korean history, politics, and economy. The Cold War International History Project (CWIHP) and the North Korea International Documentation Project (NKIDP) of the Woodrow Wilson International Center for Scholars have added enormously to our knowledge of North Korea in recent years by bringing to light relevant documents from Russia, Eastern Europe, China, and elsewhere, as well as organizing conferences and workshops on North Korea and the Cold War. I thank especially CWIHP director Christian Ostermann and James Person of NKIDP for their pioneering work in this area, without which this book would not have been possible.

I have learned a great deal from the perspectives and research materials shared with me by scholars and experts around the world, including Chen Jian, Karoly Fendler, Kim Dong-gil, Kim Seongbo, Heonik Kwon, Sergei Kurbanov, Andrei Lankov, Hans Maretzki, Helga Picht, Sonia Ryang, Bernd Schaefer, and Shen Zhihua, among others. I owe a special thanks to the late Chris Marker, who passed away shortly before this book went to press, for permission to reproduce photographs from his book *Coréennes* and for spending a day with me discussing

North Korea, film, photography, socialism, and many other matters over some of the best vodka to be had in Paris.

At various stages of this project's development, parts of the book were presented in seminars and other forums at universities in the United States and abroad, including Columbia, Harvard, Yale, Vanderbilt, George Washington University, the Naval War College, University of Washington in Seattle, University of Toronto, St. Thomas University, Hanyang University, East China Normal University, and Renmin University. I am grateful to my hosts and audiences at all these presentations for their valuable feedback. My colleagues and students at Columbia have provided encouragement, criticism, and above all an unparalleled environment of intellectual inquiry and stimulation. Two graduate research assistants, Dajeong Chung and Piri Gordon, helped with research in Korean and German sources, respectively. Caroline Marsburger aided my research in the German Federal Archives in Berlin.

As always, my greatest thanks go to my wife, Elia, and to our children, Mira and Sara, whose love, understanding, and good humor have constantly sustained and inspired me.

An earlier version of chapter 2 appeared as "'Fraternal Socialism': The International Reconstruction of North Korea," *Cold War History* 5, no. 2 (May 2005): 161–87 (by permission of Taylor & Francis, www.tandfonline.com), and of chapter 5 as "*Juche* and North Korea's Global Aspirations," Woodrow Wilson International Center for Scholars, North Korea International Documentation Project, Working Paper No. 1 (February 2009).

Korean terms have been transliterated according to the McCune-Reischauer romanization system, except for words with commonly accepted alternative spellings (e.g., Kim Il Sung, Juche). Unless otherwise noted, all translations from Korean, German, Chinese, Russian, Japanese, French, and Spanish are my own.

Introduction

NORTH KOREA IN
THE INTERNATIONAL SYSTEM

Certain places in the world act as fractures in the international system, points of
contact between the tectonic plates of historical change that erupt periodically
into conflicts that spread beyond the region to draw in the Great Powers, and
which remain in constant tension even in times of relative peace. In modern Europe, the Balkans are one such place, where local and seemingly trivial disputes
over territory and ethnicity triggered the First World War at the beginning of
the twentieth century, and where the disintegrating state of Yugoslavia brought
a more contained war to the continent at century's end.[1] During the Cold War,
there were numerous places where local conflicts drew in—or were provoked
by—the superpowers, whether directly or indirectly: Indochina, Cuba, Angola,
the Horn of Africa, and Afghanistan, to name only a few. In most of these cases,
these conflicts subsided and the areas retreated into relative obscurity and neglect. But in some cases, conflict has appeared endemic and irresolvable, outlast-
ing the Cold War that fueled so many clashes in the second half of the twentieth
century, and posing a perennial danger of regional or even global warfare. A
combination of bitter and ongoing local disputes, strategic location, and rivalry
among the major powers has made these places sites of systemic conflict. One
such place is the Middle East; another is the Korean Peninsula.

---

1. As Mark Mazower points out, "the Balkans" as a metaphor for endemic ethnic and territorial
conflict is a European term of fairly recent vintage, although built on earlier images of the region.
Mazower, *The Balkans: A Short History* (New York: Modern Library, 2000), xxxi. In other words, the
Balkans as "the Balkans" is a product of modern history, not of eternal enmities.

In the first two decades after the Cold War, the Middle East (specifically Iraq) and the Korean Peninsula (specifically North Korea) were the two places where the world's remaining superpower, the United States, came most consistently to the point of military conflict. This occurred in both places, almost simultaneously, on two occasions: the Gulf War of 1990–91, followed by a near-war over North Korea's nuclear program in 1993–94; and the Iraq War of 2003, which occurred in the midst of a second North Korean nuclear crisis that began in October 2002. Of course, in many respects the origins, nature, and (potential) resolution of these regional-cum-global conflicts are vastly different. The post–Cold War struggles in the Middle East, and the Persian Gulf in particular, are related to strategic natural resources, disputed postcolonial national boundaries, and religion, none of which have much relevance in Korea and Northeast Asia. The Middle East has been explosive, the site of continuous low-intensity warfare and terrorism when not embroiled in outright war; conflict on the Korean Peninsula, since the Korean War armistice of July 1953, has been much more contained, despite the high level of constant tension. Nevertheless, whether as "rogue states" or members of the "axis of evil," Iraq and North Korea tended to be viewed by post–Cold War US policymakers as regimes beyond the pale of normal diplomacy, oppressive toward their own people and threatening to the stability of the international system.[2] The two regimes were certainly linked in the minds of US political leaders and in the American media, if not in the states of concern themselves.

As of May 2003, the Iraqi regime of Saddam Hussein ceased to exist, toppled by a US-led invasion. But the Democratic People's Republic of Korea (DPRK, North Korea), despite acute poverty, isolation, and a political system that seemed a throwback to the Stalinist 1950s, remained in place.[3] In 2012, more than twenty years after the collapse of the Soviet Union, the DPRK celebrated the hundredth anniversary of founding leader Kim Il Sung's birth, under the new leadership of Kim's grandson, Kim Jong Un. The world had changed dramatically, but North Korea, it seemed, had not. This book is about North Korea's troubled and troubling place in the world during the Cold War era, which set the pattern by which North Korea still deals with the world in the twenty-first century. From a North Korean perspective, in fact, there was not one Cold War, but three: the global

---

2. North Korea and Saddam Hussein's Iraq were the only "evil regimes" singled out by name in the Bush administration's major policy statement of September 2002, *The National Security Strategy of the United States of America* (Falls Village, CT: Winterhouse Editions, 2002), section 5.

3. As I have argued elsewhere, the survivability of the North Korea regime is partly the result of the way the DPRK was founded, which was much less along the lines of a Soviet "satellite" than is commonly assumed. See Charles K. Armstrong, *The North Korean Revolution, 1945–1950* (Ithaca: Cornell University Press, 2003).

Cold War between the United States and its allies and the Soviet bloc; the Sino-Soviet rivalry from the late 1950s to the end of the 1980s, which was more localized but at times at least as bitter as the US-Soviet conflict; and the intense rivalry between North and South Korea. After the 1953 armistice ended the fighting in the Korea War, the two Koreas expressed their mutual animosity through military buildup, threats and propaganda, espionage and diplomatic competition, rather than all-out war. In that sense, inter-Korean relations were very much the global Cold War in microcosm. North Korea's foreign relations were to a great extent a reflection of these three Cold Wars. The last of these three, the inter-Korean conflict, still has not ended.

At a more general level, this book explores the role of small states, or "weak actors," in the modern system of interstate relations, of which North Korea is one of the most striking examples in the period since World War II. Much of the vast literature in history and political science on the interactions of Great Powers assumes, as Thucydides famously remarked, that "the strong do what they have the power to do and the weak accept what they have to accept."[4] Much less explored is the ability of certain small or weak states to resist and even manipulate the more powerful.[5] In her study of the power of weak states in the international system, Annette Baker Fox argues that such ability depends above all on "the existence of competition among the great states."[6] Using the examples of Turkey, Finland, Norway, Sweden, and Spain in World War II, Fox suggests that the success of weak states to resist the pressure of great powers even in times of crisis "lay in their capacity to convince the great-power belligerents that the costs of using coercion against them would more than offset the gains."[7] By threatening either to deprive a Great Power of something the latter values, invoking retaliation by a competing Great Power, or shifting allegiance to the other side, a weak state is able to maintain its neutrality in Great Power conflict while gaining economic, military, or other benefits from one or more of the competing powers. This describes almost perfectly North Korea's position in the Sino-Soviet conflict of the late 1950s

---

4. Thucydides, *The Peloponnesian Wars*, trans. Rex Warner (New York: Penguin Books, 1972), 402.

5. Among the more important studies of this subject in the political science literature are Robert L. Rothstein, *Alliances and Small Powers* (New York: Columbia University Press, 1968); David Vital, *The Survival of Small States: Studies in Small Power/Great Power Conflict* (London: Oxford University Press, 1971); Michael Handel, *Weak States in the International System* (London: Frank Cass, 1981); Hans H. Indorf, *Strategies for Small-State Survival* (Kuala Lumpur: Institute of Strategic and International Studies, 1985); Sheila Harden, ed., *Small Is Dangerous: Micro States in a Macro World* (New York: St. Martin's Press, 1985); Colin Clarke and Tony Payne, eds., *Politics, Security, and Development in Small States* (London: Allen and Unwin, 1987); and Jeanne A.K. Hey, ed., *Small States in World Politics: Explaining Foreign Policy Behavior* (Boulder, CO: Lynne Reiner, 2006).

6. Annette Baker Fox, *The Power of Small States: Diplomacy in World War II* (Chicago: University of Chicago Press, 1959), 8.

7. Ibid., 9.

to the late 1980s, when the DPRK was able consistently to extract economic, political, and security concessions from both China and the USSR without fully siding with either. What is particularly interesting about the North Korean case, however, is that the DPRK was able to continue extracting concessions even after the end of Cold War from the new Great Power rivals in the East Asian region, China and the United States.[8]

A shift of focus from Great Power conflict to the role of smaller actors in the international system might give us a very different view of recent international history. In the field of Cold War studies, the political scientist Tony Smith has called this a "pericentric" view—that is, a view from the periphery, rather than from the perspective of the superpowers or from the central Cold War conflict in Europe.[9] The Cold War cannot be explained by US-Soviet rivalry alone. Certain local actors—including North and South Korea, East and West Germany, Cuba, Israel, the Mujahadin in Afghanistan, the Solidarity movement in Poland, and many others—were not merely manipulated objects, but active subjects shaping, exacerbating, prolonging, or helping to terminate the Cold War at the local and even global levels. North Korea was one of the first such cases of this phenomenon of "tail wagging the dog" or "tyranny of the weak" in the Cold War. It is now clear that the impetus for the North Korean attack on the South in June 1950 came not from Stalin or Mao but from Kim Il Sung.[10] Far from the Kremlin determining every action in the Communist bloc, it is increasingly evident that Soviet control was much weaker than previously thought even with regard to East European satellites, let alone distant and highly nationalistic third-world regimes in Asia and Africa.[11] Moscow's power over its "empire" was usually neither very advantageous to the USSR—economically, it was almost always a drain— nor very effective in cultivating local support. And part of the Soviet Union's

---

8. By the late 1990s, the DPRK was the largest recipient of US economic aid in East Asia—despite the fact that the two countries lacked diplomatic relations and were still technically at war with each other. China has long been North Korea's largest aid donor overall.

9. Tony Smith, "New Bottles for New Wine: A Pericentric Framework for the Study of the Cold War," *Diplomatic History* 24, no. 4 (fall 2000): 567–91.

10. The Soviet documents on the Korean War have yet to be synthesized into a major study of the subject, although there have been some important steps in that direction. In English see especially Alexandre Mansourov, "Communist War Coalition Formation and the Origins of the Korean War," Ph.D. diss., Columbia University, 1997, as well as the work by Kathryn Weathersby, Shen Zhihua, Kim Donggil, and others published through the Cold War International History Project and its spin-off, the North Korea International Documentation Project. The definitive studies in Chinese and Russian are, respectively, Shen Zhihua, *Chaoxian Zhanzheng Jiemi* [Secrets of the Korean War Revealed] (Hong Kong: Tiandi chuban youxian gongsi, 1995); and A. V. Torkunov, *Zagadochnaia voina: Koreiskii konflikt 1950–1953 gg.* [Secret War: The Korean Conflict, 1950–1953] (Moscow: Rosspyen, 2000).

11. Randall W. Stone, *Satellites and Commissars: Strategy and Conflict in the Politics of Soviet-Bloc Trade* (Princeton: Princeton University Press, 1996); Sheldon Anderson, *A Cold War in the Soviet Bloc: Polish–East German Relations, 1945–1962* (Boulder, CO: Westview Press, 2001); Margot Light, ed. *Troubled Friendships: Moscow's Third World Ventures* (London: British Academic Press, 1993).

ineffectiveness abroad and vulnerability to local resistance was the crude and transparent nature of Soviet attempts at domination. If the Soviet Union was quasi-imperial, the United States was (for the most part) postimperial—much more subtle and effective in asserting and maintaining its global hegemony.[12] For reasons this book will explore, the DPRK has successfully resisted, at great cost to the North Korean people, both types of imperial formation. North Korea's ability to survive for six decades in a precarious international position, extracting maximum concessions from its major allies (and occasionally even its enemies) despite its objective weakness, has in its own way been a remarkable achievement. Yet very few works have attempted to explain North Korea's foreign relations in an extended and systematic fashion. Some of the political science literature has been good on comparative foreign relations of the two Koreas or specific aspects of North Korean foreign policy.[13] There has also been some solid work on North Korea's domestic society and politics, although little by historians, and none that have taken full advantage of post-Soviet archives.[14] In fact, no book-length, single-authored study of North Korean foreign relations has appeared in English since the 1970s.[15]

The structure of this book is chronological, beginning with the outbreak of the Korean War and ending with the collapse of East European communist states and the Soviet Union in 1989–91 and the two Koreas' joint entry into the United Nations in 1992. The year 1972 is roughly the top of the arc in the "rise and fall" of North Korea in the international system. Until the early 1970s, the DPRK was deeply embedded in the socialist family of states and had few formal relations outside that bloc. But, while North Korea was more isolated diplomatically than South Korea, it was probably ahead of South Korea economically up to that point. With US-China rapprochement in the early 1970s, the global Cold War became less bipolar and more multidirectional, and this had important effects

---

12. Martin Shaw, "Post-Imperial and Quasi-Imperial: State and Empire in the Global Era," *Millennium: Journal of International Studies* 34, no. 2 (2002): 327–36. The United States was also subject to manipulation by its Cold War "clients," and South Korea at various times has practiced its own "tyranny of the weak" vis-à-vis the United States.

13. See, among others, B.K. Gills, *Korea versus Korea: A Case of Contested Legitimacy* (London: Routledge, 1996); and Scott Snyder, *Negotiating on the Edge: North Korean Negotiating Behavior* (Washington, DC: United States Institute of Peace Press, 1999).

14. For example, Adrian Buzo, *The Guerrilla Dynasty: Politics and Leadership in North Korea* (Boulder, CO: Westview Press, 1999); Kong Dan Oh and Ralph C. Hassig, *North Korea through the Looking Glass* (Washington, DC: Brookings Institution Press, 2000); and Balazs Szalontai, *Kim Il Sung in the Khrushchev Era: Soviet-DPRK Relations and the Roots of North Korean Despotism, 1953–1964* (Stanford: Stanford University Press, 2006).

15. Chin O. Chung, *Pyongyang between Peking and Moscow: North Korea's Involvement in the Sino-Soviet Dispute, 1958–1975* (Tuscaloosa: University of Alabama Press, 1978); Wayne Kiyosaki, *North Korean Foreign Relations: The Politics of Accommodation, 1945–1975* (New York: Praeger, 1976).

on the two Koreas. First, Seoul and Pyongyang entered into official dialogue for the first time since the Korean War and announced a joint communiqué on inter-Korean relations in July 1972. Second, the two Koreas dropped their policies of refusing to allow other countries to recognize both Seoul and Pyongyang, and engaged in competition for diplomatic ties around the world, especially among newly independent countries in Asia and Africa.

In the 1970s North Korea reached parity with the South in diplomatic relations, and for many postcolonial countries North Korea was a more attractive model of independent economic development than was South Korea. North Korea's global position reached a plateau at that point and would soon face a rapid fall. In the 1980s South Korea leapt far ahead of the North economically, and by the 1990s, after the collapse of North Korea's socialist allies in Eastern Europe and the Soviet Union, the DPRK had become an economic basket case and international pariah. North Korea appeared to be alone against the entire world.

The first four chapters of this book concentrate on North Korea's position within the Communist bloc and its confrontation with South Korea and the United States from the Korean War to the Sino-US rapprochement in the early 1970s. Chapters 1 and 2 examine the Korean War and the postwar reconstruction of the DPRK. Chapters 3 and 4 trace the emergence of *Juche*, or "self-reliance" (although the word signifies much more than this), as the guiding principle of North Korea, and the rise of Kim Il Sung's dictatorship, amidst the Sino-Soviet split and the struggle against US "imperialism." Chapter 4 ends with the 1972 Sino-US rapprochement and North-South Korean joint communiqué. Chapter 5 examines the rise of North Korea's status in the Third World, including Pyongyang's attempts to transfer its economic model to a number of developing countries, as well as North Korea's new overtures to advanced capitalist countries in the 1970s. In the early 1980s, as recounted in chapter 6, the DPRK announced the accession of Kim Jong Il as heir apparent to national leadership, while North Korea renewed its close ties to the USSR and Eastern Europe. The Chinese, to the dismay of their Korean allies, followed an increasingly "revisionist" path of market-oriented development and pro-US alignment. Meanwhile, South Korea pulled rapidly ahead of North Korea in economic development and international recognition. Chapter 7 deals with the continued economic and diplomatic decline of North Korea relative to the South in the late 1980s, the shift toward recognition of Seoul even by North Korea's communist allies, the collapse of state socialism in Eastern Europe and the USSR, and the devastating consequences of communism's collapse for North Korea's economy and diplomatic position in the post–Cold War years. An epilogue concludes the book with a brief overview of North Korean foreign relations in the 1990s and 2000s, focusing on North Korea's ability to survive and even gain substantial concessions from the international community despite its severe disadvantages—a "power of the weak" cultivated in decades of maneuvering amongst allies and enemies during the Cold War.

One of the major challenges for writing this book has been finding sources. It is often said that North Korea—where few foreign scholars are even allowed into libraries, much less archives—lacks anything that can be considered "real" scholarly sources, especially for historians. This is not quite accurate. It is true that the DPRK remains closed to archival research by foreigners, or for that matter by most North Korean citizens. But there are two ways of overcoming this limitation, ideally used in tandem.

First, as scholars of the USSR and other communist states have long known, there are ways of carefully reading official publications from a closed society to get a reasonably accurate picture of, or at least revealing glimpses into, that society.

Second, there are many important sources outside North Korea that have yet to be fully exploited in studies of the DPRK. These include Western diplomatic and intelligence sources, testimonies of North Korean refugees and defectors, and above all materials from North Korea's present and former allies. The richest sources of information to date, and the ones most open to research, are the archives of the former Soviet Union and North Korea's allies in Eastern Europe, including East Germany, Romania, Bulgaria, Albania, Hungary, Czechoslovakia, and Poland.[16] Vast numbers of Soviet and East European documents have been translated and published, and more continue to be collected, by the Cold War International History Project (CWIHP) and the North Korea International Documentation Project (NKIDP) at the Woodrow Wilson Center in Washington, DC.[17] These materials, especially translations from languages with which I am unfamiliar (Hungarian, Romanian, Polish, Czech, etc.) have been extremely valuable in the research for this book. The NKIDP has also organized several "Critical Oral History" conferences, bringing together scholars and government officials from South Korea, the United States, and Eastern Europe, which have shed much light on North Korea's past from the memories of Pyongyang's former interlocutors.

China, Pyongyang's closest ally to the present day, has been slower to open its archives to foreign researchers, and material related to North Korea is often

---

16. For North Korean history until the Korean War, the most important available archival source is the collection of documents captured by the US Army during the war, which was the main source of research materials for my earlier book. See Armstrong, *North Korean Revolution*.

17. Many of these documents are also available online. See www.wilsoncenter.org/document-collections.

sensitive. But beginning in the 1980s, the PRC released memoires and scholarly studies that were much more candid about its relationship to the DPRK than the official propaganda previously had been.[18] Chinese documents intended for "inner circulation only" (*neibu*) informed the pioneering work of Shen Zhihua and other Chinese scholars in the 1990s, and since 2004 the Chinese Foreign Ministry has made declassified documents available to independent and foreign scholars.[19] Cross-checking of these various archival sources against each other and against published materials from North Korea, South Korea, China, Japan, the United States, and the United Nations makes possible a rich synthetic picture of North Korea's foreign relations history. It is still a view from the outside in; perhaps a better subtitle for this book would have been "the world and North Korea." But it is a much closer view than we have had before, and until the DPRK opens its own archives to scholars, the perspective from North Korea itself can be inferred only through this multiarchival, multiperspectival assemblage.[20]

For more than a century, Korea has been a singularity in the international system, a "black hole" that has periodically drawn Japan, China, Russia, and the United States into war.[21] It is one of the few places in the post–Cold War world that could still be the site of a major war between great powers. Yet Korea, for all its real and potential importance, is poorly understood and rarely studied deeply in the West. The urgency of the "Korea problem," meaning in recent decades especially North Korea, has more often than not been met by hasty assumptions based on faulty analogies. Thus, in the immediate aftermath of the end of the Cold War, the most common expectation in the West was that North Korea would soon and suddenly collapse like East Germany.[22] A more optimistic view held that North Korea would follow the Chinese and Vietnamese path of

---

18. The Chinese role in the Korean War was of particular interest to both Chinese and foreign scholars, as new information from the Soviet Union had triggered a major reassessment of this event. See Steven M. Goldstein, "Chinese Perspectives on the Origins of the Korean War: An Assessment at Sixty," *International Journal of Korean Studies* 14, no. 2 (fall/winter 2010): 45–70.

19. See Shen, *Chaoxian Zhanzheng*, as well as Shen Zhihua and Danhui Li, *After Leaning to One Side: China and Its Allies in the Cold War* (Stanford: Stanford University Press, 2011). The Chinese Foreign Ministry materials cover the period 1949–65 and are accessible onsite in the CFMA research room. See People's Republic of China, Ministry of Foreign Affairs, *Zhongguo waijiaobu jiemi dangan* (Archives of China's Ministry of Foreign Affairs, Declassified Diplomatic Files).

20. An official DPRK history of North Korean foreign relations explains that the DPRK is "guided by the Kim Il Sung principles of independence, friendship, and peace going back to the anti-Japanese struggle." Once these terms are decoded this does, in fact, rather accurately reflect the way North Korea has dealt with the world. Pak T'aeho, *Chosŏn Minjujuŭi Konghwaguk taewae kwanggyesa* [Foreign Relations History of the DPRK], vol. 1 (Pyongyang: Saehoe kwahak ch'ulp'ansa, 1985), 3.

21. Cumings, *The Origins of the Korean War*, vol. 2, *The Roaring of the Cataract: 1947–1950* (Princeton: Princeton University Press, 1990), 620.

22. Aidan Foster-Carter, *Korea's Coming Reunification: Another East Asian Superpower?* (London: Economist Intelligence Unit, 1992); Nicholas Eberstadt, *The End of North Korea* (Washington, DC: American Enterprise Institute, 1999).

market-oriented reform under the guidance of the ruling party.[23] But more than two decades after the fall of the Berlin Wall, North Korea had neither collapsed nor engaged in a dramatic, Chinese-style economic opening.

The continued existence of an "unreformed" North Korea into the twenty-first century suggests several things. First, as with any other country, North Korea's historical trajectory is distinctive; the DPRK is not East Germany or China, any more than South Korea is Japan or South Vietnam. This is especially the case for a country that has deliberately and insistently followed its own path of self-reliance, despite the enormous human cost this has entailed. Second, for all its internal weaknesses, North Korea for most of its history has managed rather effectively to deal with the outside world to its maximum advantage, whether playing off China and the USSR against each other in the Cold War, or China and the United States after the end of the Cold War. Third, North Korea is a vivid reminder that the homogenizing forces of globalization, and the reach of American power, have their limits. North Korea may change, but this change will come from within, not as the result of threats or pressure from without.[24] Finally, North Korea's defiance of both American power and conventional wisdom alike is the result of its history, especially the history of confrontation with the outside world—and the United States in particular—since the outbreak of the Korean War in 1950. Sixty years after the war, Korea remains a flashpoint for conflict, and North Korea remains on a war footing. To be sure, this state of conflict is used by the North Korean regime to justify internal oppression; as is often the case, tyranny within is directly related to a sense of weakness toward external threats. But the Korean conflict is real, an unresolved legacy of post–World War II division and the Cold War. The "Korea problem," at the epicenter of armed confrontation among countries great and small, continues to be a danger to the region and perhaps to the world. Its resolution remains no less urgent now than when it began.

---

23. Sung Chull Kim, "Is North Korea Following the Chinese Model of Reform and Opening?" *Institute Reports*, East Asian Institute, Columbia University, 1994.

24. Andrei Lankov, "Changing North Korea," *Foreign Affairs* (November/December 2009). Available at http://www.foreignaffairs.com/articles/65506/andrei-lankov/changing-north-korea.

THE UNFINISHED WAR, 1950–53

If a war is inevitable, then let it be waged now, and not in a few years when Japanese militarism will be restored as an ally of the USA and when the USA and Japan will have a ready-made bridgehead on the continent in the form of the entire Korea run by Syngman Rhee.

—Joseph Stalin, October 1950

The War for Liberation

On June 25, 1950, in a predawn drizzle at the beginning of the rainy season, the Korean People's Army (KPA) of North Korea attacked South Korean positions on the Ongjin Peninsula in the west with an artillery barrage and moved eastward across the Thirty-eighth parallel in a series of artillery and ground attacks.[1] By around 5:00 a.m., the KPA had taken the medieval Korean capital of Kaesŏng, just south of the Thirty-eighth parallel; shortly thereafter, a full-scale invasion force moved down the road toward Seoul, while other North Korean detachments invaded across the center of the peninsula and the East Coast. By June 28, just three days after the invasion began, the KPA had taken Seoul from the city's scattered, outnumbered, and outgunned South Korean defenders.

The invasion of June 25 was far from the first armed clash between North and South Korean military forces. Initiated by both sides, fighting had been fierce along the Thirty-eighth parallel for more than a year, including particularly pitched battles in the area of the Ongjin Peninsula in the summer of 1949.[2] But

---

The epigraph comes from a letter from Stalin to Kim Il Sung, 8 October 1950, APRF, Fond 45, Opis 1, Delo 347, Listy 65–67. Cited in *Cold War International History Project Bulletin* 5–6 (winter 1995–96): 116.

1. Korea Institute of Military History, *The Korean War,* vol. 1 (Lincoln: University of Nebraska Press, 2000), 156; Roy E. Appleman, *South to the Naktong, North to the Yalu* (Washington, DC: Office of the Chief of Military History, Department of the Army, 1961), 21.

2. Bruce Cumings, *The Origins of the Korean War,* vol. 2, *The Roaring of the Cataract, 1947–1950* (Princeton: Princeton University Press, 1990), 388–98.

the KPA blitzkrieg was qualitatively different from the uncoordinated skirmishes and guerrilla warfare that had beset Korea since the two regimes were established in 1948. To many in the West, particularly the United States, the North Korean action was a perfidious attack by international communism against the Free World, an attack that could only have been masterminded by Moscow to test Western resolve and expand communist territory in the newly emerging Cold War. The United States and its allies in the United Nations were quick to condemn the invasion, and two days after the North Korean attack, the UN Security Council called on "members of the United Nations to furnish such assistance to the Republic of Korea as may be necessary to repel the armed attack and to restore international peace and security in the area."[3]

The communists responded by accusing the Americans and their South Korean clients of starting the war, and condemning US "aggression."[4] The Soviets maintained that the United States had no business intervening in a civil war, and the Chinese leadership, in a kind of mirror-image reversal of the American perspective, saw the American intervention in Korea as part of a general plot to expand the US military presence in mainland Asia, including the areas of greatest strategic concern to China: the Korean Peninsula, Indochina, and especially Taiwan.[5] Naturally, the North Koreans were the most vocal critics of the United States and South Korea for "starting" the war, and their official line on June 25 has been exactly the opposite of the American and South Korean view: on that morning, North Korean histories assert, "The South Korean puppet army, under the direct command of the 'US military Advisory Group,' launched an armed invasion all along the Thirty-eighth parallel in a preconceived war plan."[6] The Soviets and Chinese tended to be less explicit about what happened on the morning of June 25, and since the collapse of the Soviet Union, Russian documents have shown conclusively that North Korea did indeed launch an all-out attack, with Moscow's blessing (and weapons)—although these documents do not entirely support the standard, anticommunist Cold War view of the event either, as we shall see. As mentioned in the Introduction, the Chinese government began releasing documents related to the Korean War in the 1980s, and the Chinese Foreign Ministry began opening its archives in 2004, in part as a response to the

---

3. Cited in William Stueck, *The Korean War: An International History* (Princeton: Princeton University Press, 1995), 12.

4. Ibid. 50.

5. Shu Guang Zhang, *Mao's Military Romanticism: China and the Korean War, 1950–1953* (Lawrence: University Press of Kansas, 1995), 56

6. *The US Imperialists Started the Korean War* (Pyongyang: Foreign Languages Publishing House, 1977), 203.

Russian material.[7] Although not as thorough and accessible as the Russian archives, Chinese documents, along with memoirs, official histories, and scholarly books and articles released since the late 1980s, give a much more detailed picture of Soviet-Chinese-North Korean dynamics in the Korean War than was previously available, even if they tend to gloss over the issue of "who started the war."[8]

Origins of War

For decades, the origins of the Korean War were as contested and mysterious as any war in the twentieth century. The idea that the North Korean invasion was a carefully preconceived conspiracy among the communist leaders, with Stalin pulling Kim Il Sung's (as well as Mao Zedong's) puppet strings, remained the orthodox view held by many Western scholars and the general public throughout the Cold War. Even during the war itself, however, the journalist I. F. Stone publicly questioned this view and suggested a more active American and South Korean role in this "surprise attack."[9] In the 1970s and 1980s, scholars strongly critical of US foreign policy and suspicious of Western orthodoxies about the Korean War, in part following Stone's lead, reexamined the Korean War as fundamentally a civil war that became internationalized through U.S. intervention— an event in which South Korea and the United States were, if not instigators, not entirely innocent victims either.[10] But until the end of the Cold War and the release of previously classified, high-level Soviet materials in the early 1990s, neither the orthodox nor the revisionist schools of thought on the Korean War could rely on a clear picture of actions and strategies on the communist side. The Chinese responded to the release of Soviet documents with more limited, but nonetheless very enlightening, revelations of their own. Even without access to North Korean archives, we now have a much better understanding of the

---

7. The publicly available Chinese Foreign Ministry documents begin with the founding of the People's Republic in 1949 and end in December 1965, before the outbreak of the Cultural Revolution in 1966. The Korean War period is covered extensively, although much about the war remains classified. See People's Republic of China, Ministry of Foreign Affairs, *Zhongguo waijiaobu jiemi dangan* [Archives of China's Ministry of Foreign Affairs, Declassified Diplomatic Files], 1949–65.

8. For example, a standard Chinese military history of the war talks about "the outbreak of the Korean Civil War" on June 25, without specifying who fired the first shot. Academy of Military Science, Research Division for Military History, *Kang-Mei Yuan-Chao zhanzhengshi* [History of the Resist-America Aid-Korea War], vol. 1 (Beijing: Junshi kexue chubanshe, 2000), 25.

9. I. F. Stone, *The Hidden History of the Korean War* (New York: Monthly Review Press, 1952).

10. Joyce and Gabriel Kolko, *The Limits of Power: The World and United States Foreign Policy, 1945–1954* (New York: Harper & Row, 1972); Bruce Cumings, *The Origins of the Korean War*, 2 vols. (Princeton: Princeton University Press, 1981, 1990); John Merrill, *Korea: The Peninsular Origins of the War* (Newark: University of Delaware Press, 1989).

processes leading up to June 25 from the communist perspective than was possible before the 1990s.[11]

And what we know is that June 25 *was* a kind of communist conspiracy—but not in the way commonly understood in the 1950s. The North Korean invasion was not initiated by Stalin and carried out by his faithful proxy Kim Il Sung, but rather, Kim Il Sung took the lead in persuading Stalin to support Kim's venture against the South. The idea that Kim initiated the Korean War is not entirely a post–Cold War revelation—Khrushchev said as much in his memoirs more than forty years ago[12]—but, strangely enough, the post–Cold War literature on the Korean War tends to reaffirm old orthodoxies and emphasize the role of Stalin (and to a lesser extent Mao) in initiating the conflict, downplaying the North Korea role, even though the evidence these studies present make it quite clear that Kim was more manipulating than manipulated. For example, the first major post–Cold War study of the Korean War, a collaboration among a Russian, an American, and a Chinese scholar and drawing heavily on the Soviet documents, acknowledges that Kim Il Sung "managed to make Moscow see the situation on the peninsula through his own eyes" and successfully lobbied for a year to win Stalin's support for the invasion.[13] Yet the authors present the war almost entirely as a Great Power conflict between the USSR, the United States, and China, and pay little attention to the role of Koreans in initiating and conducting the war. Like the orthodox reading of the Korean War in the 1950s, much of the post–Cold War, postrevisionist literature on the Korean War relegates the Koreans to the

---

11. English translations of important Soviet documents on the origins and outbreak of the Korean War were first published through an initiative of Columbia University's Center for Korean Research and the Cold War International History Project (CWIHP) in *CWIHP Bulletin* 5–6 (winter 1995–96), part of a larger collection compiled by Alexandre Y. Mansourov under the auspices of the Center for Korean Research. So far the best English-language analysis based on these Soviet materials, yet to be published in book form, is Mansourov's 1997 Columbia University Ph.D. dissertation, "Communist War Coalition Formation and the Origins of the Korean War." For a Russian-language account, much less analytical but reproducing many of the documents in the original, see A. V. Torkunov, *Zagadochnaia Voina: Koreiskii konflikt 1950–1953 gg.* [Secret War: The Korean Conflict, 1950–1953] (Moscow: Rosspyen, 2000).

12. Khrushchev stated emphatically, "I must stress that the war was not Stalin's idea, but Kim Il-Sung's. Kim was the initiator." *Khrushchev Remembers*, trans. and ed. Strobe Talbott (Boston: Little, Brown, 1970), 368. See also *Khrushchev Remembers: The Glasnost Tapes*, trans. and ed. Jerrold L. Schechter with Vyacheslav V. Luchkov (Boston: Little, Brown, 1999), 145–47, which goes into greater detail on the subject, and William Taubman, *Khrushchev: The Man and His Era* (New York: W. W. Norton, 2003), 332.

13. Sergei N. Goncharov, John W. Lewis, and Litai Xue, *Uncertain Partners: Stalin, Mao, and the Korean War* (Stanford: Stanford University Press, 1993). Note that only the names of Stalin and Mao, not Kim, are in the subtitle.

margins and treats the event almost entirely as a clash of major countries and personalities.[14]

The fact that North Korea under Kim Il Sung initiated the war is crucial for our understanding of not only the Korean War itself, but the history of subsequent events on the Korean Peninsula, especially in North Korea. DPRK histories call the war "the Fatherland Liberation War" (*Choguk haebang chŏnjaeng*), and claim that the war was a heroic defense of Korea against the American imperialists.[15] This is how Kim Il Sung and the DPRK leadership presented the war to the Korean people, before and after June 25, and how Kim justified his planned invasion to Stalin: as a war to liberate the people of South Korea from the American occupiers and their Korean collaborators. Although the war ended in stalemate, the North declared victory, claiming to have foiled the American scheme to "recolonize" the entire peninsula. Yet in practice, North Korea, like South Korea, has always acted on the premise that the war was unfinished, "liberation" incomplete. It is most likely that by the 1990s, unification on North Korean terms was little more than an abstraction to the DPRK leaders, who were preoccupied with the sheer survival of their regime.[16] But for decades after the Korean War armistice ended the fighting in July 1953, much of North Korean foreign policy (and domestic policy as well) was driven by the ambition to extend the revolution to the South, to complete the task initiated by the June 25 attack and frustrated by the US intervention. The massive military buildup in the 1960s, and the tragic long-term consequences for the DPRK economy that resulted, was only one expression of this overriding ambition.[17]

The attack of June 25 was a North Korean invasion, planned in advance with the Soviet Union, and supported by China. This much confirms the "orthodox" understanding of the Korean War. But it is also important not to forget the Korean political context of the war, including the ongoing guerrilla war in

---

14. Richard C. Thornton has even argued that Stalin wanted Kim Il Sung to *lose* the war in order to weaken China against the United States and keep Mao dependent on Moscow. Thornton, *Odd Man Out: Truman, Stalin, Mao and the Origins of the Korean* War (Washington, DC: Brassey's, 2000). While keeping China weak may have been a useful result of the war from Stalin's perspective, there is no evidence that the Soviets preferred North Korea to fail in its bid to conquer the South—quite the contrary, Stalin saw this as a golden opportunity to unify Korea under Soviet influence at minimal cost to the USSR.

15. See, for example, *Hyŏngmyŏng ŭi widaehan suryŏng Kim Il-sŏng Tongji kkeso yŏngdo hasin Chosŏn inmin ŭi chŏngŭi ŭi choguk haebang chŏnjaeng sa* [History of the Korean People's Righteous Fatherland Liberation War led by Comrade Kim Il Sung, the Great Leader of the Revolution] (Pyongyang: Sahoe Kwahak Ch'ulp'ansa, 1972).

16. David Kang, "North Korea's Military and Security Strategy," in Samuel S. Kim, ed., *North Korean Foreign Relations in the Post-Cold War Era* (Hong Kong: Oxford University Press, 1998), 177–79.

17. This military buildup was sharply criticized by North Korea's socialist allies in Eastern Europe, criticisms the DPRK leaders ignored, as we will see in chapter 3.

South Korea, the perception of the illegitimacy of the Rhee regime by many in the South, and the perception in the North that South Korea would launch an attack against the North if the communists did not strike first. In other words, to North Korea June 25 was, in a sense, a preemptive strike, and not merely a war of aggression. Readers in the early twenty-first century need hardly be reminded that the difference between a war of aggression and a war of preemption may be largely in the eye of the beholder. Nevertheless, it is not necessarily justifying the North Korean action to point out that there was already a de facto war going on between North and South Korea well before June 25, that Kim's concerns about a South Korean attack were not completely unfounded, and that neither the North nor the South, nor even the United Nations before the war began, considered the Thirty-eighth parallel an international boundary. In that sense the UN defense of South Korea may be less clearly justified than the UN-sanctioned coalition war in 1991 against Saddam Hussein's Iraq, which incontrovertibly had violated an accepted international border, that between Iraq and Kuwait. Korea was a civil *and* an international conflict simultaneously, not just an international war fought by local proxies, and not just a civil war that became internationalized.[18] In June 1950, Koreans invaded Korea—or rather, Soviet-sponsored Koreans attacked territory administered by American-sponsored Koreans, and in the process nearly triggered World War III.

Although much has been written during the past few decades about the origins and outbreak of the Korean War, the orthodox and revisionist accounts of the war have tended to speak past each other rather than come together to create a synthetic picture of the war.[19] Attempting in part to move toward such a synthesis, it is worth recounting here the events leading up to June 25. Until the end of 1949, Stalin was more concerned about preventing a South Korean attack on the North than supporting a North Korean invasion of the South. Kim had begun lobbying Stalin for support for an invasion as early as March 1949, informing Stalin during a meeting in Moscow that "we believe that the situation makes it necessary and possible to liberate the whole country through military means."[20]

---

18. Stueck therefore misses the point when he argues, against Cumings, that the Korean War should be understood primarily as an international conflict. William Stueck, *Rethinking the Korean War: A New Diplomatic and Strategic History* (Princeton: Princeton University Press, 2002), 82–83.

19. The South Korea–based scholar Pak Myŏng-nim has attempted such a synthesize in his monumental, and still incomplete, study of the Korean War, *Hanguk chŏnjaengŭi palbal kwa kiwŏn* [The Outbreak and Origins of the Korean War] (Seoul: Nanam, 1997), and *Hanguk 1950: Chŏnjaeng kwa p'yŏnghwa* [Korea 1950: War and Peace] (Seoul: Nanam, 2002). See also Wada Haruki, *Chōsen sensō zenshi* [Complete History of the Korean War] (Tokyo: Iwanami, 2002).

20. Cited in Evgueni Bajanov, "Assessing the Politics of the Korean War, 1949–51," *CWIHP Bulletin* 5–6: 54.

Stalin replied that North Korea was too weak for a quick and decisive victory, and that a war would draw in the Americans, who still maintained a large military presence in the South. He suggested that Kim wait until the South make the first move and counterattack in force: "Then your move will be understood and supported by everyone."[21] The Soviet ambassador to Pyongyang, Terentii Fomich Shtykov, warned the Soviet Foreign Ministry that the frequent South Korean incursions north of the Thirty-eighth parallel between April and June of that year were a test of the rapidly growing Republic of Korea (ROK) Army against the North, as the southern military prepared itself for all-out war. Supplementing the regular ROK army, Shtykov noted, "South Korea set up subversive and guerrilla bands in every province in North Korea."[22] But, far from supporting a North Korean counterattack, Stalin chastised Shtykov for not doing enough to maintain peace on the Thirty-eighth parallel, lest the Soviet Union be dragged into an unwanted clash with the United States. In August and September, Kim again lobbied Stalin to support an attack, arguing that North Korea was sufficiently strong to conquer the ROK on its own, and now that the United States military had withdrawn from Korea, the United States would not intervene to support the South.[23] Shtykov relayed to Stalin North Korean concerns that South Korea was planning to seize the whole of the Ongjin Peninsula, part of which lay in South Korean territory, from which it could launch further attacks in the North. Kim Il Sung suggested in turn Soviet support for a North Korean takeover of the Ongjin Peninsula–Kaesŏng area, and then see if conditions were favorable for a more general attack on the South.[24] Stalin again demurred, but ordered the Pyongyang embassy to review the situation on September 11, without informing Kim. Ever the realist, Stalin wanted to ensure the situation was overwhelmingly in his favor before he sanctioned such a move.

In the latter half of 1949, several factors helped to convince Stalin that the situation would now favor a North Korean attack on the South with minimal cost to the USSR. These included the Soviets' successful testing of an atomic bomb in August; the communist victory in China in October (followed by the Sino-Soviet Friendship Treaty signed in February 1950); the exclusion of the USSR from the postwar Japanese settlement; the rearmament of Germany; and the establishment of NATO and the clear American commitment to the defense of Western

---

21. Cited in Kathryn Weathersby, "'Should We Fear This?' Stalin and the Danger of War in Korea," Cold War International History Project Working Paper No. 39 (July 2002), 4.

22. Center for Korean Research, Shtykov telegram to Vishinsky, 2 May 1949.

23. Bajanov, "Politics of the Korean War," 54.

24. Zhihua Shen and Danhui Li, *After Leaning to One Side: China and Its Allies in the Cold War* (Stanford: Stanford University Press, 2011), 17; Jonathan Haslam, *Russia's Cold War: From the October Revolution to the Fall of the Wall* (New Haven: Yale University Press, 2011), 121.

Europe, including the Berlin airlift of 1948–49.[25] Secretary of State Dean Acheson's speech at the National Press Club on January 12, 1950, in which he seemed to suggest that Korea and Taiwan lay outside the US defense perimeter, has often been cited as encouraging a communist attack on the South.[26] Recent research in the Chinese and Russian archives suggests, however, that neither the Chinese nor the Soviet leadership believed the Acheson speech necessarily signaled that the US would not intervene in Korea.[27] But the American security commitment to Asia did appear to be weakening, opening a window of opportunity for the communist side. The ideal scenario would be a swift North Korean victory without US intervention; even if in the worst case the US did intervene, with Chinese assistance a war in Korea would divert US resources from Europe and bog down American forces in an unwinnable war in Asia.[28] For the Soviets, a North Korean attack was worth the risks. For Kim Il Sung, Soviet support for an attack meant his dream of unification would soon be fulfilled. The Chinese had been cut out of planning for the attack, but they still supported it as a defense of the Chinese revolution, a means to secure their Eastern periphery, and an opportunity to deal a telling blow to the American imperialists.

Thus, in January 1950, Stalin moved to support Kim's military action against the South. After a final plea from Kim Il Sung for assistance in "liberating" South Korea, relayed through Ambassador Shtykov on January 17, Stalin telegrammed Shtykov on January 30, telling him to inform Kim "that I am ready to help him in this matter." However, Stalin warned that the "action should be organized in such a way that there won't be too much risk involved," meaning that the war would be swift, decisive, and not trigger an American intervention.[29]

Stalin's aversion to direct confrontation with a major enemy was quite consistent with his earlier insistence on neutrality in the war against Japan until the final days of the Pacific War, and before that, his pact with Nazi Germany.[30] Far from a wild-eyed promoter of world revolution, Stalin was a consummate

---

25. Vladislov Zubok and Constantine Pleshakov, *Inside the Kremlin's Cold War: From Stalin to Khrushchev* (Cambridge: Harvard University Press, 1996), 65–66; Bajanov, "Politics of the Korean War," 87.

26. James I. Matray, "Dean Acheson's Press Club Speech Reexamined," *Journal of Conflict Studies* 22, no. 1 (spring 2002). Available at http://journals.hil.unb.ca/index.php/JCS/article/view/366/578.

27. Kim Donggil, "Stalin's Korean U-Turn: The USSR's Evolving Security Strategy and the Origins of the Korean War," *Seoul Journal of Korean Studies* 24, no. 1 (June 2011): 95–96.

28. See Kim Donggil and William Stueck, "Did Stalin Lure the United States into the Korean War? New Evidence on the Origins of the Korea War," North Korea International Documentation Project e-dossier no. 1 (2008). Available at http://www.wilsoncenter.org/publication/nkidp-e-dossier-no-1.

29. Center for Korean Research, Shtykov telegram to Vyshinsky, 19 January 1950.

30. According to Gorodetsky's exhaustive analysis, Stalin's neutrality pact with Japan, along with the dissolution of the Comintern, were originally intended to appease Hitler in the hopes of avoiding war altogether. Gabriel Gorodetsky, *Grand Delusion: Stalin and the German Invasion of Russia* (New Haven: Yale University Press, 1999), 320.

realist, and it seems he expected others to be the same. His overriding concern was Soviet national interest, as he perceived it, and his failure to grasp the "irrational" motivations for Hitler to launch a two-front war led to the greatest military disaster in Soviet history, and the greatest loss of life of any belligerent in World War II. Similarly, Stalin's apparently rational calculation that the United States would not intervene in Korea, because it was not in America's interest, turned out to be wrong. Stalin ended up with the worst of both worlds: a remilitarized United States, ready to confront the Soviet Union and perceived communist threats around the world, and a loss of prestige among Moscow's Asian allies. The American Cold War military buildup, outlined in the seminal national security document NSC 68, was implemented as a direct result of the Korean War.[31] And while the USSR's refusal to support North Korea with combat troops may have averted a disastrous clash with the United States, it permanently damaged the Soviets' relationship with both North Korea and China. The Korean War probably ranks second only to the Nazi-Soviet pact among Stalin's biggest foreign policy miscalculations.[32]

A realist to the core, Stalin was not averse to using wild-eyed revolutionaries when it suited his purpose. The Soviet and Chinese accounts now available of the events leading up to the Korean War show a great deal of mistrust and mutual manipulation among Stalin, Kim, and Mao. Kim went to Moscow secretly and met three times with Stalin between April 10 and 25 to discuss war plans. Stalin agreed to support the North Korean invasion with arms, advisors, and air cover, but under two conditions: that the United States would not interfere, and that the Chinese would agree to assist with combat forces if North Korea needed direct military support. Kim then visited Beijing, again in secret, on May 13. On the fifteenth he met with Mao, who agreed to Stalin's plan and recommended that the KPA adopt a strategy of avoiding major cities and surrounding and destroying enemy forces in the countryside—in other words, the "People's War" strategy that had defeated the Nationalists in the Chinese Civil War.[33]

In fact, the North Koreans did not take Mao's advice on this and many other matters. Notwithstanding the constant refrain of a relationship "as close as lips and teeth," conflicts over strategy, tactics, and leadership personnel would color

---

31. Robert Jervis, "The Impact of the Korean War on the Cold War," *Journal of Conflict Resolution* 24 (December 1980): 563–92.

32. Interestingly enough, the final Soviet decision for the June 25 invasion was made on June 22, 1950—the anniversary of "Operation Barbarossa," Hitler's invasion of the Soviet Union. Mansourov, "Communist War Coalition," 395.

33. Weathersby, "'Should We Fear This?'" 12; Shen Zhihua, "Sino-North Korean Conflict and Its Resolution during the Korean War," *Cold War International Project Bulletin* 14–15 (winter 2003–spring 2004): 13.

China-North Korean cooperation throughout the Korean War.[34] The Chinese political and military leaders tended to see the North Koreans as headstrong and incautious, while the North Koreans saw the Chinese as heavy-handed and imperious. In some ways, this mutual perception was a continuation of the "big brother–little brother" relationship of past centuries of Sino-Korean relations. But this relationship, in both its agreements and its tensions, took on new attributes in the context of a shared revolutionary history and a global communist movement led by Moscow. Koreans' suspicion of Chinese motives arose both from the long history of Chinese domination over Korea, and the more recent trauma of Korean communists' persecution in Manchuria in the early 1930s, the so-called Minsaengdan Incident.[35] On the one hand, Korean and Chinese communists from the mid-1930s to the Korean War had a history of close cooperation against "imperialists," both Japanese and American; on the other hand, the North Koreans chafed at being junior partners to the Chinese (Mao liked to call Kim Il Sung, affectionately but condescendingly, *Xiao Jin*—"Little Kim") and have downplayed the role of China in the Korean War ever since. After the war, North Korean official histories would all but erase the participation of the Chinese forces from public memory. The Chinese, for their part, would—like most of North Korea's allies—come to resent the North Koreans' lack of acknowledgment and gratitude for the help and sacrifice given them.

The DPRK leadership had important roots in the Chinese communist revolution. Kim Il Sung himself, and many other leaders of the North Korean military, party, and government, had been members of the Chinese Communist Party (CCP) before 1945. Unlike the Soviet-trained Koreans, who were mostly educators and civilian advisors, the CCP-Koreans were experienced guerrilla fighters. Kim's Manchurian guerrilla group, however, was somewhat marginal to the mainstream Chinese communist movement, and Kim also had close ties to the Soviet military, which had been responsible for bringing Kim to power in North Korea. Perhaps for that reason, Kim's instinct was to rely first on the Soviets to back him up, and only when Soviet support was secure to seek Chinese aid.

The first Korean guerrilla group associated with the Chinese Eighth Route Army, the main communist fighting force in China, was the North China Korean Youth Association, formed in the Shanxi Province redoubt of the Eighth

---

34. Shen and Li, *After Leaning to One Side*, 52. The authors draw extensively on recently declassified Soviet and Chinese documents, as well as oral history, for their account.

35. Hongkoo Han, "Wounded Nationalism: The Minsaengdan Incident and Kim Il Sung in Eastern Manchuria," Ph.D. diss., University of Washington, 1999. In 1932–34, thousands of Korean communists were arrested, and hundreds killed, by the CCP as suspected Japanese agents. Kim Il Sung was one of those detained. Although the Chinese and Koreans in Manchuria formed a unified army shortly thereafter, mutual suspicions lingered on.

Route Army in January 1941, under the leadership of Mu Chŏng. This group was renamed the Korean Independence League in July 1942, led by Kim Tu-bong and Ch'oe Ch'ang-ik. Mu Chŏng commanded the league's military branch, the Korean Volunteer Army (KVA), with Pak Hyo-sam and Pak Il-u as his deputies. The Korean Independence League leadership moved to Yan'an, the CCP headquarters, toward the end of World War II. After the Korean War, these Korean guerrillas would be attacked and purged as the "Yan'an faction" by Kim Il Sung and his associates.[36] But before the war, KVA veterans offered invaluable skills and experience for enabling North Korean to build up a military capable of defeating the South. Former KVA fighters became the leading officers and crack troops of the North Korean Army.[37] US military intelligence estimated in early 1947 that at least 80 percent of the officers in the North Korean security forces at the time were veterans of the Chinese civil war.[38]

The North Koreans began requesting the return of ethnic Korean soldiers from China in the spring of 1949, when Kim Il, political director of the KPA, visited Beijing. Two Korean divisions of the Chinese PLA were dispatched to North Korea in July 1949, and a third was sent in the spring of 1950.[39] According to Chinese records, slightly more than thirty-five thousand ethnic Korean returned to North Korea before the outbreak of the Korean War, fewer than US intelligence reports of the time and scholars later have estimated, but still a substantial number.[40] What was critical is that these Korean Volunteer Army veterans had the training and combat experience to take leading roles in the Korean People's Army. Two-thirds of the political cadres in the KPA were KVA veterans.[41] When the Chinese intervened to defend North Korea against the Americans in October 1950, using a "Volunteer Army" of their own, it was partly out of reciprocity for Korean assistance to the Chinese communists.[42]

---

36. Shen and Le, *After Leaning to One Side*, 52–53. See also Donggil Kim, "Prelude to War? The Repatriation of Koreans from the Chinese PLA, 1949–50," *Cold War History* 12, no. 2 (May 2012): 227–44.

37. United States Department of State, *Foreign Relations of the United States 1949*, vol. 7 (Washington, DC: United States Government Printing Office, 1976), part 2, 974.

38. National Archive and Record Administration, United States Army, Record Group 319, *Intelligence Summaries—North Korea* (ISNK) no. 31 (15–28 February 1947), 4.

39. Kim, "Prelude to War," 228. Kim bases his account on newly released Chinese materials.

40. Ibid., 237–38. Kim suggests that US intelligence overestimated the number of ethnic Korean returnees based on misreading the movement of Chinese forces *through* North Korea in the final stages of the Chinese Civil War. He also points out that regular North Korean army troops were never dispatched to China, as US intelligence incorrectly reported. See Cumings, *Origins*, vol. 2, 446.

41. National Archive and Record Administration, Record Group 242, "Record Seized by US Military Forces in Korea," shipping advice 2009, item 9/120. KPA Cultural Cadre Bureau, *Munhwa kanbu sŏngwon t'onggyep'yo* [Statistical Table of Cultural Cadre Members]. December 15, 1949 ("top secret").

42. See Cumings, *Origins,* vol. 2, 363, 357–64

Of course, China intervened as well for the sound practical reasons of defending Chinese territory against a UN force advancing toward its borders.[43] But reciprocity and self-defense were mixed with a powerful belief that the United States was an unremittingly hostile power, that war was inevitable at some point, and that a confident revolutionary power such as China could defeat the technologically far superior American forces. This was Mao's perception of a Sino-American clash in Korea long before the clash actually occurred. In May 1950, according to Soviet reports, Mao told the DPRK ambassador to Beijing, Yi Chu-yŏng, that Korean unification was now possible only by military means, and there was no reason to be frightened of the United States. The Americans, Mao asserted, "would not unleash a Third World War because of such a tiny piece of territory." But if a conflict with the United States did come, China would be ready and would give "sufficient assistance" to North Korea to defeat the imperialists.[44] If Stalin was a realist, even a "hyper-realist," Mao was a military romantic.[45] Or rather, romanticism and pragmatism together shaped CCP attitudes toward war and foreign policy, creating an optimism that underlay Chinese support for fighting Americans and their surrogates in Korea and Indochina, with far-reaching consequences for the Cold War.[46] Stalin exploited this romanticism quite shrewdly, in effect promising Kim that the USSR would defend North Korea to the last Chinese.

In February 1950, after Stalin had given his blessing for a North Korean attack, Lieutenant-General Vasilyev arrived in Pyongyang and took over from Ambassador Shtykov the role of chief military advisor to the KPA.[47] The North Korean strategy now focused on conventional war, the pro-North guerrillas in South Korea having been largely decimated in the winter of 1949–50, as the southern guerrilla leader Kim Tal-sŏng reported in Pyongyang on March 3.[48] Plans for the war were confined to the upper echelons of the DPRK and KPA leadership, and even frontline commanders were informed of the invasion only at the last moment. KPA cultural officers taught—and probably believed themselves—that the war had been provoked by the South, under orders of the Americans, and that the North Korean invasion was a counterattack.[49]

---

43. The classic "realist" explanation for China's intervention in the Korean War, based on official Chinese publications and US documents, is Allen Whiting, *China Crosses the Yalu: The Decision to Enter the Korean War* (New York: Macmillan, 1960).

44. Center for Korean Research, Shtykov to Vishinsky, 12 May 1950.

45. The apt expression "hyper-realism" is from Anders Stephanson, "Stalin's Hyper-Realism," *Diplomatic History* 25, no. 1 (winter 2001): 129 39, a review of Gorodetsky's *Grand Delusion*.

46. Zhang, *Mao's Military Romanticism*, 11, 251.

47. Center for Korean Research, Shtykov to Vishinsky, 23 February 1950.

48. Center for Korean Research, Ignatiev to Vishinsky, 10 April 1950.

49. RG 242, shipping advice 2010, item 1/62. Korean People's Army, Cultural Section. "Lecture Notes."

Meanwhile, on the political front, North Korea revitalized the Democratic Front for the Unification of the Fatherland (Choguk t'ongil minju chŏnsŏn, DFUF). According to Shtykov, Kim Il Sung and DPRK vice-premier Pak Hŏn-yŏng had proposed the creation of the DFUF at the end of May 1949. The DFUF would unite all "patriotic parties and social organizations" to support the withdrawal of the US troops and UN Temporary Commission on Korea (UNTCOK), supervise new general elections in the North and South, and create a new, all-Korean national government.[50] Kim and Pak had insisted that if all left-wing parties in the South were allowed to organize and political prisoners released, such elections would give the DPRK and its allies decisive power in both North and South. And if the Americans and South Korean leaders refused to cooperate, they would be seen as opposed to unification. Either way, the North would score a political victory. Shtykov felt that this was a "reasonable" proposal and supported the creation of the DFUF, which was launched on June 25, 1949—a year to the day before the Korean War began.[51] Not surprisingly, Syngman Rhee and the Americans flatly refused the DFUF proposal, and the ROK continued to keep a tight lid on the left, holding national assembly elections of its own in May 1950. On June 1, 1950, the DFUF renewed its appeal for unification and called for a conference of North and South Korean political leaders and new elections, leading to a national unity government by August 15, the fifth anniversary of Korean independence from Japan. Rhee once again refused the offer, and the three DFUF representatives who had come south to extend the invitation were arrested.[52]

North Korea also made two other proposals: the exchange of two leading southern communists held prisoner in the ROK for the release of Cho Man-sik, the Pyongyang-based Christian nationalist leader who had been under house arrest since January 1946; and a merger of the ROK National Assembly and the Supreme People's Assembly of the DPRK.[53] The prisoner exchange was blocked by Rhee, and the legislative merger was obviously a nonstarter, as it would have given equal representation to the North, with half the population of the South. Conversely, southern proposals for national elections would have given greater voice to the more populous South and were rebuffed by the DPRK. This latter impasse established a pattern of North-South proposals on legislative unity for the next sixty years.

50. Center for Korean Research, Shtykov to Vishinksy, 5 June 1949.
51. Mansourov, "Communist War Coalition Formation," 125.
52. Merrill, *Korea*, 76.
53. Stueck, *Korean War*, 40.

In any event, North Korea's initiatives seem more a means of distracting the Americans and South Koreans than serious peace proposals. As we have seen, Soviet–North Korean joint planning for an invasion had been underway since February.[54] Once again, however, it is important to appreciate the differing motives of the two allies in going to war. For Kim, the war was a means of overcoming the division of Korea, eliminating the "reactionary" forces of Syngman Rhee and other conservative and pro-American elements, and consolidating his power over the whole Korean Peninsula. Extending the world socialist revolution, much less Soviet power, was at most a secondary concern. For Stalin, the main concern was eliminating the potential security threat of a revitalized and remilitarized Japan, allied with pro-Japanese elements in the South and backed by the United States. Russia had been defeated by Japan in war forty-five years earlier, and Stalin was determined to prevent Korea once again becoming a security threat to his country.[55] If the Americans stayed out of Korea, as it seemed they most likely would, a northern conquest of South Korea could expand the zone of Soviet influence in the Far East and might even trigger revolution in Japan itself, offsetting recent American gains in Western Europe.[56] A unified Korea under Kim's regime would also give the Soviets new access to railways and warm-water ports in Northeast Asia, especially important now that China was demanding the return of the Changchun Railway and the Port Arthur naval facilities that had long been under Russian control.[57] In other words, the unification of Korea on North Korean terms would consolidate the Soviet zone of security on the Korean Peninsula and deter American and Japanese aggression in the Far East for the foreseeable future.

For Mao, a supporter of this venture if not a participant in its planning, a successful northern invasion would remove the Americans from this sensitive area of China's frontier, encourage revolutionary forces throughout Asia, and return all of Korea to its "natural," historical position as China's ally. Unfortunately for Mao, assisting North Korea would mean losing Taiwan, which US forces blocked the PLA from "liberating" as soon as the Korean War broke out. For Stalin, helping North Korea conquer the South, creating a unified Korean Peninsula

---

54. In addition to the Soviet documents, useful accounts of the war preparation may be found in Lim Un, *The Founding of a Dynasty in North Korea: An Authentic Biography of Kim Il-sung* (Tokyo: Jiyu-sha, 1982), 171–74; and Yu Sŏng-chŏl, "My Testimony," *Hanguk Ilbo*, November 1, 1990. "Lim Un" (a pseudonym) and Yu were both Soviet Koreans in the early years of the DPRK, who were later purged and went into exile in the USSR.

55. Mansourov, "Communist War Coalition Formation," 248

56. Wada Haruki, "The Korean War, Stalin's Policy, and Japan," *Social Science Japan Journal* 1, no. 1 (April 1998): 12.

57. Shen and Li, *After Leaning to One Side*, 22.

allied to the USSR, was preferable to helping Mao liberate Taiwan, which would strengthen China as a potential rival in Asia. Thus Stalin pressed the Chinese to support the North Korean attack and set aside China's own unification with Taiwan for the time being.[58] Mao could not have known that Taiwan would be lost to the communists indefinitely, and that Kim's gambit to conquer South Korea would ultimately fail. Nevertheless, for all three, the potential gains of a North Korean invasion outweighed the risks. Furthermore, the possibility could not be discounted that the South would strike first if it felt in a position to conquer the North, as Syngman Rhee vowed he would do in his frequent calls for a "northern advance" (*pukchin*). For China and the USSR as well as North Korea, June 25 was in no small part a preemptive move.

It was not entirely out of deception, then, that General Vasilyev and his Soviet and North Korean staff referred to their plan to attack the South as a "Preemptive Strike Operational Plan."[59] If the South Koreans and Americans did not think North Korean peace initiatives were genuine, the northerners had no reason to trust Rhee and the Americans either. For a year, both sides increasingly had acted as if war were inevitable. The difference is that, unlike the Americans, the Soviets gave full support to their Korean clients to launch hostilities. Typically, Stalin approved an attack only when he saw overwhelming force advantage, which the KPA had in June 1950—an advantage it could lose to the South in the near future. Stalin had hoped for, and Kim had promised, a swift and decisive victory. At first, it appeared they would be successful beyond their wildest dreams.

The North Korean Occupation of South Korea

Kim Il Sung did not follow Mao's advice to avoid the cities; instead, the KPA, under Soviet advice, followed a classic blitzkrieg approach and went straight for the South Korean capital. By the middle of June 25, Soviet YAK fighter planes were already bombarding Seoul. By the end of the day on June 27, Seoul's defenses were on the verge of collapse. Kim had assured Stalin that he could take Seoul in three days, and he lived up to his promise. This time, unlike the Nazi invasion in World War II, the blitzkrieg worked to the Soviet advantage; perhaps Stalin saw the KPA's success as vicarious revenge for Operation Barbarossa.

From the beginning of the war, North Korean media insisted that the South had attacked first. On June 26, the newspaper *Chŏson Inmingun* (Korean

---

58. Ibid., 28.
59. Kathryn Weathersby, "Soviet Aims in Korea and the Origins of the Korean War, 1945–1950: New Evidence from Russian Archives," Cold War International History Project Working Paper No. 8 (Woodrow Wilson International Center for Scholars, November 1993), 25.

People's Army), under the headline, "The Korean People's Army is Gloriously and Heroically Fighting for the Benefit of Our People and the Unification of the Fatherland," reported that the "so-called National Defense Army" of the South Korean "puppet government" crossed the Thirty-eighth parallel on June 25 and had been repelled by North Korean forces.[60] On June 28, Kim Il Sung made a radio address to "the people of all Korea," stating once again that "on June 25, the army of the puppet government of the traitor Syngman Rhee crossed the 38th parallel in order to conquer the area north of 38. The border defense forces of the heroic Republic [i.e., North Korea] resisted the attack and routed the army of the Syngman Rhee puppet government." Kim went on to say that the KPA had launched a counteroffensive, penetrating "ten to fifteen kilometers" south of the Thirty-eighth parallel, liberating the areas of Ongjin, Kaesŏng, and Paekch'ŏn.[61] By this time, in fact, the KPA had already taken Seoul.

The KPA's main propaganda theme was national unity and liberation. Internal directives to KPA cultural officers make little if any reference to the Soviet Union and focus instead on the role of the Korean People's Army in liberating Korea, giving effusive praise to the "Supreme Leader," General Kim Il Sung.[62] On the ground, the KPA generally administered "liberated" areas through reinstating the People's Committee (PC) structure that had emerged in Korea shortly after liberation in August 1945. The PCs had developed into a pan–North Korean system of administration under Soviet guidance by 1947, while being dismantled by the Americans in South early in the US occupation.[63] The KPA-installed chairman of the Seoul PC was a former southerner, Yi Sŭng-yŏp. According to his lieutenant, Yi Ku-yŏng, who was later arrested as a spy in South Korea, one of Yi Sŭng-yŏp's first acts as PC chairman was to execute some of his former Communist Party colleagues whom he had just released from Seoul's Sŏdaemun prison, fearing they might reveal his past collaboration with the Japanese.[64] Likewise, many of the released prisoners took out personal vendettas against members of the

60. *Chosŏn inmingun*, June 26, 1950, 1.

61. RG 242, SA 2005, item 2/67. Broadcast transcript of Kim Il Sung's "Appeal to the People of All Korea," June 26, 1950. See also the KWP journal *Kŭlloja* 12 (June 30, 1950): 3.

62. RG 242, shipping advice 2009, item 6/8. Kyŏnggi Province Interior Ministry, "Propaganda and Explanation for People in the Liberated Areas," July 15, 1950.

63. For the northern PCs, see Armstrong, *North Korean Revolution*, chapter 2; for the South, see Cumings, *Origins*, vol. 1, especially chapters 4 and 8.

64. Sim Chi-yŏn, *Sanjŏnge paerŭl maego: Noch'on Yi Ku-yŏng sŏnsaengŭi saraon iyagi* [Mooring the Ship to the Mountain Peak: Conversations with Yi Ku-yŏng] (Seoul: Kaema sŏwon, 1998). As it turned out, after the war Yi Sŭng-yŏp himself was arrested and executed in North Korea for keeping KPA forces tied down in Seoul, rather than moving South before the Americans intervened.

(South) Korean national police and right-wing youth groups, who were tried by Peoples' Courts and often summarily executed.[65]

But overall, the three-month KPA occupation of Seoul and a large part of South Korea was far from a reign of terror. In late fall 1950, sociologists John W. Riley Jr. and Wilbur Schramm, sponsored by the U.S. Air Force, led a team of social scientists to conduct a survey of Seoul residents who had lived through the northern occupation, in order to evaluate the nature and impact of communist rule there. The resulting book, *The Reds Take a City*, paints a rather benign picture of the occupation despite its Cold War sensationalism. For example, even though Riley and Schramm refer to "millions of Koreans trapped by the Reds" in Seoul, they note that "even those who had most reason to hate the forces from the North typically reported their conduct courteous and reasonable."[66] Among the KPA's policies, land reform, equal rights for women, and Korean unification "seem to have made the greatest impression" on the people of Seoul.[67]

Overt resistance to the occupation could be punished severely, and those deemed "traitors to the Korean nation"—former Japanese collaborators, high-ranking members of the Rhee regime, the National Police, members of right-wing youth groups, and the like—were beyond redemption. But the KPA and their collaborators were careful, at least in the initial occupation, to avoid arbitrary and brutal dispensation of justice. "Discipline and order," says one directive to occupation security forces, "should be strictly observed. Never be offensive or bureaucratic towards the people and do not infringe on the people's rights."[68] Many of the moderate South Korean politicians stayed in Seoul and joined the People's Committee, including such prominent figures as O Mang-sŏp, staff officer from Kim Ku's conservative Korea Independence Party; Cho So-ang, National Assembly member from the Socialist Party; and Kim Kyu-sik, veteran of the Korean Provisional Government in Shanghai and chairman of the Interim Legislative Assembly under the US Military Government.[69] The US Air Force survey suggests that the majority of South Korean factory workers, and perhaps

65. National Archives and Records Administration, Record Group 59. "Records of the Department of State." US Embassy, Seoul, to State Department, 19 October 1950, "Communist Atrocities against Civilians in Seoul," 1.

66. John W. Riley Jr. and Wilbur Schramm, *The Reds Take a City* (New Brunswick, NJ: Rutgers University Press, 1951), 65, based on "A Preliminary Study of the Impact of Communism on Korea," United States Air Force, Air University, 1950.

67. Riley and Schramm, *Reds Take a City*, 35.

68. National Archives and Records Administration. United States Army, Far East Command. Allied Translator and Interpreter Section (ATIS), box 6, item 38. "Documents on Organization and Formation of North Korean Interim Committee," n.d. Captured Sinchon-Miryang area, received 16 February 1951, 7.

69. US State Department, Record Group 59, 759A Series. Ambassador Muccio to State Department, 8 July 1950.

two-thirds of the students, actively supported the KPA.[70] Similarly, US military intelligence observed that support for the northern occupation in Seoul "comes mostly from the working class and university and high school students including females," and that 60 percent of Seoul students were active supporters of the KPA.[71]

The North Korean occupation forces set about re-creating the North Korean system in the South. A key element of this was land reform, which they began in early July.[72] Occupation cadres and local officials were given detailed instructions on how to implement the land reform, and directives from Pyongyang stressed the importance of this move for "motivating the people's support of the government as a people's government."[73] Implemented at the local level by "village committees," the KPA-sponsored South Korean land reform was almost identical to the land reform implemented in North Korea in the spring of 1946. Land was to be taken away from large landlords and redistributed to tenants and landless farmers, families would receive land according to the number of "labor points" in each family, and the newly redistributed land would be taxed at the rate of about 25 percent of the annual harvest. The one major difference was that some large landowners would be able to keep their holdings of up to twenty *chongbo* (about fifty acres, a rather substantial farm by Korean standards), whereas in the North, everything over five chongbo had been confiscated.[74] The KPA occupation also formed or reconstituted labor, farmer, youth, and women's groups in the South to correspond to the mass organizations in North Korea.[75] In addition to the Korean Workers' Party, the women's and youth organizations seem to have been the most active in political work, as they had been in the North.

The North Korean system brought to the South was a system of mass mobilization. As they had in the North, the party and People's Committees in the South utilized coercion, a well-organized police force, and networks of surveillance to keep the populace in line. The security organs were under the authority of the Ministry of the Interior in Pyongyang, which had been extremely effective at eliminating dissent in North Korea. But the occupation authorities invested a great deal of their energies and resources into what the American analysts called "thought control," a set of techniques that would soon be known in the West

---

70. Riley and Wilbur Schramm, *Reds Take a City*, 166–67.

71. Cited in Cumings, *Origins*, vol. 2, 670.

72. Local ad hoc land reform programs were instituted even earlier in areas occupied by the KPA. See for example RG 242, shipping advice 2012, item 6/105. Ongjin County People's Committee, "On Punishment and Property Settlement for Reactionaries," June 28, 1950.

73. ATIS, "North Korean Interim Committee," 8.

74. For the complete text of the South Korean land reform under the North Korean occupation, see RG 242, shipping advice 2009, item10/66.

75. Cumings, *Origins*, vol. 2, 673–80.

as "brainwashing."[76] KPA control of mass media, meaning at that time primarily radio and newspapers, was immediate and pervasive. The Seoul Symphony Orchestra was pressed into service of the regime, and all available artists were recruited to paint propaganda posters. Mass rallies, parades, musical events, and other public spectacles were frequently used in the occupied South, as they had been in the North, to bring political messages to the largest possible audience. Frequent "study sessions" were held in cities and occupied villages. Citizens were asked to give "voluntary confessions" of past crimes and pledge their loyalty to the DPRK.[77] Denunciation was encouraged, but the US-sponsored social science survey found that "the system relied more upon inducements than upon deterrents," including such prizes as extra food rations, professional training, public praise, and certificates for good behavior.[78]

The occupation authorities put special emphasis on education. Schools were important sites for political indoctrination, but attacking illiteracy and backwardness, especially among the poor and underprivileged, was also a major priority of the regime. Seoul, long the educational capital of Korea, was a true prize in this regard. The KPA regarded Seoul's "211 schools, 7,000 teachers and 260,000 students" as key instruments in the struggle for unification.[79] Educators and students, as we have seen, were among the most welcoming supporters of the new regime. Throughout occupied South Korea, the KPA was able to rebuild the education system in the occupied areas with "politically acceptable" local teachers quite rapidly.[80]

On the whole, the North Korean occupation authorities and their agents preferred to rule through a system of rewards and psychological pressure rather than punishment and coercion. But discipline broke down after the Inch'ŏn landing on September 15, 1950, and widespread killing and destruction of property took place as the North Koreans retreated from the advancing UN forces. KPA morale collapsed everywhere after Inch'ŏn. On September 18, the head of the local Workers' Party branch in Yŏnch'ŏn County, Kangwŏn Province, reported "strengthening of anti-Republic activities" and "repeated attacks by the American

76. Riley and Schramm, *Reds Take a City*, 103–20. The term *brainwashing*, supposedly a favored technique of Asian communists, was first popularized by Edward Hester's book *Brainwashing in Red China* (New York: Vanguard, 1951).

77. A large number of such testimonies can be found in RG 242, shipping advice 2009, item 10/55. "List of Confessions," Iksan County, August 1950.

78. Riley and Schramm, *Reds Take a City*, 144.

79. RG 242, shipping advice 2009, item 7/14. Hŏ Min, "On the Democratic Education System being Implemented in the DPRK," Education Section, Inch'ŏn City People's Committee, July 30, 1950, 2.

80. See for example RG 242, SA 2012 8/67, list of schools in South Chŏlla Province, 1 July 1950.

imperialists."[81] According to US military and other sources, hundreds of political prisoners were massacred in the southwestern port city of Mokp'o, the eastern industrial city of Wŏnsan, and elsewhere, and buried in mass graves; the largest slaughter apparently took place in Taejŏn, where thousands of Korean civilians, ROK soldiers, and American soldiers were reportedly executed at the end of September.[82] In mid-October, after Seoul was retaken by UN forces, the US embassy estimated that at least one thousand civilians, including women and small children, had been executed by the KPA in the vicinity of Seoul in the final week of September.[83] Such killings went on as the UN forces swept up the peninsula in October; one victim was Cho Man-sik, the leading conservative nationalist in North Korea, who had been under house arrest in Pyongyang since January 1946.[84]

Mutual accusations of atrocities and war crimes have poisoned the relations between North and South Korea, and between North Korea and the United States, ever since the Korean War began. There is little doubt that all sides committed atrocities, although the Chinese People's Volunteers were perhaps the least guilty in this regard.[85] South and North Korea accused each other of killing thousands, even tens of thousands, of civilians and POWs in cold blood, in numerous horrific massacres. Few of these allegations were ever thoroughly investigated, and we will never know how many were true, how many exaggerated, and how many simply fabricated. Whether one side or the other committed more atrocities, and is therefore "more guilty" than its counterpart, is an academic question in the worst sense of the term, rather like determining that communism is "worse" than fascism because the former "killed more people."[86] But there is little reason to doubt that both the ROK and DPRK armies committed heinous acts against soldiers and civilians on the other side. Most of the civilian victims were guilty of nothing more than being in the wrong place at the wrong time, or being forced to choose sides in a confusing and rapidly shifting civil war environment. The sense of understandable outrage each side has felt against the other—along with the fear of reprisals—has been no small hindrance to Korean moves toward

81. RG 242, shipping advice 2013, item 1/191. Chairman's Report, Korean Workers' Party, Kangwŏn Province, Yŏnch'ŏn County Branch, September 18, 1950.

82. Appleman, *South to the Naktong*, 587–88.

83. Embassy to State, 19 October 1950, 3.

84. Chung'ang Ilbo, *Pirok: Chosŏn Minjujuŭi Inmin Konghwaguk* [Secret Record: The Democratic People's Republic of Korea] (Seoul: Chung'ang Ilbosa, 1991), 102–3.

85. Cumings, *Origins*, vol. 2, 697.

86. Stephane Courtois and Mark Kramer's *Black Book of Communism* (Cambridge: Harvard University Press, 1999) takes such a "body count" approach to condemning communism. Whatever communism's crimes, this kind of specious empiricism is not much help in understanding a political system.

unification, one important reason Korea remains divided, unlike the two Germanies, who never fought a war with each other.

American atrocities, on the other hand, were by and large of a different order. It is clearly the case that Americans did, in several instances, kill large numbers of Korean civilians at close range, most famously near the village of No Gun Ri in July 1950, as revealed in a detailed press investigation nearly fifty years later.[87] North Korean accusations of systematic American massacres, such as the murder of two thousand villagers in Yŏndong County, have never been independently verified.[88] But the act that inflicted the greatest loss of civilian life in the Korean War by far, one which the North Koreans have claimed ever since was America's greatest war crime, was the aerial bombardment of North Korean population centers. American control of the skies over Korea was overwhelming. Soviet MIGs, flown by Soviet, Chinese, and North Korean pilots, were sometimes effective against American air power. But under Stalin's orders, the Soviet fighter planes were strictly limited in number and in the range they were allowed to fly, lest US-Soviet air battles lead to a larger war.[89] And in any case, Soviet air support did not come until the end of 1950. During the summer and fall, North Korean air defenses were virtually nonexistent. Lightly armed, local self-defense units in occupied South Korea could only watch and suffer as their towns and villages were obliterated from the air.[90] Hundreds of tons of ordinance, including millions of gallons of napalm, were dropped on North Korea as the UN forces advanced. By the end of the war, North Korea claimed that only two modern buildings remained standing in Pyongyang.

For the Americans, strategic bombing made perfect sense, giving advantage to American technological prowess against the enemy's numerical superiority. The American command dismissed British concerns that mass bombardment would turn world opinion against them, insisting that air attacks were accurate and civilian casualties limited.[91] Russian accusations of indiscriminate attacks on civilian targets did not register with the Americans at all. But for the North

---

87. Charles J. Hanley, Sang-Hun Choe, and Martha Mendoza, *The Bridge at No Gun Ri: A Hidden Nightmare from the Korean War* (New York: Henry Holt, 2001).

88. *Haebang Ilbo*, August 10, 1950.

89. The extent of Soviet air involvement in the Korean War was long a secret of the Cold War, whose details only become known after the collapse of the USSR. See Xiaoming Zhang, *Red Wings over the Yalu: China, the Soviet Union, and the Air War in Korea* (College Station: Texas A&M University Press, 2002).

90. RG 242, shipping advice 2013, item 1/191. Organization of Armed Home Defense Units, September 1950. Reports include graphic descriptions of an air attack on the city of Yŏch'ŏn on August 26, and the bombing of an elementary school on September 1.

91. Conrad C. Crane, *American Airpower Strategy in Korea, 1950–1953* (Lawrence: University Press of Kansas, 2000), 42–43.

Koreans, living in fear of B-29 attacks for nearly three years, including the possibility of atomic bombs, the American air war left a deep and lasting impression. The DPRK government never forgot the lesson of North Korea's vulnerability to American air attack, and for half a century after the Armistice continued to build up antiaircraft defenses, underground installations, and eventually nuclear weapons, to ensure that North Korea would not find itself in such a position again. The long-term psychological effect of the war on the whole of North Korean society cannot be overestimated. The war against the United States, more than any other single factor, gave North Koreans a collective sense of anxiety and fear of outside threats that would continue long after the war's end.

The US-UN-ROK Occupation of North Korea

Crossing the Parallel

When the United States decided to enter the war to defend South Korea, the Americans did not have an explicit plan to retake the North. A few days after the war broken out, the United States announced that its intention was simply to restore the Republic of Korea to the status quo antebellum.[92] The UN resolution to defend Korea was to "repel aggression," suggesting that the North Korean forces merely be pushed back across the Thirty-eighth parallel. But some in the State Department wanted to retain the option of crossing the Thirty-eighth parallel into the North, and both the Joint Chiefs of Staff and General MacArthur were in favor of the idea. For its part, the ROK government was unequivocal about the South Korean position: the United Nations should enter the North, bringing the entire peninsula under the jurisdiction of the ROK. The ROK ambassador to the United States, John M. Chang (Chang Myŏn), relayed to the State Department on September 18 the message that his government wanted the UN forces to push as far as the Chinese and Soviet borders of Korea, that North Korea must surrender unconditionally, and that UN-supervised elections should be held in the North; in this process the ROK "should assume sovereignty over North Korea after the defeat of the North Korean forces."[93] On September 26, ROK foreign minister Limb told Warren Austin, the US ambassador to the United Nations, that "my government has always considered and now considers itself to be the only legitimate government of all of Korea."[94] Therefore the entrance of UN forces into the

---

92. Stueck, *Korean War*, 6.
93. United States, Department of State, *Foreign Relations of the United States, 1950*, vol. 7, *Korea* (Washington, DC: US Government Printing Office, 1976), 735. Hereafter FRUS.
94. Ibid., 787.

North would automatically bring the reconquered areas under the administration of the ROK. However, as John M. Allison, US delegate to the UN General Assembly, pointed out, such a claim contradicted the US and UN position since December 12, 1948, that the ROK only had "effective control and jurisdiction over that part of Korea where the UN Temporary Commission on Korea was able to observe and consult."[95] In short, ROK jurisdiction extended only as far north as the Thirty-eighth parallel, and any question of the North coming under ROK control would have to be an issue for future discussion. Austin suggested to Secretary of State Dean Acheson that the extension of ROK jurisdiction into North Korea not be automatic and further suggested that after the surrender of North Korean forces "free elections [should] be held in *all of Korea* within one year."[96]

The issue of who would be in sovereign control of North Korea was thus still a point of dispute between the ROK and the United States at the end of September 1950, but the question of a UN advance across the Thirty-eighth parallel into North Korea itself had already been resolved in favor of crossing the parallel by the United States weeks before. On September 11, President Truman approved National Security Council decision NSC 81/1, which authorized the UN forces to enter the North. But the Joint Chiefs of Staff (JCS) strongly cautioned the UN commander to be circumspect in provoking the Russians and the Chinese in the process. In a memo to MacArthur on September 27, the JCS warned that "under no circumstances, however, will your forces cross the Manchuria or USSR borders of Korea, and as a matter of policy, no non-Korean ground forces will be used in the northeast provinces bordering the Soviet Union or in the area along the Manchurian border." Further, any "political question such as the formal extension of sovereignty over North Korea should await action by UN to complete the unification of the country."[97]

The UN General Assembly had met on September 19 to discuss crossing into North Korea. At that point, the British position had been for holding new elections throughout Korea and creating a new unified government, whereas the United States supported new elections only in the North.[98] The issue of postwar Korean government still undecided, the United Nations authorized on October 6 the entry of US-led forces into North Korea. On October 9 the US Eighth Army crossed the Thirty-eighth parallel, and MacArthur broadcast a surrender message to the supreme commander of the Korean People's Army: "The early and

---

95. Ibid., 789.
96. Ibid., 825. Emphasis added.
97. *Records of the Joint Chiefs of Staff, Part II, 1946–53: Reel 9* (Washington, DC: Microfilm, University Publications of America, 1979), 578, 580 (hereafter JCS); Michael Hickey, *The Korean War: The West Confronts Communism* (Woodstock, NY: The Outlook Press, 2000), 84.
98. Stueck, *Korean War*, 92.

total defeat of your forces is now inevitable. In order that the decision of the United Nations may be carried out with a minimum further loss of life and destruction to Korea, the United Nations Commander in Chief calls upon you and the forces under your command, wherever situated, to lay down your arms and cease hostilities forthwith."[99] Kim Il Sung, safe in his Kanggye redoubt near the Chinese border, did not respond.

It should be noted that MacArthur's surrender message made no mention of the ROK. The US position was that the United Nations, not the ROK, had jurisdiction over the conquered areas of the North. A top secret State Department memo of October 2 held that Koreans would play a dominant role in administering the North but "the sovereignty of the Republic of Korea over the northern areas will not be legally extended until elections are held. During this interim period North Korea will therefore be in a status of occupation and will be subject to the authority of the Commanding General of the Unified Forces."[100] North Korea, in other words, would for the time being be under the authority of General MacArthur, not Syngman Rhee. In the meantime, the US Department of Army drafted a proposal on October 3 for a three-phase occupation of North Korea: (1) from the entry into the North until the end of significant guerrilla activity; (2) from the end of guerrilla activity until national elections are held; and (3) from national elections until the ROK has assumed responsibility for the North. During the first two phases, MacArthur would be "Military Governor of that part of Korea which lies North of the 38th Parallel" in the name of the United Nations.[101] For a brief period, MacArthur was in the unique position of being the authorized commander of two military occupation governments, one in Japan and one in North Korea.

Administering the North

In fact, however, jurisdiction over North Korea was not such a simple matter. Not only were the UN command and the ROK government at odds over who should be administering the conquered North, MacArthur himself expressed reluctance to assume the role of military governor. MacArthur envisioned a six- to eighteen-month period of interim civil administration in North Korea, until elections could be held and the ROK government itself take control.[102] But he and the Joint Chiefs wanted to avoid any appearance of a unilateral US military

---

99. JCS, 582.
100. FRUS, 835.
101. Ibid., 854–5.
102. JCS, 700.

government. The JCS advocated "the participation of as many as possible of the UN nations in post-hostilities activities in Korea,"[103] especially Asian members. This allied effort would administer the newly unified Korea through a UN Interim Committee on Korea, later replaced by the UN Commission for the Unification and Rehabilitation of Korea (UNCURK), established October 7, 1950, whose members included Australia, Chile, the Netherlands, Pakistan, the Philippines, Turkey, and Thailand.

In mid-October the army brought in Colonel Alfred Conner Bowman, formerly head of the postwar Allied government in Trieste, to assist with the construction of a civil administration in North Korea. Bowman arrived in Japan on October 16 and discussed the situation in North Korea with members of MacArthur's occupation administration in Tokyo, who informed him that "'something is cooking' on MG [military government] for North Korea" despite MacArthur's "very strong protest against the term 'Military Government.'"[104] Bowman's clear impression was that, protests to the contrary, MacArthur and those around him were planning a "full-scale military government" for North Korea along the lines of the 1945–48 military government in South Korea and the current US occupation administration in Japan. Members of MacArthur's Japan team echoed the officials in Washington in their "misgivings" about allowing the ROK troops free reign in the North.[105] The preferred alternative, already in the works, was a temporary American-led administration that would begin with an "intensive education and reorientation program" for the residents of North Korea before eventually handing over the administration of the North to the ROK.[106]

When Bowman visited North Korea itself, however, he received a slightly different impression. It was clear that, whatever American intentions may have been, ROK representatives were already in control of civil administration in much of the North. On his flight to Pyongyang on a US Air Force plane, Bowman was accompanied by the ROK minister of education, minister of welfare, minister of defense, and Helen Kim (Kim Hwal-lan), president of Ewha Women's University and public information officer in Syngman Rhee's government.[107] American commanders on the ground told him that "ROKS are carrying out MG procedures in an orthodox manner" and that the South Koreans were utilizing local people, not their own, to run civil affairs.[108]

---

103. Ibid., 652.

104. Hoover Institution, Stanford University. Alfred Conner Bowman Papers, box 1. Diary of Visit to Japan and North Korea, 1, 3.

105. Ibid., 5.

106. Ibid., 31.

107. Ibid., 7.

108. Ibid., 12–13.

The South Korean Role

Syngman Rhee had agreed on July 14, 1950, to place ROK forces under UN command, although technically the ROK Army was not part of the UN forces because Seoul was not a UN member.[109] In practice, ROK forces were often on the ground in the North ahead of the US and other UN troops, and took over local governance. The reality was, in many areas, a South Korean occupation of the North. ROK forces had crossed the Thirty-eighth parallel in the west as early as October 1, 1950, a week before the UN forces entered the North. South Koreans captured the port city of Wŏnsan on October 11, more than two weeks ahead of the US Tenth Corps, which found the ROK forces already running a civil administration in the city. The US State Department was informed on October 10 that the ROK National Police "already are patrolling nine towns liberated in Red North Korea by troops of the Republic." According to Home Minister Cho Pyŏng-ok, these police were part of a force of thirty thousand "being recruited to keep order in all Red territory as it is freed from Communist rule."[110] Thus, despite the UN position that ROK jurisdiction be confined to the area below the Thirty-eighth parallel, in fact the Rhee government was reconstituting civil administration in the recaptured areas of North Korea as well.

Just as the KPA conquest of Seoul had been the key symbolic and strategic victory in the initial North Korean attack on the South, the UN capture of the North Korean capital of Pyongyang was central to the allied conquest of the North. Here again it was ROK forces who led the way. The First Division of the ROK Army, led by General Paik Sun Yup, was the first Allied military force to enter Pyongyang, on October 19. Paik recounted later the thrill he felt that his forces had "beaten everyone to Pyongyang," including the US First Cavalry, who had been expected to liberate the city.[111] This was an especially sweet victory for Paik, who was a native of Pyongyang and had fled south in December 1945. Paik set up First Division headquarters in the North Korean Supreme People's Assembly building, and he sat in Kim Il Sung's own chair.[112] After the US First Cavalry joined the ROK troops in Pyongyang, the two forces retreated to the outskirts of the city and left the administration of Pyongyang to local citizens. Colonel Archibald W. Meldon was the First Cavalry's civil affairs officer, and he helped to establish a provisional

---

109. For the "Taejŏn Agreement" on the status of ROK forces in relation to the UN alliance see Appleman, *South to the Naktong*, 112. The ROK Army was technically under the administration of the US Eighth Army, which was of course the leading force in the UN alliance, but in actual practice the ROK forces often acted independently.

110. "Secretary of State to the Embassy in Korea," 12 October 1950. FRUS, 939.

111. Paik Sun Yup, *From Pusan to Panmunjom* (Dulles, Virginia: Brassey's, 1999), 73.

112. Ibid., 82.

city council under acting mayor Im Chang-dŏk.[113] Rhee flew to Pyongyang later that month and announced that the people of North Korea were now united with their southern brethren as one nation, the Republic of Korea, and would begin the task of rebuilding a unified country.[114]

The extension of ROK sovereignty over the North was, as mentioned earlier, something that the US viewed ambivalently and about which other Alliance members clearly opposed. The British and the French, in particular, had been highly critical of the Rhee government before war broke out, and were much more reluctant than the Americans to recognize the jurisdiction of the ROK over the occupied areas of the North as the war progressed.[115]

Press reports of ROK Army behavior in the recapture of South Korea from the communist forces had been extremely critical, although less so in the American than in the British and Western European media. British and French journalists reported mass arrests and indiscriminate torture and killing of suspected collaborators.[116] The British journalist Reginald Thompson wrote that the recapture of Seoul by ROK forces was so marred by violence that "few people can have suffered so terrible a liberation."[117] Accompanying UN forces into Pyongyang, Thompson witnessed "self-styled United Nations North Koreans . . . conducting witch hunts throughout the city."[118] While reports of atrocities by the North Koreans were commonplace in the Western press as well, the image of Rhee's government and the ROK was hardly any better. Under these circumstances, opinion among UN allied governments was poorly disposed toward allowing Rhee to extend his government into the North.

Secretary of State Dean Acheson was incensed by press reports that Rhee was setting up an ROK civil administration in the North, including the appointment of five provincial governors. On October 18 Acheson cabled John Muccio, US ambassador to Seoul, that if such reports had been correct and if Rhee insisted on "outright defiance of principles laid down by the UN," the US would find it difficult to support Rhee against pressure from the United Nations and elsewhere to hold new elections throughout Korea.[119]

---

113. Henry Chung, *Korea and the United States through War and Peace, 1943–1960* (Seoul: Yonsei University Press, 2000), 188.

114. Ibid., 192.

115. State Department, "Draft Memorandum to the National Security Council," 30 August 1950. FRUS, 671.

116. See for example the London *Times,* 9 October and 24 October 1950; Serge Bromberger et al., *Retour de Coree* (Paris: Juillard, 1951), 138–39; *New York Times,* 17 November 1950.

117. Reginald Thompson, *Cry Korea* (London: MacDonald, 1951), 94.

118. Ibid., 182.

119. "Secretary of State to the Embassy in Korea," 18 October 1950, FRUS, 979.

The instruments for enforcing law and order, Rhee announced on October 18, 1950, were the South Korean police and volunteer youth leagues.[120] Rhee also declared that, contrary to the US-UN plan, land reform in North Korea would be overturned and land returned to the former landlords. The entire apparatus of political mobilization in the North, beginning with the government and party and going down to the local social organizations, was to be dismantled. The problem was, however, that the North Korean system penetrated far more deeply into the society than had the system in the South. Millions of North Korean residents belonged not only to the Worker's Party, but to various government-sponsored front organizations such as the Women's League, the Peasant League, the Worker's League, and the Democratic Youth League. Almost any of them could be considered "communist." The daunting task of demobilizing this highly mobilized society, and creating a new social system in its place, led to acts of violence that could be more indiscriminate than in the North Korean occupation of the South.[121] While allegations of atrocities on both sides have been a point of bitter contention between North and South Korea since the war broke out, North Korea has consistently argued that hundreds of thousands of civilians were indiscriminately killed by US and South Korean forces in the fall of 1950.[122] Whatever the truth of these allegations, they have served as a rallying point for North Korea's anti-American sentiment that remains salient to this day.

Reeducation and Reorientation

By October 27, the Korean War appeared to be over. As far as the UN forces were concerned, the war had been won and Korea was reunified.[123] MacArthur announced that the UN mission was now to clear the North of any remaining pockets of resistance and to begin the task of reconstruction, reeducation, and reorientation. *Reorientation* was a term often used by the US military occupation forces in Germany and Japan, and indicated the political, economic, and above all psychological transformation of a conquered enemy society toward liberal democracy. The Korean War was, like World War II before it but in the new communist/anticommunist Cold War context, a war of propaganda as well as arms. This was especially true for the US and Allied forces during the occupation of North Korea, where a major priority was convincing a population subjected to

---

120. Callum MacDonald, "'So Terrible a Liberation': The UN Occupation of North Korea," *Bulletin of Concerned Asian Scholars* 12, no. 2 (April–June 1991): 10.

121. Ibid., 5.

122. See, for example, *US Imperialists Started the Korean War*.

123. Thompson, *Cry Korea*, 190.

five years of intensive communist "brainwashing" to accept the positive role of the United Nations, United States, and Republic of Korea in uniting their country. A State Department draft memorandum to the National Security Council had noted this as early as August 1950, well before the entry of UN forces into North Korea, recommending that "the United States should make every effort, utilizing all information media, to turn the inevitable bitterness and resentment of the war-victimized Korean people away from the United States and direct it toward the Korean Communists, toward the USSR and, depending upon the role they play, toward the Chinese Communists, as the instigators of the destructive conflict."[124] For the United States, the occupation of North Korea from September to November 1950 offered an unprecedented opportunity for Americans to study the "psychology of communism." The US Air Force commissioned a psychological study of refugees from North Korea and South Koreans who had lived through the ninety-day communist occupation of the South. The study concluded that the communist "monopoly of information" had been "at least 90 percent effective."[125] Nevertheless, there were "cracks" in this monolithic information control. People secretly listened to radio broadcasts from the South; rumors from the outside spread through well-established networks of friends, relatives, and neighbors; even if active resistance was minimal, there were those who quietly refused to believe the propaganda.

After five years of a highly compressed revolutionary experience in society, economy, politics, and culture, enthusiasm for the North Korean system had already begun to wane. According to interviews with North Korean residents during the UN occupation, mainly in the areas of Wŏnsan and Hŭngnam, support for the communists had fallen most sharply among the peasants, who had originally been the greatest beneficiaries of the reforms.[126] Among industrial workers, support for the communist program had lessened but was still substantial. But support was highest among intellectuals and students, both in North Korea itself and in the areas of South Korea that had been occupied by the Korean People's Army. A new kind of "reorientation" was an urgent task for the UN forces occupying the North, a task the UN Command suggested had to be pursued in conjunction with, and was as equally important as, the military operation itself.

The ROK Department of National Defense first proposed a plan for "the conversion of communists north of the Thirty-eighth parallel" in October 1950, a

---

124. State Department, "Draft Memorandum," 665–66.
125. Wilbur Schramm and John W. Riley Jr., "Communication in the Sovietized State, as Demonstrated in Korea," *American Sociological Review* 16, no. 6 (December 1951): 765.
126. National Archives Record Group 497, box 464. Headquarters, 181st Counter-Intelligence Corps Detachment, 1st Marine Division, Fleet Marine Force. "Communist Indoctrination of North Korean Civilian Populace," 30 November 1950, 2–5.

translation of which the US Eighth Army in Korea forwarded to the commander-in-chief, Far East on October 28.[127] The ROK plan called for a multimedia operation that would eliminate all visual and aural evidence of the communist regime in every province, county, and village. Propaganda units at each provincial seat would consist of two painters, two theater artists, two musicians, and one religious leader, and would make extensive use of returned, and strongly anticommunist, refugees from the North. After the "cleansing and extinction of communist-inspired music," for example, "newly made songs, martial music and lyrics inspiring racial spirit" would be "propagated and publicized throughout the broadcasting system and various recitals, street marches and broadcast cars." Individuals would be categorized according to ideological orientation and re-educated accordingly: in descending order of political reliability, "(a) patriots (political criminals, underground political workers), (b) general people, (c) communist sympathizers, (d) communist indoctrinated one [sic], and (e) communist soldiers and policeman."[128] "All should be tolerated but those who are the enemy of our race and who ran to the communism by his will," the plan stated, and "those who are tolerated should be persuaded to make public his reconversion through the communiqué, radio broadcast, message, etc."[129]

The United States responded with its own, slightly less ominous-sounding plan for changing the hearts and minds of the North Koreans. In November, the State Department drafted a "Reorientation Plan for Korea"—all of Korea—acknowledging that "we must admit that communist propaganda developed a certain degree of success in both North and South Korea."[130] The State Department priority would be on information, and the reconstruction of the educational system would be handled by UNESCO as part of postwar rehabilitation. There was an enormous information vacuum to fill: the State Department Plan noted that "the North Koreans have been shut off from the outside world since 1941," when the Pacific War led to the Japanese blackout of Western news; the North Koreans were not even aware that the United States—not the Soviet Union—had defeated Japan in World War II.[131] Under such conditions "it may be assumed that among the uneducated people shut off from the rest of the world there has been a good

127. RG 319, box. 18. US 8th Army to CINCFE, "Plan Developed by Information and Education Bureau, Department of National Defense, Republic of Korea, For the Conversion of Communists North of the Thirty-eighth Parallel to the Democratic Form of Government," 28 October 1950.

128. Ibid., 4.

129. Ibid., 8.

130. RG 319, box 18. Department of State, "Reorientation Plan for Korea," November 1950, 9.

131. Ibid., 7.

deal of acceptance of the communist line."[132] Therefore an extensive, intensive, and appropriate program of reorientation had to be implemented immediately. "The mistakes of the United States Information Service (USIS) in concentrating on too sophisticated media and on the cities must be avoided," the State Department noted, without stating explicitly that this is where the Soviet and North Korean communists had been more strategically successful.

The priority media of reeducation would be (1) motion pictures, (2) puppet and marionette shows, (3) speaker programs, (4) exhibits, and (5) Korean vernacular script (hangŭl) publications. In particular, motion pictures "offer the best media for use during the short-term re-education period." The USIS motion picture production unit in Seoul should resume operation, and the USIS puppet section should also "be resumed as quickly as possible."[133] A key role would be played by returned North Korean refugees, who were to be sent back to their home regions to give public talks on the evils of communism and the benevolence of the United Nations. The USIS would coordinate this program through the use of mobile propaganda units and the establishment of reorientation centers in Seoul, Pusan, Taejŏn, Taegu, Kwangju, and Chŏnju in the South, and Pyongyang, Hamhŭng, Wonsan, and Ch'ŏngjin in the North.

At the forefront of reorientation would be Christians, both native Christians and Western missionaries. Most Korean Christians were seen as strongly anticommunist, especially those who had fled from the North, although perhaps a third of the Christians in North Korea had joined the progovernment Korean Christian Federation led by Kim Il Sung's mother's cousin, Kang Yang-uk. The State Department plan was, in effect, to unleash the missionaries on North Korea. "As part of the program, missionaries, should not only be allowed but should be assisted in reestablishing the large education and medical centers which were once maintained in the North," recovering their old denominational division of labor: Methodists and Presbyterians in Pyongyang; Presbyterians in Sunchŏn, Kangye, and Chaeryong; Methodists in Wŏnsan; Canadian Presbyterians in Hamhŭng.[134] Particularly important would be the Protestant Audio-Visual Community, with its substantial equipment and experience in reaching the countryside.

Although State Department and US Military Government personnel would run the reorientation program at the center, seven of the nine members in charge of field operations were children of Western missionaries born in Korea, including Horace G. Underwood and his brother Richard, and E. Otto De Camp of the Protestant Audio-Visual Committee. The metaphors of religion and war, as

132. Ibid., 10.
133. Ibid., 17.
134. Ibid., 8.

well as the concerted use of Christian propagandists, gave the reorientation plan the flavor of a crusade: "Above all, those who direct the program must be adaptable and good Americans willing to tackle the work with evangelical zeal. Given proper weapons and adequate supplies and equipment, a few qualified Americans can accomplish a great deal in all of Korea and can lay a foundation which will facilitate the reconstruction and unification of the country."[135]

On November 27 and 28, representatives of the State Department, United States Information Service–Korea, General Headquarters (GHQ) Far East, and the Department of the Army met to finalize the reorientation plan. They proposed an Information and Education Program that would be run by State Department personnel "but [was] not to be identified as a US program," in other words, it was to be a UN operation. A ten-man State Department team was ready to be airlifted to Korea around December 1 to carry this out. On the one hand, the obvious model for the Korean reorientation and the source of much of its human and material resources would be the still-ongoing occupation of Japan. On the other hand, the task would in some ways be far greater. For one thing, there was no private ownership of media in North Korea, and thus private ownership and operations of newspapers and other media would have to be developed. For another, there was still a great distrust of Americans and ongoing propaganda being broadcast from behind enemy lines to the North, as well as from China and Russia. The lack of material resources was acute, and much would have to be brought in from Japan. But reorientation, though onerous, was a priority "no less important than the maintenance of peace and order or economic rehabilitation." To begin with, a short "intensive" period of not more than twelve months of deprogramming would be implemented by forces on the ground, followed by a long-term consolidation and rehabilitation with the assistance of UN member states and international organizations. Priority would be given to visual media and reaching the countryside.

The United States was faced with, in fact, a triple burden of reorientation, and the American planners seemed determined to make up for the mistakes and short-sightedness of the initial occupation of South Korea. The new reorientation plan would be no less than to "undo whatever has been done to the minds of the people by the communist regime, the Japanese regime, and even the heritage of the pre-Japanese regime which stands in the way of their becoming adequate participants in an orderly, responsible, progressive and peace-loving democratic society."[136] It was, to say the least, an ambitious program. But in the end, it was

---

135. Ibid., 23.

136. RG 319, box 18. General Headquarters, United Nations Command. Operations Order No. 2, "Reorientation and Reeducation Program" (Confidential), 1.

never implemented. On the very day reorientation plans were finalized, November 28, 1950, the US Eighth Army began a headlong retreat south, in the face of a massive Chinese offensive.[137] The Korean War from this point onward became less a political conflict than a massive military struggle between conventional armies, and "reorientation" would have to be postponed for the indefinite future.

Chinese Intervention, Counterattack, and Stalemate

China's entry into the Korean War changed the war dramatically and came neither suddenly nor without warning. As we have seen, Mao had suggested to Kim Il Sung as early as May 1950 that China would assist the KPA if requested. On June 28, just three days after war broke out, Nie Rongzhen, acting chief of the People's Liberation Army (PLA) General Staff, proposed sending a military observation group to North Korea.[138] In early July, China's Central Military Commission decided to establish a Border Defense Army in the northeast of the country, with some 260,000 soldiers.[139] The Chinese became even more concerned in August, after the North Korean advance was slowed and the US-UN-ROK forces established their defense cordon at the Pusan perimeter. Mao noted that the US forces might make an amphibious landing at Inch'ŏn, thus turning the tide of war.[140] On August 11–14, Chinese military leaders in the northeastern region, under CCP Northeastern Bureau Chief Gao Gang, convened a meeting in which Gao proposed sending troops to Korea "in the name of the Volunteer Army."[141] Still, the Chinese would not send their troops into Korea without a Korean request for them to do so, along with a clear Soviet commitment of support.

Chinese-Korean-Soviet war preparations, far from reflecting the harmonious cooperation of fraternal allies, were fraught with mutual suspicion and lack of communication. Zhou Enlai appointed General Chai Chengwen chargé d'affaires to North Korea on July 10 and head of the PRC military mission in Pyongyang on August 12, to coordinate defense planning with the North Koreans, but Chai found the Koreans frustratingly uncooperative and reluctant to give the Chinese

137. Stueck, *Korean War*, 128.

138. Zhang, *Mao's Military Romanticism*, 72. See also Chai Chengwen and Zhao Yongtian, *Banmendian Tanpan* [Panmunjom Negotiations] (Beijing: Jiefangjun chubanshe, 1989).

139. Shen and Li, *After Leaning to One Side*, 34–35.

140. Ibid. 36. Soviet advisors had also warned the North Koreans about the possibility of a US landing at Inch'ŏn. See Goncharov et al., *Uncertain Partners*, 171–72.

141. *Kang-Mei Yuan-Chao zhanzhengshi*, 91–92.

necessary information.[142] The Soviets were hesitant to offer air cover as the Chinese requested, in the event of Chinese deployment to Korea.[143] The North Koreans preferred Soviet assistance to Chinese and turned to the Chinese only after the Soviets refused to send in their own troops. The KWP Politburo held an emergency meeting on September 28, as the KPA lines were being decimated by advancing UN troops, and the following day Kim Il Sung and Pak Hŏn-yŏng wrote a telegram to Stalin asking for "direct military aid from the Soviet Union," but "if for some reason this is impossible, then assist us in the creation of international volunteer units in China and in other people's democracies."[144]

The Soviets refused North Korea's request. On October 1, Kim and Pak sent a long, pleading telegram to Mao, a copy of which is on display at the Korean War museum in Dandong, China, across the Yalu River from North Korea. The tone of the message is urgent and almost obsequious, full of Confucian deference to "respected Comrade Mao Zedong" and pointing out the threat to China of the UN advance across the Thirty-eighth parallel. Pak then met Mao and Zhou in Beijing and asked directly that Chinese troops be sent to Korea. That same day, Stalin telegrammed Mao requesting China send "at least five or six divisions" of "volunteers."[145] On October 3, Zhou sent a message to the United States through Indian ambassador K. M. Pannikar, warning that "the Chinese people absolutely will not tolerate foreign aggression, nor will they supinely tolerate seeing their neighbors being savagely invaded by the imperialists."[146] Beijing was committing itself to "oppose America and defend Korea," as the war would be known in China.

For several days the Chinese leadership debated the dispatch of troops to Korea. Mao had already made up his mind to send troops, and on October 8 established a Chinese People's Volunteer Army (CPVA) under the command of Peng Dehuai. Lin Biao opposed the move, arguing that the Chinese military was underequipped and vulnerable to US airstrikes and atomic weapons on Chinese soil. Zhou Enlai was hesitant as well.[147] Zhou was dispatched to Moscow to discuss Soviet-Chinese military cooperation on Korea, and on October 11 met with Stalin at the Soviet leader's dacha in Sochi. Stalin explained that the USSR could

142. Shen, "Sino-North Korean Conflict," 3, based on interviews with Chai.

143. Ibid. 6.

144. Kathryn Weathersby, "The Soviet Role in the Early Phase of the Korean War: New Documentary Evidence," *Journal of American-East Asian Relations* 2, no. 4 (winter 1993): 453–44.

145. Shen and Li, *After Leaning to One Side*, 39.

146. Nie Rongzhen, *Inside the Red Star: The Memoirs of Marshal Nie Rongzhen* (Beijing: New World Press, 1988), 635; Zhou Enlai, *Zhou Enlai Nianpu* [Chronology of Zhou Enlai] (Beijing: Zhongyang wenxian chubanshe, n.d.), 82.

147. Peng Dehuai, *Memoirs of a Chinese Marshall: The Autobiographical Notes of Peng Dehuai* (Beijing: Foreign Languages Publishing House, 1984), 472.

not send its own troops to Korea, lest they trigger a major war with the United States, nor would he commit himself to proving air support for the Chinese. Zhou, for his part, conveyed China's reluctance to enter the war due to its economic difficulties and the need to rebuild after it own recent civil war. Stalin responded that in that case, it would be better for Kim and his troops to give up on North Korea and retreat to Northeast China and the Russian Far East, where his guerrilla movement had operated before 1945. On October 13, Stalin telegrammed Kim via Ambassador Shtykov, suggesting Kim evacuate his forces from Korea and move farther north.[148]

Meanwhile Mao held an emergency meeting of the Politburo to discuss the dispatch of Chinese forces to Korea. The group reaffirmed China's commitment to defending Korea, but Soviet air cover and material support were critical matters that remained uncertain. Zhou stayed in Moscow until October 16 to discuss these issues with the Soviet leadership. Still lacking a firm commitment of Soviet air cover, Zhou met with other member of the CCP Central Committee on October 18 for a final discussion of troop deployment to Korea. Mao declared that, whatever the limitations of Soviet support, the Chinese could no longer stand back while enemy forces besieged Pyongyang. That evening, Mao ordered CPVA forces to cross the Yalu River into Korea.[149] Within a few days, the CPVA encountered and decisively defeated South Korean troops in their first battle with the enemy.[150] Chinese offensives in November would send the US Eighth Army reeling, in what Roy Appleman accurately calls "a series of disasters unequaled in our country's history."[151]

By this time, Kim had moved his headquarters to the vicinity of Kanggye, in the north central province of Chagang near the Chinese border. Mountainous and sparsely populated, Chagang was a new province, established in February 1949 "for the purpose of accelerating the exploitation of the inexhaustible underground as well as forestry resources which the province possesses," according to the North Korean media.[152] US intelligence before the Korean War speculated

148. Alexandre Y. Mansourov, "Stalin, Mao, Kim and the Chinese Decision to Enter the Korean War, September 16–October 15, 1950: New Evidence from the Russian Archives," *Cold War International History Project Bulletin* 6–7 (winter 1995–96): 103–4. Khrushchev remembered Stalin as saying, "If Kim Il Sung falls, we are not going to participate with our troops. Let it be. Let the Americans now be our neighbors in the Far East." Khrushchev was appalled by this cold-blooded abandonment of a communist ally. *Khrushchev Remembers: The Glasnost Tapes* (New York: Little, Brown, 1990), 147.

149. Shen and Li, *After Leaning to One Side*, 46.

150. Peng, *Memoirs*, 473.

151. Roy E. Appleman, *Disaster in Korea: The Chinese Confront MacArthur* (College Station: Texas A&M University Press, 1989), 5.

152. RG 59, 795A series. Embassy to State, 7 March 1950.

that the Soviets had appropriated the region as a timber and mineral concession, noting that it covered much of the same area as the 1896 Yalu Timber Concessions of Czar Nicholas II, and that an internal "Iron Curtain" cut off Chagang from the rest of North Korea.[153] But this region was also near the area where Kim's guerrilla movement had been active in the 1930s and, virtually impregnable from the South but well connected by road to Manchuria, was an ideal redoubt for Kim. Chagang remained a militarily restricted region after the Korean War, the only province to which foreign aid workers were not allowed access during the famine of the 1990s, and the site of suspected underground nuclear activity near the village of Kŭmchang-ri in 1998.

The Central Committee of the KWP held its Third Plenum at Kanggye in late December 1950. The purpose of the plenum was to assess the state of the war, and several top military and party leaders were criticized and punished for "errors" and "crimes" in their conduct of the war. The biggest victim of these purges, the first of a series of potential rivals eliminated by Kim Il Sung throughout the 1950s, was Mu Chŏng, commander of the Second Corps. A veteran leader of the Korean Volunteer Army in Yan'an and arguably the most experienced military commander in the KPA, Mu Chŏng was chastised for failing to defend Pyongyang, dismissed from his post, and forced into exile in China, where he died shortly afterward.[154] Eleven months later, at the Fourth Plenum of the KWP Central Committee in November 1951, Kim proposed a more inclusive party recruitment process in order to enlarge a KWP devastated by war, defections, and flight to the South. Hŏ Ka-i, the leading Soviet Korean, was attacked for having promoted overly restrictive recruitment policies as party secretary. Hŏ was accused of "liquidationism," removed from his post, and committed suicide (or possibly was murdered) in July 1953.[155] The war thus became an opportunity for Kim to consolidate his personal power within the DPRK leadership, and by the end of 1951 he had effectively eliminated two of his most serious rivals, Mu Chŏng and Hŏ Ka-i, leading figures of the "Yanan" and "Soviet" factions, respectively. Shortly after the war ended, Kim removed his biggest rival, "domestic" communist leader Pak Hŏn-yŏng, who was also accused of aiding the enemy in the war, among other charges. We will return to the subject of North Korea's intraelite struggles in the following chapters.

153. Ibid.

154. Dae-Sook Suh, *Kim Il Sung: The North Korean Leader* (New York: Columbia University Press, 1988), 122–23; Chungang ilbo, *Pirok*, 135–48.

155. Andrei Lankov, *From Stalin to Kim Il Sung: The Formation of North Korea 1945–1960* (New Brunswick: Rutgers University Press, 2002), 148–52.

The Armistice

After the Chinese entered the war, Kim Il Sung wanted the Chinese forces under his direct command, but the Soviets and Chinese overruled him. The Chinese–North Korean allied forces were led by CPVA commander Peng Dehuai, and Kim would take this as another slight against North Korean sovereignty by the overbearing Chinese.[156] But in any case the CPVA-KPA combined forces were immediately effective in turning back the enemy tide. The Chinese–North Korean counterattack of November–December 1950 drove UN forces south of the Thirty-eighth parallel once again, recapturing Seoul at the end of December. But the communist offensive reached its limits in January 1951; the UN forces then pushed back, and by mid-1951 the two sides had reached a stalemate roughly across the middle of the peninsula. For two years, from July 1951 to July 1953, the two coalition armies engaged in a war of position along this shifting central front, as they simultaneously attempted to work out a cease-fire arrangement. This "negotiating while fighting," linked to issues of POW repatriation and international opinion, accomplished little except further destruction. Nevertheless, the destruction remained confined to the Korean Peninsula, although at several points it could have easily spread into China, or even triggered a global US-Soviet conflict. MacArthur, as is well known, wanted permission to attack the Chinese mainland and requested permission to do so in December 1950.[157] He did not believe the Soviets would respond, and even suggested using atomic weapons on Manchuria to block Chinese reinforcements.[158] But Truman was more restrained than MacArthur and also more sensitive to the concerns of America's European allies, who deeply feared a Soviet counterattack on Europe if the war expanded in East Asia.[159] MacArthur was removed from his command on April 11, replaced by General Matthew B. Ridgeway, and within a few weeks the Americans began secret talks with the Soviets and Chinese about a negotiated end to the fighting.

After the CPVA intervention, the North Koreans expected a quick and total victory, as Kim Il Sung and Pak Hŏn-yŏng made clear to Peng Dehuai in January 1951.[160] Kim and Park opposed Peng's policy of graduate advancement, giving the troops time to rest and regroup, and urged Peng instead to continue pursuing the Americans until they withdrew from the peninsula. Peng lost

---

156. Shen and Li, *After Leaning to One Side*, 70–76.

157. FRUS, 1630–33.

158. Cumings, *Origins,* vol. 2, 750. According to MacArthur's proposal, the atomic bombing would be accompanied by a US-backed Chinese Nationalist invasion of the mainland, rolling back the Chinese communist revolution permanently.

159. Stueck, *Rethinking the Korean War*, 124–25.

160. Hong Xuezhi. *Kang-Mei Yuan-Chao zhanzheng huiyi* [Recollections of the Resist-America Aid-Korea War] (Beijing: Jiefangjun wenyi chubanshe, 1991), 110–13.

patience and shouted back, "Your underestimation of the enemy is a serous mistake and I will not tolerate it. If you think I am not doing my job, you can fire me, court-marshal me, or even kill me."[161] In the end Peng's more cautious approach, supported by the Soviets as well as the Chinese, won the day and was reluctantly accepted by the North Korean leadership. As the North Koreans saw it, China's failure to press their advantage against the Americans in early 1951 may have cost them the total liberation of Korea. Even though China and the USSR saved the DPRK from destruction, their assistance was not enough for Pyongyang to permanently unify the country, the goal for which the North Koreans had launched the war in the first place.

The Soviets, for their part, went out of their way to avoid a direct clash with the United States, even if it meant profoundly disappointing their Korean and Chinese allies. Although the Soviets did supply air cover and equipment, neither the CPVA nor the KPA got the full support from the Soviet military that they had hoped for, and "total victory" eluded them. It may have served Stalin's purpose to keep the Korean conflict protracted, ensuring that China (and North Korea) would remain weak and dependent. But if this was Stalin's plan, Soviet parsimony did not prevent an acrimonious Sino-Soviet split from emerging a few years after the war ended, and probably did much to encourage it. Chinese influence remained strong in North Korea after the war, not least because of the thousands of CPVA soldiers who participated in the postwar reconstruction and stayed in North Korea until 1958. Although not without its own tensions, Chinese–North Korean cooperation in the war created a bond much deeper than the correct but rather distant Soviet-DPRK ties. Once again, Stalin may have been too clever by half.

This "limited war" was for Koreans a total war. The human and material resources of North and South Korea were used to their utmost. The physical destruction and loss of life on both sides was almost beyond comprehension, but the North suffered the greater damage, due to American saturation bombing and the scorched-earth policy of the retreating UN forces.[162] The US Air Force estimated that North Korea's destruction was proportionately greater than that of Japan in the Second World War. American planes dropped 635,000 tons of bombs on Korea, compared to 503,000 in the entire Pacific theatre of World War II, including 32,557 tons of napalm.[163] The number of Korean dead, injured, or missing by war's end approached 3 million, 10 percent of the overall population.

---

161. Shen and Li, *After Leaning to One Side*, 80, citing Peng's memoirs.

162. Far East Command ordered General Walker to "destroy everything that might be of use to the enemy" as the Eighth Army fled south in December 1950. Appleman, *Disaster in Korea*, 360.

163. Cited in Rosemary Foot, *A Substitute for Victory: The Politics of Peacemaking at the Korean Armistice Talks* (Ithaca: Cornell University Press, 1990), 207–8.

The majority of those killed were in the North, with half of the population of the South; although the DPRK does not have official figures, possibly 12 to 15 percent of the population was killed in the war, a figure close to or surpassing the proportion of Soviet citizens killed in World War II.[164] Ironically, North Korea's "Fatherland Liberation War" resembled the Soviet Union's "Great Patriotic War" in its devastating effect on the country, and did not even end in victory—exactly the outcome Kim and Stalin had wanted to avoid when they planned the attack of June 25, 1950.

North Korea's considerable economic achievements since liberation were all but completely wiped out by the war. By 1949, after two years of a planned economy, North Korea had recovered from the postliberation chaos, and economic output had reached the level of the colonial period.[165] Plans for 1950 were to increase output again by a third in the North, and of course the DPRK leadership had expected integration with the agriculturally more productive South as a result of the war. According to DPRK figures, the war destroyed some 8,700 factories, 5,000 schools, 1,000 hospitals, and 600,000 homes.[166] Most of the destruction occurred in 1950 and 1951. To escape the bombing, entire factories were moved underground, along with schools, hospitals, government offices, and much of the population. Agriculture was devastated, and famine loomed. Peasants hid underground during the day and came out to farm at night. Destruction of livestock, shortages of seed, farm tools, and fertilizer, and loss of manpower reduced agricultural production to the level of bare subsistence at best. The *Rodong Sinmun* newspaper referred to 1951 as "the year of unbearable trials," a term revived in the famine years of the 1990s.[167] Worse was yet to come. By the fall of 1952, there were no effective targets left for US planes to hit. Every significant town, city, and industrial area in North Korea had already been bombed. The Air Force therefore decided in the spring of 1953 to target irrigation dams on the Yalu River, both to destroy the North Korean rice crop and to pressure the Chinese, who would have to supply more food aid to the North. Five reservoirs were hit, flooding thousands of acres of farmland, inundating whole towns and laying waste to the essential food source for millions of North Koreans.[168] Only emergency assistance from China, the USSR, and other socialist countries prevented widespread famine.

The war also had an important effect on the DPRK leadership's relationship with the North Korean people. As many as 3 million North Koreans fled South

---

164. Jon Halliday, "The North Korean Enigma," *New Left Review* 127 (May–June 1981): 29.

165. RG 59. U.S. Embassy to State, "Economic Conditions in North Korea," October 11, 1949, 8.

166. "The Three Year Plan," *Kyŏngje kŏnsŏl* [Economic Construction], September 1956, 5–6.

167. *Rodong Sinmun*, March 16, 1952, 1.

168. Callum MacDonald, *Korea: The War before Vietnam* (London: Macmillan, 1986), 241–42.

during the war; many fled to escape the bombing, but there were certainly many others who left the North and stayed in the South for political reasons.[169] On the one hand, this exodus siphoned off many of the potential dissenters. On the other hand, such a massive emigration did not reflect well on the regime's ability to mobilize and maintain popular support. The leadership's anxiety about the trustworthiness of its own people was reflected in some of Kim Il Sung's public statements during the war, calling for heightened vigilance against "reactionaries" and rallying around the party.[170] After the war, Kim and other leaders put much emphasis on the need for "reeducation" to ensure the loyalty of North Korea's citizens, as we will discuss in the next chapter. The war created a new class of potentially untrustworthy citizens who had cooperated with the enemy or whose relatives had fled to the South. Together with North Koreans having ties to the Japanese colonial regime, these suspect people formed a "hostile class" that comprised as much as 20 percent of the DPRK population, a group that suffered severe discrimination in decades to come.[171]

In addition to its effects on North Korean society internally, the Korean War profoundly colored the DPRK's relations with the outside world, particularly the USSR and China. As mentioned earlier, China's direct participation in the war increased Chinese influence over North Korea relative to the influence of the Soviet Union, a subject we will explore in further in the following chapters. Other socialist countries also gave North Korea assistance, including medical and technical support from East Germany, Czechoslovakia, Hungary, Romania, Bulgaria, Poland, and the Mongolian People's Republic. The Korean War was the first major test of Soviet-bloc solidarity against the West, and the only time China, the Soviet Union, and Eastern Europe were to cooperate so closely in a military endeavor. In his 1951 New Year message, Kim declared North Korea's great debt to its fraternal allies:

> We Korean people are not standing alone in our righteous struggle. Headed by the great Soviet people, the peoples of popular democracy and all the freedom loving peoples have been giving us their sympathy and support since the first day of the war. Particularly, the people of China, our great neighbor, sent their Volunteer units at a difficult time

---

169. Robert A. Scalapino and Chong-Sik Lee, *Communism in Korea*, vol. 1, *The Movement* (Berkeley: University of California Press, 1972), 414.

170. See for example Kim Il Sung, "The Tasks and Roles of Local Government at the Present Stage," *Rodong Sinmun*, February 19, 1952, 1–3.

171. The division of North Korean society into "core," "wavering," and "hostile" classes is not publicly acknowledged by the DPRK, but has been frequently and consistently noted by North Korean defectors. See for example the testimonies in *Human Rights in the Democratic People's Republic of Korea* (Minneapolis: AsiaWatch, 1988).

when we were retreating, and acting together with the Korean People's Armed Forces, frustrated the advance of the enemy.... The great Soviet people have consistently extended great aid to the Korean people in our struggle, while the people of China, our neighbor, have dispatched their valiant Volunteer units for direct participation in the war to annihilate and clean up the common enemy of the Korean and Chinese peoples, the American imperialist aggressor forces.[172]

It is worth noting that Kim here acknowledged the USSR as the "head" of the countries aiding North Korea, and spoke of Moscow's "great aid," but his speech focused much more on the blood sacrifices of China, "our neighbor." China had certainly been more forthcoming in aiding North Korea than the USSR, whose caution and reticence were a deep disappointment to Kim. But the North Koreans, as we have seen, had reason to be suspicious of China as well. In the years to come, Kim Il Sung's lack of trust for *both* the Soviet Union and China would become increasingly apparent. North Korea during and after the Korean War was a country deeply dependent on other countries for its very survival, but craving independence, and ready to express that independence as soon as the opportunity arose—as it did, fortuitously for Kim, in the Sino-Soviet split of the late 1950s and 1960s.

An armistice putting an end to the fighting was signed by the UN command, the CPVA, and the KPA at the village of Panmunjŏm on July 27, 1953. The armistice extended the cease-fire line on either side to a four kilometer-wide Demilitarized Zone (DMZ), a boundary that would become the most militarily fortified area on earth. The DMZ was intended to be a temporary demarcation pending a political solution to Korea's division, which the warring sides hoped would be reached within a year of the armistice. Between April and June 1954, the nineteen belligerent nations of the Korean War met in Geneva to discuss the process of Korea's unification. The Geneva Conference failed to resolve the Korea question, and in future years became much better known for its discussion of the war in Indochina that began immediately after the Korea talks broke down in June. Division became the enduring status quo on the Korean Peninsula.

As the solution to an international war, the armistice worked. For the United States, China, and the Soviet Union, the inconclusive end of the war was a manageable if unsatisfactory compromise. At least a more general war had been averted, and the questions of a permanent end to the state of war and of Korean unification could be put off to the indefinite future. As the solution to a civil war,

---

172. RG 59, 795A Series. State Department Memorandum, January 3, 1951. "Kim Il Sung's New Year Message."

the armistice made the Korean War a pointless tragedy. In the end, the attempts by both North and South Korea to unify the peninsula by force had failed. After more than three years of enormous physical destruction and loss of life, the Korean War ended more or less where it began, with the peninsula divided between two mutually hostile states, each claiming to be the legitimate government of all of Korea. The continued hostility and mistrust between the two Koreas to this day is in no small measure a result of the experience of each being occupied by the military forces of the other side in 1950; however brief the periods of occupation were, the negative aspects of these experiences have been evoked by each government to reinforce among its people a negative view of the other Korean state. Far from resolving Korea's division, the war made it the most complete, enduring, and dangerous national division in the world. For decades this hostile division served to justify repression and tyranny on both sides of the DMZ.

A few prescient observers at the time of the armistice appreciated the long-term consequences of solidifying the division of Korea. The British author Kingsley Amis, for example, comparing divided Korea to Kashmir and Palestine, wrote that "it is dangerous to allow a cease-fire line to harden into a frontier. . . . India and Pakistan cannot indefinitely endure the tension of indecision in Kashmir, while relations between Israel and its neighbors remain dangerously bitter on a frontier that was never intended to do more than recognize a temporary *fait accompli.*" Without a workable solution to Korea's division, the peninsula "would long remain a danger spot, unless from the beginning the United Nations can at least lay down the basis of a program for eventual political collaboration between North and South."[173] Such a program was never realized, and over the next sixty years, the boundaries of Kashmir, Palestine, and Korea would remain the most contested and conflict-ridden frontiers in the world.

---

173. *The Nation*, August 8, 1953, 105–6.

POSTWAR RECONSTRUCTION AND A DECLARATION OF SELF-RELIANCE, 1953–55

> The point is that we should not mechanically copy the forms and methods of the Soviet Union, but should learn from its experience in struggle and from the truth of Marxism-Leninism. So, while learning from the experience of the Soviet Union, we must put stress not on the form but on the essence of its experience.

—Kim Il Sung, December 1955

Rebuilding from the Rubble

When the fighting stopped in the summer of 1953, the entire Korean Peninsula lay in utter ruin. South of the DMZ, the United States and its allies led an ambitious, well-funded effort to rehabilitate South Korea under the auspices of the United Nations Korea Reconstruction Agency (UNKRA).[1] North Korea, even more devastated than the South and suffering as well from a labor shortage caused by the population hemorrhage of the war, had far fewer resources with which to rebuild itself. Yet through a combination of tremendous work and sacrifice on the part of the North Korean people, generous economic and technical assistance from the "fraternal" socialist countries, and the advantage of a prewar industrial infrastructure more developed than that of South Korea, the DPRK soon achieved economic growth rates that far surpassed South Korea's into the 1970s. Indeed, in the late 1950s North Korea's growth rate of total industrial output was probably the highest in the world.[2]

Epigraph comes from Kim Il Sung, "On Eliminating Dogmatism and Formalism and Establishing Juche in Ideological Work," *Works*, vol. 9 (Pyongyang: Foreign Languages Publishing House, 1982), 403–4.

1. The postwar reconstruction of South Korea was the world's largest multilateral development project at the time. See Steven Hugh Lee, "The United Nations Korea Reconstruction Agency in War and Peace," in Chae-Jin Lee and Young-ick Lew, eds., *Korea and the Korean War* (Seoul: Yonsei University Press, 2002), 357–96.

2. John Yoon Tai Kuark, "A Comparative Study of Economic Development in North and South Korea during the Post-Korean War Period," Ph.D. diss., University of Minnesota, 1966, 32; Joseph S. Chung, *The North Korean Economy: Structure and Development* (Stanford: Hoover Institution Press, 1974), 146–47.

North Korea's long descent from an economic "miracle" in the 1950s to an economic catastrophe in the 1990s, while South Korea simultaneously rose from third-world poverty to first-world affluence, is one of the great reversals of the twentieth century. Many external factors contributed to this reversal, including the US embargo against North Korea from the Korean War onward, the favorable international climate for South Korean development, and the decline in economic assistance from socialist countries after the late 1950s. But North Korea's slide into economic disaster is due in no small part to the insistence of the DPRK government on "self-reliance," or Juche, which was first articulated in the mid-1950s and became official policy in the mid-1960s. It is perhaps ironic that self-reliance was announced at the peak of North Korea's dependence on foreign aid. Yet, the roots of Juche lie deep in Korea's modern history and in the experiences of Kim Il Sung and the DPRK leadership. National independence and self-reliance were among the foremost slogans of the North Korean communists from the time of the anti-Japanese guerrilla war; overwhelming dependence on the Soviet Union before the Korean War and on socialist-bloc assistance after would have only reinforced this desire for self-assertion. North Korea was probably never as self-reliant as its leaders claimed, but far more than was prudent for sustained economic growth after the postwar reconstruction period.[3] Self-reliance was a common aspiration among postcolonial nations striving for independence, and for a time North Korea's Juche program gained a degree of popularity as a model for newly independent third-world states, an issue I will explore in chapter 5. Self-reliance may also have been an understandable reaction to Korea's long dependence on Japan and the Soviet Union (and even earlier, on imperial China).[4] But no other country has carried self-reliance as far, and for as long, as North Korea. Juche has been the most extreme and uncompromising expression of national political and economic sovereignty in the world. The fateful decision to move toward self-reliance was made at the end of the 1950s, and the consequences of Juche would, over time, be almost as devastating for the North Korean people as the Korean War itself.

North Korean sources claimed a reduction in industrial output at the end of the war of nearly 40 percent compared to 1949 levels.[5] The production of consumer goods declined similarly, and the production of agriculture by some 24 percent.[6]

---

3. The economist Marcus Noland, among others, has called North Korea "the world's most autarkic economy," with a ratio of trade to the overall economy less than one-quarter of South Korea's. Noland, *Avoiding the Apocalypse: The Future of the Two Koreas* (Washington, DC: Institute for International Economics, 2000), 61.

4. Bruce Cumings, "Corporatism in North Korea," *Journal of Korean Studies* 4 (1982–83): 269–94.

5. *Postwar Reconstruction and Development of the National Economy of DPRK* (Pyongyang: Foreign Languages Publishing House, 1957), 8.

6. Natalia Bazhanova, *Kiroe sŏn Puk Han kyŏngje* [North Korean Economy at the Crossroads], trans. Yang Chu-yong (Seoul: Hanguk kyŏngje sinmunsa, 1992), 8.

Nearly three-quarters of homes had been destroyed, along with hundreds of thousands of acres of farmland. Electricity production was down to 26 percent of its prewar level, chemical production 22 percent, fuel and metallurgical production 11 percent and 10 percent respectively. The transportation infrastructure was in chaos, with 70 percent of trains and 85 percent of ships destroyed and much of the railway system unusable.[7] The DPRK estimated that war-related damage amounted to 420 billion won, or nearly $170 million by then-current exchange rates.[8] Such a statistic is as impressive as it is meaningless. The simple fact was, North Korea had been virtually destroyed as an industrial society. The first priority of the DPRK leadership was to rebuild industry.

Within days of the armistice, Kim Il Sung sent a report to the Soviet embassy in Pyongyang, detailing the extent of war damage and the need for Soviet assistance to rehabilitate North Korea's industrial economy.[9] At the Sixth Plenary Meeting of the KWP Central Committee on August 5, Kim outlined the DPRK plan for postwar reconstruction.[10] Economic planning would give priority to the rehabilitation and expansion of heavy industry, as it did before the war. Light industry would also be restored and developed in order to improve the people's livelihood. "Distorted" development from the latter part of Japanese colonial rule would be redirected to better suit the needs of the North Korean people. In a foretaste of North Korea's future policy of local self-reliance, Kim proposed that "every provincial People's Committee should work for the development of local industry to ensure the production in large quantities of daily necessities for the people."[11] This application of what would later be called Juche at the local level, first as a policy and later as a necessity when the DPRK economy began to crumble in subsequent decades, resonated with—and was possibly inspired by (although without acknowledgment)—the Japanese colonial-era practice of local "self-strengthening," or *jiriki kōsei*.[12] This term, pronounced *charyŏk*

7. Soviet Embassy to the DPRK, Diary Report, 7 July 1954. AVPRF Fond 0102, Opis 10, Papka 53, Delo 8.

8. *Postwar Reconstruction*, 8.

9. Kim Il Sung to Soviet Ambassador Suzdalev, "General Report on Basic Reconstruction of Important Enterprises Relating to Heavy Industry," July 31, 1953. AVPRF, Fond 0102, Opis 9, Papka 44, Delo 4.

10. Kim Il Sung, *All for the Postwar Rehabilitation and Development of the National Economy* (Pyongyang: Foreign Languages Publishing House, 1961). A slightly different translation may be found in Kim Il Sung, *Works*, vol. 8 (Pyongyang: Foreign Languages Publishing House, 1982), 9–54.

11. Kim, *Postwar Rehabilitation*, 17.

12. Gordon Mark Berger, *Parties Out of Power in Japan, 1931–1941* (Princeton: Princeton University Press, 1977), 69. O Wŏn-ch'ŏl, leading economic advisor to South Korean President Park Chung Hee in the 1970s, has explicitly linked North Korea's self-reliance policies to the *jiriki kōsei* of the Japanese Government-General in the late colonial period, criticizing the DPRK for its outdated "Japanese-style industrialization." O Wŏn-ch'ŏl, "The Reasons for the Collapse of the North Korean Economy," *Sin Tonga* (January 1995), 150.

gaengsaeng in Korean and *zili gengsheng* in Chinese, would be a slogan for self-reliance in the DPRK and Mao's China as well.

As Kim outlined it, the new economic program would move in three stages: first would be a "preparatory" period of six months to a year, during which a thorough assessment of needs would be undertaken and plans for reconstruction drafted. Next would come a three-year economic plan intended to bring the economy up to prewar levels. Finally, the Three-Year Plan would be followed by a Five-Year Plan for the general industrialization of the entire country.[13] Kim acknowledged the great sacrifices the North Korean people would have to make in order to achieve these ambitious goals. But he cited three advantages North Korea possessed for successful postwar reconstruction: the experience of economic construction between 1945 and 1950, as well as the experience of the war itself in teaching the North Korean people sacrifice and ingenuity; the abundance of natural resources in the DPRK; and the fact that "we can count on the reliable support and aid from the international democratic camp."[14] Both the Soviet Union and China, as well as Poland, Czechoslovakia, Hungary, and other Soviet-aligned socialist countries, had promised as much assistance as possible to North Korea's rehabilitation effort, Kim announced. The USSR alone would give the DPRK 1 billion rubles in aid, and other countries would give—if we may paraphrase Marx—from each according to its ability, to North Korea according to its need.

Fraternal Assistance

As we have seen in the previous chapter, fraternal aid to the DPRK began during the Korean War. Of course the great bulk of direct military assistance came from the USSR and China, but the Soviet-bloc countries in Eastern Europe also contributed to the war effort with logistical support, technical aid, medical supplies, and the like. The German Democratic Republic, for example, which had just established diplomatic relations with the DPRK in November 1949, began assisting North Korea in September 1950 with the formation of the Committee for Assisting Korea (Korea-Hilfsausschuss) in the National Assembly.[15] By the end of March 1952, the GDR had sent 11.6 million deutschmark worth of supplies to the DPRK, including 150,346 kilograms of medicine and two ambulances.[16] Among

---

13. Robert Scalapino and Chong-Sik Lee, *Communism in Korea,* vol. 1 (Berkeley: University of California Press, 1972), 528.

14. Kim, *Postwar Rehabilitation,* 36–37.

15. In November 1954, this committee was folded into the Solidarity Committee for Korea and Vietnam (Solidaritätsausschuss für Korea und Vietnam). SAPMO-BA, DY 30, J IV 2/3/371.

16. Rüdiger Frank, *Die DDR und Nordkorea: Der Wiederaufbau der Stadt Hamhung von 1954–1962* (Aachen: Shaker, 1996), 7.

the most poignant forms of assistance was the taking in of thousands of Korean war orphans. Romania alone reportedly sheltered some 1,500 of these children, who were returned to the DPRK with the completion of North Korea's 1957–61 Five-Year Plan.[17] The first group of 205 Korean children were sent to the GDR in January 1953.[18] These and hundreds of others were also returned to North Korea several years later.

Kim Il Sung led a delegation to Moscow in September 1953, primarily to settle the terms of Soviet assistance. The Soviet government agreed to cancel or postpone repayment for all of North Korea's outstanding debts and reiterated its promise to give the DPRK 1 billion rubles in outright aid, both monetary and in the form of industrial equipment and consumer goods.[19] Soviet technicians were sent to North Korea to help with the rehabilitation effort, and the majority of factory reconstruction in postwar North Korea was supervised by Soviet experts. Pyongyang also received promises of aid from East European countries and the Mongolian People's Republic, the latter promising to send North Korea some 86,500 head of livestock.[20] The third-largest contributor of external assistance after the Soviet Union and China was East Germany, which played a major role in the rebuilding of Hamhŭng, North Korea's second-largest city and an important industrial center, a project we will discuss in some detail shortly.

Kim visited Beijing in November and received similar terms from the PRC, reflecting in part the Chinese government's interest in competing with the USSR for influence in North Korea. China canceled North Korea's debts from the Korean War and offered the DPRK 800 million yuan in aid for the period 1954–57, of which 300 million would come in the first year.[21] North Korea and China also signed an agreement on economic and cultural cooperation similar to the one signed between the DPRK and USSR in March 1949.[22] China helped North Korea in factory reconstruction, although not on the scale that the USSR did, and became a major source for North Korean consumer goods, including textiles, cotton, and foodstuffs. Chinese technical experts went to North Korea, and

---

17. Key P. Yang and Chang Bo Chee, "North Korean Education System, 1945 to Present," *China Quarterly* 14 (1963): 128.

18. GDR Embassy in Beijing, 20 January 1953. MfAA, A 5566.

19. Soviet Foreign Ministry, Far East Department. "Interview with Counselor Yang Yŏng-sun of the DPRK Embassy," 29 September 1953. AVPRF, Fond 0102, Opis 9, Papka 44, Delo 7.

20. Soviet Embassy in DPRK, Report, 22 January 1954. AVPRF, Fond 0102, Opis 10, Papka 52, Delo 8. See also Karoly Fendler, "Economic Assistance from Socialist Countries to North Korea in the Postwar Years, 1953–1963," in Han S. Park, ed., *North Korea: Ideology, Politics, Economy* (Englewood Cliffs, NJ: Prentice Hall, 1996), 167–69.

21. Scalapino and Lee, *Communism in Korea*, 529.

22. Fendler, "Economic Assistance," 167.

Koreans traveled to China for technical training. But perhaps the most important contribution that China made to North Korea's reconstruction, in addition to monetary aid and debt cancellation, was the manpower supplied by PLA troops who remained in North Korea until 1958. These troops, who numbered in the hundreds of thousands, helped repair roads and rail lines damaged by war and rebuild schools, bridges, tunnels, and irrigation dams. In labor-short North Korea, the physical assistance of Chinese People's Volunteers was invaluable for the rehabilitation of the war-damaged infrastructure.[23]

The period of postwar reconstruction in North Korea was the first and only time the Soviet Union, China, and the Soviet-aligned countries of Eastern Europe and Mongolia cooperated on a large-scale economic project of this nature. It was the historical high point of "international socialist solidarity," one that would never be repeated after the USSR and China fell out in the early 1960s. Contemporary Soviet sources give a breakdown in foreign assistance to the DPRK between 1953 and 1960 as dividing roughly into thirds, no doubt a division of labor suggested by Moscow. Exactly one-third (33.3 percent) of reconstruction aid came from the USSR, 29.4 percent from China, and 37.3 percent from other countries.[24] More specifically, the aid came from the following sources:

TABLE 2.1 Foreign Assistance from Socialist Countries to DPKR, 1953–60 (in rubles)

USSR	292.5
China	258.4
GDR	122.7
Poland	81.9
Czechoslovakia	61.0
Romania	22.0
Hungary	21.0
Bulgaria	18.7
Albania	0.6
Mongolia	0.4
North Vietnam	0.1
TOTAL	879.3 million

Source: SSSR i Koreia [The USSR and Korea] (Moscow: USSR Academy of Sciences, 1988), 256.

---

23. This contribution was warmly acknowledged in the DPRK media when the Chinese troops left Korea in the spring of 1958. See "Farewell to the Chinese People's Volunteers!" *New Korea* 5 (1958): 33–36.

24. Bazhanova, *North Korean Economy*, 22, based on statistics from the USSR Trade Ministry archives.

North Korea was dependent on fraternal assistance for more than 80 percent of its industrial reconstruction needs between 1954 and 1956, the period of the Three-Year Plan.[25] As we can see, by far the most important source of this assistance was the USSR. Among other projects, Soviet aid and technical assistance built or rebuilt the Sup'ung hydroelectric power plant (the largest such plant in East Asia at the end of World War II, destroyed by the Americans in the Korean War); the chemical works in Hŭngnam (also destroyed in the war); the steelworks at Sŏngjin (renamed Kimch'aek in 1957, after a DPRK hero killed in the Korean War); the port at Namp'o; and a textile factory in Pyongyang. Soviet aid was both extensive and diverse:

TABLE 2.2 Soviet aid to the DPRK, 1953–57

TYPE	AMOUNT/VALUE	QUANTITY
Technical assistance and equipment	10 million rubles	601
Oil products	1,000 tons	113.6
Rolling metal	1,000 tons	134.8
Rope and steel cable	1,000 tons	4.9
Tubing	1,000 tons	22.8
Rolling nonferrous metals	1,000 tons	3.8
Fertilizer	1,000 tons	122.1
Tires	1,000	59.6
Lumber	1,000 cubic meters	113.3
Cotton weave	1 million meters	11.9
Cotton thread	1,000 tons	2.9
Livestock	1,000 head	16.9
Rice	1,000 tons	39.8
Cooking oil	1,000 tons	4.6
Sugar	1,000 tons	9.0
Medicine and medical equipment	1 million rubles	23.4

Source: SSSR i Koreia [The USSR and Korea] (Moscow: USSR Academy of Sciences, 1988), 257.

North Korea could not possibly have rebuilt its economy as quickly as it did without this massive inflow of aid into nearly every sector of production and consumption. But the DPRK did not remain aid-dependent for long. Partly this was out of necessity, as socialist-bloc aid was intended from the beginning to be phased out as reconstruction was completed. Yet it is remarkable how quickly North Korea's aid dependency dropped—North Korea's declaration of "self-reliance" by the end of the 1950s was not without substance. In 1954, 33.4 percent of North Korea's state revenue came from foreign aid; in 1960, the proportion was down to a paltry 2.6 percent. By contrast, well over half of South Korea's government revenue came from foreign assistance in 1956.[26] By the early 1960s,

---

25. Ibid., 24.
26. Kuark, "Economic Development," 55.

according to American officials, South Korea appeared to be a "black hole" for aid assistance, while the North had impressively reindustrialized.[27] This difference cannot be explained by foreign aid alone, which was far greater in absolute terms in South Korea than in the North. The regime's ability to mobilize the North Korean population was also indispensable for the success of this project. As Kim Il Sung had warned, economic reconstruction would require all the work and resources the North Korean people could muster.

Mobilizing the Masses

North Korea by 1950 had already become a society of mass mobilization. The postwar reconstruction effort was carried out with much the same militaristic methods as the war itself and the prewar economic program before that. Indeed, the line between the army and the civilian reconstruction workforce was often a blurry one: KPA draftees were sometimes retained in factory work rather than sent into the army, and active KPA troops were utilized in civilian reconstruction projects.[28] Local peasants were involved in clearing rubble from factories and repairing streets. Hundreds of office works labored after hours to repair the main thoroughfare of Stalin Street in Pyongyang (renamed Victory Street in 1956).[29] The Democratic Youth League (DYL), which had played a central role in political organization before the war, mobilized children and young people to rebuild schools and cultural facilities.[30]

The reconstruction effort rehabilitated North Korea's industrial sector in a remarkably short time, but the effect on the standard of living of ordinary North Koreans was mixed. In December 1953, the DPRK government canceled all pre–Korean War debts owed by the peasantry, a decree that was understandably well received by the hard-pressed Korean farmers.[31] But the party leadership debated fiercely about the priorities to be given to overall industrialization versus focusing on the increasing production of consumer goods and improving the livelihood of the masses. At the Sixth Plenum of the KWP Central Committee, for example, some representatives advocated eliminating the ration system and

---

27. For analysis of South Korea's aid-dependency in the Syngman Rhee period, see especially Jung-En Woo, *Race to the Swift: State and Finance in Korean Industrialization* (New York: Columbia University Press, 1990), chapter 3.

28. Soviet Embassy in DPRK Report, 30 June 1954. AVPRF, Fond 0102, Opis 10, Papka 52, Delo 8.

29. Soviet Embassy in DPRK Report, 15 October 1953. AVPRF, Fond 0102, Opis 9, Papka 44, Delo 9. As it happened, the mobilization of local workers to construct East Berlin's "Stalinallee" triggered the first popular uprising in the Soviet bloc, the Berlin uprising of June 17, 1953. No such problems affected reconstruction work in Pyongyang.

30. Soviet Embassy in DPRK Report, 7 October 1953. AVPRF, Fond 0102, Opis 9, Papka 44, Delo 9.

31. Soviet Embassy in DPRK Report, 13 January 1954. AVPRF, Fond 0102, Opis 9, Papka 44, Delo 9.

increasing wages, while others wished to increase quantities of rations instead. Ultimately the Central Committee decided to keep the rationing system in place but to reduce the price of certain consumer items and increase wages. In April, the regime increased workers' wages an average of 25 percent, although there were still complaints of excessively high prices.[32]

North Korea had embarked on a Stalinist program of rapid industrialization as early as its first economic plan of 1947, with particular emphasis on heavy industry, including chemicals, steel, and hydroelectric power.[33] The DPRK after the Korean War would again put first priority on rebuilding heavy industry. Kim Il Sung's report to Soviet ambassador S. P. Suzdalev at the end of July 1953 emphasized the need for rapidly rebuilding North Korea's heavy industrial base, particularly machine tools.[34] In the first two years of postwar reconstruction some 80 percent of industrial investment, or nearly 40 percent of total investment, went into heavy industry, a proportion quite similar to China at the time or East European countries a few years earlier.[35] North Korea's emphasis on heavy industry was partly due to the existence of a prewar industrial infrastructure built in the latter part of the Japanese colonial period. Although much of this infrastructure had been heavily damaged or destroyed in the Korean War, rebuilding was a simpler task than building from scratch—the plans and technical knowledge already existed, and experts from more advanced fraternal countries were there to help. But, as Kim had expressed earlier, the North Korean leadership was keen on redirecting industry from the distortions of colonial development. For example, Kim pointed out, the Japanese had built major factories on the coasts, convenient for shipping to Japan but far from the sources of raw materials and poorly suited for Korea's domestic needs. Therefore existing plants should not merely be reconstructed, but new factories and the infrastructure serving them should be built to better serve the needs of North Korea.[36] The new economic plans laid out a careful sequence of rehabilitation and development leading toward industrial self-sufficiency, beginning with sources of power and raw materials (especially electricity generation and mining), and moving on to the production of basic industrial goods such as iron, steel, machine tools, ships, automobile parts, and chemicals, including chemical fertilizer.[37] Oil supplies were also critical, and one of the first tasks of rehabilitation was the reconstruction of the Korea-Soviet Oil

---

32. Soviet Embassy in DPRK Report, 28 May 1954. AVPRF, Fond 0102, Opis 9, Papka 44, Delo 9.

33. Charles K. Armstrong, *The North Korean Revolution, 1945–1950* (Ithaca: Cornell University Press, 2003), chapter 5.

34. Kim Il Sung to Suzdalev, 31 July 1953, enclosure, 1–3.

35. Masai Okonogi, "North Korean Communism: In Search of Its Prototype," in Dae-Sook Suh, ed., *Korean Studies: New Pacific Currents* (Honolulu: University of Hawaii Press, 1994), 185–86.

36. Kim, *Postwar Rehabilitation*, 11.

37. Ibid., 11–14; Kim to Suzdalev, enclosure.

Company and the Aoji Artificial Oil Plant in the northeastern city of Aoji, near the Soviet border.[38]

The Soviet Union supplied much of the technical advice and material assistance, but the North Koreans' ambitions did not always follow Soviet guidelines. Until the war, North Korea had largely been a source of primary goods for the USSR, but North Korean planners after the war wanted to focus on manufactured goods, including goods for export outside the Soviet bloc, something the Soviet advisors did not think practical. The 1954–56 plan paid a great deal of attention to textile production, an area that had overwhelmingly been concentrated in the South before division, in order to make the DPRK more self-sufficient in clothing and textiles, another policy which the Soviets advised against.[39] The thrust of the postwar rehabilitation plan was toward autarky rather than incorporation into a Soviet-centered international division of labor. The establishment of a "socialist division of labor" was not something that had been of much interest to Stalin, who preferred to extract what the USSR needed from occupied territories after World War II and otherwise let the "satellite" countries fend for themselves. Khrushchev attempted much more forcefully to rationalize economic relations among socialist states, an attempt North Korea resisted to the end. North Korea never joined the Soviet-directed Council on Mutual Economic Assistance (CMEA), for instance, and even scheduled its economic plans so as not to coincide with those of the other socialist countries.

It is useful to contrast North Korea's postwar industrialization program with contemporary projects in Eastern Europe, about which the North Koreans were reasonably well informed—the DPRK had diplomatic relations only with other socialist countries until 1958, when it established diplomatic ties to Algeria and Guinea.[40] In 1953, there were major workers' protests in East Germany and Czechoslovakia, and partly as a response to this, the Soviet Union reduced its demand for reparations from the GDR, and the Czech and East German governments redirected resources toward improving living standards of ordinary citizens to some extent.[41] North Korean planners, meeting with Soviet advisors in the spring of 1954, said that they had paid careful attention to the experiences and mistakes of the "people's democracies" in economic planning, particularly the need to pay attention to the livelihoods of ordinary citizen.[42] In fact, however,

---

38. DPRK Foreign Ministry to Soviet Embassy, "Description of Aoji Artificial Oil Plant," AVPRF Fond 0102, Opis 9, Papka 44, Delo 4.

39. Soviet Embassy in DPRK Report, 30 March 1956. AVPRF, Fond 0102, Opis 12, Papka 68, Delo 5.

40. George Ginsburgs and Roy U.T. Kim, *Calendar of Diplomatic Affairs, Democratic People's Republic of Korea* (Moorestown, NJ: Symposia Press, 1977), 51–52.

41. See for example Martin McCauley, *The German Democratic Republic since 1945* (London: Macmillan, 1983), 69.

42. Soviet Embassy in DPRK Report, 19 April 1954. AVPRF, Fond 0102, Opis 10, Papka 52, Delo 8.

DPRK economic planning was heavily skewed toward developing North Korea's independent industrial base, and in particular its military complex.

Reconstruction was, in a sense, war by other means. Kim Il Sung and his group of former Manchurian partisans at the center of power in the DPRK were, after all, people who had never known anything but guerrilla war, conventional war, and a brief period of Stalinist economic construction between (which could also be seen as a species of war mobilization). The production of consumer goods and the improvement of everyday life among the masses was a secondary concern to the creation of a powerful industrial state. In postwar North Korea, unlike in Eastern Europe, there were no messy workers' protests with which to contend. The population itself was a resource to be channeled into industrialization for the sake of state power, including military power.

Soviet assistance was primarily directed toward North Korea's basic industries, including power, iron, and chemicals, rather than to machine production.[43] Machine-building factories were helped more by Eastern Europe; Moscow, in fact, was more forthcoming toward China than to North Korea in help with plans and technology for the production of tools, vehicles, and defense-related products.[44] The Soviets were more interested in rebuilding North Korea's prewar industrial base than creating a new industrial structure in the DPRK. Nevertheless, the Soviets helped with the construction of more than forty new factories in North Korea after the war. The East European countries, for their part, gave assistance to a number of specific industries. For example, the GDR supplied materials for North Korea's chemical and synthetic textile industries. North Korea and East Germany signed a trade agreement in 1954, renewed annually until a long-term agreement was reached for 1958–61.[45] Poland and Czechoslovakia signed similar trade agreements with the DPRK in 1954. The terms were quite favorable to the DPRK, including barter (North Korea supplying metals, agricultural goods, and marine products in exchange for manufactured goods and technology) and credits for technological assistance. As a result, North Korea benefited considerably, and at little cost to itself, from the transfer of technology and expertise from the more advanced East European countries.[46]

The Koreans had a great deal of input into what sorts of plants were to be built, and where. As we have seen, one of Kim Il Sung's complaints about

---

43. Okonogi, "North Korean Communism," 181.

44. Shu Guang Zhang, "Sino-Soviet Economic Cooperation," in Odd Arne Westad, ed., *Brothers in Arms: The Rise and Fall of the Sino-Soviet Alliance, 1945–1963* (Stanford: Stanford University Press, 1998), 201.

45. GDR Ministry of Foreign Affairs, Far Eastern Department, Korea Section. "Overview of Relations between the GDR and DPRK," 28 April 1966. MfAA, C 1026/73.

46. Barry K. Gills, *Korea versus Korea: A Case of Contested Legitimacy* (London: Routledge, 1996), 56–57.

Japanese colonial industrialization was that factories had been built close to the coasts but far from the sources of power and raw materials. North Korean officials told the East European advisors in Pyongyang that they wanted to establish new industrial centers in mountainous areas of the interior, where they would be close to the mines and also less vulnerable to attacks from enemy naval forces, which had created so much damage during the Korean War.[47] Thus Czechoslovakia, Hungary, and other fraternal countries helped to build plants in Kusŏng, Tŏkch'on, Hŭich'on, and other inland areas of North Korea. The major exception to this relocation to the interior was the industrial city of Hamhŭng and its port of Hŭngnam, North Korea's most important center of industry outside of Pyongyang, which was rebuilt with East German aid and was far too extensive to be abandoned or relocated. At this time China was also in the process of resituating much of its industry from the coastal areas and the Northeast to the interior, partly for reasons of military security and partly to bring the plants closer to mines and energy sources, and the Chinese may have inspired the North Koreans to take a similar approach.

Despite North Korea's attempts to move toward self-sufficiency—or at least the production of its own industrial necessities—as quickly as possible, postwar rehabilitation in the DPRK was overwhelmingly dependent on aid from abroad, and from the Soviet Union in particular. In 1955 Moscow agreed to transfer technology to North Korea virtually for free. Between 1956 and 1958 alone the USSR gave North Korea grants and credits in the range of 300 million rubles, and by 1959 the total amount of Soviet aid may have been as high as 2.8 billion rubles, or $690 million dollars at then-current exchange rates.[48] According to contemporary Soviet sources, by the end of the Five-Year Plan in 1960, Soviet aid accounted for 40 percent of North Korea's electricity generation, 53 percent of coke production, 51 percent of cast iron, 22 percent of steel, 45 percent of reinforced concrete blocks and 65 percent of cotton fabric.[49] Thousands of North Koreans received technical training in the USSR and Eastern Europe, and more than ten thousand North Korean students were enrolled in universities and colleges in Soviet-bloc countries during the reconstruction period.

And yet despite—or perhaps because of—this dependence, the DPRK leadership was bitterly divided over North Korea's economic relations with the Soviet

47. GDR Embassy in DPRK, Report on Conversation with Hungarian Ambassador, 29 October 1957. MfAA A 6979.

48. Erik Van Ree, "The Limits of *Juche*: North Korea's Dependence on Soviet Industrial Aid, 1953–76," *Journal of Communist Studies* 5, no. 1 (March 1989): 68.

49. Karoly Fendler, "Economic Assistance and Loans from Socialist Countries to North Korea in the Postwar Years 1953–1963," *Asien* 42 (January 1992): 42.

Union and Eastern Europe in the late 1950s. Between 1956 and 1958, as we will explore further in the next chapter, Kim Il Sung and his group opposed integration into an international division of labor led by the USSR, in which North Korea would exchange its primary products for manufactured goods from the European socialist countries. Kim's opponents argued against excessive self-reliance, and called for less emphasis on heavy industry and more on light industry and consumer goods. These arguments over economic policy became embroiled in turn with power struggles among pro-Soviet, pro-Chinese, and Manchurian guerrilla factions within the DPRK ruling group, as well as the debate over collective leadership inspired by Khrushchev's "de-Stalinization" in the USSR. In the end, Kim's line of collectivization, nationalism, self-reliance, and heavy-industry-first development won the day, and those opposed to him paid, in many cases, with their lives.

Although foreign aid was drastically reduced in the early 1960s, North Korea remained dependent on long-term loans from the USSR and other socialist countries until the Soviet Union collapsed. By 1989, half of DPRK foreign trade was with the USSR, and North Korea's debts to the Soviet Union amounted to nearly a year's worth of exports.[50] It seems that DPRK planners did not seriously take into account the loss of foreign assistance when they formulated the first seven-year economic plan (1961–67). As a result, the plan could not be fulfilled and had to be extended three years, making it a de facto Ten-Year Plan (1961–70). Thereafter North Korea would never fulfill its economic plans on time, and after the mid-1960s would not even publish concrete statistics on economic output (as opposed to percentage increases). We can see this as the beginning of North Korea's long, protracted economic decline. The socialist economic showcase of the 1950s sputtered out in the 1960s, just as South Korea's modernization program was beginning to take off. North Korea was, in a sense, a victim of its own early economic success, entering a cul-de-sac of underdevelopment from which it would never recover.

This grim fate could hardly have been foreseen by anyone in or outside of North Korea in the mid-1950s. As late as 1974, a pair of Western economists could declare the DPRK an economic success story offering "an alternative development theory which turns upside down all the accepted premises of Western economic thinking."[51] North Korea announced its Three-Year Plan completed after a breathtaking (and back-breaking) two years and eight months. Official production statistics were dazzling and, for the most part, probably even true. Industry was, of course, the centerpiece of the plan, and industrial production

---

50. Fendler, "Economic Assistance," 43.
51. Ellen Brun and Jacques Hersh, *Socialist Korea: A Case Study in the Strategy of Economic Development* (New York: Monthly Review Press, 1976), 21.

in 1956 was 2.9 times that of 1953 and double the last full prewar year of 1949. Agricultural production had increased 124 percent compared to 1953 and 108 percent compared to 1949, helped by massive increases in irrigation, supplies of chemical fertilizer, tractors, and farm equipment. More than eighty new large and medium-sized industrial establishments had been built, along with hundreds of schools, hospitals, theaters, and cinemas. Entirely new industrial towns had been established in Hŭich'on and Kusong. New centers of light industry in East Pyongyang and of machine building in the Nagwŏn-Pukchung region had sprung up.[52]

All of this was in the name of "socialist transformation," meaning that the state directed the economy and the people were moved into collective forms of association. State-run and cooperative industry, which had accounted for 90.7 percent of North Korea's industry before the war, was now up to 98 percent. By the end of 1956, 80.9 percent of peasant households were in agricultural cooperatives. Shiny new farmhouses on efficient cooperative farms had replaced the ramshackle huts of traditional villages, and "Korea's countryside has now been freed forever from poverty." In the cities, North Korea's factory and office workers had received an average wage increase of 35 percent between November 1956 and June 1957 alone.[53] The propaganda about a "heroic new age" for the North Korean people was not entirely unjustified, but to get a sense of the complexity and human cost of North Korean reconstruction, we will examine in some detail two of the biggest and best-documented projects of postwar rehabilitation: the reconstruction of Pyongyang, the capital and largest city of the DPRK; and the reconstruction of Hamhŭng, North Korea's second-largest city and most important industrial complex. The Pyongyang project was built largely with Soviet assistance, the Hamhŭng project with East German. The two cities exemplify the multinational nature of the postwar reconstruction effort, and literally expressed in concrete the goals, methods, and priorities of the DPRK regime in building this new, socialist, industrial society.

Socialist Modern: Urban Reconstruction in Pyongyang and Hamhŭng

The New Capital

The city, especially the capital city, had long played a central role in state socialist projects, beginning with "Red Moscow" in the 1920s.[54] For Marxist-

---

52. Kim Il Chan, "Economic Reconstruction in North Korea," *New Korea* 6 (June 1957): 11–13.
53. Ibid., 13.
54. Timothy J. Colton, *Moscow: Governing the Socialist Metropolis* (Cambridge: Belknap Press of Harvard University Press, 1995).

Leninists, modern industrial cities exemplified the evils of capitalist exploitation and held the potential for planning and reordering urban life according to rational, "scientific" socialist ideals.[55] The idea of a city as a laboratory for building utopia had deep roots in the European Enlightenment, going back as far as Tommaso Campanella's *City of the Sun* from the early seventeenth century, a book viewed favorably by Soviet planners in the 1930s—just as the Soviet Union's most radical urban experiment, the entirely planned industrial city of Magnitogorsk in the Ural Mountains, was taking shape.[56] Pyongyang would also be a "City of the Sun," in this case of the Great Leader Kim Il Sung, "Sun of the Nation." The utter destruction of Pyongyang gave North Korean urban planners a virtual blank slate to create an ideal city. The only comparable urban experiment in the postwar socialist world was East Berlin, which had faced similar devastation but was only half a city; in Pyongyang, North Koreans had an entire capital to reconstruct. As Pyongyang evolved in succeeding decades, it would be a unique showcase of Korean-style socialism, full of monuments, straight streets, clean parks, and pastel-colored high-rise buildings. Pyongyang rebuilt from the ashes looked like no other city in Asia, with the possible exception of Singapore, another carefully planned and policed city under authoritarian rule. And unlike other socialist third-world countries such as China and Cuba, the DPRK did not have an antiurban bias in its ideology or economic policies; on the contrary, North Korean leaders consistently emphasized that the center of national life lay in Pyongyang, the heart of the social organism in which only the privileged and politically well-behaved could reside. At times, such as the famine of the 1990s, the appendages of the country—the outer provinces—could even be sacrificed so that the heart would live.

Pyongyang, in fact, was not declared the capital of the DPRK—that is, the capital of all Korea—until the new North Korean constitution of 1972. But from the end of the Korean War, North Korean planners clearly saw Pyongyang as being in competition with Seoul for reconstruction as a capital city. Pyongyang had been Korea's second city for centuries. It is probably the oldest continuously settled urban area on the Korean Peninsula, going back to the semilegendary Chinese exile Kija (Qizi), who established a kingdom called Chŏson, with its capital at

55. David M. Smith, "The Socialist City," in Gregory Andrusz, Michael Harloe, and Ivan Szelenyi, eds., *Cities after Socialism: Urban and Regional Change and Conflict in Post-Socialist Societies* (Oxford: Blackwell, 1996), 70–99.

56. Stephen Kotkin, *Magnetic Mountain: Socialism as a Civilization* (Berkeley: University of California Press, 1995), 364–65.

Pyongyang, around 1000 BC.[57] In the fifth century AD the city became the capital of Koguryŏ, which occupied the northern part of the Korean Peninsula and extended well into Manchuria, until its defeat by the southeastern Korean kingdom of Silla in the late seventh century. In AD 929 Wang Kŏn, founder of the Koryŏ dynasty, established Pyongyang as a secondary capital, with the main capital of his kingdom at what is now Kaesŏng in southwestern North Korea. Throughout the succeeding Chosŏn dynasty (1392–1910), Pyongyang remained the second-largest city in Korea next to the capital, Seoul. In some ways Pyongyang was at the forefront of modernity in the early twentieth century: the home of many of Korea's leading writers and intellectuals, the center of Protestant Christianity, and the site of many new manufacturing and industrial concerns under Japanese colonialism. This legacy, and the opportunity to rebuild a city from the ruins, made the North Korean capital a very different kind of place from the southern capital—not decadent, compromised, Confucian Seoul, but pure, modern, Christian, revolutionary Pyongyang.

Pyongyang was the center and showcase of North Korea's postwar rehabilitation effort. According to later DPRK sources, during the Korean War the US Air Force dropped 428,748 bombs on Pyongyang, or approximately one for every resident of the city.[58] The greatest devastation came in the spring of 1951, when much of the city was reduced to ashes. Rehabilitation of the capital began within a few days of the armistice under DPRK Internal Decision Number 125, "On the Reconstruction of Pyongyang," announced July 30, 1953.[59] This decision was supposed to fulfill "the spirit of the Sixth Plenum" of the Korean Workers' Party Central Committee, which outlined the priorities for postwar reconstruction in all of North Korea in early August. In particular, the rebuilding of Pyongyang was intended to correct the "unenlightened, exploitative and oppressive character" of Japanese colonial development, and bring order, reason, and improvement of quality of life to the citizens of the capital.[60] For example, under the Japanese, 67 percent of factories were built in residential areas inside the city, while Pyongyang's workers lived in poverty on the city's outskirts. There was a sharp divide between the Korean and Japanese residents of Pyongyang, as there was in other Korean colonial cities, with the Japanese living in privileged neighborhoods and

---

57. In 1993 North Korean archeologists claimed an even older pedigree for Pyongyang, allegedly discovering the bones of the (heretofore thought mythical) King Tangun near Pyongyang, dating from about 3000 BC. This "proved," therefore, that Pyongyang was the original capital of Korea and the cradle of the Korean race. See *Pyongyang Review* (Pyongyang: Foreign Languages Publishing House, 1995), 26.

58. Ibid., 25.

59. P'yŏngyang Hyangt'osa P'yŏnjip Wiwŏnhoe, *P'yŏngyangji* [Pyongyang Gazetteer] (Pyongyang: Kungnip ch'ulp'ansa, 1957), 501.

60. Ibid., 502.

occupying most of the top positions in industry, commerce, and government administration. Even though the Japanese constituted no more than 2–3 percent of the population of colonial Korea, nearly one-quarter of the residents of Pyongyang were Japanese by 1925. In Seoul, the proportion was even higher.[61] The new plans for Pyongyang would separate residential from industrial districts and create tens of thousands of new "workers' apartments" for city dwellers. The numerous historical sites of Pyongyang would be preserved, new architecture would harmonize with the old, and Pyongyang's "special character" would be preserved as both Korea's oldest city and a "heroic and modern" new capital.[62]

The chairman of the Pyongyang City Rehabilitation Committee (PCRC), established to oversee this urban reconstruction project, was none other than Premier Kim Il Sung himself, a native of the city. But reconstruction was carried out with the assistance, advice, and close supervision of Soviet technicians and Soviet ambassador Suzdalev.[63] The GDR also sent a team of urban planners to help with the project.[64] The first task was the creation of a 3,600-square-meter Kim Il Sung Square to commemorate "victory" in the Fatherland Liberation War and establish a new central space for the city. Work on Kim Il Sung Square began the day after the armistice was signed, July 28—two days before the official plans for urban reconstruction were announced. Kim Il Sung Square would be bisected by the city's main North-South axis, Stalin Street, which terminated in the north at the reconstructed Liberation Tower, originally built in 1946 to commemorate Korea's liberation by the Soviet army.[65] The first phase of urban reconstruction culminated with the construction of the Pyongyang Grand Theatre at the southern terminus of Stalin Street in 1960. Like its namesake in East Berlin, Stalinallee, Pyongyang's Stalin Street was to be lined with multistory showcase residential buildings.[66]

The PCRC claimed some thirteen thousand new residences had been built by the end of 1953, but the priority of the initial reconstruction period was on public

61. Eckart Dege, "P'yŏngyang—Ancient and Modern—the Capital of North Korea," *GeoJournal* 22, no. 1 (September 1990): 26.

62. Pyongyang Gazetteer, 502; *P'yŏngyangŭi ŏje wa onŭl* [Pyongyang, Yesterday and Today] (Pyongyang: Sahoe kwahak ch'ulp'ansa, 1986), 106.

63. Soviet Embassy in DPRK, "Interview with Pyongyang City Committee Vice-Chairman Comrade Kim Sŏng-yong," 25 February 1955. AVPRF, Fond 0102, Opis 11, Papka 60, Delo 8.

64. Dege, "P'yŏngyang," 26.

65. Pyongyang Gazetteer, 502; Pyongyang, Yesterday and Today, 106. A "Friendship Tower" to the Chinese People's Volunteers was erected in 1959. Stalin Street was renamed "Victory Street" (*Sŭngni toro*), and the Soviet role in the liberation and reconstruction of Pyongyang was rarely mentioned after this point.

66. Pyongyang's Stalin Street apartment blocks were four or five stories tall, more modest than Berlin's. Stalinallee in Berlin also changed its name after Stalin's death, to Karl-Marx-Allee.

spaces and structures rather than private dwelling places.[67] These included, in addition to Kim Il Sung Square, a Mao Zedong Square, a People's Army Square, a National Theater, two new department stores, a sports stadium on Moranbong Hill, a movie studio, an international hotel, and the reconstruction and expansion of Kim Il Sung University and Moranbong Theatre. All of these projects were completed within a year, an astonishing tempo that later came to be called "Pyongyang Speed."[68] Under the slogans "Let us rapidly rehabilitate and reconstruct the heroic city of Pyongyang!" and "All for the postwar rehabilitation and development of the national economy!" the citizenry of Pyongyang attacked reconstruction as if it were a military campaign. This campaign began in earnest in June 1954, when the PCRC launched a competition to achieve the major goals of reconstruction by the ninth anniversary of Korea's liberation from colonial rule, August 15, 1954.[69] The PCRC even published a newspaper, *Kŏnsolja* (The Constructionist) to report news of the rehabilitation effort. The 1954 competition culminated in the opening of the Memorial Hall for the Fatherland Liberation War on August 13, just two days before the August 15 anniversary.[70] Still there was no time to rest. The Fourth Decision of the PCRC on February 10, 1955 called for even more accomplishments by the tenth anniversary of liberation on August 15, 1955. These goals focused more on citizens' amenities, including homes, schools, parks, libraries, hospitals, bathhouses, beauty parlors, and social and cultural centers. The 144-day campaign of 1955 mobilized some 4,210,000 soldiers, technicians, students, and workers; Kim Il Sung himself allegedly visited all the construction sites in June 1955.[71] All of these tasks too were fulfilled on time, marking the completion of Pyongyang's basic rehabilitation by mid-August 1955, which coincided with the completion of the Three-Year Plan for the national economy.[72]

Economic reconstruction as war could be effective but had its limits. Although few complaints about the rehabilitation effort appeared in the North Korean media, and the patriotic fervor of much of the population was probably genuine, the strain on the citizens of Pyongyang must have been tremendous. Throughout its history, the DPRK never successfully moved from an economy of war mobilization to a more relaxed form of economic development, and was still

---

67. Pyongyang Gazetteer, 504.
68. This "Pyongyang Speed" included the alleged construction of twenty thousand apartments with materials for seven thousand in 1958, and the assembly of a single flat in fourteen minutes. The quality of these apartments received little comment. *Pyongyang Review* (1985), 25.
69. Pyongyang Gazetteer, 508.
70. Ibid., 510.
71. Pyongyang, Yesterday and Today, 107; Pyongyang Gazetteer, 511.
72. Soviet Embassy in DPRK, "Interview with Kim Sŏng-yong," 1–2. In fact, the 1954 plan had been "overfulfilled by 123 percent," according the Soviet embassy's North Korean informants.

approaching economic problems with the language and tactics of warfare half a century later. Once again, we can see North Korea as a victim of some of its early success. In 1957, when the Five-Year Plan was launched, yet more government directives called for dramatic achievements in urban development by the twelfth anniversary of liberation on August 15 and exhorted all "patriotic workers, students and citizens" to contribute to the struggle. Every office was supposed to devote 15 percent of its workforce to reconstruction every workday, and all citizens were supposed to volunteer their efforts on Sundays as well. Students from Kim Il Sung University, the Korean Workers' Party Central Party School, the People's Economic University, and Kimch'aek Technical College held competitions for reconstruction work, and students from the provinces also participated "with loving hearts."[73] Every year more Pyongyang residents participated in the reconstruction effort: 505,624 in 1954, 584,624 in 1955, 625,431 in 1956, and some 670,000 in 1957.[74] If these numbers are to be believed, out of Pyongyang's population in the late 1950s of about 1 million, all but the very young and the very old were active in the project of urban rehabilitation.

In the reconstruction of Pyongyang, as in the North Korean economy more generally, fraternal assistance was massive, diverse, and crucial. At the time, this help was warmly and extensively acknowledged in the DPRK media. After the 1960s, when self-reliance became both the dominant slogan and the lens through which all previous North Korean experiences were filtered, the role of foreigners in postwar reconstruction was rarely if ever mentioned. Broadly speaking, China contributed mainly manpower and light consumer goods, the Soviets and East Germans supplied technical assistance and supervision, and the other East European countries gave equipment and technical assistance for specific industries. Kim Il Sung publicly thanked the Chinese People's Volunteers, who had fought "shoulder-to-shoulder" with the Korean People's Army, for their continued role in the postwar reconstruction effort.[75] CPV soldiers helped rebuild bridges, elementary schools, factories and apartments. In February 1955, for instance, the Forty-seventh Brigade of the CPV rebuilt the Pyongyang Electric Train Factory.[76] A group of more than 770 Chinese construction experts stayed in Pyongyang from November 1954 to the end of 1956 to help oversee reconstruction. Albania donated asphalt for paving roads, Czechoslovakia gave buses, Hungary built a precision tool factory, East Germany gave telephones and switchboards for the city's communication services and modernized the National Film Production

73. Pyongyang Gazetteer, 514.
74. Ibid., 515.
75. *Nodong Sinmun*, March 28, 1955.
76. Pyongyang Gazetteer, 523.

Center. Poland built the West Pyongyang Railway Factory, Bulgaria built a factory for wooden tools, Romania built up Pyongyang Central Hospital, and the USSR, Czechoslovakia, China, and East Germany each contributed engines and freight and passenger cars to develop the North Korean railroad industry.[77] During the period of the Three-Year Plan, many of the East European leaders, including Otto Grotewohl of the GDR, Enver Hoxha of Albania, and Gheorghe Gheorghiu-Dej of Romania, visited Pyongyang, where they were warmly thanked for their countries' contributions to postwar reconstruction.[78]

The effect of this breakneck pace of urban reconstruction on the lives of ordinary Pyongyangers, and the degree of real enthusiasm about these efforts, is not easy to assess given that no dissenting views appeared in the public record, or for that matter in the reports of the planners that are currently extant. Nevertheless, from the records that do exist we can get some sense of the nature and impact of development on everyday urban life. Like elsewhere in the postwar sphere of Soviet domination, housing construction in Pyongyang was for the most part centrally planned, publicly owned, relatively homogeneous, affordable, and functional, tending to emphasize quantity over quality.[79] What is distinctive about the Pyongyang experience, however, is the speed at which public housing was built. The bulk of housing construction in the central area of Pyongyang was completed in the period of the Three- and Five-Year Plans (1954–61); later projects in the 1970s and 1980s were concentrated outside the city center. In this early phase, Pyongyang's residential architecture was very much modeled on Berlin, Warsaw, and Moscow, and there were even a few graduates of the German architectural school of Bauhaus advising North Koreans on urban planning and architecture.[80] Of the entire budget for postwar reconstruction, housing constituted 10.9 percent in 1955, 14.6 percent in 1956, and 14.9 percent in 1957, dropping to 12.8 percent in 1958.[81] The total area of urban housing construction in all of North Korea amounted to 4,720,000 square meters in 1954–56, and in the 1957–60 period constituted 6,220,000 square meters, of which 1.87 million square meters was for Pyongyang alone.[82] Housing for seventeen thousand families was constructed in a single twelve-day period in February 1958.[83] With ready-made

77. Ibid., 524.

78. Ibid., 528.

79. See for example Peter Marcuse and Wolfgang Schumann, "Housing in the Colours of the GDR," in Bengt Turner, József Hegedüs, and Iván Tosics, eds., *The Reform of Housing in Eastern Europe and the Soviet Union* (London: Routledge, 1992), 74–144.

80. Frank, *DDR und Nordkorea*, 49.

81. "The Struggle in the Area of Basic Construction," *Kŏnsŏlja*, April 1958, 4.

82. *Chosŏn chungang nyŏngan* (Pyongyang: Chosŏn chungang t'ongsinsa, 1959), 202, 333.

83. *Pyongyang Sinmun*, May 10, 1958.

parts and an assembly line of workers, one apartment could be constructed in fourteen minutes. Hence, "Pyongyang Speed" became the slogan for rapid housing construction.[84]

Obviously, at that speed there was little room for variety or quality control. Apartments were thrown together on a standardized model, and as in the *kommunalka* (communal apartments) of the USSR, several families shared a single bathroom and kitchen—as many as twelve families, in the case of Pyongyang.[85] Walls were thin, roofs leaked, electricity was erratic at best. Shoddy, hastily built, and dangerously unmonitored construction was not unique to North Korea, of course, and South Korea would later become notorious for poor oversight of construction as well, the most famous incident being the collapse of an entire department store in Seoul in 1995. But whatever the drawbacks of reconstruction at "Pyongyang Speed," in a few short years the city had emerged from rubble to become a well-ordered, visibly modern metropolis. Except for the carefully preserved historical monuments, including two of the traditional city gates, hardly anything of colonial or precolonial Pyongyang remained. The narrow, crooked streets and chaotic marketplaces that characterized other Asian cities, including even parts of Seoul to this day, had been eliminated, replaced by heroic boulevards, monumental buildings, spacious parks, and state-run department stores. Pyongyang was and would remain the nerve center and showpiece of socialist Korea and the model for other DPRK cities, including "beautiful, magnificent Hamhŭng," capital of South Hamgyŏng Province and North Korea's second city.[86]

Hamhŭng and the "Hamhungers"

In the last decade of colonial rule, the city of Hamhŭng in northeastern Korea was the site of perhaps the most impressive industrial development in the Japanese empire. Much of it was dedicated to supporting the military, as the empire went to war first with China, then with the United States. The flow of the mighty Yalu River was diverted to supply hydropower for these industrial concerns, most of which involved processing mineral resources from elsewhere in Korea and beyond, such as American and later Southeast Asian oil refined at the port of Wŏnsan. Population growth in the region exploded in the 1930s, and at the time of liberation in 1945, Hamhŭng and Wŏnsan had the highest proportions of factory workers of any cities in Korea. Several towns along the northeast coast were developed into important trading and shipping ports in the late colonial

84. Ibid., June 7, 1958.

85. "On the Results and Progress of Reconstruction in Pyongyang in 1958," *Chŏson chungang nyŏngam* (1959), 77.

86. "Hamhŭng becomes a Beautiful, Magnificent City," *Kŏnsŏlja* (June 1958), 45.

period, including the small fishing village of Hŭngnam, the shipping port for nearby Hamhŭng.[87] Hŭngnam became a major port under the Japanese, exporting Hŭngnam's most important product, chemical fertilizer. The nitrogen fertilizer plant built in Hamhŭng by the Japanese entrepreneur Noguchi Jun was one of the largest fertilizer plants in the world in the early 1940s. Nitrogen fertilizer can also easily be converted into explosives for military use, and for this reason Hamhŭng in general, and the Noguchi fertilizer plant in particular, were targeted for destruction by the US Army in the Korean War.[88] When the fighting ended, Hamhŭng and Hŭngnam were little more than ruins.

In the face of the Chinese advance in late November and December 1950, the US Army Tenth Corps withdrew toward the Hamhŭng/Hŭngnam area to be evacuated by sea. Hamhŭng had already been bombed by the US Air Force, but the Tenth Corps had been ordered to "deny the Communist troops supplies and transportation facilities" before they left the area.[89] For several days, beginning December 11, the 185th Engineering Battalion of the Tenth Corps hauled some four tons of dynamite to the industrial outskirts of Hŭngnam and began to destroy what remained of the factories. On December 15, the railroad bridge leading south from Hamhŭng was blown up. All the highway bridges in the vicinity were similarly demolished. Three days later, the First Platoon burned all the buildings and destroyed all aviation supplies at Hamhŭng's Yongp'o airport, about five miles south of Hŭngnam, with gasoline, tracer bullets and grenades; for good measure, a naval bombardment hit the airport later that afternoon.[90] Meanwhile, some 100,000 North Korean refugees were transported from Hŭngnam to South Korea by US navy ships, in the so-called "Christmas Evacuation" of December 19–24.[91] Out of the rubble of a destroyed and depopulated Hamhŭng, the North Koreans and East Germans built a new industrial city.

It is not clear exactly when, or by whom, the decision was made for East German aid to focus on the city of Hamhŭng. It appears that GDR prime minister Otto Grotewohl personally promised Kim Il Sung help in rebuilding a city when the two men met at the Geneva Conference in 1954. Later that year, in late June or early July, a North Korean leader (presumably Kim Il Sung) wrote to Grotewohl:

---

87. Shannon McCune, *Korea's Heritage: A Regional and Social Geography* (Rutland, VT: Charles E. Tuttle, 1956), 135–38.

88. National Archives and Records Administration, Record Group 497, box 462. Eighth United States Army, 533rd Engineer Technical Intelligence Team. "General Investigation Forms," 30 December 1950, 23.

89. United States Army, Center for Military History. 8–5.1A BA 24, "Destruction in Hamhung and Hungnam, 11 November 1950–19 December 1950," 1.

90. Ibid., 19–20.

91. Bong Hak Hyun, "Christmas Cargo: A Civilian Account of the Hungnam Evacuation," MacArthur Archives, Norfolk, VA, 6.

> The government and the whole Korean people are endlessly touched and thankful for the promise given by you, dear comrade Prime Minister, to our delegation at the Geneva Conference, to rebuild one of the destroyed towns by the efforts of the German Democratic Republic. . . . The government of our Republic has decided as the object of reconstruction and recovery by your government the city of Hamhŭng, one of the provincial centers of our Republic.[92]

Perhaps Grotewohl, presiding over a war-damaged country himself, was moved by a sense of common bond with the Koreans; perhaps he was pressured by the Soviets to give East German aid to a major industrial reconstruction project, but not in the capital, which would be a showcase of Soviet aid. In any case, Grotewohl appointed his own son Hans Grotewohl, an architect, as head of a "German Work Team" (Deutsche Arbeitsgruppe, DAG) to direct the project. Hundreds of East German engineers, technicians, craftsmen, and their families were sent to Hamhŭng, some residing for several years, and gained the collective, ironically German-sounding nickname "Hamhunger." In the fall of 1954 a GDR delegation visited Hamhŭng to lay the groundwork for the reconstruction project, and the following year the East German government announced its plan to help in the reconstruction of Hamhŭng for the period 1955–64.[93] By the time the project ended in 1962 (two years ahead of schedule), the total monetary value of East German aid to Hamhŭng was 118,000,000 deutschmark.[94]

The Germans found a city that had been destroyed even more thoroughly than Pyongyang. Eighty-five percent of Hamhŭng's factories had been demolished, along with 90 percent of its housing. The Soviets helped rebuild some of the industry in the city, particularly the chemical works.[95] But the German planners and engineers redesigned the city as a whole, and were involved in every aspect of reconstruction, from residential housing to public monuments and factories. The DAG included city planners, architects, engineers, and master craftsmen. Koreans were involved with planning, project work, and construction as well, and Soviet advisors also participated. By mid-1955, a general plan for city redevelopment had been drawn up jointly by the Germans, Koreans, and Soviets. Some 350 German specialists and technicians directed the project, under the auspices of the Ministry of Mechanical Engineering in Berlin.[96] The Germans

92. Cited in Frank, *Die DDR und Nordkorea*, 23.
93. GDR Embassy in Pyongyang, 4 November 1954. MfAA A 5575; GDR Ministry of Foreign Affairs, "Reference Material on the Fifteenth Anniversary of the Founding of the Democratic People's Republic of Korea," 29 July 1960, 9. MfAA A 7135.
94. GDR Foreign Ministry, "GDR Assistance to the DPRK," 8 September 1962. MfAA A 17343.
95. *SSSR i Koreia* (Moscow: USSR Academy of Sciences, 1988), 256.
96. GDR Embassy in DPRK Report, 29 October 1959. MfAA A 10264.

arrived in Hamhŭng on April 10, where they were greeted by a delegation of Workers' Party and social organization representatives, led by Hamhŭng People's Committee Chairman Kim Myŏng-ho.[97] The DPRK press welcomed the fraternal assistance of the German people, and GDR ambassador Richard Fischer promised that "we will work together with the Korean people to make Hamhŭng into the most beautiful city."[98]

The German visitors found their Korean hosts both hospitable and demanding, welcoming and at the same time aloof. Part of this ambivalence was undoubtedly a product of cultural differences. The Germans and Koreans worked together but lived apart; photographs from the time show technicians and their families living like European colonialists (or missionaries), sequestered in foreigners' neighborhoods, vacationing at beaches on the East Coast in shockingly revealing swimwear, Koreans nowhere to be seen.[99] East Germany itself was undergoing great hardship as it recovered from war while giving reparations to the Soviet Union, yet the DPRK leadership seemed to think that the GDR was obligated to give generously to North Korea because Germany was a "rich country," Korea a poor one. Ambassador Fischer wrote to the GDR Foreign Ministry in 1956 that "the Korean friends feel that the GDR is one of the richest countries in the Peace Camp," implying that East Germany should give even more.[100] This would not be the last time that North Korea appeared ungrateful for international assistance. But such an attitude made perfect sense in Korean cultural terms, under which the better-off were expected to be generous and magnanimous toward the less fortunate.[101] Despite its recent urbanization and development, North Korea was still largely rural, and the socialist camp was a kind of Korean village writ large: the USSR was the village headman, demanding respect but protecting and providing for the poorer villagers in turn; the GDR, closer to the Soviet Union in terms of geography, culture, and economic development, was expected to behave similarly. Later, when the DPRK saw itself as a model for Third World development, it tried to assist several African countries in much the same way that East Germany and the Soviet Union had helped postwar North Korea—DPRK engineers, for example, rebuilt a large part of the Ethiopian capital

97. *Hamnam Ilbo*, April 13, 1955.

98. *Minju Chosŏn*, June 15, 1955.

99. The East German architect and amateur photographer Erich Robert Ressel (1919–75), who worked with the DAG in Hamhŭng and Hŭngnam from 1956 to 1957 (and defected to West Germany in 1959) left behind a valuable photographic record of the "Hamhungers" that was later compiled into a book by a South Korean historian. Paek Sŭng-jong, *Tongdok top'yonsu Ressel ŭi Puk Han ch'uok* [East German Architect Ressel's North Korean Reminiscences] (Seoul: Hyohyŏng ch'ulp'ansa, 2000).

100. Telegram from Ambassador Fischer to Foreign Minister Bolz, 31 May 1956. MfAA 7135.

101. See Vincent S. Brandt, *A Korean Village between Farm and Sea* (Cambridge: Harvard University Press, 1971).

of Addis Ababa during that country's Marxist phase in the late 1970s. It was in this broader sense of "generalized reciprocity," not tit-for-tat exchange, that the North Koreans seemed to understand their obligations to their European socialist benefactors, whereas the latter saw merely selfishness and ingratitude.[102]

Much of the East German assistance was for the construction of housing. In 1956, the first full year of the Hamhŭng project, housing made up half of total investment:

TABLE 2.3 East German Aid to DPRK, 1956

TYPE OF INVESTMENT	AMOUNT (IN THOUSANDS OF *WON*)	PERCENTAGE OF TOTAL
Housing	411,933	50.0%
Civil engineering works	247,159.8	30.0%
Public buildings	67,557	8.2%
Industrial sites	49,431	6.0%
Assistance for basic industry	25,538	3.1%
Electrification	22,244	2.7%

Source: Ruediger Frank, *Die DDR und Nordkorea; Der Wiederaufbau der Stadt Hamhung von 1954–1962* [The GDR and North Korea: The Reconstruction of Hamhung City, 1954–1962] (Aachen: Shaker, 1996), 45.

By mid-1959, the Hamhŭng project had built some six thousand new residences; waterworks to produce twenty thousand cubic meters of drinking water, supplied by pumps and electric equipment from the GDR; an elementary school; a high school; crèches; public baths; laundry facilities; and a cultural center for youth. Industrial projects included stone quarries in Hamhŭng and Hŭngnam, cement works, housing and furniture factories, and the reconstruction of the chemical plant.[103]

Korean-German cooperation was not without its difficulties. Alfred Förster, the third director of the DAG, complained in 1958 that his Korean coworkers were overly committed to dogmatic, formal decision making and failed to listen to their German advisors, who for their part were convinced of their own superior expertise and efficiency. "Overcoming these contrary tendencies costs overall in patience, energy and time," Förster wrote.[104] GDR-DPRK differences on the ground in Hamhŭng partly reflected differences within the socialist camp in the late 1950s. The year 1956 in particular was a turbulent one in the socialist camp, with the Hungarian uprising and Khrushchev's "secret speech" at the Twentieth

---

102. I am grateful to Fred Carriere of the Korea Society for providing this insight at the Cold War International History Project Conference "Inside North Korea," Washington, DC, March 8, 2003.

103. GDR Foreign Ministry, Extra-European Department, Korea Section. "Support of the German Democratic Republic for the Korean People's Democratic Republic," 19 August 1960. MfAA 7135, Fiche 1, 26–27.

104. Alfred Förster to Professor Liebknecht, July 7, 1958. Bauhaus Archives, Dessau. 22/58/14.

Congress of the CPSU leading to two contrary tendencies: a degree of liberalization ("de-Stalinization") in the USSR and its close allies in Eastern Europe, on the one hand, and on the other continued centralization and a growth in the "cult of personality" in the DPRK and China. The broader impact of this split will be taken up in the next chapter. But the effect on the Hamhungers and other Eastern Europeans in the DPRK was immediate. The Pyongyang government limited contact between foreigners and Koreans, and East European "brothers" began to feel as if they resided in enemy territory.

De-Stalinization in the Soviet Union and East Germany contrasted with what the Germans and Soviets considered Korean and Chinese "dogmatism" not only in politics, but even in urban planning. Konrad Püschel, head of city planning for the Hamhŭng project, wrote that the Koreans' "false understanding and false decisions" about city planning "had their roots in Pyongyang." The Korean friends, obsessed with monument-building and rapid construction, "forget above all that here will be the heart of a socialist city to live and work."[105] And "Pyongyang Speed" had its impact on Hamhŭng as well. The Germans complained that the Koreans built apartments, 98 percent of which were in high-rise buildings, so fast that one had to constantly recheck the quality.[106] As the Germans saw it, the Koreans were simply in too much of a hurry to "construct socialism."

Püschel modeled Kim Il Sung Street, the main thoroughfare of Hamhŭng, on East Berlin's Stalinallee, and planned Hamhŭng's central square along the lines of Alexanderplatz. A student of Wassily Kandinsky's at Bauhaus, Püschel argued that "social order stands on the shape of a socialist city," and planners should pay careful attention to traditional Korean city form and spatial relationships. Rather than modernity effacing tradition, "tradition finds a new context in our society."[107] Not all the planners agreed with Püschel's organic conception of the socialist city. His successor as head of the German planning team, Karl Sommerer, was critical that Püschel's plan centered on a cultural and shopping area rather than an administrative center. A "correct" city plan, Sommerer argued, would demonstrate the movement toward a socialist, then a communist, society rather than focus on such petty pursuits as entertainment and commerce.[108] The German planners also had disagreements with their Korean counterparts, and in particular Chu Sang-chŏl, head of the Hamhŭng City Planning Commission. Despite these differences, the end result by the early 1960s was a city fully recovered from the devastation of war, with a revived industrial core, plentiful

105. Letter from Konrad Püschel, 30 June 1958. Bauhaus Archives, Dessau. 22/58/15.
106. "Report on Housing in Hamhŭng," 26 October 1959. Bauhaus Archives, Dessau. 15/59.
107. Konrad Püschel, 30 June 1958. Bauhaus Archives, Dessau. 22/58/15.
108. Karl Sommerer to Konrad Püschel, 21 March 1960. Bauhaus Archives, Dessau. 6/60/2.

modern housing, and new roads and parks, a city that in some ways looked like it belonged in Eastern Europe more than in Eastern Asia.

In 1960, the East German press called North Korea "an economic miracle in the Far East."[109] But if the Germans expected public gratitude from the Koreans for their role in reconstruction, they were disappointed. Until around 1960, North Korean officials and media often acknowledged this fraternal assistance. In June 1956, Kim Il Sung visited the GDR and personally thanked the East Germans for their help.[110] After the 1957–61 Five-Year Plan, however, the DPRK pretended that reconstruction had been achieved by the Koreans themselves without outside help, as if saying this would make history retroactively conform. From the beginning, the DPRK leadership had seen foreign assistance as a limited process that would gradually give way to North Korean self-reliance, yet the East Europeans were taken aback at how the Koreans insisted that they had achieved self-reliance even while their fraternal socialist allies were contributing toil and treasure to North Korean reconstruction. In early 1961, the Czech ambassador to the DPRK told his East German counterpart, Kurt Schneidewind, that Koreans had said to him, presumably with straight faces: "There have been two periods in the development of our country: the first period was in the last year of the war and in the following two years. Here the socialist brothers gave us a lot of help. We appreciate that. But in the period of the Five-Year Plan we have achieved everything through our own strength, without any foreign help."[111] Around the same time Ambassador Schneidewind, writing on "some questions of personality cult, dogmatism and nationalist tendencies in the DPRK," noted that

> All successes, not least those achieved with the great assistance of the fraternal socialist countries, especially with the aid of the Communist Party of the Soviet Union and the Soviet people, are propagated as their own successes. Accordingly, great feats that were accomplished by the Soviet Union, the CSSR, Poland, and the GDR, are described as accomplishments of the Korean workers "without foreign assistance". . . international cooperation in all fields and the fraternal aid from the socialist countries are not mentioned and not appreciated.[112]

---

109. Martin Radmann, "Ein Wirtschaftswunder im Fernen Osten," *Neues Deutschland*, December 27, 1960.

110. GDR Foreign Ministry, Korea section. "Visit of a Government Delegation of the DPRK in the GDR, June 1956." MfAA A 6927, Fiche 1.

111. GDR Embassy in DPRK, "Notes on Discussion with the Ambassador of the CSSR, Comrade Kohousek, 3 February 1961." MfAA.

112. GDR Embassy in DPRK, "On some questions of personality cult, dogmatism and nationalist tendencies in the DPRK," 30 January 1961. SAPMO-BA. DY 30, IV 2/20/137.

The DPRK and GDR governments declared the Hamhŭng project completed in 1962, two years ahead of schedule. The German specialists and their families went home. At the same time, the thousands of Korean orphans taken in by German, Romanian, and other East European families were sent back to Korea. Some North Korean students remained in Eastern Europe and the USSR, but the era of close "fraternal cooperation" had come to an end. From this point onward, North Korea would chart its own idiosyncratic course.

Internal Repression

Purges and the Party

One of the distinctive characteristics of the North Korean political system, compared to other Marxist-Leninist polities, has been what we might call the "truncated pyramid" of the ruling party: since its inception in the summer of 1946, the KWP has been a socially broad-based party with a relatively large membership (12–15 percent of the population, a proportion much higher than the Communist parties of the USSR or China) and a small, tightly knit ruling elite bound by close personal ties. In the post–Korean War years, the grassroots base of the KWP was rebuilt after heavy losses due to deaths and defections, with an emphasis on "steel-like" unity for the sake of economic reconstruction.[113] At the beginning of 1956, party members numbered 1,164,945, of whom more than half had joined since the war.[114] Nearly 60 percent were classified as poor peasants, 22.6 percent workers, 13 percent white-collar workers, and 3.7 percent "other."[115] The KWP was therefore widely represented among the rural and working classes. At the top, however, the party leadership became increasingly less diverse and more centered around the Manchurian partisan comrades of Kim Il Sung. This was accomplished through a series of purges, culminating in the August 1956 KWP Plenum that eliminated Kim's Soviet- and Chinese-aligned rivals once and for all, and permanently consolidated Kim's leadership. That Kim was able to liquidate rivals with close ties to the USSR and China while utterly dependent on the two communist giants for economic reconstruction, and consolidate absolute power

---

113. See for example the front-page *Rodong Sinmun* editorial of December 18, 1953, entitled "Our Party Has Been Solidified like Steel in Organization and Ideology."

114. See *Rodong Sinmun* report on the KWP Third All-Party Congress, April 24, 1956.

115. There were two other major "fraternal" parties in the DPRK political system: the Korean Democratic Party, established as a party of moderate Christian nationalists in November 1945, and the Young Friends' Party, the political arm of the native Korean religion of Ch'ŏndogyo. Both had become subordinate to the Workers' Party even before the war, and afterward held little more than token significance in the ruling structure.

and an untouchable cult of personality just as the Soviet Union and its East European allies were undergoing "de-Stalinization," are among his and his faction's most remarkable political feats.

As we have seen in the previous chapter, purges in the DPRK leadership began during the Korean War itself. The first targets of the purges were former members of the South Korean Workers' Party (SKWP) who had come North before the war. The SKWP leader, Pak Hŏn-yŏng, was foreign minister in the first DPRK cabinet and Kim's most important rival. But the first victims were southern intellectuals, including the novelist Im Hwa and poet Kim Nam-ch'on, who were arrested in October 1952. Im confessed to conspiring with certain high-ranking party members against the regime.[116] In mid-December, at the Fifth Plenum of the KWP Central Committee, Kim Il Sung attacked "factional elements" within the party, his target clearly being the former SKWP members and Pak Hŏn-yŏng in particular.[117] In late February 1953, Pak himself was arrested, along with other high-ranking southerners, including Central Committee secretary Yi Sŭng-yŏp, former head of the Seoul People's Committee during the wartime occupation.[118]

The purges spread through the government ministries and social organizations during the first months of 1953, as various alleged "hostile elements" and "factionalists" were exposed. Altogether some four hundred KWP members were expelled from the party.[119] Lesser victims were forced to give public self-confessions and were demoted, not always permanently. Others faced long-term imprisonment and execution. On July 30, 1953, three days after the armistice was signed, Yi Sŭng-yŏp and eleven alleged coconspirators were officially indicted for treason. Put before a show trial in early August, they were accused of being spies for the Americans and subsequently executed. Pak Hŏn-yŏng did not face trial until later, charged with (among other things) being a spy for the American missionary Horace Underwood from as early as 1919, and was sentenced to death in December 1955.[120] Some of the purged leaders were from the pro-Soviet and pro-Chinese factions of the DPRK leadership, including Mu Chŏng of the "Yanan" group and the Soviet Korean Hŏ Ka-i; until 1956, however, most of the victims

---

116. Bran Myers, *Han Sŏrya and North Korean Literature: The Failure of Socialist Realism in the DPRK* (Ithaca: Cornell University, 1994) 84–85; Scalapino and Lee, *Communism in Korea* 432–438.

117. Scalapino and Lee, *Communism in Korea*, 439.

118. Soviet Embassy in DPRK, Report, 13 March 1953, AVPRF, Fond 0102, Opis 11, Papka 60, Delo 5.

119. According to Pak Yong-bin, head of the Organizational Department of the KWP. Soviet Embassy in DPRK, Annual Report, 15 April 1954. AVPRF, Fond 0102, Opis 10, Papka 62, Delo 7.

120. Koon Woo Nam, *The North Korean Communist Leadership, 1945–1965: A Study of Factionalism and Political Consolidation* (Tuscaloosa: University of Alabama Press, 1974), 92; Scalapino and Lee, *Communism in Korea*, 440, 447.

of these factional purges were from the "domestic," or South Korean, faction, who had the weakest base in North Korea and no foreign patron to protect them.[121]

These early purges were particularly damaging to the intellectual class in North Korea, as many of North Korea's leading intellectuals had migrated from the South before and during the Korean War.[122] Among the most prominent intellectuals caught up in the postwar purges were Im Hwa, a veteran of the Korea Artista Proleta Federatio (KAPF), the leading left-wing cultural group in the 1920s and 1930s, and former vice chairman of the DPRK Writers' Union; Sŏl Chŏng-sik, who had studied English literature in Ohio and translated Shakespeare into Korean and had been the chief North Korean interpreter at the Panmunjŏm armistice talks; and Kim Sŭng-nam, a composer strongly influenced by Bartok and other European modernists, who was perhaps the greatest composer in Korea at the time.[123] Virtually the only major active cultural figure of southern origin (as opposed to those no longer active in the cultural arena, like the novelist and former DPRK culture minister Hong Myŏng-hŭi) to survive the postwar purges, and perhaps the least talented among them, was the novelist Han Sŏr-ya. Han led some of the most vicious attacks against his fellow writers and artists while writing some of the most obsequious homilies to the Great Leader, Kim Il Sung.[124] Han himself was finally purged in 1962, as if to prove the adage that the revolution always eats its own.

Han began his attack at the First Congress of Writers and Artists, held on September 26–27, 1953. By this time Im Hwa had already been arrested and executed, and Han accused Yi T'ae-jun, another KAPF veteran, of having been a follower of Im Hwa and therefore guilty by association. Yi was subsequently kicked out of the Writers' Union. Han also attacked Kim Sŭng-nam, the composer, accusing him of abandoning Korean musical traditions and blindly emulating Western musical forms. Visual artists were similarly accused of neglecting Korean traditions and lacking patriotism.[125] Here we can see nationalism in the arts, or the lack of it, used as a political weapon for the first time in postwar North Korea, a tactic that would reach its apogee in Kim Il Sung's speech to propaganda workers in December 1955, the speech that launched North Korea's "Juche" ideology.

---

121. Lim Un, *The Founding of a Dynasty in North Korea: An Authentic Biography of Kim Il Sung* (Tokyo: Jiyu-sha, 1982), 216–17.

122. Scalapino and Lee, *Communism in Korea*, 890.

123. This was the opinion of, among others, Ely Haimowitz, the music advisor for the Department of Education of the US Military Government in South Korea, where Kim Sŭng-nam lived until he went North in 1948. Author's interview with Ely Haimowitz, November 11, 2002.

124. Han was probably the first writer to use the term *Sun of the Nation* (*Minjogŭi t'aeyang*) for Kim Il Sung, as early as 1946, and contributed more than anyone to the development of Kim's hagiography, until Han's fall from grace in the early 1960s.

125. Yang and Chee, "North Korean Education System," 127–35.

The postwar period was one of considerable anxiety on the part of the regime about politically suspect elements in the society as a whole. A campaign to weed out pro–South Korean and pro-American agents was announced the day after the armistice, on July 28, by Minister of the Interior Pang Hak-se, who offered amnesty to spies who surrendered as well as rewards to those who helped in apprehending them. Denunciation was apparently widespread, as was its abuse. At the Sixth Plenum of the KWP Central Committee in April 1954, Kim Il Sung criticized the unauthorized seizure of property of those whose relatives had fled to the South.[126] Nevertheless, the families of defectors, ROK soldiers, and anticommunist guerrillas remained under suspicion, and would face discrimination for decades to come. Techniques of social surveillance, policing, and control, already strong before the war, became further consolidated afterward and enabled the DPRK to become one of the most tightly controlled societies in the world.

The extension of political control over society was linked to an ongoing process of social engineering. In the spring of 1946, North Korea had introduced rapid, universal, and relatively moderate land reform that eliminated large landowners and gave land to hundreds of thousands of poor farmers. Collectivization was announced in the spring of 1950 but interrupted by the war. The regime began to organize peasants onto collective farms shortly after the war ended, and by 1956 some 40 percent of North Korea's farming population had been collectivized. By 1958, the process of collectivization was essentially complete, as was the nationalization of industry. At this point, as we will see in the next chapter, the DPRK declared the arrival of "socialism." According to DPRK statistics, North Korea was rapidly transformed after the war into a nation of "workers" and cooperative farmers:

TABLE 2.4 Change in class composition of DPRK (in percentages)

Category	1946	1949	1953	1954	1955	1956
Workers	12.5	19.0	21.1	25.7	28.4	27.3
Office employees	6.2	7.0	8.5	10.4	12.2	13.6
Members of agricultural cooperatives	—	—	—	17.1	26.1	40.0
Independent farmers	74.1	69.3	66.4	44.2	31.2	16.1
Members of handicraft cooperatives	—	0.3	0.5	0.48	0.95	1.1
Independent craftsmen	1.5	0.8	0.6	0.59	0.35	0.3
Industrialists	0.2	0.1	0.1	0.1	0.05	0.03
Merchants	3.3	1.7	1.2	0.87	0.58	0.57

Source: *Postwar Reconstruction and Development of the National Economy of DPRK* (Pyongyang: Foreign Languages Publishing House, 1957), 60–61.

---

126. Soviet Embassy in DPRK, Report, 19 April 1953. AVPRF, Fond 0102, Opis 11, Papka 60, Delo 5.

The New "Hermit Kingdom"

While the DPRK regime consolidated its control internally, North Korea became increasingly reticent toward its East European allies. The Soviet-bloc diplomats found North Korea to be much less fraternal than the East Europeans were among themselves. The East German embassy noted that even the Soviet representatives had more difficulty carrying out their work in Pyongyang than in other "People's Democracies."[127] The Hungarian ambassador remarked that the North Koreans "would like to curtail the operation and activity of the whole diplomatic corps and keep its operation under a rather strict control."[128] The DPRK frequently rotated the Korean employees of the East European embassies, a problem Soviet ambassador Suzdalev told his Hungarian counterpart there was little the East Europeans could do to address.[129] Unlike the Soviet-aligned People's Democracies, the North Koreans did not discuss internal party purges with other fraternal parties, except in the most minimal and oblique ways. East Europeans found themselves more isolated in Pyongyang than in hostile capitals in the West; the only similarly suspicious and closed fraternal country was Albania.[130] Unlike Albania, however, North Korea was never excommunicated from the Soviet bloc.

This suspicious and reticent attitude can be seen in part as the reemergence of Korea's long-standing "Hermit Kingdom" tradition of isolation, expressed in a new language of fierce defense of national sovereignty. But it was also related to Kim Il Sung's wariness of and disdain for "de-Stalinization" in the Soviet Union and Eastern Europe, already apparent in late 1953, well before Khrushchev made it official. "Collective leadership," the slogan of the post-Stalin era, was not in the least appealing to Kim, although he did pay some lip service to the idea in the late 1950s, as we will see. While the leaders of Bulgaria, Romania, Poland, and even Albania and Mongolia relinquished some of their multiple leadership posts, Kim did not follow suit, retaining the posts of premier and Central Committee chairman as his cult of personality continued to grow.[131] Kim was also the only North Korean leader to maintain these multiple positions.

The First North Korean Food Crisis

As we have seen, North Korea's postwar economic program was extremely successful in the aggregate, especially in the area of industrial development. But at

---

127. GDR Embassy in DPRK, Report, 15 November 1954. MfAA A 5566.

128. Hungarian Embassy to the DPRK, Annual Report, 26 February 1955, KTS, 4. doboz, 5/a, 004076/1955. Translated by Balázs Szalontai for the Cold War International History Project.

129. Soviet Embassy in DPRK, Report, 29 September 1954. AVPRF, Fond 0102, Opis 10, Papka 44, Delo 9.

130. GDR Embassy in DPRK, Report, 22 December 1953. MfAA A 5566.

131. GDR Foreign Ministry, Memorandum, January 1954. MfAA A 5576.

the microlevel there were numerous problems, some of them quite severe. A few of the other party leaders questioned the autarkist and heavy-industry-oriented policies promoted by Kim, and this debate emerged as early as the Central Committee plenum of August 1953.[132] Critics included Minister of Finance Ch'oe Ch'ang-ik, Chairman Pak Ch'ang-ok of the State Planning Commission, and Minister of Light Industry Pak Ŭi-wan (Ivan Pak). All three were appointed vice premiers in March 1954. None were to survive the purges of the late 1950s, nor were their ideas of emphasizing light industry and consumer goods over heavy industry and self-reliance ever put seriously into practice.

Agricultural policy in particular was little short of disastrous in the first few years after the war, culminating in a serious food shortage in 1955. After the war ended, the DPRK began its long-delayed program of agricultural collectivization. By September 1953, there were a thousand cooperatives in the DPRK. In November 1954, in the midst of a bumper harvest, the Central Committee decided to accelerate collectivization, to coincide with a decision to complete the Three-Year Plan by the end of 1955, half a year ahead of schedule.[133] In fact, however, neither the production nor the distribution of food grains was as successful as Kim and the KWP leadership suggested. Local food shortages began to appear early in 1955; within a few months, much of the country was in the midst of a food crisis, and the traditional "barley hill" (*pori kogae*) of spring famine loomed.[134]

Several factors contributed to North Korea's first food crisis, prefiguring the much more severe food disaster of the mid-1990s. First, the labor shortage caused by the war and the diversion of the workforce into industry hit hard the agricultural sector, which was still very labor-intensive in the mid-1950s despite glowing reports of mechanization. Indeed, much of the agricultural labor was carried out by women and young children, the adult males either lost or working in the cities.[135] Second, bad weather in 1954, including insufficient rainfall in the normally rainy summer, led to a poor harvest, especially for rice. This was less the case for the southwestern regions of North Korea than the northern and eastern regions, but nevertheless the overall crop was badly hit.[136] Third, the postwar reconstruction program depended on agricultural taxes and compulsory grain deliveries to the cities; a poor harvest squeezed even more out of the already hard-pressed agricultural sector. In April 1955, Soviet ambassador A. M. Petrov remarked to a

132. Okonogi, "North Korean Communism," 181–83.

133. Ibid., 184.

134. Soviet Embassy in DPRK, Report, 10 May 1955. AVPRF, Fond 0102, Opis 11, Papka 60, Delo 5; GDR Embassy in DPRK, Report, 27 May 1955. MfAA A 5631.

135. Soviet Embassy in DPRK, Report, 10 May 1955; Soviet Embassy in DPRK, Report, 17 August 1955. AVPRF Fond 0102, Opis 11, Papka 60, Delo 5.

136. oviet Embassy in DPRK, Report, 22 October 1954. AVPRF, Fond 0102, Opis11, Papka 60, Delo 8.

group of East European diplomats that the KWP's report of 3 million metric tons of grain harvested in 1954 was certainly false. At best, Petrov said, the crop had been 2.3 million metric tons, and even that might be an exaggeration. As a result of these exaggerated production figures, the state often took 50 percent of local harvests as tax, rather than the 25 percent required by law, depleting peasants of what little reserve they might have had. Similarly, compulsory grain deliveries were based on higher production figures than were in fact the case, and the state had to take grains at times by force.[137]

The production of grain in 1953 was 24 percent less than in 1949, and declined even further in 1954. As Scalapino and Lee put it, "Serious food shortages continued through 1954 and 1955, a fact not admitted by the government until the end of 1956."[138] Government attempts to address the problem only made it worse. For example, a decree of October 1954 prohibiting private trade in grain, combined with the state's decision to withhold rice from government shops in order to maintain ration levels, led inevitably to a shortage of rice in state shops and skyrocketing inflation. A kilogram of rice that had cost forty won in state-owned stores soon became four hundred won on the black market, equivalent to roughly one-third of the average worker's monthly income.[139] Meanwhile, collectivization of peasant households rapidly increased, and productivity correspondingly declined. By the end of 1954, one-fifth of peasant households were in collective farms; two years later, the proportion had risen to 40 percent.[140]

The province hit hardest by the food shortage was North Hamgyŏng, the DPRK's most remote and mountainous area. This had long been the part of Korea where rural life was poorest and most precarious, and the site of greatest hunger once again in the famine of the 1990s. But the whole country was affected by the crisis. East European diplomats reported a large internal migration of North Koreans searching for food, and many instances of death by starvation. Peasants, even in the relatively affluent provinces of South P'yŏngan and Hwanghae, supplemented their diets with—or tried to live entirely on—wild grains, grasses, and tree bark.[141] Rations were sharply cut back, even for state employees in Pyongyang. Beggars, thieves, and homeless children proliferated.[142]

---

137. Soviet Embassy in DPRK, Report, 13 April 1955. AVPRF, Fond 0102, Opis 11, Papka 65, Delo 45.

138. Scalapino and Lee, *Communism in Korea*, 533.

139. Soviet Embassy in DPRK Report, 24 February 1955. AVPRF, Fond 0102, Opis 11, Papka 60, Delo 8.

140. Soviet Embassy in DPRK, Annual Report, 26 February 1955. AVPRF, Fond 0102, Opis 11, Papka 65, Delo 45.

141. Soviet Embassy in DPRK, Report, 10 May 1955. AVPRF, Fond 0102, Opis 11, Papka 60, Delo 5.

142. Ibid.

Although the total number of victims will never be known with certainty, the 1955 North Korea food shortage was not nearly as severe as the food crisis of the 1990s, or proportionately as disastrous as China's Great Leap Forward famine in the early 1960s. Nevertheless, the DPRK leadership was forced to reexamine the policies that led to the disaster; among other steps, the regime put a stop to compulsory grain deliveries while distributing rice from China and the USSR to the regions hit hardest by hunger.[143]

There was also a search for scapegoats. In early April 1955, the KWP Central Committee held a plenum in which it admitted that the 1954 harvest had been poorer than previously announced. Kim Il Sung attacked the "bureaucratism" that had led to such falsifying of the data. Kim Il Sung's old comrade-in-arms Kim Il, minister of agriculture, was singled out for criticism and disappeared from public view for a time, although he was to reemerge later. A number of other high-ranking leaders, including Pang Ho-san of the Yanan group, were demoted permanently.[144] Needless to say, Kim Il Sung himself came away blameless, admonishing all party members to study the principles of Marxism-Leninism and apply them to the actual conditions of North Korea. Many party members, Kim said, had "made the dogmatic error of mechanically applying the experiences of other countries to the reality of our country."[145] This vague criticism prefigured Kim's speech at the end of 1955, in which the individual party members who had made these "errors," and the "other countries" they were emulating, would be singled out by name.

Nevertheless, the food situation continued to deteriorate after the April plenum. An April 26 editorial in the *Rodong Sinmun* mentioned the food crisis for the first time, suggesting that citizens supplement their diets with grass and tree bark. The issue was quickly withdrawn from circulation.[146] The Soviets and their East European allies were becoming increasingly critical of the North Korean leadership for its handling of the crisis. In a discussion with Hungarian diplomats in April, Soviet ambassador Petrov railed against Kim Il Sung's one-man rule and cult of personality, which prevented mistakes from being openly admitted and addressed. Production targets were inflated to the point of absurdity, Petrov said; the grain crop target for 1955, for example, was originally 4 million metric tons, double the output in 1954 and completely impossible to attain.[147]

---

143. Soviet Embassy in DPRK, Report, 5 May 1955; Report, 13 April 1955. AVPRF, Fond 0102, Opis 11, Papka 60, Delo 5.

144. Scalapino and Lee, *Communism in Korea*, 469–471; Andrei N. Lankov, "Kim Il Sung's Campaign against the Soviet Faction in Late 1955 and the Birth of *Chuch'e*," *Korean Studies* 23 (June 1999): 46.

145. Cited in Okonogi, "North Korean Communism," 194.

146. Soviet Embassy in DPRK, Report, 10 May 1955; Report, 26 May 1955. AVPRF, Fond 0102, Opis 11, Papka 60, Delo 5.

147. Soviet Embassy in DPRK, Report, 13 April 1955. AVPRF, Fond 0102, Opis 11, Papka 60, Delo 5.

Emergency grain shipments and agricultural goods from the USSR and China saved North Korea from an even worse food crisis than it already faced. Under Soviet pressure, the DPRK rescinded its prohibition on private trade in grains, and the price of rice declined as food sources increased. More resources were put into irrigation, and the production of chemical fertilizer was stepped up, improving agricultural production. Agricultural taxes were reduced, peasant debts were canceled, and small merchants were allowed to resume their business.[148] Combined with better weather in the summer of 1955 and the mobilization of soldiers for the fall harvest, these policies alleviated the worst of the rural suffering. North Korea's first postwar food crisis was over.

Against De-Stalinization

In their standard, Cold War–era study of Korean communism, Scalapino and Lee suggest that in the mid-1950s the DPRK was still essentially a faithful Soviet satellite, an Asian Bulgaria.[149] In fact, it is quite clear from the East European documents that North Korea at this time was not very amenable to Soviet control despite its dependency on Soviet and fraternal aid. North Korea's reluctant retreat from its single-minded pursuit of heavy industry in 1955, under strong Soviet pressure, cannot be compared to the reformist "New Course" carried out by regimes in Eastern Europe in the first three years after the death of Stalin. While in Poland or Hungary the Soviets could reduce or even remove the power of wayward local leaders, in North Korea Kim Il Sung was able to reinforce his personal control and eliminate the very rivals who were closest to the USSR. In a conversation at the Soviet embassy in Pyongyang in July 1955, Soviet ambassador Ivanov informed his East European colleagues that the Soviets were well aware of North Korea's extreme sensitivity to any perceived interference in their internal affairs, and that therefore Soviet and other foreign advisors had to be wary of pushing too hard or appearing to scold or lecture the Koreans for their "errors."[150]

As we will explore further in the next chapter, one of the ironies of Soviet-DPRK relations is that the North Korean leadership—and Kim Il Sung in particular—always held a soft spot for Stalin but came to loathe Khrushchev, despite the fact that Khrushchev was much less assertive of Soviet influence over North Korea than Stalin had been. Part of this difference was perhaps personal,

---

148. Soviet Embassy in DPRK, Report, August 1955; Report, 17 August 1955. AVPRF, Fond 0102, Opis 11, Papka 60, Delo 5.

149. Scalapino and Lee, *Communism in Korea*, 546–558.

150. Soviet Embassy in DPRK, Report, 17 August 1955. AVPRF, Fond 0102, Opis 11, Papka 60, Delo 5.

as Kim held up Stalin as his role model and considered Khrushchev a boor. Another factor is that Stalin helped Kim come to power in the late 1940s, whereas Khrushchev's support for Kim was at best ambivalent. Khrushchev was at first openly critical of North Korea's heavy-industry approach to industrialization, its hostile stance toward South Korea, and Kim Il Sung's cult of personality. Although Khrushchev would come around to unconditional support of Kim by 1957, the damage had already been done, and Kim remained deeply suspicious of the Soviet leader throughout Khrushchev's time in office.[151]

On the surface, Soviet policies toward North Korea in the mid-1950s strengthened the DPRK's autonomy and economic position. The post-Stalin leadership tried to create a more equal relationship between the Soviet Union and its Asian allies. In September 1955, the USSR gave North Korea full control of Sokav, the Soviet-Korean airline.[152] During the same year, the Soviet-Korean transport company Mortrans, as well as jointly owned oil refining companies established before the Korean War, were also handed over to the Koreans.[153] This was the same time at which the Soviet Union relinquished control of the Lüshun naval base and Soviet-Chinese joint companies in Xinjiang and Manchuria to the PRC.[154] Clearly the new Soviet leadership was trying to distance itself from the "big-power chauvinism" of the Stalin era, a move at first welcomed by both Kim and Mao Zedong.[155]

De-Stalinization in the USSR gave Kim a window to further consolidate his domestic leadership position in the fall of 1955, mostly at the expense of the "Soviet Koreans." The USSR did little to prevent the fall of their loyalists in North Korea; after all, the Soviets were working to replace the "Muscovites" in Eastern Europe with national leaders, and it would have been unseemly to take the opposite tack in Korea, blocking nationalists associated with Kim in favor of more Moscow-oriented local leaders. Only the following summer, when Kim initiated a serious crackdown on his Soviet- and Chinese-aligned rivals, did the Moscow and Beijing become alarmed. Despite sending two high-ranking officials, Anastas Mikoyan and Peng Dehuai, in an unprecedented joint intervention into North Korea's domestic political affairs, the Soviets and Chinese were unable in the end

151. Nobuo Shimotomai, "Kim Il Sung's Balancing Act between Moscow and Beijing, 1956–1972," in Tsuyoshi Hasegawa, ed., *The Cold War in East Asia, 1945–1991* (Washington, DC: Woodrow Wilson International Center for Scholars, 2011), 125–26.

152. Soviet Embassy in DPRK, Report, 19 October 1955. AVPRF, Fond 0102, Opis 11, Papka 60, Delo 5.

153. Yoon T. Kuark, "North Korea's Industrial Development During the Postwar Period," in Robert Scalapino, *North Korea Today: Strategic and Domestic Issues* (Berkeley: Institute of East Asian Studies, University of California, Berkeley, Center for Korean Studies, 1983), 54–62.

154. Odd Arne Westad, "Introduction," in Westad, ed., *Brothers in Arms*, 15–16.

155. Ree, "The Limits of *Juche*," 52–53.

to prevent Kim's purge. The "August Incident" of 1956 is something we will take up in the following chapter.

In September 1955 Kim proposed the promotion of Ch'oe Yong-gŏn, one of his former colleagues in the anti-Japanese guerrilla struggle of the 1930s, to the Central Committee of the KWP. This proposal was strongly opposed by Pak Ch'ang-ok, Pak Yŏng-bin, and other Soviet Koreans, who argued that Ch'oe was not even a member of the Workers' Party—he had been appointed chairman of the noncommunist Korean Democratic Party (KDP) in January 1946, after the founder of the KDP, the Christian nationalist Cho Man-sik, was placed under house arrest.[156] This was technically true but largely irrelevant. Everyone knew that Ch'oe's membership in the KDP was a means for the communists to control this "bourgeois" party, and that his true loyalties were with the KWP. More significantly, the Soviet Koreans, under the influence of de-Stalinization in the USSR, were beginning to criticize Kim Il Sung's cult of personality and suggest a more moderate, collective orientation for the DPRK leadership.[157] Such criticism would, within a year, be their undoing. In any event, Ch'oe did ultimately win his promotion, and would remain at the top of the DPRK leadership for many years to come. The campaign against "factional elements" continued at the KWP Central Committee Plenum in December 2–3. There, the Kim loyalist Im Hae attacked Pak Il-u, one of the prominent "Yanan" Koreans, and Kim Yŏl, a Soviet Korean member of the Central Committee. Kim Yŏl was expelled from the party and arrested.[158] Pak Il-u, a former minister of the interior, had already been removed from power during the Korean War.

The Articulation of Self-Reliance

It is in this context that we can understand Kim Il Sung's "Juche" speech of December 1955. Kim delivered this speech, entitled "On Eliminating Dogmatism and Formalism and Establishing Juche in Ideological Work," at an extended session of the Presidium of the KWP Central Committee held December 27–28. The Presidium was a small group of Central Committee members ranking above the Political Council (North Korea's version of the Politburo), normally consisting of a few dozen people, although at the December 1955 meeting there were more than four hundred present, according to Soviet records.[159] The speech was not

156. Lankov, "Kim Il Sung's Campaign against the Soviet Faction," 47.

157. Ibid., 47–49; Okonogi, "North Korean Communism," 187.

158. Soviet Embassy in DPRK, Report, 1 March 1956. AVPRK, Fond 0102, Opis 12, Papka 68, Delo 6.

159. Cited in in Lankov, "Kim Il Sung's Campaign against the Soviet Faction," 51.

made public until some time later, and in subsequent North Korean publications the venue was vaguely cited as a "speech to propaganda and agitation workers."[160] The Juche speech was much more than a critique of current cultural policy, its ostensible subject. It was also more than an attack on Kim's political opponents, which is the way it has most often been interpreted.[161] Over subsequent decades, the December 1955 speech became the touchstone of North Korea's self-reliance policy in all areas of life, including economic development, diplomacy, military affairs, and cultural production.[162] Although not seen as particularly noteworthy by Pyongyang's allies the time, the Kim's speech marked in retrospect the beginning of North Korea's divergence from the Moscow-dominated international socialist community, a declaration of independence from Soviet control and influence.

The domestic political targets of the speech could not have been more explicit: they were high-ranking party members with close Soviet ties. Pak Hŏn-yŏng had just been sentenced to death on December 15 (although the sentence was not carried out until 1956), effectively eliminating the SKWP faction in the North Korean leadership. Although the "Pak Hŏn-yŏng—Yi Sŭng-yŏp spy clique" was mentioned in Kim's speech,[163] the main targets named in Kim's attack were all Soviet Koreans still active in the DPRK leadership: Pak Yŏng-bin, Ki Sŏk-bok, Chŏng Yul, Chŏn Tong-hyŏk, and above all the chairman of the State Planning Commission, Pak Ch'ang-ok.

Kim began his speech with reference to "serious errors on the literary front," which represented the problem of propaganda work in general. This problem stemmed from "the failure to delve deeply into all matters and the lack of Juche."[164] Propaganda and agitation workers "merely copy and memorize things foreign," instead of paying attention to things Korean. Juche meant, in essence, a Korea-centered view of the world.

---

160. Kim, "On Eliminating Dogmatism," 395–417.

161. Lankov, "Kim Il Sung's Campaign against the Soviet Faction"; Scalapino and Lee, *Communism in Korea*, 500–503.

162. As a Bulgarian diplomat in Pyongyang remarked some twenty years later, "Since 1955, the Juche ideology of Kim Il Sung has become, to an ever-increasing degree, the foundation of all social life in the DPRK." GDR Embassy in Pyongyang, 19 September 1975. "Notes on a conversation between comrade Tuparov, attaché of the Embassy of the PRB, and comrade Stark, Second Secretary of the Embassy of the GDR, on 29 August 1975 in the Embassy of the GDR," 2. MfAA C6854.

163. Kim, "On Eliminating Dogmatism," 397.

164. Ibid., 395. Here and in other official North Korean texts in English, "Juche" is left in untranslated romanization. Although the DPRK attempted in the early years to translate "Juche" as "self-identity," by the late 1960s Juche was apparently considered untranslatable, the ineffable essence of North Korean identity and ideology. Perhaps DPRK publishers thought (or hoped) that foreigners simply knew what "Juche" meant.

> We are not engaged in any other country's revolution but solely in the Korean revolution. This, the Korean revolution, determines the essence of Juche in the ideological work of our Party. . . . To make revolution in Korea we must know Korean history and geography as well as the customs of the Korean people. Only then is it possible to educate our people in a way that suits them and to inspire in them an ardent love for their native place and motherland.[165]

Kim accused "Pak Ch'ang-ok and his kind" of neglecting Korean history in the area of literature. They had "closed their eyes" to the struggle of the KAPF literary group in the colonial period, to the 1929 student uprising against the Japanese, to the March First 1919 Independence Movement. Instead, these "factionalists" were lavishing praise on foreigners (i.e., Russians) and blindly emulating the Soviet Union.

> Once I visited a People's Army rest home, where there was a picture of the Siberian steppe on the wall. Russians probably like that landscape. But we Korean people like the beautiful scenery of our own country. . . . One day this summer when I dropped in at a local democratic publicity hall, I saw diagrams of the Soviet Union's Five-Year Plan on show there, but not a single diagram illustrating our own Three-Year Plan . . . I noticed in a primary school that all the portraits on the walls were of foreigners, such as Mayakovsky and Pushkin, but there were none of Koreans. If children are educated in this way, how can they be expected to have national pride?[166]

Koreans must apply Marxism-Leninism "creatively" to the conditions specific to Korea, in both domestic and foreign matters. "Some advocate the Soviet way and others the Chinese," Kim said, "but is it not high time to work out our own?"[167] Here again a Soviet Korean was singled out for criticism:

> Pak Yŏng-bin, on returning from the Soviet Union, said that as the Soviet Union was following the line of easing international tension, we should also drop our slogan against US imperialism. Such an assertion has nothing to do with revolutionary initiative. It would dull our people's revolutionary vigilance. These US imperialists scorched our land, massacred our innocent people, and are still occupying the southern half of our country. They are our sworn enemy, aren't they?[168]

---

165. Kim, "On Eliminating Dogmatism," 395–96.
166. Ibid., 399.
167. Ibid., 403.
168. Ibid., 401.

Kim insisted that different approaches to "imperialism" did not mean that Soviet and North Korean efforts were in conflict; rather, "loving Korea is just as good as loving the Soviet Union and socialist camp and, likewise, loving the Soviet Union and the socialist camp is just as good as loving Korea." Internationalism and patriotism were mutually reinforcing; a true patriot is also an internationalist, and vice versa.[169]

The speech had its intended domestic effect. Pak Ch'ang-ok and Pak Yŏng-bin were expelled from the Politburo in January 1956. Pak Yŏng-bin was also expelled from the Central Committee, and Pak Ch'ang-ok resigned as chairman of the State Planning Commission. Ki Sŏk-bok and Chŏng Yul also lost their positions. Kim loyalists such as Im Hae, Pak Kŭm-chol, and Ch'oe Yong-gŏn advanced at their expense. But in light of the international conditions in late 1955 and early 1956, it is difficult to argue, as Scalapino and Lee have done, that "Kim's new nationalism was the product at this point of internal, not international, considerations."[170] First, Kim's nationalism was hardly new; he had spent his entire youth until the age of thirty-three as an anti-Japanese guerrilla fighter, only the last three or four years of that period in the USSR, and had never been particularly close to the pro-Soviet or pro-Chinese factions of the DPRK leadership (although he was adept at aligning with one or both of these groups when it suited his purpose). Nothing in his Juche speech was a radical departure from Kim's earlier statements on Korean nationalism, going back to the immediate postliberation period.

Furthermore, internal and international considerations were inextricably mixed. Kim was well aware of the moves toward collective leadership, internal liberalization, and relaxation of tensions with the United States in post-Stalin Soviet Union. He also clearly disapproved of all these measures, which were diametrically opposed to the direction he wanted to take the DPRK: a leadership more under his control, mass mobilization for rapid industrialization, and unification with South Korea. To achieve these goals, the advocates of the "Soviet path"—those high-ranking party members with close ties to the USSR—had to be eliminated, but in a way that did not provoke the Soviet Union to break its ties to North Korea or cut off aid, on which North Korea was deeply dependent. Culture was a shrewd point of entry through which to attack the Soviet group, an area that the Soviets were unlikely to strongly defend. As long as the DPRK appeared to be following Soviet advice in economic matters, North Korea going

169. Ibid., 404–5.
170. Scalapino and Lee, *Communism in Korea*, 502.

its way in the cultural arena was not of great concern. From the Soviet perspective, maintaining North Korea as an ally in East Asia was more important than the positions of a handful of Soviet-aligned North Korean leaders. Few could have seen at the time that Kim's Juche speech was not merely an assertion of Korean cultural distinctiveness or an attack on his pro-Soviet rivals, but would be the very foundation of North Korea's independent position in the international socialist community.

A SINGULAR PATH

North Korea in the Socialist Community, 1956–63

> **Party propaganda is not oriented toward studying the works of Marxism-Leninism, but rather is solely and completely oriented toward the "wise teachings of our glorious leader, Comrade Kim Il Sung" . . . Dogmatism in the Korean Workers' Party is closely linked to mystical ideas of Confucianism, which extend to certain nationalist tendencies.**

—East German Embassy in Pyongyang, March 1961

De-Stalinization and the Rise of Kim

Khrushchev's "secret" speech denouncing Stalin at the Twentieth Congress of the Communist Party of the Soviet Union in February 1956, widely disseminated to fellow Communist parties and leaked to the Western press, sent shock waves through the socialist world. Its effects on North Korea were ambiguous. At first, the de-Stalinization campaign in the USSR encouraged rumbles of dissatisfaction with Kim Il Sung's paramount leadership in North Korea, particularly among those with close ties to the Soviet Union, but also from some of the "Yanan" group who were equally unhappy with the direction of Kim's policies and the growing influence of the former Manchurian partisans. This perceived opportunity to reform Kim's rule, however, soon turned into a debacle for his critics, who were harshly denounced at the August 1956 Plenum of the KWP Central Committee. The personal intervention of Deputy Premier Anastas Mikoyan of the USSR and Chinese defense minister Peng Dehuai temporarily forced Kim and his allies to relent and reinstate the critics, but this reversal lasted less than two years, until March 1958, when the First National Conference of KWP Representatives reinforced the decisions of the August plenum and eliminated Kim's major Soviet- and China-aligned rivals once and for all.[1] From that time onward, Kim ruled without any public challenge.

Epigraph from Embassy of GDR in DPRK, Report, 14 March 1961. SAPMO-BA, DY 30, IV 2/20/137.

1. Robert A. Scalapino and Chong-Sik Lee, *Communism in Korea,* vol. 1, *The Movement* (Berkeley: University of California Press, 1972), 514–23.

Kim Il Sung did not attend the CPSU Twentieth Congress, and the Korean Workers' Party was represented by a delegation led by Ch'oe Yong-gŏn, Kim's old guerrilla comrade.[2] This put Kim in good company, as Mao Zedong and Ho Chi Minh also missed the Congress. In March, Ch'oe reported his visit to the KWP Central Committee. Very little of Ch'oe's speech, or of the other speeches at the Central Committee session (including that by Kim Il Sung) was reported in the North Korean media. Shortly thereafter some articles critical of the "cult of personality" appeared in *Rodong Sinmun* and elsewhere, but only in the form of translations from the Soviet and Chinese press.[3] Stalin was never criticized by name. Indeed, Stalin probably maintained a more favorable image in North Korea than in any other country in the world, not least in the writings of Kim Il Sung. As late as 1998, in the eighth volume of Kim's posthumous "autobiography," Kim attributes the successful development of the Soviet Union into a great power to the wise leadership of Stalin, "faithful comrade and disciple of Lenin." Unfortunately, Kim recounted, "Things began to go astray after Khrushchev came to power. Modern revisionism appeared in the Soviet Party, and the Soviet people began to suffer from ideological maladies. . . . [Khrushchev] forgot the care with which his leaders had brought him up, he vilified Stalin on the excuse of the personality cult."[4] Kim Il Sung would tolerate neither "revisionism" nor any other "ideological malady" in his own rule and would remain a faithful follower of his mentor Stalin throughout the turmoil of de-Stalinization.

In late April the KWP held its own Third Party Congress. In contrast to previous congresses, this time visiting East European and Soviet delegates were not allowed to mingle with the Koreans.[5] The KWP Congress did not discuss the problem of the cult of personality, nor did it pay much attention to shifting economic priorities from heavy industry to raising the standard of living for ordinary citizens, two major issues of the Twentieth CPSU Congress. Soviet ambassador Ivanov, in his discussions with other Soviet-bloc diplomats, complained of North Korea's reluctance to take up this latter issue and its insistence on a misguided heavy-industry-first approach to economic development, as well as the lack of attention paid by the DPRK leadership to economic cooperation

2. According to Soviet ambassador Vladimir Ivanov, Kim Il Sung told the Soviets he could not attend the CPSU Congress as he was busy preparing for the KWP Third Party Congress, scheduled to begin April 23. Diary of Ambassador V. I. Ivanov, February–March 1956, RGANI, Fond 5, Opis 28, Delo 411, 1.163. Cited in Nobuo Shimotomai, "Pyeongyang in 1956," *Cold War International History Project Bulletin* 16 (fall 2007–winter 2008), 456.

3. Soviet Embassy in DPRK, Report, 19 April 1956. AVPRF, Fond 0102, Opis 12, Papka 68, Delo 6.

4. Kim Il Sung, *With the Century: Reminiscences*, vol. 8 (Pyongyang: Foreign Languages Publishing House, 1998), 290–91.

5. Andrei Lankov, "Kim Il Sung's Campaign against the Soviet Faction," *Korean Studies* 23 (1999): 59–60.

between North Korea and the other fraternal countries.[6] Meanwhile, in elections to the new Central Committee, the number of Kim loyalists from his Manchurian guerrilla days more than doubled. Proportions of former Manchurian guerrillas went up comparably as well in the KWP Political Council, renamed the Standing Committee. Nevertheless, the "Soviet Korean" Pak Ch'ang-ok, despite Kim's attacks on him the previous December, was retained on the Central Committee (perhaps to placate the Soviets), although he was demoted in rank. Many members of the Yanan group, and even a few of Pak Hŏn-yŏng's former followers, were also reelected to the Central Committee.[7] The vicious "anti-factional struggles" of earlier months had abated, but only temporarily.

What the DPRK did put into practice, however, was a new nationalist orientation in culture and the arts, which after all had been the ostensible theme of Kim's December 1955 "Juche speech." The Korean-Soviet Friendship Association closed down its provincial offices at the end of 1955. Broadcasts of Radio Moscow were drastically reduced in February 1956, coinciding with the Twentieth CPSU Congress. Soviet plays were no longer performed.[8] In a speech at the Third KWP Congress, Minister of Education Kim Ch'ang-man, also vice chairman of the Central Committee and a long-time ally of Kim Il Sung, criticized the lack of Korean geography, history, and literature in North Korean university education.[9] The "Koreanization" of North Korean culture was underway, at the expense of Soviet—and indeed all European—cultural influence. A music festival celebrating the tenth anniversary of the founding of the GDR, sponsored by the East German embassy in Pyongyang in October 1959, would be among the last such large-scale performances of European music in North Korea.[10] Characteristically, the speeches by GDR officials at this event went into great detail about the amount and variety of East German assistance to the DPRK, whereas the North Korean speeches never mentioned it.

The August Incident

The rift between North Korea and the USSR predated the Twentieth CPSU Congress in 1956, going back to the immediate aftermath of Stalin's death in 1953. The new post-Stalinist leadership, pursuing consumer-oriented economic policies at home and peaceful coexistence abroad, criticized both North Korea's radical

6. Soviet Embassy in DPRK, Report, 4 June 1956. AVPRF, Fond 0102, Opis 12, Papka 68, Delo 6.

7. Dae-Sook Suh, *Kim Il Sung, The North Korean Leader* (New York: Columbia University Press, 1988), 147–54.

8. Lankov, "Kim Il Sung's Campaign against the Soviet Faction," 61–62.

9. Soviet Embassy in DPRK, Report, 18 July 1956. AVPRF, Fond 0102, Opis 12, Papka 68, Delo 6.

10. GDR Embassy in Pyongyang, Report, 26 October 1959. MfAA A 10264.

domestic agenda and its continued advocacy of "liberating" the South—by force if necessary. The Soviets were also concerned about losing their influence within the DPRK power structure, as "Soviet-Koreans" were purged from the inner circles of leadership, beginning with Hŏ Ka-i, driven to suicide (or possibly killed outright) in July 1953. Hŏ successor in charge of party personnel, the Soviet-Korean Pak Yŏng-bin, was dismissed in April 1955. Kim's frontal attack on the Soviet "faction" in December 1955 led to a corresponding rise in the status of the pro-Chinese elements in the KWP.[11] But by the middle of 1956, both the Soviet- and the China-aligned KWP elites were deeply dissatisfied with the direction of Kim Il Sung's rule, and their dissatisfaction would soon go public.[12]

In the summer of 1956 the challenge to Kim Il Sung's leadership came out into the open. On June 1, Kim led a delegation to Moscow and several East European capitals to discuss economic aid and other issues. During Kim's absence, which lasted nearly three weeks, his opponents conspired to put a stop to his growing one-man rule, perhaps even replace Kim with a collective leadership. Yi Sang-cho, then DPRK ambassador to the USSR, tried to win Moscow's backing for the conspiracy. Meeting with Soviet foreign ministry personnel in mid-June, Yi criticized Kim's cult of personality and his repressive rule, and asked for Soviet help in bringing reform to the DPRK. In July, opponents of Kim—including Pak Ch'ang-ok, Ch'oe Ch'ang-ik, Kim Sŭng-hwa, and Yun Kong-hŭm—informed diplomats at the Soviet embassy in Pyongyang that they planned to criticize Kim at the next Central Committee plenum and hoped for Soviet support in their venture. This support, however, was not forthcoming.[13] In fact, the Soviets thought they already saw signs of reform in Kim's approach to economic policies, and they did not want to risk alienating a foreign leader who was both loyal to the Soviet Union and popular at home.[14] Overly emboldened by the example of de-Stalinization in the USSR and some of the "satellite" countries, the conspirators miscalculated

---

11. Nobuo Shimotomai, "Kim Il Sung's Balancing Act between Moscow and Beijing, 1956–1972," in Tsuyoshi Hasegawa, ed., *The Cold War in East Asia, 1945–1991* (Stanford: Stanford University Press, 2011), 124–26.

12. As James Person notes, it is important not to overstate the group identities of the Soviet and Yanan "factions," which are largely post hoc labels affixed by Kim Il Sung to tarnish his enemies. It is true that the main challengers to Kim Il Sung in the 1950s were individuals who had been associated with the Soviet and Chinese Communist parties, but they did not necessarily see themselves as making up distinct "factions." If there was any communist group in North Korea with a strong sense of collective identity it was the former members of the South Korean Workers' Party, but by 1955 their leader Pak Hŏn-yŏng had been purged and their power eradicated. See James Person, " 'We Need Help from Outside': The North Korean Opposition Movement of 1956," Cold War History Project Working Paper No. 52, August 2006.

13. Andrei Lankov, *From Stalin to Kim Il Sung: The Formation of North Korea, 1945–1960* (New Brunswick, NJ: Rutgers University Press, 2002), 156–62.

14. Soviet Embassy in DRPK, Report, 12 September 1956. AVPRF, Fond 0102, Opis 12, Papka 68, Delo 6.

their degree of both foreign backing and domestic support in reducing Kim's power. The result, as in the purges of 1952–55, was victory for Kim Il Sung and utter disaster for his opponents.

The attack on Kim Il Sung came at the KWP Central Committee plenum in the final days of August. One by one, Kim's opponents gave speeches criticizing various aspects of his rule. Pak Ch'ang-ok had a particularly lengthy document detailing the errors of Kim Il Sung's rule, which he was not allowed to read in its entirety.[15] Nevertheless, the charges were harsh and numerous, covering three main areas. First, there was the question of the personality cult, which persisted in North Korea despite the call for eliminating such "deformities" of Marxism-Leninism after the Twentieth CPSU Congress. Second, there was the lack of attention to improving living standards. Ch'oe Ch'ang-ik alluded to the food shortages and lack of consumer goods, the direct results of the overemphasis on heavy industry.[16] Third, party officials were selected on the basis of cronyism and factional affiliation rather than merit. Another issue, less important politically but perhaps more insulting to members of the Soviet and Yanan groups personally, was the fact that Kim Il Sung had distorted history by portraying his Manchurian guerrilla group as the true representative of the Korean revolution, at the expense of the communist movements in Korea, the Soviet Union, and elsewhere in China.[17]

Some of these criticisms were refuted by Kim at the Plenum. In the area of economic policy, for example, Kim referred to his experiences in Eastern Europe and the USSR and assured the committee he would continue the process of reform in Korea. The plenum did take up several issues of economic reform, including reducing the agricultural tax, slowing down the pace of collectivization, and paying more attention to ordinary living standards.[18] In other areas, Kim was not about to give ground. The opposition speakers were booed and shouted down.[19] Kim still had plenty of support within the Central Committee, even among those in the Yanan and Soviet groups. Member of Kim's Manchurian group were not going to shift their loyalties, and the surviving members of the SKWP group refused to side with the critics as well. Far from creating a swell of opposition to Kim's rule, the anti-Kim conspirators found themselves isolated. Pak Ch'ang-ok, Ch'oe Ch'ang-ik, and Yun Kong-hŭm were expelled from the Central Committee and

15. Soviet Embassy in DPRK, Report, 31 October 1956. AVPRF, Fond 0102, Opis 12, Papka 68, Delo 6.

16. Soviet Embassy in DPRK, Report, 10 June 1956. AVPRF, Fond 0102, Opis 12, Papka 68, Delo 6.

17. Scalapino and Lee, *Communism in Korea*, 511.

18. Soviet Embassy in DPRK, Report, 31 October 1956. AVPRF, Fond 0102, Opis 12, Papka 68, Delo 6.

19. Lim Un, *The Founding of a Dynasty in North Korea: An Authentic Biography of Kim Il Sung* (Tokyo: Jiyu-sha, 1982), 226; Lankov, *From Stalin to Kim Il Sung*, 164–65.

the party, and Yun—along with Sŏ Hŭi (chairman of the Federation of Unions), Kim Chang-il (deputy minister of culture), and Yi P'il-gyu (head of the Department of Construction), who were also expelled from the party—fled to China to escape further punishment.[20]

At this point, China and the USSR intervened. On August 31, Ambassador Yi Sang-cho delivered a letter to the Soviet Foreign Ministry, addressed to Khrushchev, detailing the abuses perpetrated by Kim and his "sycophants." Yi suggested a senior CPSU representative come to Pyongyang and convene a plenum of the KWP Central Committee, at which the unfair treatment of Kim's critics could be addressed and "specific steps worked out directed at removing the shortcomings in our party."[21] The Soviets leadership consulted with Ambassador Ivanov on the matter, and following meetings between Soviet and Chinese leaders at the CCP Congress in Beijing later in September, the two parties decided to send a joint delegation to Pyongyang, led by Mikoyan and Chinese defense minister Peng Dehuai, former head of the combined Chinese-Korean forces in the Korean War.[22]

Peng and Mikoyan met with Kim Il Sung and told him to cease his attacks on the Soviet-Korean and Yanan groups, reinstate the expelled party members, and publish the decrees of the August and September KWP Central Committee Plenums. Kim's response was half-hearted at best. Attacks on Kim's critics ceased, but only temporarily. Pak Ch'ang-ok and Ch'oe Ch'ang-ik were readmitted to the Central Committee, but not to their former positions as vice prime ministers. Sŏ Hŭi, Yun Kong-hŭm, Yi P'il-gyu and Kim Chang-il were readmitted to the party as well.[23] Kim never published the decrees of the August and September plenums and did not even make public the visit of Mikoyan and Peng to the "party masses."[24] As it turned out, the conspirators' reprieve was a Pyrrhic victory, and the results of this Sino-Soviet intervention were soon reversed; indeed, this blatant interference in North Korea's internal affairs probably made Kim even more determined to punish his opponents. Ultimately Kim would not yield to Soviet and Chinese pressure even when combined, much less when the Soviets

---

20. "Memorandum of Conversation with Ambassador of the People's Republic of China to the DPRK, Qiao Xiaoguang, 4 September 1956." RGANI, Fond 5, Ops 28, Delo 410, Listy 322–25. Translated and reproduced in Person, "'We Need Help from Outside,'" 69–72.

21. "Report by N. T. Federenko on a Conversation with Yi Sang-jo, Ambassador of the DPRK to the USSR, 5 September 1956." RGANI, Delo 5, Opis 28, Delo 412, Listy 224–228. Translated and reproduced in Person, "'We Need Help from Outside,'" 75.

22. Person, "'We Need Help From Outside,'" 44–45. Kim probably did not take kindly to criticism and "advice" from Peng, who had overridden his authority by taking command of Korean forces during the war.

23. Scalapino and Lee, *Communism in Korea*, 513–14; *Rodong Sinmun*, September 29, 1956, 1.

24. "Memorandum of Conversation with the Charge d'Affaires of the Chinese Embassy in the DPRK, Chao Ke Xian." RGANI, Fond 5, Opis 28, Delo 411, Listy 344–346. Translated and reproduced in James Person, "'We Need Help from Outside,'" 82.

and Chinese were later in competition with one another. Kim's "big brothers" were much less influential than they appeared, and Kim's ability to manipulate and circumvent his Great Power patrons—while continuing to benefit from their aid and support—would henceforth be a constant theme in North Korea's relations with China and the USSR.

One of the most significant unintended consequences of the CPSU Twentieth Congress was the Hungarian uprising of October—November 1956. A spontaneous revolt against the pro-Soviet Hungarian government in Budapest escalated into the greatest threat to Soviet dominance in Eastern Europe since 1948, and nearly led to the breakup of the Warsaw Pact before being crushed by Soviet forces (with the strong encouragement of Mao Zedong).[25] The event reverberated throughout the communist world and might have potentially inspired a similar opening in the DPRK, as a prominent North Korean defector later argued; but the actual result was a kind of preemptive counterrevolution in the DPRK.[26] The unrest in Budapest—just five months after major anti-Soviet protests in Poland, and three years after unrest in East Germany—made the Soviet leadership anxious that other allied states, including North Korea, be kept within the Soviet orbit. For the North Korean leaders, these events sent a message that their own positions might be vulnerable to popular opposition and led to a clampdown on potential dissidents, especially students. A small number of North Korean students in Hungary defected to the West at the time of the uprising, and most of those remaining were brought back to North Korea. The KWP Central Committee resolved in December to step up mandatory physical labor for students and intellectuals.[27] Several North Koreans were tried as "American spies" and charged specifically with trying to instigate a rebellion like that in Hungary.[28] Fears of a spillover effect from the Hungarian uprising were not unfounded; even before the event, North Korean students in Hungary had attempted to defect to the West, and months after their recall to North Korea, a great many of the students who had been in Hungary were considered sympathetic to the "counterrevolution."[29] The DPRK leadership must have been greatly relieved when the uprising subsided, and quickly recognized the Soviet-supported Kadar regime.

It was not only the students, however, who showed signs of dissatisfaction. Workers had to be carefully monitored lest they be influenced by the workers' uprisings in Hungary, Poland, and East Germany. Perhaps more important, North

---

25. John Lewis Gaddis, *The Cold War: A New History* (New York: Penguin, 2005), 109.
26. Lim, *Founding of a Dynasty in North Korea*, 231.
27. Soviet Embassy in DPRK, Report, 14 May 1959. AVPRF, Fond 0102, Opis 15, Papka 8, Delo 7.
28. Scalapino and Lee, *Communism in Korea*, 546–58.
29. Soviet Embassy in DPRK, Report, 2 July 1957. AVPRF, Fond 0102, Opis 15, Papka 8, Delo 7.

Korea's long-suffering peasants were becoming increasingly discontented with the hardships brought on by the food shortages and other postwar difficulties. Soviet counselor Petrov noted in April 1955 that there was "strong dissent" among the peasantry, which could be exploited by "hostile elements" opposed to the current regime.[30] In particular, the issue of compulsory grain deliveries had diminished the reputation of the party in the eyes of the peasant population.[31] Despite these rumblings of discontent, or perhaps because of them, the collectivization of agriculture and the nationalization of industry proceeded apace, as we have seen. By the end of 1958, almost nothing of North Korea's private sector remained in either agriculture or industry. With the collectivization of nearly the entire economy, the DPRK declared the "complete victory of the socialist revolution."[32]

In North Korea, as in Albania, Romania, China, and North Vietnam, the hardline leadership was able to contain—and even reverse—the destabilizing effects of liberalization triggered by the Twentieth Congress.[33] The DPRK experienced its own leadership crisis, but this was confined to the upper echelons of the KWP, and news of the intraparty disputes barely reached the population at large. Little of the discussion in the August plenum, or for that matter the de-Stalinization campaign in the Soviet Union itself, entered the North Korean press.[34] There were other, unofficial channels of communication; students, for example, knew of the intervention of Peng and Mikoyan, and of course word spread among intellectual circles of the Hungarian unrest.[35] In May and June 1957, according to Soviet sources, a small group of Kim Il Sung University professors declared sympathy with anti-Kim critics in the party but were immediately condemned by other students and professors at the university.[36] Little attempt was ever made

---

30. Soviet Embassy in DPRK, Report, 13 April 1955. AVPRF, Fond 0102, Opis 11, Papka 60, Delo 7.

31. Soviet Embassy in DPRK, Report, 26 May 1955. AVPRF, Fond 0102, Opis 11, Papka 60, Delo 7.

32. Joseph S. Chung, *The North Korean Economy: Structure and Development* (Stanford: Hoover Institution Press, 1974), 62.

33. A few weeks after the August Incident, Albanian leader Enver Hoxha visited Pyongyang, and noted approvingly Kim Il Sung's success at removing the "poisonous wasp" of revisionism, although Hoxha was startled to learn that two of the malefactors had been given sanctuary in China, Albania's close ally. Hoxha claims later to have convinced the Chinese to return the North Korea exiles to the DPRK. Jon Halliday, ed., *The Artful Albanian: Memoirs of Enver Hoxha* (London: Chatto & Windus, 1986), 177–79.

34. Soviet Embassy in DPRK, Report, 31 October 1956. AVPRF, Fond 0102, Opis 12, Papka 68, Delo 6.

35. Soviet Embassy in DPRK, Report, 5 October 1956. AVPRF, Fond 0102, Opis 12, Papka 68, Delo 6.

36. Embassy of the People's Republic of Poland in Pyongyang, "Conversation with Comrade Pimenov, First Secretary of the Embassy of the USSR, on 15 October 1957," translated and reproduced in James Person ed., *New Evidence on North Korea's Chollima Movement and First Five-Year Plan (1957–1961)*, North Korea International Documentation Project Document Reader (2009), 16.

to connect intellectual criticism with popular discontent. There was no popular alternative to Kim Il Sung, who had developed an impressive cult of personality around himself since well before the Korean War, and the elites were divided among themselves. "Collective leadership" was one thing in the Soviet Union after Stalin's death, quite another in North Korea while Kim was very much alive and retained a good deal of support within the leadership. After Pak Hŏn-yŏng's execution in 1956, the only veteran communist in the top ranks of the Workers' Party with a strong domestic base was former labor minister O Ki-sŏp.[37] But O had been criticized and demoted within the KWP as long ago as 1948 and had kept a relatively low profile since then; despite this, he too would be caught up in the final "factional purge" of 1958.

The Mikoyan-Peng intervention only temporarily slowed Kim's amassing of personal power and his elimination of critics and potential rivals. It was just a matter of time, and as it turned out not much time, before Kim and his supporters resumed their attack. The attack came at the First Conference of KWP Representatives in March 1958. At the conference, Pak Kŭm-ch'ŏl, who had been a close ally of Kim since Kim's Manchurian guerrilla days in the mid-1930s, asserted that the decisions of the August plenum had been correct and that Pak Ch'ang-ok and Ch'oe Ch'ang-ik were indeed factionalists, counterrevolutionaries and dangerous revisionists. They should be severely punished, just as the "Pak Hŏn-yŏng—Yi Sŭng-yŏp clique" had been in 1955.[38] Once again, Ch'oe Ch'ang-ik, Pak Ch'ang-ok, and their allies were expelled from the party. Added to their number for the first time was Kim Tu-bong, one of the most senior veterans of the Korean communist movement in China and former chairman of the North Korean Communist Party. Kim Il Sung himself attacked Kim Tu-bong, his erstwhile superior in the Communist Party, in the concluding address of the March 1958 conference. Kim Tu-bong was accused of "undermining our Party" and leading astray "no small number of young people." He, like the others, had to be punished severely. In addition, O Ki-sŏp was accused of "individual heroism" and purged.[39] According to Soviet reports, nearly four thousand KWP members were purged.[40] This time, no outside intervention saved Kim Il Sung's opponents, and the so-called

---

37. O Ki-sŏp had been a labor organizer based in South Hamgyŏng Province during the colonial period, imprisoned for thirteen years under the Japanese, and was one of the two most prominent communists of northern origin in the early years of the DPRK. The other, Hyŏn Chun-hyŏk, was assassinated in 1946.

38. Scalapino and Lee, *Communism in Korea*, 522–23.

39. Kim Il Sung, "For the Successful Fulfillment of the First Five-Year Plan, Concluding Speech at the First Conference of the Workers' Party of Korea, March 6, 1958," *Selected Works*, vol. 1 (Pyongyang: Foreign Languages Publishing House, 1965), 364–66.

40. See Yuri Andropov's report to the Twenty-first CPSU Congress in January 1959. Cited in Shimotomai, "Kim Il Sung's Balancing Act," 129, fn.20.

"factionalists" were eliminated for good. There would never again be open criticism of Kim Il Sung's leadership in the DPRK.

The Flying Horse

In the summer of 1958, the DPRK launched a new campaign to fulfill the Five-Year Plan ahead of schedule. The campaign was dubbed "Ch'ŏllima," after a mythical winged horse that could fly a thousand *li* in a single day, a kind of East Asian Pegasus. This was shortly after the Great Leap Forward had begun in China, and the similarities between the two campaigns were evident. But China's Great Leap Forward was short-lived and its results were immediately disastrous, leading to the deaths of tens of millions of people.[41] The outcome of the North Korean economic campaigns of the late 1950s was more ambiguous, and for decades Ch'ŏllima remained the enduring symbol of North Korea's "human wave" approach to economic development. Even amidst the economic catastrophe of the 1990s, a bronze statue of the flying horse loomed over Moranbong Hill in Pyongyang, urging the North Korean people toward ever-greater sacrifices.

The Ch'ŏllima movement, like the Great Leap Forward, was a campaign of mass mobilization dependent on "volunteer" labor. White-collar workers and students were required to assist in crop harvesting and irrigation works, urbanites sometimes going to the countryside for as long as two months to work in the fields.[42] Ministries were asked to send as many as half of their employees to work directly in the factories. Ch'ŏllima was "Pyongyang Speed" for the whole economy. In September 1959, Kim Il Sung declared that the Five-Year Plan should be fulfilled in less than three and a half years, and factories were asked to double their output over the 1958 level.[43] This meant the introduction of new work methods and elimination of idle capacity, a subject we will turn to shortly.

The Ch'ŏllima movement resembled the Great Leap Forward in rhetoric as well as in practice. Just as Mao had declared that the Chinese economy would

---

41. Perhaps 30 million, and possibly as many as 45 million, Chinese died in the famine brought on by the economic dislocations of the Great Leap Forward, a fact not publicly revealed until several decades later. See Frank Dikötter, *Mao's Great Famine: The History of China's Most Devastating Catastrophe, 1958–1962* (New York: Walker & Company, 2010).

42. This was similar to the "down to the countryside" (*xiafang*) movement in China in the 1950s and 1960s, except that in the Chinese case, sending urban workers, bureaucrats, and students to work in the villages was often a form of punishment and could last for years. In North Korea, the system of urbanites assisting in agricultural production was more regularized—more evenly distributed socially and limited temporally—and perhaps for that reason lasted longer and inspired less resentment than the Chinese practice.

43. Soviet Embassy in DPRK, Report, 7 October 1958. AVPRF, Fond 0102, Opis 14, Papka 75, Delo 6.

soon surpass that of Britain, in November 1958 Kim Il Sung spoke of catching up with and outstripping Japan in industrial output in 1959.[44] Ch'ŏllima, like the Great Leap Forward, also promoted the decentralization of industry and local self-sufficiency. More than 40 percent of North Korea's consumer goods were reportedly produced locally by the fall of 1959, and every province had its own steel and cement works.[45] Even power generation was pushed to the local level, with farmers' cooperatives using corn to fuel power plants. This took some of the burden off of the large hydroelectric generators, whose power could be used instead for the state-run heavy industries.[46] Indeed, the central state benefited considerably from the decentralization of industry; the proportion of revenue collected from local industry rose from 9.2 percent in 1958 to 16.5 percent in 1959.[47]

The effect of this breakneck-paced industrial campaign on North Korean living standards was mixed at best. Government policy attempted to improve living conditions to a certain extent: in August, the prices of dozens of consumer goods were cut by an average of 20 percent (although not basic foodstuffs, such as rice and flour), and the government announced on January 1, 1959, that wages would be raised by 40 percent overall.[48] But the consumer economy was based on a rationing system that was highly regulated and relatively Spartan. In 1959, ordinary workers received 700 grams of grain (rice and wheat) per day, skilled workers 800 grams, and miners 1,000 grams. Children received 350–400 grams.[49] This was not much higher than the rations distributed before the war. The North Korean journal *Minju Chosŏn* noted in September 1959 that, even with rationing, ordinary citizens had to spend 75 percent of their incomes of food, leaving little to spend on rent and consumer goods, much less new industrial products.[50] Agricultural cooperatives were expected to maintain a savings rate of some 30 percent, and although peasants were allowed to keep small plots for private use, they were not permitted to sell their products or to raise domestic livestock.[51] Rapid industrialization drew many young peasants from the country to the city, which both aggravated the agricultural labor shortage

44. Kim Il Sung, "On Communist Education, Speech at a Short Course for the Agitators of the City and Prefecture Party Committees of the Country, November 20, 1958," *Selected Works*, vol. 1, 406–8.

45. Soviet Embassy in DPRK, Report, 15 September 1959. AVPRF, Fond 0102, Opis 15, Papka 81, Delo 7.

46. Soviet Embassy to the DPRK, Report, 10 November 1959. AVPRF, Fond 0102, Opis 15, Papka 81, Delo 7.

47. Chung, *North Korean Economy*, 68–69.

48. Soviet Embassy in DPRK, 24 February 1959. AVPRF, Fond 0102, Opis 15, Papka 81, Delo 7.

49. Soviet Embassy in DPRK, Report, October 1959. AVPRF, Fond 0102, Opis 15, Papka 81, Delo 7.

50. Cited in GDR Embassy in Pyongyang, "Report on Conditions in the DPRK," 2 November 1960. MfAA, A6982.

51. Chung, *North Korean Economy*, 10–12.

and put strains on urban services.[52] East German advisors noted that "volunteer" labor had become more demanding and less productive. On top of the enforced labor were the frequent political meetings and study sessions, adding even more hours to the day. Complaining about any of this was, of course, strictly punished.[53]

The increase in industrial output was impressive, but the inefficiencies and human costs were severe. Even more acute than the labor shortage overall was the shortage of skilled technicians and managers.[54] The Ch'ŏllima campaign was launched after students were recalled from Eastern Europe, meaning that many of those who had studied abroad had not yet completed their training, and in any case they were not trusted because of their exposure to "counterrevolutionary influences."[55] Poor supervision combined with impossible production quotas resulted inevitably in shoddy output as well as frequent industrial accidents, which (as in the Soviet Union under Stalin) were often blamed on sabotage. Alleged saboteurs were arrested and punished severely.[56]

The Ch'ŏllima campaign coincided with a new wave of political repression. Thousands were imprisoned or executed as saboteurs and spies. In a conversation with a Soviet diplomat in 1960, Pang Hak-se, minister of the interior, referred to some 100,000 "reactionaries" detained between October 1958 and May 1959 alone.[57] Among the upper ranks of the KWP, more than ninety members were removed from their positions in the 1958–59 period, often on charges of collaborating with the enemy during the Korean War.[58] Some were merely purged or demoted, others sent to the countryside for physical labor, and others were executed. New provincial courts were set up to try collaborators, and those condemned to death faced public executions.[59] Factory directors and heads of factory party committees who failed to reach the planning targets were replaced and often publicly criticized as "hostile elements."[60]

52. Soviet Embassy in DPRK, Report, 15 December 1959. AVPRF, Fond 0102, Opis 15, Papka 81, Delo 7.

53. GDR Embassy in DPRK, "Political and Economic Conditions in DPRK," 4 June 1959. MfAA A 6979.

54. Soviet Embassy in DPRK, "Report on Political Conditions in DPRK," 26 September 1959. AVPRF, Fond 0102, Opis 15, Papka 83, Delo 33.

55. Soviet Embassy in DPRK, "Report on Political Conditions in DPRK," 3 June 1960. AVPRF, Fond 0102, Opis 20, Papka 35, Delo 5.

56. Soviet Embassy in DPRK, "Political Conditions DPRK," 5 February 1959. AVPRF, Fond 0102, Opis 15, Papka 83, Delo 33.

57. Scalapino and Lee, Communism in Korea, vol. 2, The Society, 833–35.

58. Ibid., vol. 1, 524.

59. Soviet Embassy in DPRK, "Political Conditions DPRK," 24 February 1959. AVPRF, Fond 0102, Opis 15, Papka 83, Delo 33.

60. Ibid.

Both the economic campaign and the political repression resembled contemporary events in China, specifically the Great Leap Forward and, before it, the Anti-Rightist campaign. This is not to say that North Korea was merely emulating China—in many respects Ch'ŏllima was also reminiscent of forced industrialization and terror in Stalin's Soviet Union, and a number East European countries at the time were also attempting to "leap forward" economically. But Kim Il Sung himself had long been an admirer of Chinese communist methods, and of Mao personally, and seemed to be convinced that Chinese methods were appropriate and effective for solving North Korea's economic problems.[61] China was an increasingly important economic partner as well. The PRC and the DPRK negotiated new terms for trade and technological cooperation in July 1958.[62] Beijing gave substantial new financial credits to the DPRK at the end of the 1950s, and military assistance from China also increased significantly.[63] Despite Chinese–North Korean friction over the purge of the Yanan Koreans, China was becoming an important counterweight to the Soviet Union for North Korea's external economic relations.

While following the Chinese lead in economic affairs, North Korea was at the same time asserting its political independence from China. In February 1958, Zhou Enlai came to Pyongyang and announced the withdrawal of the Chinese People's Volunteer Army (CPVA) from North Korea, then more than 400,000 strong.[64] Kim Il Sung and Mao Zedong had discussed the Chinese troop withdrawal at the Moscow Conference in November 1957, and by early 1958 a three-phase troop removal plan had been worked out between the two governments.[65] The last of the CPVA forces left Korea in October, to a warm farewell with much talk of "eternal friendship." In reality there had been considerable tension between Chinese and North Korean forces, as well as between the CPVA and the Korean civilian population. A half-million-man foreign army amidst a native population of some 10 million could not have but appeared as an occupation force.[66] By comparison, there were less than a quarter as many American troops

---

61. Chin O. Chung, *P'yongyang between Peking and Moscow: North Korea's Involvement in the Sino-Soviet Dispute, 1958–1975* (Tuscaloosa: University of Alabama Press, 1978), 45.

62. Chinese Foreign Ministry Archive (CFMA), "Report on a Visit by a Korean Government Delegation," July 29, 1958. CFMA, Document No. 116–00230–03.

63. Scalapino and Lee, *Communism in Korea*, 944–947.

64. Shimotomai, "Kim Il Sung's Balancing Act," 128.

65. Shen Zhihua, "Alliance of 'Tooth and Lip' or Marriage of Convenience? The Origins and Development of the Sino-North Korean Alliance, 1946–1958," unpublished paper, 35.

66. North Korean officials even complained to the Soviets that the Chinese soldiers acted like occupiers and were no longer welcomed on Korean soil. Cited in Zhihua Shen and Danhui Li, *After Leaning to One Side: China and Its Allies in the Cold War* (Stanford: Stanford University Press, 2011), 214–15.

in South Korea, with twice the population of the North. North Korean leaders had chafed under Chinese command during the war and criticized the CPVA for not pushing for the "final liberation of Korea" in 1951, and Soviet military advisors reported lack of communication and contact between the Korean military and the CPVA command after the war.[67] As early as 1955, North Korea was publicly downplaying the role of Chinese assistance in the Korean War, much to the dissatisfaction of the Chinese.[68] Well before the "August Incident," and even before the end of the war, Kim Il Sung and other North Korean leaders were concerned about the undue influence of Koreans with Chinese military backgrounds, particularly while the CPVA presence in Korea gave them tacit support.[69] The Chinese troop withdrawal reduced the potential influence of China in North Korean politics, especially in the military. It also gave Pyongyang a propaganda edge over South Korea, as now only the southern half of the divided peninsula hosted foreign military forces.

North Korea rhetorically distanced itself from China in the late 1950s, albeit less overtly than with Kim's anti-Soviet "Juche" statements, reflecting again the rise of Korean nationalism. The Ch'ŏllima movement was touted in the North Korean media as a great success, a truly original and uniquely Korean approach to economic development. Its indebtedness to Chinese methods was not acknowledged. Nor, as we have seen in the previous chapter, did the DPRK at this time give much credit to the fraternal socialist countries in assisting North Korea. Indeed, contact between individual North Koreans and East European visitors and advisors was carefully restricted, which not only strained or prevented personal friendships between North Koreans and East Europeans, but also made technical cooperation more difficult.[70]

As usual, it was in the area of culture that nationalism was most clearly visible. By 1957 there were virtually no performances of foreign theater or music in the DPRK. An Mak, the DPRK deputy minister of culture and a veteran KAPF writer, attempted to reverse the trend somewhat by strengthening ties between the North Korean cultural world and the East European embassies. An was ousted in 1958, and around 1960 he and his wife, the dancer and choreographer Ch'oe Sŭng-hŭi, were purged. Ch'oe had been the preeminent modern dancer

67. RGANI, Fond 5, Opis 28, Delo 314, listi 34–59. Translated and reproduced in James Person, ed., "Limits of the 'Lips and Teeth' Alliance: New Evidence on Sino-DPRK Relations, 1955–1984," Woodrow Wilson International Center for Scholars, North Korea International Documentation Project Working Paper (March 2009), 2.

68. Ibid., 3.

69. Ibid.

70. Soviet Embassy in DPRK, "Political Conditions DPRK," 24 February 1959. AVPRF, Fond 0102, Opis 15, Papka 83, Delo 33.

in the colonial period, trained in Japan, and was widely known abroad. In the early 1940s she had toured Europe, the United States, and Latin America. In 1946, after approaching the US Military Government in South Korea for help in setting up a dance studio and being refused, she migrated to the North, where she was lavishly welcomed by the Soviets and the North Korean People's Committee.[71] After the war, Ch'oe headed the State Dance School and her husband became a leading figure in the Ministry of Culture. But, in part because of their South Korean origins and ties, as well as their apparently less-than-enthusiastic embrace of the new revolutionary nationalism in North Korean culture, both lost their positions at the end of the 1950s: An was removed from his post in the Culture Ministry, and Ch'oe lost her seat in the Supreme People's Assembly. Shortly afterward the two disappeared under mysterious circumstances. Following An and Ch'oe's departure, modernism in the theater gave way to politically themed works along the lines of Jiang Qing's revolutionary operas in China. The big show of 1959–60 in Pyongyang was a ballet celebrating rapid industrialization, entitled—of course—*Ch'ŏllima*.[72]

Self-reliance, or what would soon be known as "Juche in economics," was one of the leading goals of the Ch'ŏllima movement. This included the domestic production of machine tools, the use of Korean anthracite rather than imported coal for fuel, and even self-sufficiency in food, no easy task given the mountainous terrain and cold climate of the northern Korean Peninsula. Kim Il Sung declared in early 1959 that grain production would soon reach 7 million metric tons, or more than twice the current output.[73] The Soviets, on their part, thought the North Koreans wildly unrealistic. When Kim Il Sung met with Khrushchev in Moscow after the CPSU Twenty-First Congress in 1959, Khrushchev chastised the Koreans for neglecting cooperation with fraternal countries and trying to produce everything by themselves. Khrushchev told Kim bluntly that the DPRK Five-Year Plan was not realistic and that the Koreans could not build a modern economy "solely on the dynamism and enthusiasm of workers," according to later Soviet reports of the meeting.[74] Khrushchev's lectures must have seemed scolding and patronizing to Kim, and no doubt contributed to Kim's negative opinion of the Soviet leader. The Koreans did not argue, but neither did they apply Soviet criticism to any change in their economic policies.

71. Charles K. Armstrong, "The Cultural Cold War in Korea, 1945–1950," *Journal of Asian Studies* 62, no. 1 (Febuary 2003): 77.

72. Scalapino and Lee, *Communism in Korea*, 885; Soviet Embassy in DPRK, Report, 24 February 1959. AVPRF, Fond 0102, Opis 15, Papka 83, Delo 33.

73. Soviet Embassy in DPRK, Report, 20 March 1960. AVPRF, Fond 0102, Opis 16, Papka 85, Delo 6.

74. Soviet Embassy in DPRK, Report, 16 December 1959. AVPRF, Fond 0102, Opis 15, Papka 81, Delo 7.

Nevertheless, despite their differences, the USSR and DPRK signed a new agreement on technical cooperation in March, and Soviet loans contributed to the building of several new factories. Although they disagreed with the economic policies North Korea was pursuing, the Soviets seemed to feel that the North Koreans, like wayward children, "should realize the mistakes on the basis of their own experiences."[75] It should be kept in mind, however, that this new Soviet-Korean agreement was based on trade and loans, not outright aid as in the first few years after the Korean War. Foreign aid had declined from nearly one-quarter of North Korea's annual budget during the postwar Three-Year Plan to less than 3 percent in 1959.[76] In part, self-reliance was a virtue born of necessity. The decline in foreign aid was one factor contributing the DPRK leadership's decision to slow down the pace of Ch'ŏllima at the end of 1959 and experiment with new economic methods in the early 1960s.

By the spring and summer of 1959, factories in North Korea were declaring that they had fulfilled the Five-Year Plan as much as two years ahead of schedule. Toward the end of the year, 1960 was designated a "buffer period," during which it would be necessary "to solidify what we have achieved, supplement the weaker sectors, further develop necessary sectors, and dramatically improve people's living conditions."[77] Throughout the year 1960, the front pages of the *Rodong Sinmun* carried the slogan, "Increase productivity with existing labor power and facilities!" With the reduction in foreign aid and North Korea's perennial labor shortage, the DPRK had little alternative. One of the most important "necessary sectors" to be developed was the machine-tool industry, understood correctly as an essential area for economic self-reliance. A Machine Tool Production campaign had begun in 1957, with the goal of doubling the production of machine tools using domestic resources only. In January 1960, the *Rodong Sinmun* announced that, indeed, the DPRK had produced some thirteen thousand machine tools in 1959, 1.8 times the number produced the previous year.[78]

Self-reliance in industry was to be practiced at both the national and local levels. In December 1960, the party announced a new Independent Accounting System (*Tongnip chaesanje*) that would make each local enterprise responsible for its own production and profit, and require it to keep strict records of its inputs and outputs.[79] One year later, Kim Il Sung introduced a new "enterprise system" based

---

75. Ibid.

76. Kim Yŏn-ch'ŏl, *Puk Hanŭi sanŏphwa wa kyŏngje chŏngch'aek* [Industrialization and Economic Policy in North Korea] (Seoul: Yŏksa wa pip'yŏngsa, 2001), 202.

77. *Rodong Sinmun*, September 7, 1959, 1.

78. bid., January 17, 1960, 1.

79. Ibid., December 1, 1959, 2–3.

on his visit to the Taean Electrical Machine Factory in Pyongyang.[80] The Taean Enterprise System prescribed reform in three areas: the establishment of a unified leadership system, with the chief engineer taking on the new role of "Chief of Staff" akin to the military; the reorganization of the mutual supply system, streamlining the supply of goods to factories; and the adjustment of the worker welfare system, to improve delivery of necessities to workplaces. New emphasis would be placed on the factory party committee in the management decision-making process, which would follow the "mass line" (kunjung nosŏn, a term borrowed from China), that is, applying criticism and suggestions from the "masses" in a collective management system.[81] Workers would be given material rewards for increased output, but the main effect of the Taean system was supposed to be ideological. Productivity increases would result less from material incentives than from enhanced enthusiasm and esprit de corps, eliminating the "old ideology of free-riding."[82] The Taean system was said to embody self-reliance, or "Jucheness" (chuch'esŏng),[83] and it remained the official industrial policy of the DPRK through to the 1990s, part of a general "Juche management theory."[84]

Agriculture had its own Kim-inspired method. In February 1960 Kim Il Sung gave "on-the-spot guidance" at a number of villages, including Chŏngsan-ri in South P'yŏngan Province. He criticized earlier government policies for making peasants less motivated to produce and declared that the DPRK needed a vast increase in the number of cadres trained in agricultural methods. Local party committees were to be reorganized, and thousands of agricultural scientists were to be sent to the countryside to improve the quality of life and increase productivity. A new system of bonuses would be introduced, and members of work units that fulfilled their quotas would get 10 percent of the crop in addition to their regular income. Workers on state farms, and later on cooperatives as well, were allowed to keep anything produced beyond what the central plan required.[85] This new system of group incentives and management reorganization

---

80. Ibid., December 18, 1961, 1–2. Kim's on-the-spot guidance (hyŏnje chido), highly publicized visits to factories and farms where he instructed workers on how to improve their methods, was a characteristic aspect of Kim Il Sung's leadership style, a practice he happened to share with Khrushchev but not with Stalin or with his own son and successor, Kim Jong Il.

81. Ibid. See also Widaehan Suryŏng Kim Il-sŏng Tongji kkesŏ changjohasin Taeanŭi saŏp chegye [The Taean Enterprise System Created by the Great Leader Comrade Kim Il Sung] (Pyongyang: Rodongdang ch'ulp'ansa, 1975).

82. Taean Enterprise System, 124.

83. Ibid., 1.

84. Pak Yŏng-gŭn et al, Chuch'e ŭi kyŏngje kwalli iron [Juche Economic Management Theory] (Pyongyang: Sahoe kwahak ch'ulp'ansa, 1992).

85. Soviet Embassy in DPRK, Report, 30 March 1960. AVPRF, Fond 0102, Opis 16, Pakap 85, Delo 6.

in agriculture was dubbed the "Chŏngsan-ri Method." Like the Taean Enterprise System, the Chŏngsan-ri Method remained a vpermanent part of North Korea's official economic policy, although actual practices differed considerably in later years—especially during the period of economic decline and food shortages in the 1980s and 1990s.

North Korea's consistency in economic policy, or less charitably its stubborn adherence to the slogans and methods of the 1950s, is a striking contrast to China, which followed similar methods at first but soon shifted course. As mentioned earlier, the Great Leap Forward was abandoned shortly after it began, so that it became essentially a phenomenon of 1958.[86] Ch'ŏllima never officially ended, and the movement was declared an unqualified success in the North Korean media. Between 1972 and 1992, Ch'ŏllima was even enshrined in the North Korean Constitution as the "general line of socialist construction in the DPRK."[87] Objectively the results of Ch'ŏllima were ambiguous, but the movement did not lead directly to a disaster on the scale of the Great Leap Forward famine. North Korea's economic experiments of the late 1950s might have been unrealistic but they were not as reckless as China's; North Korea's great famine would come much later, in the 1990s, as the result of long-term structural flaws (compounded by natural disasters and the loss of socialist economic partners) rather than short-term policy changes.[88]

Pyongyang between Beijing and Moscow

The USSR and China contributed such enormous resources to the reconstruction of North Korea partly out of solidarity, and partly—especially on the part of China—out of competition. North Korea was an area of crucial strategic importance to China and one place where the potential for Chinese influence, built on the "blood-cemented friendship" of the Korean War, was considerable. But China's ambitions extended well beyond Korea. After Stalin's death in 1953, Mao saw himself as international socialism's senior statesmen and the natural leader of the world communist movement. Even before then Mao had seen the Chinese revolution as the natural model for revolution in the developing world; as it turned out, this was where communism would make its greatest advances in the

---

86. Dali Yang, *Calamity and Reform in China: State, Rural Society, and Institutional Change since the Great Leap Famine* (Stanford: Stanford University Press, 1998), 44.

87. Ryu Kiljae, "The Ch'ŏllima Movement and Socialist Economic Construction Campaigns," in *Pukhan sahoejuŭi konsol ŭi chŏngch'i kyŏngje* [The Political Economy of North Korean Socialist Construction] (Seoul: Kyungnam University Far East Institute, 1993), 75.

88. Stephan Haggard and Marcus Noland, *Famine in North Korea: Markets, Aid, and Reform* (New York: Columbia University Press, 2007).

third quarter of the twentieth century, and the Chinese leadership understood their country to be at the forefront of this revolutionary trend.[89]

The competition between China and the USSR for leadership of global communism became increasingly apparent in the late 1950s, leading to an open rift between the two countries by 1960. China's criticism of Khrushchev's de-Stalinization campaign, opposition to détente with the West, support for Third World revolution, and promotion of rapid industrialization internally gave the PRC a great deal in common with North Korea, and during this period Sino–North Korean relations were particularly close. But North Korea was also dependent on the USSR for economic and military aid, and was wary of alienating Moscow. Alone among smaller communist countries caught up in the Sino-Soviet split, the DPRK managed to maintain a rough balance between the two communist giants throughout the three decades of Sino-Soviet alienation. It is not so much that North Korea "leaned toward" one or the other of its patrons, although at times it did, but rather that the DPRK maintained a certain distance from both, while gaining from each the benefits of its strategic position vis-à-vis the other. In this respect the DPRK was a shrewd practitioner of what Annette Baker Fox has called "the power of small states," playing off the competition between its two much larger neighbors to its own advantage.[90]

Sino-Soviet competition was mixed with a kind of division of labor in intra-communist economic relations. As mentioned previously, Kim Il Sung led a delegation to the Soviet Union and Eastern Europe in June 1956 to negotiate renewed assistance in economic reconstruction. As a result of this visit, the USSR cancelled some of North Korea's debts, postponed repayment of other debts amounting to more than a billion rubles, and offered new aid in both money and goods.[91] China, at the time, did not renew its pledge of aid, although in September 1958 China extended $25 million in credits to North Korea.[92] In July 1955, China had offered 800 million yuan in assistance to North Vietnam, roughly twice as much aid as Hanoi got at the time from the USSR.[93] This seemed to reflect an understanding between the Soviet Union and China, in which the latter would take the lead in assisting revolutionary movements and regimes in Southeast Asia, while

---

89. Chen Jian and Yang Kuisong, "Chinese Politics and the Collapse of the Sino-Soviet Alliance," in Odd Arne Westad, ed., *Brothers in Arms: The Rise and Fall of the Sino-Soviet Alliance, 1945–1963* (Stanford: Stanford University Press, 1998), 264.

90. Annette Baker Fox, *The Power of Small States: Diplomacy in World War II* (Chicago: University of Chicago Press, 1959).

91. Yoon T. Kuark, "North Korea's Industrial Development During the Postwar Period," in Robert Scalapino, *North Korea Today: Strategic and Domestic Issues* (Berkeley: Institute of East Asian Studies, University of California, Berkeley, Center for Korean Studies, 1983), 62.

92. Chung, *P'yŏngyang between Peking and Moscow*, 29.

93. Qiang Zhai, *China and the Vietnam Wars, 1950–1975* (Chapel Hill: University of North Carolina Press, 2000), 71–73.

the USSR would focus on Eastern Europe and Mongolia. From the Korean War onward, the Soviet Union and China shared responsibility for the DPRK. North Korea, more than any other small communist state, was the object of cooperation—and competition—between Moscow and Beijing.

Soviet and Chinese policies in East Asia were becoming more divergent than complementary by the latter 1950s.[94] Even more vexing than differences about support for revolution in the East was the glaring divide between Mao's anti-imperialism and Khrushchev's peaceful coexistence with the West. The rumblings of this clash could already be heard in 1957, although few in the West recognized this at the time. By the end of the decade, the split within the communist world would come out into the open, and the DPRK had to tread a careful path along the rift. But unlike North Vietnam, for example, with which North Korea shared some obvious parallels, the DPRK never fell fully into the "Soviet camp" nor clashed directly with China.

Soviet economic support for the DPRK declined sharply after the end of the Three-Year Plan, both because of Soviet parsimony and because of North Korean insistence on self-reliance. But the Soviet Union also wanted to maintain its influence in Pyongyang, partly as a counterweight to China, and partly out of concern about centrifugal forces in the Soviet bloc after the 1956 Hungarian uprising. This resulted in what might be called a negative policy toward the DPRK: the Soviet Union reduced the number of advisors and level of assistance to North Korea after 1956, but it also refrained from criticizing or interfering in North Korea's domestic affairs. De-Stalinization was no longer an open issue. On the contrary, a new KWP internal purge in the spring of 1958 elicited no response from the Soviets. In fact, the North Korean purge coincided with Khrushchev's attacks on his own rivals in the Presidium and a renewed Anti-Rightist movement in China, ending China's short-lived "Hundred Flowers" campaign. The direction of the communist regimes abroad, especially the USSR and China, appeared to be in sync with Kim Il Sung's own hard-line policies. In fact, both Moscow and Beijing seemed ready to denounce the 1956 Mikoyan-Peng intervention into North Korean affairs. Yuri Andropov, CPSU secretary responsible for relations with fraternal parties (and a future party general secretary) assured North Korea that the Soviet Union would oppose "factionalists" in the DPRK.[95] Zhou Enlai, meeting with Kim Il Sung in November 1958, similarly promised Kim China's noninterference in North Korea's internal affairs.[96]

---

94. Constantine Pleshakov, "Nikita Khrushchev and Sino-Soviet Relations," in Westad, ed., *Brothers in Arms*, 234.

95. Shimotomai, "Kim Il Sung's Balancing Act," 128–29.

96. Record of Meeting between Premier Zhou Enlai and Premier Kim Il Sung, 22 November 1958. CFMA No. 204–0064–02.

The purge of 1958, culminating in the KWP Conference in March, was a kind of mopping up from the August Incident of 1956: Kim Tu-bong, the elder states-man of the Yanan group, was removed as chairman of the Supreme People's As-sembly and replaced by Ch'oe Yong-gŏn, Kim Il Sung's old guerrilla comrade; Pak Ch'ang-ok, alleged ringleader of the Soviet faction, had been demoted to running a provincial factory and was finally arrested. Yi Sang-cho, former North Korean ambassador to Moscow, was expelled from the party and became an exile in the USSR.[97] A number of high-ranking academics were also expelled from the party, for supposedly siding with the anti-Kim oppositionists. Purges took place as well within the upper ranks of the military.[98]

The release of many of the relevant documents from the Russian and Chinese archives since the early 1990s gives us a much clearer picture of the Sino-Soviet split now than was possible before the end of the Cold War.[99] The Moscow Con-ference of Communist Parties in November 1957 was a key turning point, the moment when Sino-Soviet differences were beginning to come out in the open. The conference produced a "Moscow Declaration" that essentially papered over these differences, declaring equality among all socialist countries, national in-dependence, respect for state sovereignty, and noninterference in each other's internal affairs. Kim Il Sung's speech at the conference was a reiteration of cli-chés about international solidarity that skirted all sensitive subjects. The con-ference was little mentioned in the DPRK media, which continued to emphasize North Korea's Juche within a supposedly unified socialist community.[100]

---

97. The DPRK asked for Yi Sang-cho's extradition but Moscow refused. Beijing similarly refused to allow the forcible return of the Chinese-aligned victims of the 1956 purges to North Korea. As Khrushchev remarked to Mao in October 1959, "both you and we have Koreans who fled from Kim Il Sung. But this does not give us ground to spoil relations with Kim Il Sung, and we remain good friends." Vladislav M. Zubok, "The Khrushchev-Mao Conversations, 31 July–3 August 1958 and 2 October 1958," *Cold War International History Project Bulletin* 12–13 (fall–winter 2001), 266.

98. Soviet Embassy in DPRK, "Interview with DPRK Foreign Ministry First Secretary Pak Kil-yŏng," 4 October 1957. AVPRF, Fond 0102, Opis 121, Papka 7, Delo 16.

99. Much of this material has been introduced to the West through initiatives of the Cold War International History Project. Soviet documents from Russian government archives have been open (more or less) to outside scholars since the early 1990s, and the Chinese Foreign Ministry archives (CFMA) are gradually opening as well, although the CFMA materials are currently inaccessible past 1965. See especially David Wolff, "'One Finger's Worth of Historical Events': New Russian and Chi-nese Evidence on the Sino-Soviet Alliance and Split, 1948–1959," Cold War International History Project Working Paper No. 30 (August 2000); Lorenz Lüthi, *The Sino-Soviet Split: Cold War in the Communist World* (Princeton: Princeton University Press, 2008), and Sergey Radchenko, *Two Suns in the Heavens: The Sino-Soviet Struggle for Supremacy, 1962–1967* (Stanford: Stanford University Press, 2009).

100. Chung, *P'yŏngyang between Peking and Moscow*, 26.

But privately, the Soviet and PRC governments, and Mao and Khrushchev personally, were at odds by the summer of 1958. The immediate cause of the conflict was a pair of Soviet proposals that Mao seemed to take as direct affronts to Chinese sovereignty: building a radio monitoring station in China to keep track of American naval activities in the Pacific and creating a joint Sino-Soviet submarine flotilla under Soviet command. On July 22, Mao invited Soviet ambassador Yudin to discuss the latter issue. The discussion quickly became a rant on the part of Mao about Soviet anti-Chinese prejudice and Great Power chauvinism. The Soviets had "extend[ed] Russian nationalism to China's coast," Mao claimed, and he told Yudin, "You have never had faith in the Chinese people, and Stalin was among the worst."[101] Khrushchev flew to Beijing to calm the waters, meeting with Mao on July 31. But the damage had already been done, and Sino-Soviet relations were on a rapid downhill spiral from July 1958 onward.

In early September, Soviet foreign minister Gromyko visited Beijing in the midst of the PRC shelling of Quemoy and Matsu in the Taiwan Straits, making no secret of Soviet disapproval of China's "adventurism" (although the Soviets were applying similar brinkmanship tactics over Berlin).[102] In September 1959 Khrushchev met with US president Eisenhower at Camp David, a major boost to peaceful coexistence, while China still took an official anti-imperialist position and was beginning to feel the disastrous effects of the Great Leap Forward. In the Sino-Indian border conflict of September–October 1959, the Soviet Union took a neutral position and was sharply criticized for this in China. By the time Khrushchev and Mao met again in Beijing for the tenth anniversary of the founding of the PRC in October 1959, the stage was set for all-out confrontation between the two communist giants.[103] The Sino-Soviet confrontation could have been a disaster for North Korea, but instead the DPRK managed to exploit this to its own advantage for the next three decades.

South Korea, Japan, and the Third World

Part of the motivation for North Korea's rapid industrialization campaign was the DPRK's competition with South Korea. Despite the problems in North Korea's consumer economy, including a serious food shortage in early 1955 and another food crisis in 1959, from the outside it appeared that the North had clearly won

---

101. Chen and Yang, "Chinese Politics and the Collapse of the Sino Soviet Alliance," 268; Wolff, "One Finger's Worth of Historical Events," 11, fn.23.

102. Zubok, "Khrushchev-Mao Conversations," 245.

103. Wolff, "One Finger's Worth of Historical Events," 14.

the inter-Korean economic competition by the end of the 1950s.[104] North Korea's stunning industrial growth in the late 1950s stood in stark contrast to the stagnation and anomie in the South.[105] South Korea appeared unable to survive at all without extensive American aid for the indefinite future, whereas North Korea was making great strides economically and becoming a growing exporter of manufactured goods in the midst of a rapid decline in Soviet-bloc aid. For all its internal repression, the DPRK was at least able to find a formula for industrial growth, while the authoritarian, corrupt, and economically incompetent Syngman Rhee regime languished.

But perhaps Pyongyang's biggest propaganda victory over Seoul at this time was the large-scale return of Koreans from Japan. The process of repatriation began in 1959, mostly as a means of alleviating North Korea's shortage of skilled labor, although the propaganda value was certainly not lost on the DPRK leadership. Immigration from Japan peaked between December 1959 and December 1961, when nearly 75,000 repatriates (including over 1,600 Japanese spouses) came to North Korea. By the time the program ended in 1984, a total of 93,340 repatriates had gone to the North.[106] In fact, the Koreans who came from Japan were not, strictly speaking, repatriates, as more than 90 percent of them were originally from the South—which made Pyongyang's propaganda victory all the more sweet. Thus, for the most part Koreans migrating from Japan to North Korea were not returning to their actual home areas, but chose to go because of their political sympathies and promises of good jobs and treatment. This also reflected the general political orientation of ethnic Koreans in Japan at the time, more than 80 percent of whom were affiliated with the pro–North Korea General Federation of Korean Residents in Japan, more than four times the proportion of those who belonged to the pro–South Korean residents' group.[107]

The DPRK and the Korean residents in Japan had been pushing for repatriation since August 1958. In the years immediately following the Korean War, North

---

104. According to Soviet sources, North Korea's 1959 harvest produced less than half of the targeted 5 million tons of grain. See Shimotomai, "Kim Il Sung's Balancing Act," 130.

105. Anne Krueger, *The Developmental Role of the Foreign Sector Aid* (Cambridge: Harvard University Press, 1979), 41–42.

106. *If I Had Wings Like a Bird I would Fly Across the Sea: Letters from the Japanese Wives of North Korea Repatriates* (New York: The American Committee for Human Rights of Japanese Wives of North Korean Repatriates), 14; Kim Yong-dal, ed., *Puk Chosŏn kŭiguk saŏp gwangye charyojip* [Materials on North Korean Repatriation] (Tokyo: Jiyusha, 1995), 341. For a detailed and moving study of this "repatriation," see Tessa Morris-Suzuki, *Exodus to North Korea: Shadows from Japan's Cold War* (Lanham, MD: Rowman & Littlefield, 2007).

107. See Sonia Ryang, *North Koreans in Japan: Language, Ideology, and Identity* (Boulder, CO: Westview Press, 1997).

Korea had been reluctant to take in Koreans from Japan; as Kim Il Sung told Zhou Enlai in November 1958, the "situation was too dire" in the DPRK to welcome repatriates. But after the initial period of postwar reconstruction, the North Korean leadership decided Korean-Japanese returnees could bring valuable skills to the DPRK while at the same time strengthening ties between North Korea and the General Association of Koreans in Japan, a group leading the "people's movement" in Japan.[108] Formal negotiations over the repatriation issue began in early 1959 between the Red Cross organizations of Japan and North Korea. On August 13 the two sides agreed on the terms of the repatriation at a meeting in Calcutta, and despite strong opposition from South Korea, repatriation began in December.[109] The DPRK asked other socialist countries for assistance in the process, and the Soviet Union agreed to provide the repatriation ships, while other countries helped out financially.[110]

The first group of 975 "repatriates" arrived at the port of Ch'ŏngjin aboard the SS *Krylion* and SS *Tobolsk* on December 16, 1959. They were greeted by an enthusiastic crowd of flag-waving local residents, and shortly after arriving traveled by train to Pyongyang, where they met with Kim Il Sung himself.[111] The returnees, many of them skilled professionals, were treated as a privileged class by the regime, receiving high-wage jobs, comfortable apartments, and access to special department stores. Such special treatment inevitably created envy and resentment among ordinary North Koreans; resentment could in turn lead to denunciation. Connections to either South Korea or Japan made one vulnerable to denunciation, and the Japanese-Koreans usually had both. After their initial welcome wore off, some of the Japanese-Koreans even ended up in the prison camps.[112]

But the repatriates were useful, not least for the remittances they received from their families in Japan, which became an important source of revenue for the North Korean government. The precise fate of many of the repatriates, after their first few months or years in the DPRK, was often unknown to their relatives and friends in Japan. In particular, the conditions and treatment of the 6,755 Japanese

108. Record of Meeting between Premier Zhou Enlai and Premier Kim Il Sung, November 27, 1958. CFMA No. 204–00064–02.

109. Soviet Foreign Ministry, Report to DPRK Embassy, 2 September 1959. AVPRF, Fond 0102, Opis 15, Papka 81, Delo 1.

110. Soviet Embassy in DPRK, Report, 29 February 1960. Fond 0102, Opis 15, Papka 81, Delo 2.

111. *Korean Returnees from Japan* (Pyongyang: Foreign Languages Publishing House, 1960), 5–7.

112. Such was the fate of Kang Ch'ŏl-hwan, who migrated from Japan to North Korea as a young boy and was later imprisoned with most of his extended family. Kang eventually defected to the South and coauthored one of the first published memoirs of the North Korean "gulag." Kang Cho-hwan and Pierre Rigoulot, *The Aquariums of Pyongyang: Ten Years in the North Korean Gulag* (New York: Basic Books, 2001).

spouses (mostly wives) of Koreans who went to the DPRK became a human rights issue in Japan in the 1970s and after.[113] Until the late 1990s, none of these spouses were allowed to return to Japan; in November 1997, the DPRK government finally allowed a group of Japanese wives to return to Japan for a two-week visit, but none of them spoke in detail publicly about their life in North Korea, and all returned.[114]

North Korea's ideological position vis-à-vis South Korea in the 1950s was that revolution in the South was inevitable, and the peninsula would be unified on North Korean terms sooner rather than later. North Korea as such was not a permanent state, but rather the temporary site for building up the "democratic base" within the North for the inevitable union with the South.[115] In the meantime, the DPRK leadership could propose a more equitable form of coexistence or unity with the ROK, believing that ultimately history would be on the side of the revolution. North Korea's proposals for inter-Korean contacts in the late 1950s included a North-South conference, a merger of the legislative bodies of the two governments, an international peace conference to establish a unification process, nondiplomatic economic and cultural contacts, and national elections under neutral nations' supervision. All of these were rejected by the Rhee regime as meaningless propaganda.[116]

In April 1960, the Syngman Rhee government collapsed under pressure from student-led protests, and Rhee went into exile, replaced by his prime minister, Chang Myŏn. From Pyongyang's perspective, this seemed to give North-South exchange, and possibly even reunification, a new opening. The DPRK called for the ROK to engage in negotiations for forming a unified government, while at the same time appealing to the "democratic forces" within South Korea to expel the US military presence from the South and establish an interim government of workers, farmers, and students.[117] None of this made any headway with the Chang Myŏn government, which was preoccupied with internal instability, economic dislocation, and a restive South Korean military. Obviously, there was a great deal of mistrust regarding North Korea's calls for negotiations on the part of many South Koreans, who remembered that the KPA invasion had been preceded by similar appeals to unity just ten years earlier.[118] But there was also some support for North Korea's position

---

113. *If I Had Wings Like a Bird.*

114. I happened to be on the same flight from Pyongyang to Beijing as the Japanese spouses in November 1997 and have never encountered a more tight-lipped group.

115. Kim Sun-gyu, "North Korea's Initial Unification Policy: The Democratic Base Line," in Kyungnam University Institute of Far Eastern Affairs, *Puk Han ch'eje ŭi surip kwajŏng* [The Process of Constructing the North Korean System] (Seoul: Kyungnam University Press, 1991), 220.

116. Barry K. Gills, *Korea versus Korea: A Case of Contested Legitimacy* (London: Routledge, 1996), 60.

117. Ibid., 71.

118. Cumings, *Origins of the Korean War,* vol. 2, 487–88.

within South Korea, especially among students and intellectuals, in particular on such broad nationalist issues as US troop withdrawal and North-South dialogue.

It is unlikely that the North at this time seriously considered another invasion of the South, which by then had built up its military forces to a comparable level with the North, backed by a security treaty with the United States.[119] Nor, as even Kim Il Sung admitted to the Soviet ambassador in 1959, was there any active, clandestine communist movement in the South that could be North Korea's fifth column.[120] Pyongyang's appeals for dialogue and the proposal of a confederation between the North and the South were probably genuine, inasmuch as North Korea was in a far weaker position to impose the terms of unification than it had been in 1950. But these appeals failed to elicit a positive response from a fragile South Korean government perched precariously atop a deeply divided society. Many of South Korea's youth, including younger members of the liberal Democratic Party, supported North-South dialogue and put forth exchange proposals of their own. The loudest voices for unification were from the students, newly emboldened by their role in toppling Syngman Rhee.[121] On the other hand, many of the older South Koreans, refugees from the North, Christians, and the military—among whom the first three categories often overlapped—were strongly opposed to any contact with the North. While the issue of North-South contact divided the southern electorate, inflation destabilized the economy, and both the South Korean citizenry and the United States became increasingly concerned about the stability of the Chang Myŏn government. On May 16, 1961, a major general in the ROK Army named Park Chung Hee led a coup against the civilian government and installed the military in power.

At first, the DPRK leadership was willing to see the Park coup in a positive light. For one thing, the nationalist orientation of the military might create a better atmosphere for dialogue.[122] For another, Park himself had been arrested as a communist in the Yŏsu Rebellion in 1948, and might be secretly sympathetic to the North's cause—a fact that caused some consternation in among American officials as well, who feared for a moment that Park might have pulled off an internal communist takeover of the South Korea.[123] On the evening of the coup,

119. Taik-Young Hamm, *Arming the Two Koreas: State, Capital, and Military Power* (New York: Routledge, 1999).

120. Soviet Embassy in DPRK, Interview with Kim Il Sung, 19 December 1959. AVPRF, Fond 0102, Opis 15, Papka 81, Delo 7.

121. For detailed discussions of the fall of Syngman Rhee and its aftermath, see Han Sung Joo, *The Failure of Democracy in South Korea* (Berkeley: University of California Press, 1974); and Se-Jin Kim, *The Politics of Military Revolution in Korea* (Chapel Hill: University of North Carolina Press, 1971).

122. Soviet Embassy in DPRK, Report, 20 May 1961. AVPRF, Fond 0102, Opis 16, Papka 85, Delo 8.

123. Cumings, *The Origins of the Korean War,* vol. 2, 266.

North Korean officials informed the Chinese embassy in Pyongyang that they believed the coup was the work of "independent progressive forces" in the South Korean military. Two days later, with the junta harshly clamping down on internal dissent, the North Koreans saw the coup as a US-led plot to quell unrest in South Korea and keep the ROK in their orbit. Although the North Koreans did not make the parallel explicit, they now saw the South Korean military coup as, in effect, the American equivalent of the 1956 Soviet intervention in Hungary. Nevertheless, there remained progressive elements in the military, even if they were not at the forefront, and South Korea retained a revolutionary potential that the North should encourage. Thus, the DPRK could talk to the new Seoul military government in the hopes of cultivating the progressive and "patriotic" (i.e., pro-Pyongyang) elements operating behind the scenes in South Korea.[124]

In September 1961, the Park regime indeed began to hold secret talks with the DPRK, and for some months the North Korean media refrained from criticizing and insulting the ROK government as it had throughout the Syngman Rhee period.[125] But Pyongyang's overtures failed to divide the South Koreans from the United States, on whom the ROK was still deeply dependent. With the Park-led junta firmly in place, and after Park's visit to Washington in November, the Kennedy administration reaffirmed its commitment to close ROK-US ties. By the end of 1961, the DPRK appears to have given up on advancing North-South dialogue, and the North Korea media was again referring to the southern regime as "fascist" and Park himself as a Japan-lover and American puppet.[126] The North's renewed hostility toward the South ended a brief period of North-South thaw, just at the time when the USSR was promoting peaceful coexistence with the United States. North and South Korea tried to retreat into the security of their respective Cold War blocs, but the rigid East-West division of the Cold War was already giving way to something more fluid and complex. It would take another decade, and the shock of Sino-American rapprochement, to bring North and South Korea back into dialogue with each other.

South Korea and Japan were not the only countries outside the socialist bloc with which the DPRK was engaged. In the mid-1950s North Korea began to cultivate

---

124. "Preliminary View of the South Korean Military Coup Situation," May 18, 1961. CFMA No. 106–00581–04.

125. Soviet Embassy in DPRK, Report, 24 September 1961. AVPRF, Fond 0102, Opis 16, Papka 85, Delo 8.

126. Soviet Embassy in DPRK, Report, 15 November 1961. AVPRF, Fond 0102, Opis 16, Papka 85, Delo 8. Park was a graduate of the Japanese military academy in Manchuria and had been a lieutenant in the Japanese Imperial Army at the end of World War II. As his future career as president of the ROK would demonstrate, Park was both an admirer of Japan and a Korean nationalist—in essence, he wanted to repeat the Japanese "miracle" of modernization in South Korea.

ties with what would soon be called the "nonaligned" nations of the Third World. Throughout the wave of independence struggles in Africa and Asia from the 1950s to the 1980s, North Korea declared its solidarity with various anticolonial and national liberation movements. The first nonsocialist Third World government with whom the DPRK established diplomatic relations was the National Liberation Front of Algeria, in September 1958.[127] A few years earlier, in April 1955, the DPRK had sent a delegation to the Asian Conference for the Relaxation of International Tension (ACRIT) in New Delhi, the first major Third World conference attended by North Koreans. Although North Korea (along with South Korea) was excluded from the Bandung Conference in Indonesia later that year, an event that effectively launched the nonaligned movement, the DPRK media covered the event quite positively.[128] The DPRK publicly supported Egypt in the Suez Crisis of 1956, and even sent a small amount of economic assistance to the Nasser government. This was a foretaste of the extensive assistance and advice North Korea would give to Third World governments in future years, especially in Africa.

Navigating the Sino-Soviet Rift

The sudden withdrawal of Soviet specialists from China in July 1960 signified a public announcement of the Sino-Soviet conflict. The North Korean response domestically was to heighten security within the DPRK and keep even closer scrutiny of the foreign—meaning almost entirely fellow socialist—presence at home. Armed security forces were sent to guard the East European embassies, a practice which, the East German embassy remarked, exceeded the security presence in East Berlin—a city much deeper in "enemy territory."[129] Despite the heightened security, fraternal embassies were sites of occasional incidents that could be construed as threatening to the regime. For example, in November 1960 a Korean visited the Bulgarian embassy, trying to send a message to the Bulgarian Communist Party critical of the KWP and asking the Bulgarians to help the North Korean Party "correct" its mistakes. North Korean security forces entered the embassy, despite the protests of the embassy staff, and arrested the Korean. This was the last such incident at the Bulgarian embassy; the Bulgarian ambassador remarked to his Soviet counterpart that he had never seen such a hostile incident in another "fraternal" country.[130] Given recent events in Hungary, that remark may have been somewhat disingenuous. But the North Korean regime

127. Gills, *Korea versus Korea*, 60.

128. *Chŏson chungang nyŏngam* [Korea Annual] (Pyongyang, 1955).

129. GDR Embassy in DPRK, Report, 15 August 1960. MfAA A 7064.

130. Soviet Embassy in DPRK, Report, 30 November 1960. AVPRF, Fond 0102, Opis 16, Papka 85, Delo 7.

was clearly concerned that East European embassies could be the locus of unwelcome contact with foreigners and possibly even defections, and took measures to reduce any potential contact between North Korean citizens and Europeans, including Russians, to an absolute minimum.

DPRK-Soviet relations had cooled after the Twentieth CPSU Congress and the reduction in Soviet assistance. But this did not mean North Korea was necessary "leaning toward" China. The PRC also was the object of criticism, although sometimes obliquely. The KWP Central Committee in October 1960 criticized obsequious attitudes toward foreign countries and mindless imitation of things foreign, a practice it labeled *sadaejuǔi*, or "flunkeyism," as the term was officially translated in later North Korean texts. This term cropped up in numerous party publications and speeches by officials over the next several months, and the "factionalists" of 1956 were also accused of practicing sadaejuǔi.[131] Both pro-Soviet and pro-Chinese behavior was condemned as "flunkeyism," but for Korean and Chinese readers, it was obvious that sadaejuǔi referred to Korea's traditional reverence for China and Chinese culture—the term *sadae* or "serving the great" originated with the ancient Chinese philosopher Mencius, and in traditional Korea referred to Korea's subordinate relationship to China. Sadaejuǔi was, in fact, the antithesis of Juche, dependence rather than self-reliance. The use of this term implied that Juche would not be directed only against the Soviet Union, which was the primary target of Kim's original 1955 Juche speech, but against any dependence on or imitation of China as well.

The litmus test of Albania also played a role in North Korea's position vis-à-vis the Soviet Union and China. At the Moscow Conference of Communist Parties in November–December 1960, where the Soviet-Albanian clash became a kind of substitute for the Sino-Soviet conflict, the North Korean delegation refused to take sides in the dispute. On the other hand, publications within North Korea around the same time praised Albania as a successful independent socialist country. For example, the DPRK newspaper *Minju Chosŏn* said in November 1960, "Our two countries are very close to each other, like real brothers, because of common ideology and aims . . . no force on earth can break the invincible friendship and solidarity between the Korean and Albanian people."[132] North Korean–Albanian ties became extremely close in 1960–62, with frequent exchanges of delegations and new agreements on technical assistance, trade, and cultural cooperation. On the one hand, the DPRK was not willing to risk an open confrontation with the USSR; on the other hand, its "real" sympathies seemed to lie

---

131. Soviet Embassy in DPRK, Report, 28 November 1960. AVPRF, Fond 0102, Opis 16, Papka 85, Delo 7.

132. Cited in Chung, *P'yongyang between Peking and Moscow*, 65.

more with Albania, another small socialist country on the periphery of the Soviet empire, and with China, with whom it shared a common view of revolution and anti-imperialism.

The Soviets, for their part, were not willing to "lose" North Korea to Chinese influence, nor risk the DPRK leaving the Soviet orbit as Albania and Yugoslavia had. Neither, however, was the USSR under Khrushchev willing to support North Korea to the point of provoking a confrontation with the United States. There was a kind of symmetry between the Soviet position and that of the United States, which was concerned throughout the Syngman Rhee period, and probably beyond, of a South Korean provocation that would draw it into another war on the Korean Peninsula.[133] The stalemate of the war had evolved into a status quo that, though potentially volatile, was sustainable and not likely to be broken by either of the main Cold War protagonists. Kim Il Sung had little choice but to accept this status quo, although he must have found it deeply frustrating. The Soviets would give the DPRK enough military and economic aid to keep it going, but not enough to encourage it to conquer the South.

Khrushchev's peaceful coexistence was perceived by the DPRK leadership as little short of capitulation to the Americans, a policy that undermined North Korea's position vis-à-vis the South. In mid-September 1959, Khrushchev visited the United States for his famous summit meeting with Eisenhower. The fact that Khrushchev went to the United States first, before visiting the PRC, did not go down well with the Chinese, who were openly "enraged" at Khrushchev when the Soviet delegation reached Beijing on September 29.[134] The North Koreans were reluctant to even publish the details of Khrushchev's visit to the United States, until pressured to do so by the Soviet embassy in Pyongyang.[135] And, to top it off, Khrushchev did not visit North Korea at this time, as he had proposed to do earlier in the year. The North Koreans had been preparing for Khrushchev's visit since the summer and expected it in October to coincide with his visit to China. It would be the first visit by a top Soviet leader to the DPRK, and virtually the entire city of Pyongyang was mobilized to clean up the city and organize the welcoming parade. But at the last minute, Khrushchev informed the North Koreans from Beijing that he would not make it to Korea after all—in part, the Soviets implied,

---

133. A declassified State Department plan from 1959 offers an elaborate evacuation order for Americans in South Korea, in case the ROK initiated hostilities against the North. See National Security Archive, "Korea—Operation USAKOM."

134. According to the recollection of one of the Soviet delegates, cited in Zubok, "The Khrushchev-Mao Conversations," 247.

135. Soviet Embassy in DPRK, Report, 16 December 1959. AVPRF, Fond 0102, Opis 15, Papka 81, Delo 7.

so as not antagonize the United States.[136] Although not an incident of great moment in concrete terms, this demonstration of insensitivity to the Koreans' pride served to reinforce the image of the Soviet Union, and Khrushchev personally, as a fickle and untrustworthy ally.

North Korea had good reason to distrust the Chinese as well, and the Soviets encouraged North Korean suspicions about Chinese motives toward the DPRK, as Moscow tried to pry North Korea away from Beijing. When Kim Il Sung visited Moscow in June 1960, Anastas Mikoyan revealed to Kim the record of Mikoyan's conversations with Peng Dehuai in 1956, suggesting that the Chinese had wanted to remove Kim from power. According to Soviet records, Kim was at first too stunned by the revelations to speak, and finally remarked that "the Chinese leadership is defective."[137] Kim went on to criticize Mao at the KWP Plenum in July 1960.[138] But within one year, North Korea was again stressing its "blood-cemented friendship" with China, while China—despite economic difficulties at home after the Great Leap Forward disaster—provided the DPRK with a long-term loan of 420 million rubles, industrial equipment, technical assistance, and entire factories for light-industry production.[139] The Chinese were doing their utmost to compete with the USSR for Pyongyang's affections, and North Korea reaped the material rewards of this competition. Publicly North Korea remained steadfastly neutral in the Sino-Soviet dispute; the Chinese embassy in Pyongyang noted that North Korean newspapers gave equal coverage to Kim Il Sung's trips to the Soviet Union and China, although references to the Soviets stressed more the economic and technical achievements of the USSR, while references to China emphasized their deep friendship forged in war.[140]

On July 6, 1961, the DPRK signed a Treaty of Friendship, Cooperation, and Mutual Assistance with the USSR in Moscow, and then, five days later, signed an almost identical treaty with China in Beijing.[141] These two alliance treaties reflected North Korea's masterful manipulation of Beijing and Moscow rather than trilateral cooperation. In fact when Kim Il Sung came to Moscow to sign the Korea-Soviet treaty, he did not even tell his Russian hosts that he planned to sign a treaty with China on his way back to the DPRK.[142] North Korea and China had

---

136. Soviet Embassy in DPRK, Report, 7 October 1959. AVPRF, Fond 0102, Opis 15, Papka 81, Delo 7.

137. Cited in Shimotomai, "Kim Il Sung's Balancing Act," 149, fn.39.

138. Ibid., 133.

139. Cheng Xiaohe, "The Evolution of Sino-North Korean Relations in the 1960s," *Asian Perspective* 34, no. 2 (summer 2010): 180; Chung, *P'yongyang between Peking and Moscow*, 56.

140. Cheng, "Evolution of Sino-North Korean Relations," 183. Kim visited Moscow and Beijing three times between 1958 and 1961.

141. Chung, *P'yongyang between Peking and Moscow*, 56–57.

142. Shimotomai, "Kim Il Sung's Balancing Act," 135.

secretly negotiated their mutual defense treaty at the end of June, before Kim left for Moscow. Had the Soviets known in advance that North Korea and China were planning to sign their own mutual defense treaty, at a time of deepening Sino-Soviet confrontation in which the Chinese viewed Moscow with nearly as much hostility as they viewed Washington, the Soviets might have been reluctant to enter into such an agreement. But once the Sino–North Korean treaty had been signed, the Soviets could not back out of their defense commitment to Pyongyang lest they be confronted by an anti-Soviet East Asian alliance. For North Korea, an alliance treaty with both Moscow or Beijing would obviously be much more reassuring than an alliance with one or the other alone, but a trilateral agreement was impossible due to the Sino-Soviet split. The two back-to-back treaties seemed to solve Pyongyang's deepening security problem. Facing a new military regime in South Korea, which had an alliance treaty with the United States dating back to 1954, North Korea by the summer of 1961 urgently needed to strengthen its military position. Building up its own military forces was one way to do this; establishing mutual defense arrangements with its two Great Power patrons was another. Pyongyang pursued both paths simultaneously.

We can thus see the early 1960s as a time when North Korea carefully steered a course between the Soviet Union and China, refusing to take sides publicly in the Sino-Soviet dispute but gaining economic assistance and pledges of military aid from both Moscow and Beijing. The USSR could offer more material support, but ideologically the Soviet Union and North Korea were much farther apart than were the DPRK and China. At the Twenty-Second Congress of the CPSU in November 1961, Khrushchev renewed his criticism of Stalin and also sharply attacked the policies and leadership of Albania. The Chinese delegation took this as an attack on China as well, and although the North Koreans did not publicly confront the Soviets over either issue, Khrushchev's remarks clearly troubled the North Korean leadership. The Soviet abandonment of Albania—Moscow recalled its diplomats from the country in December—was an object lesson for Kim Il Sung. According to East European reports, Kim told the KWP Central Committee in the spring of 1962 that the Soviet Union might one day cast aside the DPRK as they had Albania, and that the North Korean people must be prepared for such an eventuality.[143]

After a brief rekindling of cultural exchange with the USSR in 1959–60, North Korea again raised the walls against revisionist influences in the wake of the Twenty-Second CPSU Congress. Radio Moscow's Korean programs were no longer broadcast in the DPRK after November 1961.[144] Issues of Soviet periodicals

---

143. Soviet Embassy in DPRK, Report, 5 April 1962. AVPRF, Fond 0102, Opis 16, Papka 87, Delo 29.
144. Chung, *P'yongyang between Peking and Moscow,* 65.

that covered sensitive subjects such as Stalinism and the Albanian question were withheld from circulation.[145] A major shake-up of the party sent many midlevel officials out to the provinces, and the East Europeans noted even greater restrictions on contact between Koreans and foreigners, and a tightening of political controls over the population as a whole.[146]

At the same time, North Korea's relations with China were on the rise. The number of PRC official delegations visiting the DPRK went up sharply after the end of 1961, beginning with a trade delegation in early January 1962.[147] Events in China were covered extensively in the North Korean media, exceeding Soviet news in quantity and level of praise. Chinese officials, such as CCP Politburo member and Beijing mayor Peng Zhen, who visited in April–May 1962, made a point of lauding North Korea's economic development efforts and the revolutionary enthusiasm of its people.[148] Kim Il Sung's birthday was celebrated prominently in the PRC in April 1962. In the Soviet Union, by contrast, media coverage of North Korea was much more muted. The differences over the cult of personality, economic policy, and confrontation toward the West strained North Korea's relations with the Soviet Union and the more pro-Soviet states in Eastern Europe, and the Soviets made no secret of their disdain for North Korea's political direction in their conversations with East European colleagues. Commenting on recent North Korean films, a Soviet diplomat in Pyongyang remarked to a Hungarian colleague in January 1962, "One cannot show films based on the personality cult when there is a fight against the remnants of the personality cult in the USSR."[149]

The Soviets and their European allies were troubled by what they saw as the excessive influence of China over the DPRK. In a lengthy analysis of North Korea's positions on issues currently dividing the socialist camp, written in December 1963, the East German Foreign Ministry remarked that at the time of the Twenty-Second CPSU Congress in 1961, North Korea "had taken a centrist position between the Marxist-Leninist Parties and the leadership of the Chinese CP and the Workers' Party of Albania." But in the two years since "the leadership of the KWP has moved step by step closer to the position of the leadership of the CCP." Whether on international issues (the leading role of the CPSU, the German question, disarmament, and the anticolonial struggle, among others), or on

---

145. Soviet Embassy in DPRK, Report, 5 February 1962. AVPRF, Fond 0102, Opis 16, Papka 87, Delo 29.

146. Soviet Embassy in DPRK, Report, 5 April 1962. AVPRF, Fond 0102, Opis 16, Papka 87, Delo 29.

147. Chung, *P'yongyang between Peking and Moscow*, 70–77.

148. Soviet Embassy to the DPRK, Report, 5 February 1962. AVPRF, Fond 0102, Opis 16, Papka 87, Delo 29.

149. Hungarian Embassy to the DPRK, Report, 19 January 1962, KTS, 5. doboz, 5/bc, 002255/1962. Translated by Balázs Szalontai for the Cold War International History Project.

questions of economic policy and cult of personality, North Korea was squarely in the Chinese camp. On the question of "peaceful coexistence," for example, although the DPRK media claimed that North Korea followed "the principle of peaceful coexistence with all states with different social systems who respect the freedom and independence of our people," North Korea also strongly criticized "modern revisionism" and "active coexistence," the same language used by the PRC in attacking Khrushchev's policies. On the question of disarmament, the KWP insisted that East-West conflict in Europe was quite different from the ongoing state of war in the Far East, which still required a high state of military readiness. On the question of the leading role of the Soviet Union, the DPRK media gave short shrift to Soviet foreign policy in general, condemning "Great Power chauvinism" as a code-word for Soviet arrogance and criticizing "some people" (meaning Khrushchev) in the Soviet leadership for this problem. And on the question of personality cult, North Korea had built up the cult of Kim Il Sung to gargantuan proportions since the CPSU Twentieth Congress in 1956, going directly against the true principles of Marxism-Leninism.[150]

The East Germans seemed incapable of giving the North Koreans credit for coming to these positions on their own but only saw them as the effect of Chinese influence. This influence was the result, the Germans argued, of the traditional closeness between the two countries as well as the strong economic dependence of the DPRK on the PRC. North Korea was following the "un-Marxist" policies of China and Albania and distancing itself from the Soviet bloc. But the Germans predicted—accurately, as it turns out—that this leaning toward China would not last indefinitely, and that North Korea would have to move back toward the Soviet position, for economic reasons if nothing else. China simply could not offer North Korea the aid and exchange the KWP leadership desired. The policy of self-reliance was not sufficient for North Korea to reach its industrial goals; unlike the Albanian leadership, satisfied with leaving Albania a backward agrarian country, North Korea's leaders had grand developmental ambitions for the DPRK economy. Despite the rhetoric of closeness to China, good economic relations with Eastern Europe were indispensable for North Korea to fulfill these ambitions. North Korea may have been closer to China ideologically, but practically speaking the DPRK would have no choice but to swing back toward the "true Marxist-Leninist camp" sooner or later.[151]

---

150. GDR Foreign Ministry, Extra-European Department, Korea Section. "The Position of Leadership of the KWP on the Fundamental Issues of Our Epoch." 2 December 1963. MfAA A 7174.

151. GDR Foreign Ministry, Extra-European Department, Korea Section. "The Influence of the Chinese Communist Party on the Politics of the KWP," 4 August 1963; GDR Embassy in DPRK, "Your Information on the Influence of the Chinese Communist Party on the Politics of the KWP," 28 May 1963. MfAA A 7174.

At the rhetoric level North Korea's relations with China were indeed close during the 1962–64 period. At times China could even make magnanimous gestures,
as in the 1962 border agreement between the PRC and DPRK, which yielded so
much territory to North Korea that local officials on the Chinese side protested.[152]
In 1963 and 1964 no less than twenty-two official delegations were exchanged between the two countries each year. Supreme People's Assembly chairman Ch'oe
Yong-gŏn visited Beijing in June 1963 at the invitation of PRC president Liu
Shaoqi. Ch'oe made a speech praising the Sino-Korean alliance in unusually ful-
some terms and appealed to the two countries' joint "struggle against revisionism." On June 23, the two issued a joint communiqué highly critical of peaceful
coexistence and essentially agreeing on the major issues of the Sino-Soviet conflict.[153] Three months later Liu Shaoqi made a return visit to the DPRK, where he
had a series of meetings with Kim Il Sung and Ch'oe Yong-gŏn. Later in the year,
the two countries carried joint military exercises and signed a new agreement on
economic exchange.[154]

Again at the level of rhetoric, Soviet–North Korean relations reached a nadir
just as Sino–North Korean relations peaked in 1963–64.[155] In October 1963, the
Rodong Sinmun published a lengthy editorial entitled "Let Us Defend the Socialist Camp," which put the DPRK squarely on the Chinese side in the Sino-Soviet
conflict, attacking Soviet arrogance, chauvinism, and blatant interference in the
affairs of sovereign socialist states. The editorial attacked Khrushchev's "socialist
division of labor," institutionalized in the Council for Mutual Economic Assistance (CEMA, or Comecon), as a direct threat to the economic independence
of fellow socialist countries. Through attacking the cult of personality in other
socialist countries, the editorial claimed, the Soviet Union had tried to overthrow
the leadership in these countries—an allusion to the failed anti-Kim putsch of
1956.[156] Although the target of these attacks was clearly the CPSU, the Soviet
Union was not mentioned by name. In August 1964, however, the *Rodong Sinmun* attacked the CPSU explicitly, over the Soviet plan to host a world conference
of communist parties that would exclude China, North Korea, and Albania.[157]

---

152. Chae-Jin Lee, *China and Korea: Dynamic Relations* (Stanford: Hoover Institution Press,
1996), 102.

153. Chung, *P'yongyang between Peking and Moscow*, 81–83.

154. "Record of Conversation between Premier Liu Xiaoqi and Premier Kim IL Sung," September
15, 1963. CFMA No. 203–00566–05.

155. At the level of economic interaction, there was no significant falling out between the USSR
and North Korea at this time. Soviet trade with the DPRK remained steadily high between 1961
and 1964, whereas Sino-Soviet trade dropped sharply. See Chung, *P'yongyang between Peking and
Moscow*, 93.

156. *Rodong Sinmun*, October 28, 1963, 1.

157. Ibid., August 31, 1964; Chung, *P'yongyang between Peking and Moscow*, 99–100.

Within North Korea, the chill in DPRK-Soviet relations was expressed through increased harassment and monitoring of Soviet and East European technicians and diplomats. Foreign specialists in the DPRK were now required to be finger-printed and had to report in detail to the North Korean authorities all of their movements, contacts, and Korean friends.[158] The DPRK even passed a law in 1963 forbidding marriages between Koreans and foreigners, meaning almost entirely marriages with East Europeans. Mixed-race couples were forced to move out of Pyongyang, and Koreans were pressured to divorce their European spouses. The GDR ambassador denounced this law, and the attitude of "racial purity" it implied, as nothing short of "Göbbelsian."[159] In retaliation, the Soviet, Hungarian, East German, and other Soviet-bloc governments restricted the activities of the North Korean embassies in their countries and refused to allow them to publicize the DPRKs antirevisionist propaganda.[160]

North Korea's belligerent and irredentist attitude toward the Park Chung Hee regime in South Korea was another point of friction with both the USSR and East Germany. In September 1962, DPRK vice premier Yi Chu-yŏn led a delegation to Berlin and criticized the recent building of the Berlin Wall as an insufficient measure against the imperialists. Rather, Yi suggested, the East Germans should have gone on the offensive and taken the entire city of Berlin once and for all.[161] In January 1964, Foreign Minister Pak Song-ch'ŏl told the East German ambassador that, while the East Germans took a passive approach to Western imperialism, the North Koreans reacted strongly to any provocation from the South.[162] It is doubtful that such aggressive remarks by North Korean officials represented an actual policy of aggression toward the South; certainly, there is no indication that the USSR was willing to support any such North Korean "adventurism." But the militaristic rhetoric of the DPRK in the 1960s did reflect a heightened militarization of North Korean society, which in turn may have come from a genuine fear of increased threat from the South and the Americans, while North Korea's own Great Power patrons—especially the USSR—were less than fully reliable. By the middle of the decade, Juche took on new meaning as a policy of military self-reliance, or as a DPRK slogan of the times put it, "turning the whole country into an armed camp."

---

158. Soviet Embassy in DPRK, Report, 18 October 1964. AVPRF, Fond 0102, Opis 16, Papka 87, Delo 230.

159. GDR Embassy Annual Report, 1963. SAPMO-BA, DY 30, IV A2/20/251.

160. GDR Embassy in DPRK, 19 December 1963. MfAA A 7126.

161. GDR Foreign Ministry, Extra-European Department, Korea Section. "The Influence of the Chinese Communist Party on the Politics of the KWP." MfAA A 7175.

162. GDR Embassy in DPRK, Report, 1 February 1964. MfAA A 7135.

Arming the Whole People

By the time of the Fourth Congress of the Korean Workers' Party in September 1961, almost no Soviet or Yanan Koreans remained in the Central Committee. Pak Ch'ang-ok and Ch'oe Ch'ang-ik had been executed secretly the previous year; the few Soviet and Yanan Koreans left in the KWP elite were those who had proven their loyalty to Kim Il Sung, such as Nam Il and Kim Ch'ang-man.[163] Twenty-five of the fifty-seven new Central Committee members were from Kim Il Sung's guerrilla group, and another twenty-one were younger cadres without any factional ties.[164] The last half-hearted gestures to collective leadership were eliminated from the KWP regulations, and with them the last obstacles to the absolutist rule of Kim Il Sung.

Among the most important matters of business for the Fourth Congress was the projected Seven-Year Plan for the North Korean economy (1961–67). Its ambitious targets took little account of the drop-off in fraternal assistance or North Korea's technological limitations. The first economic plan formulated since Juche had become the cornerstone of North Korean ideology, the Seven-Year Plan set out to produce machine tools, electric trains, and other sophisticated industrial goods all with local materials and manpower.[165] But external assistance, especially from the USSR, was indispensable for the Seven-Year Plan to work. Soviet credit was expected to underwrite numerous heavy-industry concerns throughout the country; Chinese assistance would still go into textiles and other light-industry production, but even if the DPRK leadership had wanted to shift its source of assistance toward China, the Soviet Union was the only ally that could offer North Korea industrial assistance of sufficient quality and quantity.[166] Unfortunately for North Korea's economic planners, the Seven-Year Plan stumbled over two major obstacles in 1964–65: the falling-out between the DPRK and the Soviet Union, resulting in a long-term reduction in East bloc aid; and the decision to put "equal emphasis" on the civilian and military economies, which diverted precious resources into a military buildup. The Seven-Year Plan had to be extended another three years, and the North Korean economy would never fully recover, beginning a three-decade descent into disaster.

North Korean rhetoric toward South Korea took on a sharply more aggressive tone in 1962, after a brief "thaw" following the fall of Syngman Rhee in April 1960. As suggested earlier, by the end of 1961 the DPRK leadership appears to

163. Adrian Buzo, *The Guerrilla Dynasty: Politics and Leadership in North Korea* (Boulder, CO: Westview Press, 1999), 64–65.

164. Suh, *Kim Il Sung*, 172.

165. GDR Embassy in DPRK, Report, 20 March 1964. MfAA A 7135.

166. Chung, *The North Korean Economy*, 123.

have abandoned its hopes that the Park regime could be conciliatory on North-South contacts. In 1963, Park was elected president, which gave him at least the appearance of greater legitimacy than the head of an unelected junta, and US president Kennedy renewed the American commitment to defense of the South. The ROK government was newly stable, firmly anticommunist, more formidable militarily than before, and even showed signs of economic growth after several years of stagnation. By contrast, North Korea's relations with the Soviet Union were openly tense, and its relations with China were less warm than they appeared. Foreign assistance was decreasing, and the domestic economy was slipping. North Korea was ahead of the South only in terms of its political stability, or rather the near-absolute control of Kim Il Sung and his partisan group. In other respects, especially on the economic front, the DPRK was losing its competitive edge. It was this combination of factors—the more threatening external environment, the weakening DPRK position vis-à-vis the South, and the need to solidify power internally—that seems to have led to the increasing militarization of North Korea at this time. Especially in contrast to the policy of peaceful coexistence in Europe, North Korea's bellicose attitude toward the South disturbed the East European officials in Pyongyang, who did not believe that the American threat had objectively increased on the peninsula.[167] An official of the DPRK Foreign Ministry told the East German ambassador bluntly that North Korea might soon have to "liberate" the South by force in order to save the suffering South Korean people; the inter-German policy of coexistence could not apply to the relationship between North Korea and the southern "fascists."[168]

As early as April 1962 the slogan *chŏnmin mujanghwa* ("arming the whole people") began to make its appearance in the DPRK, in the provinces as well as in the capital.[169] By the middle of the year, the KPA was put on a permanent state of high alert.[170] Major new defense facilities were built in the vicinity of Kanggye in Chagang Province, where the remnants of the DPRK government had retreated during the darkest days of the Korean War. All foreigners, including East European allies, were expressly forbidden from entering Chagang Province after November 1962.[171] Kim Il Sung, through the Soviet ambassador

---

167. Reflecting what was apparently a common opinion among the East Europeans, Karoly Fendler, a Hungarian diplomat stationed in Pyongyang in the 1960s, has said that the military threat was "non-existent," and was simply a tool used by Kim Il Sung for domestic purposes and to ensure economic and military support from both the Soviet bloc and China. Author's interview with Karoly Fendler, Budapest, 27 July 2002. See also Fendler, "The North Korean Phenomenon: Pyongyang Waits for its 'Own' Park Chung Hee?" *Puk Han Hakbo* [Seoul] 22 (1999).

168. GDR Embassy in DPRK, Report, 29 March 1962. MfAA A 7126.

169. Ibid.

170. GDR Embassy in DPRK, Report, August 1962. MfAA A 7126.

171. GDR Embassy in DPRK, Report, 12 November 1962. MfAA A 7135.

in Pyongyang, asked the USSR to increase its military assistance to the DPRK in mid-October, citing the critical position of North Korea's half-million-man army on the front lines against imperialism.[172] However, Khrushchev cut off Soviet military aid to North Korea in the last two years of his leadership of the USSR; it wasn't until after the fall of Khrushchev in October 1964 and the visit of Alexei Kosygin to Pyongyang in February 1965 that Soviet military assistance was resumed.[173]

The Cuban Missile Crisis of October 1962, and more specifically Khrushchev's capitulation to the United States over the crisis, dealt a damaging blow to the Soviet Union's reputation in North Korea and was harshly criticized in China as well.[174] From the perspective of the North Korean leadership, Soviet behavior over Cuba suggested that the USSR would be willing to sacrifice the interests of small socialist allies for the sake of peaceful coexistence with the United States.[175] The Soviets' continued refusal to supply North Korea with modern arms and military hardware, despite further requests from the DPRK government, reinforced this suspicion of the USSR's reliability as an ally. North Korea would therefore practice "juche in self-defense." At the KWP Central Committee plenum of December 1962, the party officially adopted the slogan of "arming the whole people." The population was told to build socialism under the slogan "Arms in the one hand and a hammer and sickle in the other!" The entire country would become a fortress, with air-raid shelters and bunkers in every population center. As in the Korean War, new factories were built underground, and a system of tunnels under Pyongyang was expanded to protect much of the city's population from attack. The KPA entrenched itself deeply in the mountains facing South Korea. And, like Mao (who perhaps inspired him with the idea), Kim boasted that his country could prevail even against a nuclear attack from the United States. North Korea's mountainous terrain, Kim told the Soviet ambassador, would weaken the effect of nuclear weapons and help his country to defend itself against the Americans.[176]

The DPRK leadership did not seriously expect an attack from the South, as North Korean officials admitted in candid conversations with some of the East European diplomats. The North Koreans recognized that the Park regime was occupied with stabilizing the political situation and improving the South Korean economy. But the urgency of the North Korean military buildup arose, in

172. GDR Embassy in DPRK, Report, 27 October 1962. MfAA A 7135.
173. Chung, *P'yongyang between Peking and Moscow*, 118.
174. Scalapino and Lee, *Communism in Korea*, 594.
175. Buzo, *The Guerrilla Dynasty*, 67.
176. Scalapino and Lee, *Communism in Korea*, 595–96.

part, from the very fact that the Park regime was becoming more stable and therefore reduced the possibility that pro-North Korean forces would take power in the South soon. "Peaceful Unification" was less likely to be in North Korea's interest than it might have been earlier, and the term itself was dropped from DPRK propaganda at the time.[177] The contrast to the situation in Vietnam, the other divided nation on the rim of East Asia, made North Korea's problems even more evident. The South Vietnamese regime was chronically unstable, and the National Liberation Front was inflicting heavy casualties on American forces there. North Koreans had long admitted in private to East European officials that there was no longer any viable communist party or guerrilla movement in South Korea. Instead, the North would have to liberate the South from without. And the fact that the Vietnamese comrades were able to fight the Americans without large-scale conventional or nuclear retaliation indicated to the North Koreans that they might be able to pull off an attack on South Korea without inviting full-scale war with the United States. Thus, from the perspective of the Pyongyang leadership, Soviet reluctance to support North Korea's military ventures was a major obstacle to the liberation of the whole peninsula.[178]

Whether or not North Korea's leaders really saw their country's situation as parallel to that of Vietnam is difficult to say. They certainly must have envied the success of the NLF in South Vietnam, and in the late 1960s North Korea stepped up its attempts to destabilize South Korea through direct action, nearly succeeding in assassinating Park Chung Hee in January 1968. "Arming the whole people" should be seen as more than a tool for domestic political control; North Korea was preparing for a renewed war with the South, and might have been ready for a swift counterattack in the event of a southern provocation, as the DPRK had been in the spring of 1950. As it turned out, such a provocation never came, and what the December 1962 Central Committee Plenum declared as a policy of "equal emphasis," or a "parallel program of economic and military development," had disastrous long-term effects on the domestic economy. The Central Committee announced that 1963 would be another "buffer year," as 1960 had been. Industrial growth was projected at 11 percent for the year, still high by world standards but less than the 18 percent projected at the beginning of the Seven-Year Plan, and much less than the Flying Horse years of the late 1950s.[179] The reduction in foreign aid and the economic drain of militarization were probably significant factors in this scaling-back of economic goals.

177. GDR Embassy in DPRK, Report, 15 February 1963. MfAA A 7126.

178. GDR Embassy in DPRK, "DPRK-USSR Relations," 15 February 1963. MfAA C 146/75.

179. GDR Embassy in DPRK, "Information on Domestic and Foreign Policy of the DPRK, July–December 1962," 15 January 1963. MfAA 1088/70.

Between 1964 and 1967, state investment in military affairs rose from 6 to 30 percent of total government expenditure. North Korea by the end of the 1960s would have one of the largest armies in the world, four times the size of the Soviet military in proportion to the population.[180] It was simply not possible for North Korea to put such enormous resources into the military and at the same time develop its civilian industry to meet the goals of the Seven-Year Plan. In April 1963 Kim Il Sung spoke to the Soviet ambassador about the state of the North Korean economy and admitted that the DPRK would have to invest more in mining and mineral extraction before they could build up manufacturing as they had hoped. Factory production was falling far short of expectations, a year into the Seven-Year Plan. Agriculture was not in the best of shape either, and the goal of "complete mechanization of agriculture," as North Korea had been announcing since the mid-1950s, was simply unrealistic. The vast majority of agricultural production was still the result of human and animal labor, and there remained an acute labor shortage in the countryside.[181]

The year 1963 looked likely to be another year of hunger, similar to 1955. East European residents observed that distribution of essential food items was scanty in towns and villages, and most of the private markets had disappeared.[182] Consumer goods in general were in short supply, and what was available tended to be of very poor quality. At a plenum in September 1963, the KWP Central Committee called for an increase in the production of consumer goods but did not allocate more resources for this production increase. Rather, the state exhorted factories to diversify and expand existing production into consumer items, and called for more necessary items to be produced at the local level. "Juche in economics" meant in effect making do with little or nothing from the central state, which is what the term would continue to mean in the long years of economic decline ahead.[183] The regime had made the choice between guns and butter, as it were, and would never veer from the priority placed on guns. If anything, the diversion of resources from the civilian to the military sectors of the economy would only increase over time, and by the 1990s, when North Korea seemed to be tilting against the hurricane winds of history itself, the DPRK would be utterly and grimly unique: a starving country with the world's fourth-largest standing army. Such a situation was by no means inevitable, but in retrospect it is clear that the wretched circumstances of North Korea in the 1990s had their roots in the "parallel economic policy" of the 1960s.

---

180. Buzo, *The Guerrilla Dynasty*, 68.
181. GDR Embassy in DPRK, Report, 8 May 1963. MfAA A 7050.
182. GDR Embassy in DPRK, Report, 2 May 1963. MfAA A 7050.
183. GDR Embassy in DPRK, Report, 21 May 1962. MfAA A 7050.

By the early 1960s it was apparent to East Europeans in Pyongyang that North Korea was not a "normal" socialist state, which meant several things. First, it meant that the DPRK did not faithfully follow the Soviet line. The DPRK was founded under the Soviet umbrella; it was Stalin's offspring almost as much as the GDR had been.[184] But North Korea was not very amenable to Soviet direction after the Korean War and would never be a faithful "satellite" like East Germany. In particular, the DPRK diverged from the Soviet-bloc states over the de-Stalinization campaign and the "cult of personality" issue. East German observers attributed Kim's ever-increasing personality cult to Chinese influence and "mystical ideas of Confucianism";[185] the Confucian part had a ring of truth, as the language of Kim's personality cult always resonated with filial piety, moral leadership, and other time-honored Confucian virtues. The "mystical" aspect of the Kim cult had other roots: in the aura of traditional Korean kingship; in a certain religiosity that held echoes of Japanese emperor-worship, traditional Korean shamanism, and even Christianity; and not least in Stalinism itself. Second, according to those who did follow the Soviet line, North Korea's "abnormality" reflected its closeness to China, itself the result of historical and cultural ties but more importantly the outgrowth of Mao and Kim's (and Hoxha's) common proclivity for "adventurism." But as we have seen, North Korea also had its differences with China, and rhetorical closeness in the 1962–64 period was not always expressed in a North Korean shift from Moscow to Beijing in any material sense. The DPRK came closest to breaking with Moscow and siding fully with Beijing in late 1963 and early 1964, but never crossed the "Albanian line" that would have meant excommunication from the Soviet bloc.

The third and most important North Korean divergence from Soviet-aligned socialism was the pronounced and growing nationalism in the DPRK from the mid-1950s onward. Self-reliance was only partly a virtue born of the necessity of getting by without foreign assistance. It was also a conscious choice made by leaders who wanted their country to avoid dependence on the Soviet Union, China, or any Great Power. Rather than see North Korea's foreign relations during the period of the Sino-Soviet conflict as one of shifting allegiances from one side to the other, it is more accurate to see North Korea as looking out for North Korea (or perhaps Kim Il Sung looking out for Kim Il Sung, which amounted to much the same thing), of never truly committing itself to one side or the other

---

184. The DPRK came into existence before the GDR, and was perhaps more of a "wanted child" than a separate state of East Germany—Stalin had much preferred a unified Germany under Soviet influence. See Wilfried Loth, *Stalin's Unwanted Child: The Soviet Union, the German Question, and the Founding of the GDR* (New York: St. Martin's Press, 1998).

185. GDR Embassy in DPRK, Report, 14 March 1961. SAPMO-BA, DY 30, IV 2/20/137.

but playing off the fear of each that its Korean ally would be "lost" to the other side. The DPRK played its very weak hand against its Great Power neighbors quite skillfully, and if the goal of the North Korean regime was to maintain its autonomy and integrity over the long haul, then it succeeded better than any other small socialist state in the world. If, on the other hand, the goal of North Korea's leaders was sustained economic development, satisfying the material needs of its people, or opening its political system to any degree of diversity, then the DPRK was an abject failure. But it was quite clear by the time of the Seven-Year Plan where the priorities of North Korea's leaders lay.

If socialism meant state ownership of the means of production, the DPRK had indeed accomplished its socialist revolution by the end of the 1950s, as the party media claimed. North Korea's accomplishment had been almost too easy. Already when the regime was founded in 1948, more than 90 percent of industrial concerns were state owned, most of the factories simply having been expropriated from their absent Japanese owners. By the end of 1958, most of the agricultural sector was also collectivized and state owned. Nationalization was more thorough in the DPRK than in any of the people's democracies of Eastern Europe; almost nothing of the private economy remained by the beginning of the 1960s. North Korea developed what Marx might have called "barracks communism," society as a kind of militarized factory under the leadership of a single Supreme Leader.

By the middle of the decade, North Korea had an impressive industrial economy by Third World standards, and a consumer economy able to supply its people with basic necessities on a generally stable basis. The country could have at that point focused its resources on improving the livelihood of its people, and shifted from a militaristic to a more diversified form of economic development. But, because of the instability in the communist bloc, the sense of growing threat from the United States and South Korea, and perhaps the difficulty of the guerrillas who now ran the DPRK in seeing economic development as anything *but* war, the regime made a conscious choice to put its resources into military buildup. The economy began to stagnate, and after a few years living conditions began gradually to decline. Perhaps if North Korea had faced a sudden shock like China's Great Leap Forward famine, the pendulum might have shifted toward economic reform and opening some years down the road. Instead, the North Korean economy suffered a protracted hollowing-out that lasted decades, the country propped up partially by Soviet bloc and Chinese assistance, its people held captive by a relentless and ubiquitous war mobilization. Fear and hope were turned outward: fear of an imminent threat from the imperialists, against which the people of North Korea were told constantly to stand guard; and hope for unification with the South, which would reward all the suffering of the present.

Workers reconstructing Pyongyang. From Chris Marker, *Coréennes* (Paris: Editions du Seuil, 1959). Courtesy of Chris Marker.

Girl in just-completed Kim Il Sung Square, Pyongyang. From Chris Marker, *Coréennes* (Paris: Editions du Seuil, 1959). Courtesy of Chris Marker.

Multiracial anti-imperialism in "great helmsman" style. Cover illustration from Korea Today, August 1976.

Moammer El Gaddafy of Libya meets Kim Il Sung, 1982. From *Korea Today*, January 1983.

Robert Mugabe of Zimbabwe in talks with Kim Il Sung, 1980. From *Korea Today*,
November 1980.

Daniel Ortega Saavedra of Nicaragua with Kim Il Sung, 1983. From *Korea Today*, May 1983.

Gifts to North Korea from Tomas Borge Martinez, minister of the interior of the Republic of Nicaragua, 1982. From *Korea Today*, August 1982.

Konstantin Chernenko of the USSR and Kim Il Sung. From *Everlasting Fraternal Friendship: The Great Leader Kim Il Sung's Official Goodwill Visits to the Soviet Union and Other European Socialist Countries* (Pyongyang: Foreign Languages Publishing House, 1984).

Kim Il Sung's "brother and best friend" Erich Honecker of East Germany, with Kim. From *Everlasting Fraternal Friendship: The Great Leader Kim Il Sung's Official Goodwill Visits to the Soviet Union and Other European Socialist Countries* (Pyongyang: Foreign Languages Publishing House, 1984).

Poster for the Thirteenth World Festival of Youth and Students in Pyongyang. By
Pak Sang Il. From *Korea Today*, June 1989.

THE ANTI-IMPERIALIST FRONT, 1963–72

> I want to point out again, however, that the Korean people are not
> alone in their struggle against the American imperialists. The mighty
> Soviet army and the armies of the socialist countries are on their side.

—Alexei Kosygin to Kim Il Sung, February 1965

Liberating the South

Pyongyang was not declared the capital of the Democratic People's Republic of Korea until the DPRK Constitution of 1972. For the first quarter-century of its existence, the North Korean government maintained the fiction that it presided over a unified nation whose capital was Seoul. According to this logic, the South was illegally occupied territory, and the North was a temporary "base area" pending a revolution that would unite the entire peninsula. This idea was first expressed in 1946 with the concept of North Korea as a "democratic base" (*minju kiji*): "In a country undergoing revolution, one area succeeds in revolution before another, establishing a revolutionary regime and accomplishing democratic reforms, and is a base for carrying out the revolutionary process through the whole country. The northern half of the Republic is such a base for anti-imperialist, anti-feudal democratic revolution in the whole country."[1] While waiting for revolution to erupt "in the whole country," the revolutionary regime should unite with sympathetic

---

Epigraph comes from "Memorandum of Conversation with USSR Ambassador to the DPRK, Comrade V.P. Moskovsky, Concerning the Negotiations between a Soviet Delegation, led by Chairman of the USSR Council of Ministers Kosygin, and the KWP Leadership, which took place on the 16th of February 1965 at the USSR Embassy in the DPRK." Archive of the Central Committee of the Czechoslovak Communist Party, Collection 02/1, File 96, Archival Unit 101, Information 13, 1962–66. Translated for the Cold War International History Project.

1. Cited in Kim Sun-gyu, "North Korea's Initial Unification Policy: The Democratic Base Line," in Kyungnam University Institute of Far Eastern Affairs, *Puk Han ch'eje ŭi surip kwajŏng* [The Process of Constructing the North Korean System] (Seoul: Kyungnam University Press, 1991), 220.

elements in the nonrevolutionary part of the country. This is the origin of Pyong-yang's United Front policy, and for decades afterward North Korea attempted to cultivate the support of antigovernment critics in South Korea. As we saw in chapter 1, this United Front strategy was initially combined with a proactive military strategy, and in June 1950 North Korea decided to invade the South, a decision that was bold but by no means irrational under the circumstances. Indeed, the war would have quickly ended in the North's favor had it not been for the US-led coalition's defense of the ROK. North Korean foreign minister Pak Hŏn-yŏng's prediction that a huge pro-Pyongyang uprising would erupt in the South in support of the Korean People's Army turned out to be wrong, and Pak paid with his life for his failure of prognostication, executed for treason in 1956.[2]

Nevertheless, the fact that the Rhee regime was saved by the US and UN forces during the Korean War could be used to support the notion that the ROK was an artificial entity propped up by the Americans, and that a combination of North Korean fortitude and subtle subversion would undermine and ultimately destroy the southern regime. This might be called North Korea's "Vietnam strategy," except that in contrast to the National Liberation Front in South Vietnam in the 1960s, there was no viable pronorthern guerrilla movement in South Korea after the Korean War. Pyongyang's approach was based on the premise that the ROK would collapse of its own contradictions sooner rather than later, and therefore the North should encourage "revolutionary forces" in the South while standing prepared for the opportunity to move in and reunify the country. But a June 25–style invasion was never again attempted, for two reasons: the clear US commitment to the defense of South Korea, and the unwillingness of the USSR and China to support such a venture.

Thus, when the student revolution of April 1960 toppled President Syngman Rhee, the DPRK leadership hoped for a subsequent collapse of the southern system that would lead to unification on North Korean terms. In order to achieve this end, the DPRK softened its rhetoric toward the interim Chang Myŏn government, which the North Koreans perceived as weak. Although this was couched in terms of "peaceful coexistence," the DPRK was at the same time preparing for a rapid regime collapse and a northern takeover of the South, stepping up the training of southern-born cadres for that end.[3] But after the military coup and

---

2. Pak was sentenced to death in December 1955, but Kim Il Sung indicated to Soviet ambassador Ivanov that Pak was still alive as late as April 1956. "Memorandum of Conversation with Kim Il Sung, 19 April 1956," AVPRF, Opis 12, Papka 68, Delo 5, Listy 64–65. Translated and reproduced in *Cold War International History Project Bulletin* 16 (fall 2007–winter 2008): 469.

3. For example, around the time of the collapse of the Rhee regime in South Korea, the DPRK began establishing "communist universities" specifically to train cadres of southern origins for leadership positions in South Korea after unification. Report of the Hungarian Embassy in the DPRK to the Hungarian Foreign Ministry, 21 July 1960. MOL, XIV-J-1-K, doboz 27/a. Translated by Balázs Szalontai for the Cold War International History Project.

the consolidation of Pak Chung Hee's rule in 1961, this window of opportunity for unification on North Korean terms appeared to have closed, except for a brief moment in April 1975 when the fall of Saigon created enthusiasm in the North that South Korea could go the way of South Vietnam. Much had changed in the quarter-century since the Korean War, however, and Kim Il Sung's proposal to move aggressively toward the South in 1975 was rebuffed by China, in contrast to Beijing's support for the North Korean attack in June 1950.[4]

Pyongyang therefore never completely abandoned a military path to Korean unification, so North Korea had to remain vigilant at all times to exploit instability in the South and to strike decisively. As noted in the previous chapter, beginning in 1962 North Korea embarked on a renewed program of military buildup under the slogan chŏnmin mujanghwa (arming the entire people), diverting precious economic resources into the military at precisely the moment when East Bloc assistance for postwar reconstruction was discontinued.[5] While a Pyongyang-led military unification never happened, the shift toward "arming the entire people" turned out to be a turning point for the DPRK economy: after an impressive period of postwar development in the 1950s and early 1960s, North Korea would lose its economic advantage over the South by the end of the decade.[6]

In the area of inter-Korean relations, both Koreas at this time practiced their version of West Germany's Hallstein Doctrine or mainland China's policy toward the Republic of China on Taiwan: refusal to recognize the rival state's existence or to maintain diplomatic ties with any foreign country that recognized it. Both Koreas were entrenched in their respective Cold War blocs, which reinforced the North-South Korean confrontation and inhibited North-South contact. This external environment changed dramatically in the early 1970s, when the Nixon administration made secret, and then public, overtures toward normalization with the People's Republic of China, North Korea's closest supporter. Motivated by these changes, and at least in part to preempt abandonment by their respective patrons, the two Koreas took matters into their own hands and began direct negotiations with each other, first through their respective Red Cross committees and then through a series of meetings between North and South Korean

---

4. Ria Chae, NKIDP e-Dossier No. 7: East German Documents on Kim Il Sung's April 1975 trip to Beijing. Available at http://www.wilsoncenter.org/publication/nkidp-e-dossier-no-7-east-german-documents-kim-il-sung's-april-1975-trip-to-beijing. Kim's ambitions for a North Vietnam–style conquest of the South, and the Chinese response, will be explored in the next chapter.

5. Karoly Fendler, "Economic Assistance and Loans from Socialist Countries to North Korea in the Postwar Years 1953–1963," *Asien* 42 (January 1992): 39–51.

6. While the CIA estimated that South Korea surpassed the North economically in the early 1970s, South Korean economists determined that per capita income in the South had surpassed that of the North by 1969. Christian Ostermann and James Person, eds., *Crisis and Confrontation on the Korean Peninsula, 1968–1969: A Critical Oral History* (Washington, DC: Woodrow Wilson International Center for Scholars, 2011), 88.

intelligence officers.[7] Almost exactly one year after Henry Kissinger's secret visit to Beijing on July 9, 1971, Seoul and Pyongyang issued a joint communiqué on July 4, 1972, outlining their principles for peaceful unification.

By the early 1970s, then, the DPRK was downplaying its southern revolution strategy for the time being.[8] This does not mean that North Korea had given up on the notion that the South Korean regime could collapse, perhaps with a nudge from North Korean forces. Attempts to destabilize the ROK government through direct action reached a peaked in January 1968, when North Korean commandoes infiltrated the grounds of the South Korean presidential compound, or Blue House. The commandoes came within a few hundred yards of their target, President Park Chung Hee, before being apprehended by ROK security forces. This was followed two days later by the North Korean capture of the American intelligence ship the USS *Pueblo* off North Korea's eastern coast. The *Pueblo*'s crew was held captive for nearly a year and was released following an American apology (swiftly rescinded) for spying on the DPRK. Then in April 1969, less than four months after the release of the *Pueblo* crew, North Korean MiG fighters shot down an American EC-121 reconnaissance aircraft over the Sea of Japan, killing all thirty-one of the crew members.[9] Tensions between North Korea and both South Korea and the United States were higher at the end of the 1960s than at any time since the 1953 armistice, yet within two years North Korea was negotiating with Seoul and making peace overtures toward Washington. This turnabout reflected the dramatic changes in Cold War dynamics between 1968 and 1972, above all the transformation of the Sino-US relationship from confrontation to strategic alignment. But the DPRK's new approach to Seoul and Washington did not mean Pyongyang had abandoned either its fervent opposition to US imperialism, or its hopes that a pro–North Korean revolution in the South was imminent.

Internationalizing the "Korean Question"

Like the decision to divide the Korean Peninsula in August 1945, the armistice signed at Panmunjŏm in July 1953 was intended to be a temporary expedient pending a long-term political solution, not a permanent state of affairs. But both

---

7. In fact, some of the Red Cross delegates *were* intelligence officers and began the process of dialogue under cover of the Red Cross meetings. Don Oberdorfer, *The Two Koreas: A Contemporary History* (Reading, MA: Addison-Wesley, 1997), 14–15.

8. Yi Chong-sŏk, *Hyŏndae Puk Hanŭi ihae* [Understanding Contemporary North Korea] (Seoul: Yŏksa pip'yŏngsa, 2000), 381.

9. Ostermann and Person, *Crisis and Confrontation on the Korean Peninsula*, 96–123.

political division and armed truce—and in the South, a large foreign military presence—would remain the status quo in Korea for more than half a century. Paragraph 60 of the Armistice Agreement had recommended that a political conference be held within three months "to settle through negotiation the questions of the withdrawal of all foreign forces from Korea, the peaceful settlement of the Korean Question, etc."[10] Not until the Berlin Conference on Germany and Austria in February 1954 did the four (formerly) allied powers (the United States, United Kingdom, France, and the Soviet Union) agree on a venue and time for a conference on the Korean Question. The place would be Geneva, and the conference would begin April 26. The four governments also agreed in Berlin that, following the talks on Korea, they would discuss the problem of restoring peace in Indochina. As it happened, the Geneva Conference would become much better known for the Indochina settlement than the Korean discussion, not least because the French defeat at Dien Bien Phu occurred shortly after the Korea conference began.

The Geneva Conference on Korea involved nineteen nations, including the Soviet Union, the People's Republic of China, North Korea, and sixteen participants from the United Nations side in the conflict (only South Africa declined to attend). Despite a hopeful beginning, the Geneva discussions became little more than the Panmunjŏm talks on a larger scale and in a more picturesque setting, with the familiar accusations of bad faith and stonewalling flying from both sides almost daily. On June 15 the talks ended as they had begun, in an acrimonious stalemate.[11] Of the four areas of occupation and division discussed by the major powers in 1954 (Austria, Germany, Indochina, and Korea), only the Austrian question was resolved peacefully and definitively—through an Allied withdrawal and the neutralization of Austria in the Cold War. Germany and Korea remained divided, and Vietnam got the "Korean Solution" of division into northern and southern regimes, leading to another two decades of warfare in Indochina.

With the collapse of the Geneva talks on Korea, the Korean Question reverted to the United Nations, where it had started in 1947. The Republic of Korea had been established under UN mandate in August 1948, and the DPRK was not recognized by the international body. The United States, the ROK, and their allies at Geneva argued that Korea should be unified through national elections sponsored by the United Nations. The North Korean–Soviet–Chinese side argued, with some justification, that the United Nations was a belligerent in the Korean War, not a neutral party to the conflict. The United States

---

10. Cited in United States Department of State, *The Korean Problem at the Geneva Conference, April 26–June 15, 1954* (Washington, DC: US Government Printing Office, October 1954), 3.

11. Steven Hugh Lee, *Outposts of Empire: Korea, Vietnam, and the Origins of the Cold War in Asia, 1949–1954* (Montreal: McGill-Queen's University Press, 1995), 213–17.

proposed a unified government elected according to proportional representation, giving a distinct advantage to the more populous South; the Communist side proposed the Koreans solve the Korean Question without outside interference, meaning that US troops would have to leave the peninsula. Although neither Korean state was a member of the United Nations, South Korea was granted observer status at the United Nations, a status denied the DPRK. The United Nations, dominated by the United States and its allies in the early Cold War years, was clearly biased toward the ROK. This would change, however, after the late 1950s.

The change in the UN position was largely a result of a change in the composition of the General Assembly, due to the growing number of newly independent, Third World states that were more critical of South Korea and more sympathetic to the North than the earlier UN members had been. From the late 1950s until the 1980s, nonaligned Third World governments such as India, Burma, Sri Lanka, Iraq, Ghana, Yemen, Morocco, and Egypt often sided with the socialist countries in condemning the UN's de facto recognition of South Korea. The Soviet-aligned states, most notably East Germany, frequently criticized the United Nations for granting only South Korea, and not the North, the right to give its position on the Korean Question at the General Assembly's debates, and welcomed the support of Afro-Asian states on the issue.[12] Of course, as the communist half of another divided nation, the GDR had its own interest in promoting the North Korean position at the United Nations.

The DPRK may have been skeptical about UN neutrality on the Korean Question, but North Korea was not opposed to the United Nations as an international body. As early as 1956, with the support of the North Korean government, the Soviet Union had proposed that the DPRK join the United Nations simultaneously with the ROK. This was a major concession on the communist side, as it would have acknowledged the legal existence of the South Korean government. But the United States refused the proposal, arguing that the DPRK was the aggressor in the Korean War, had violated the armistice, and did not recognize the authority of the United Nations.[13] China, for its part, also opposed the Soviet–North Korean proposal for UN mediation between the two Koreas, arguing that the United Nations was a party in the dispute and not a neutral arbiter.[14] A quarter-century, and much shifting of positions on all sides, would pass before

---

12. GDR Ministry of Foreign Affairs, Korea Section. "Statement by a Spokesman for the Minster of Foreign Affairs of the German Democratic Republic on the United Nations' Again Illegally Considering the So-Called Korean Question." MfAA A 6927, Document 114.

13. Barry Gills, *Korea versus Korea: A Case of Contested Legitimacy* (London: Routledge, 1996), 73.

14. Zhihua Shen and Danhui Li, *After Leaning to One Side: China and Its Allies in the Cold War* (Stanford: Stanford University Press, 2011), 214.

the two states simultaneously joined the United Nations precisely as the Soviet Union had proposed.

Despite its exclusion from the UN debates on Korea, the DPRK benefited from the change in the international system from the late 1950s to the late 1970s by greatly expanding its ties with the Third World, a subject we will return to in the next chapter. Whatever its internal repressiveness, and despite its continued dependence on Soviet and East Bloc trade and assistance, North Korea's outspoken advocacy of independence, self-reliance, anti-imperialism, and national liberation resonated with the aspirations of many newly independent states in a rapidly decolonizing world.[15] North Korea's international support, primarily in the Third World, reached a peak in the mid-1970s; after that, the undeniable economic success of South Korea and the growing economic difficulties of the DPRK pulled many Third World states toward supporting the South.

North Korea's diplomatic relations had been confined solely to other socialist states until the late 1950s, but from the early 1960s onward the DPRK began actively expanding economic and political ties with the newly emerging nations of the Third World. Regionally, this meant for North Korea primarily a focus on South and Southeast Asia, the Middle East, and Africa; Latin America, dominated overwhelmingly by the United States, was essentially off-limits to North Korea influence. The major exception to this was Cuba after the 1960 revolution, with which North Korea developed strong relations, the two regimes seeing themselves on the front lines against US imperialism.[16]

North Korea in the 1960s and 1970s could have appeared a model of postcolonial nation-building, having been founded by anti-imperialist fighters, built up an impressive industrial economy, and successfully resisted (albeit with considerable Chinese assistance) the military might of the United States in the Korean War. With no foreign troops on its soil after the withdrawal of the Chinese People's Volunteers in 1958, North Korea looked particularly good in contrast to the South, which was heavily dependent on US economic assistance and host to tens of thousands of American troops. Externally, the DPRK propaganda line was consistently in favor of anticolonial nationalism and independence throughout the Third World. In his frequent commentary on the Juche idea, Kim Il Sung regularly pointed to "US imperialism" as the main enemy of the Third World peoples and advocated Juche as the very embodiment of anti-imperialism. The DPRK portrayed the North Koreans' struggle against the United States and South Korea as identical with the struggle of Third World peoples for independence and

---

15. See the essays in praise of Juche, mostly by Third World writers, in *Immortal Juche Idea* (Pyongyang: Foreign Languages Publishing House, 1979).

16. Che Guevara visited the DPRK twice in the early 1960s; thirty years later, Che Guevara postage stamps were still for sale in Pyongyang.

completely compatible with "proletarian internationalism": "We should unite closely with the peoples of all the socialist countries; we should actively support the Asian, African and Latin American peoples struggling to throw off the imperialist yoke, and strengthen solidarity with them."[17] This revolutionary spirit was very much in sync with a good many movements for Third World solidarity in the age of decolonization; unfortunately, North Korea's foreign policy, like its economic policy, failed to change with the times in subsequent decades.

Over the course of the 1960s, North Korea normalized relations with some two dozen new governments, mostly in Africa and the Middle East. The DPRK tried to use its new diplomatic stature to advance its agenda in the United Nations, advocating DPRK participation in General Assembly debates on the Korean Question, an end to US dominance in UN activities on the Korean Peninsula, and the removal of US forces from South Korea. Outside the UN forum, North Korea tried with some success to play a leading role in the nonaligned movement, launched in Belgrade in 1961. Trade and military exchange with nonsocialist Third World countries was also of some economic benefit to North Korea, although economic relations with the Soviet-bloc states remained far more important to the DPRK until the very end of the Soviet Union. June 1961 was a particularly fruitful month for North Korea's Third World diplomacy: DPRK trade minister Yi Chu-yŏn visited Indonesia and India, opening trade and consular relations with these two countries, while also establishing a trade agreement with Burma. On a tour through West Africa that summer, North Korean officials signed similar trade agreements with Guinea, Mali, and Ghana. Guinea, in fact, had been the first sub-Saharan African country with which the DPRK established full diplomatic relations, in October 1958 (and only the second non–East Bloc country after Algeria, earlier that year). In October 1961, North Korea and Mali produced a joint communiqué on "Afro-Asian solidarity against US imperialism."[18]

In the Middle East, North Korea's first diplomatic success was with the Nasser government of Egypt, to which the DPRK had given token financial assistance during the Suez Crisis. In 1961, a DPRK delegation visited Egypt to discuss establishing consular relations, and North Korea sent similar preliminary missions to South Yemen, Morocco, and Iraq. North Korea officially condemned Israeli actions in the Middle East as complicit with US imperialism; the DPRK strongly sided with the Arab states against Israel in the 1967 war, for example.[19]

---

17. Kim Il Sung, *On the Juche Idea* (New York: The Guardian, 1980), 262.

18. George Ginsburg and Roy U.T. Kim, *Calendar of Diplomatic Affairs, Democratic People's Republic of Korea, 1945–1975* (Moorestown, NJ: Symposia Press, 1977), 71.

19. GDR Embassy in Pyongyang, "Action Report on a Talk with Comrade Pak Kwang-chŏl, Section Chief for Middle Eastern and North African Countries," 27 July 1967. MfAA C 1028/73.

By 1963, the fifteenth anniversary of the founding of the DPRK, North Korea was no longer the isolated outpost of the Soviet bloc that it had been in the aftermath of the Korean War. Twenty-two foreign delegations participated in the fifteenth-anniversary celebrations in Pyongyang, representing for the first time many Asian, African, and Middle Eastern countries outside the socialist bloc. The following year, Pyongyang hosted the Asian Economic Conference, attended by delegates from thirty-four Asia-Pacific and African countries. Kim Il Sung proclaimed the DPRK a model of self-reliant development and anti-imperialist independence for the entire Third World.[20]

Kim's most important Third World summit appearance of the 1960s was in Indonesia in April 1965, the tenth anniversary of the Bandung Conference on Afro-Asian Solidarity. This was Kim's first visit outside the socialist bloc since the founding of the DPRK. Indonesian president Sukarno had visited Pyongyang the previous year, where he seems to have been greatly impressed by both North Korea's self-reliance strategy and Kim Il Sung's leadership. Kim gave a major speech in Jakarta, where he outlined the basic principles of Juche, called for the withdrawal of all foreign forces from Korea, and vowed to strengthen the anti-imperialist movement in Asia, Africa, and Latin America. Kim, it seemed, had suddenly emerged as a leader of the nonaligned countries of the Third World, a development that both encouraged and concerned North Korea's European socialist allies, who worried that the DPRK might become too independent of the Soviet bloc.[21] Kim and Sukarno, North Korea and Indonesia were newfound allies at the forefront the anti-imperialist struggle. This moment turned out to be short-lived, however. Kim happened to have visited Indonesia during that country's infamous "year of living dangerously," and Sukarno's left-leaning government was soon toppled in a coup blamed on the Indonesia Communist Party. The resulting anticommunist bloodbath, led by the military, brought the pro-American general Suharto to power.[22] Suharto would remain Indonesia's strongman leader for the next thirty years. The overthrow of Sukarno and the American military escalation in Vietnam created a much more volatile and dangerous atmosphere for North Korea's interests in Asia.

---

20. *Chosŏn chungang nyŏngam* [Korea Central Yearbook] (Pyongyang, 1964), 34–35; GDR Foreign Ministry, Extra-European Department, Korea Section. "Information on Conversations with the Chairman of the Supreme People's Assembly, Ch'oe Yong-gŏn, regarding Several African and Asian States, 19 November–22 December 1964." MfAA C 1028/73.

21. GDR Embassy in Pyongyang, "On the Position of the DPRK at the Second Bandung Conference," 26 July 1965. MfAA C 1028/73.

22. John Roosa, *Pretext for Mass Murder: The September 30th Movement and Suharto's Coup d'Etat in Indonesia* (Madison: University of Wisconsin Press, 2006).

Confronting the Americans

Korea in the Mirror of Vietnam

The DPRK had identified Korea's position with that of Vietnam from the beginning of the American military intervention in Vietnam in 1961. Of course, the Western countries had linked together the Korean and Vietnamese questions as early as the 1954 Geneva Conference. The Soviet-aligned countries also tended to conflate Korea and Vietnam in the 1950s and 1960s, as for example in East Germany's "Committee for the Assistance of Korea and Vietnam." Two divided countries on the periphery of China, Korea and Vietnam seemed strikingly, even confusingly, alike in the minds of Europeans and Americans. From a Chinese perspective as well, Vietnam and Korea were two of a kind: for centuries important buffer states on the southern and northeastern flanks of the Chinese empire, respectively, the two countries had been traditionally the most faithful members of the Sinocentric tributary system, acknowledging the titular supremacy of the Chinese emperor over their own kings and borrowing heavily from Chinese models of politics, social organization, and elite culture.[23] More recently, the Chinese communist movement had been a kind of "elder brother" to the Vietnamese and Korean—both Ho Chi Minh and Kim Il Sung had spent years in China working with the Chinese Communist Party—and the PRC leadership saw Korea and Vietnam, along with Taiwan, as the three most important fronts in the struggle against US imperialism.[24]

The Koreans and Vietnamese themselves often pointed to the parallels between their two situations, and the solidarity of both in the face of US imperialism, although the North Korean leadership was perhaps more enthusiastic than Hanoi about their common struggle. In 1963, North Korea established a committee to support the South Vietnamese resistance movement; as we have seen in the previous chapter, the DPRK at the same time built up its own defense forces in a new policy of "equal emphasis" on the civilian and military sectors of the economy. The Park Chung Hee military regime in South Korea showed no signs of weakening, and indeed was consolidating its hold with massive US economic and military support. Under these circumstances, North Korea's buildup of both

---

23. Alexander Woodside, *Vietnam and the Chinese Model: A Comparative Study of Vietnamese and Chinese Government in the First Half of the Nineteenth Century* (Cambridge: Harvard University Press, 1971); James Palais, *Politics and Policy in Traditional Korea* (Cambridge: Harvard University Press, 1975). However, the traditional Sino-Vietnamese relationship was much more fraught with conflict than the Sino-Korean one; given this history of tension and rivalry, it should not have been surprising that China and Vietnam came again to clash after Vietnamese unification in the 1970s. Vietnam's modern national identity was formed against China much more than was Korea's, which tended to be juxtaposed against Japan. See Keith W. Taylor, *The Birth of Vietnam* (Berkeley: University of California Press, 1983).

24. Qiang Zhai, *China and the Vietnam Wars, 1950–1975* (Chapel Hill: University of North Carolina Press, 2000), 20.

military forces and militant rhetoric was more than a means for Kim Il Sung to consolidate power by keeping his people on a war footing and extracting aid from the outside.[25] They also reflected a real concern about the threat from the South, and Pyongyang's support for North Vietnam was a means of weakening the United States in the region—and perhaps a way of living vicariously through a guerrilla movement in South Vietnam that, unlike the long-defunct guerrilla movement in South Korea, showed signs of real success.

Blocked from any significant direct engagement on the Korean Peninsula itself, the two Koreas played out a kind of proxy war in Vietnam. In 1965, under strong US pressure and with promises of lavish American aid, the ROK began to dispatch combat troops to aid the American effort in Vietnam.[26] The South Korean intervention was condemned in the strongest possible terms by Pyongyang. The DPRK for its part sent medicines, clothes, and other goods to aid the South Vietnamese guerrilla movement, but North Korea's military involvement was much more modest and discrete than that of the South. Pyongyang's only direct military participation in the Vietnam War was in providing pilots for air defense, a fact not revealed publicly until the People's Army of Vietnam (PAVN) published an official history of the subject more than forty years after the event.[27] In September 1966, North Korea offered to send an air force regiment to help defend North Vietnam against American air strikes. The chief of the North Korean General Staff led a delegation to Hanoi to discuss this with PAVN officials, and the two sides agreed that North Korea would provide pilots while Vietnam would provide aircraft, equipment, and logistics. Between 1967 and 1969, a total of eighty-seven North Korean air force personnel went to Vietnam. The North Koreans lost fourteen men and claimed to have shot down twenty-six American planes. An unspecified number North Korean military observers also went to South Vietnam in order to study the South Korean army "and to use propaganda against the South Koreans," according to a Vietnamese diplomat in Pyongyang.[28] While not insignificant, this appears to be the full extent of North Korea's active

25. East European observers often took a cynical view of North Korea's military buildup, seeing it as a tool for Kim Il Sung to strengthen his hold over the country rather than a response to any objective change in the region. See for example the remarks by Horst Brie, East German ambassador to the DPRK in the mid-1960s, in Ostermann and Person, eds. *Crisis and Confrontation on the Korean Peninsula*, 79.

26. See Charles K. Armstrong, "America's Korea, Korea's Vietnam," *Critical Asian Studies* 33, no. 4 (December 2001): 527–39.

27. Merle Pribbenow, "North Korean Pilots in the Skies over Vietnam," North Korea International Documentation Project e-Dossier No. 2 (November 2011). Available at http://www.wilsoncenter.org/publication/nkidp-e-dossier-no-2-north-korean-pilots-the-skies-over-vietnam.

28. Romanian Foreign Ministry Archive, Telegram No. 76.247, July 6, 1967. Obtained and translated for North Korea International Documentation Project by Eliza Gheorghe. Available at http://www.wilsoncenter.org/article/romanian-document-confirms-north-korea-sent-troops-to-vietnam.

military contribution to the war in Vietnam. South Korea, in contrast, sent some 325,000 soldiers to Vietnam, with a loss of more than five thousand men, between September 1964 and March 1973 when the ROK troop deployment ended.[29] But whereas the South Korean participation in the war created an economic windfall for Seoul, the North Korean contribution was only an economic drain.

By the mid-1960s, not only was North Korea "arming the whole people" internally, it was sending economic and military assistance to Vietnam, which the DPRK portrayed as fighting a struggle identical to that of Korea. South Korea meanwhile normalized diplomatic relations with Japan in 1965, in an agreement that provoked violent protests in South Korea but showered the ROK with an enormous aid package. South Korea's policy of export-oriented economic development was beginning to bear fruit, and the Vietnam intervention also gave a huge boost to the South Korean economy in the form of American aid, loans, and payments to individual soldiers. In short, North Korea's foreign and domestic policies were putting a severe strain on its economy at precisely the moment when the South Korean economy, after nearly two decades of stagnation, was beginning to take off.

Kim Il Sung gave a frank assessment of the state of North Korea's economy to Alexei Kosygin, chairman of the USSR Council of Ministers, when Kosygin visited Pyongyang in February 1965 on his way back from Hanoi. The Seven-Year Plan for the DPRK economy, launched with much fanfare in 1961, was unlikely to be fulfilled. Kim blamed North Korea's economic difficulties primarily on the lack of assistance from other socialist countries, and secondarily on the diversion of resources to the military. Based on the model of the postwar Three and Five-Year Plans, Kim said that "the targets of the Seven Year Plan presupposed assistance from and deepened cooperation with you and other socialist countries. We counted on this assistance, but unfortunately didn't get it. This . . . was the substantial reason why the plan has not been fulfilled." Meanwhile, "in connection with the Caribbean crisis [i.e., the Cuban Missile Crisis] and the US aggression in Vietnam, we have been forced to accelerate the buildup of our defense industry . . . As much as 30 percent of the entire budget is consumed by the army."[30] In a special session of the Korean Workers' Party Representative Conference in October 1966, the Seven-Year Plan was extended another three years. All subsequent economic plans would be delayed as well, until the planning system itself collapsed in the 1990s. North Korea's "Economic Miracle in the Far East," as the East Germans had called it a few years earlier, would never return. South Korea, not North Korea, would henceforth be the "Economic Miracle" on the peninsula.

---

29. Institute for Military History Compilation, "The Vietnam War and the Korean Military," 115. Available at http://www.imhc.mil.kr/imhcroot/upload/resource/V27.pdf.

30. "Memorandum of Conversation with USSR Ambassador to the DPRK." See footnote 1 above.

Following Kosygin's visit to the DPRK, Soviet–North Korean relations improved rapidly, helped above all by renewed Soviet aid. The Soviet embassy in Pyongyang reported that by the end of 1964, North Korean had sensibly chosen "to abandon a one-sided orientation toward China" and return to the Soviet camp. This was more for economic than strictly ideological reasons: leaning toward China had damaged North Korea's economic ties with the Soviet Union and Eastern Europe, which "in turn, became one of the reasons for serious economic difficulties of the DPRK." This gave Moscow an opportunity to strengthen its strategic position on the Chinese periphery in Asia, but improvement in Soviet–North Korean relations depended on Moscow's continuing generosity. As the Soviet embassy report noted, "The intensity of this process is, evidently, in direct proportion to the volume of all kinds of aid to the DPRK from the Soviet Union."[31] Soviet aid underwrote a military buildup that North Korea's domestic economy alone could no longer support. This military buildup intensified in 1966, and the following year a final purge in the DPRK leadership eliminated all but Kim's most loyal partisans from the inner circles of power. North Korea had truly become a "guerrilla-band state," led by former anti-Japanese partisans who saw themselves confronted by a growing threat from the outside, including the threat of a revived "Japanese militarism."[32] Seoul-Tokyo normalization in 1965 and the American escalation in Vietnam proved, as the North Koreans saw it, that a Washington-Tokyo-Seoul axis posed an imminent threat to peace in East Asia in general and the Korean Peninsula in particular. Foreign Minister Hŏ Sŏk-tae told Soviet officials that "a new war on the Korean Peninsula is inevitable," due in part to the rise of Japanese militarism, and that was why North Korea had to sacrifice economic growth to strengthen its defense capability.[33]

The *Pueblo* Incident

It was in this atmosphere of growing tension and unease in East Asia, caused above all by the escalating war in Indochina, that an incident between North

31. Soviet Embassy in Pyongyang, "Some New Aspect of Korean-Chinese Relations in the First Half of 1965," AVPRK, fond 0102, opis 21, papka 106, delo 20, listy 14–27. Translated and reproduced in Sergey Radchenko, "The Soviet Union and the North Korean Seizure of the USS Pueblo: Evidence from the Russian Archives," Cold War International History Project Working Paper No. 47 (April 2005), 45–51.

32. For North Korea as a "guerrilla-band state," which had been incipient from the time the DPRK was founded in 1948 but not fully realized until the final victory of Kim Il Sung's ex-partisan group in 1967, see Wada Haruki, Kita Chosen: Yugekitai Kokka no Genzai [North Korea: Partisan State Today] (Tokyo: Iwanami, 1998).

33. Cited in Nobuo Somotomai, "Kim Il Sung's Balancing Act, between Moscow and Beijing, 1956–1972," in Tsuyoshi Hasegawa, ed., The Cold War in East Asia, 1945–1991 (Stanford: Stanford University Press, 2011), 142–43.

Korea and the United States nearly precipitated a second Korean War. On January 23, 1968, North Korean forces captured the USS *Pueblo*, a converted cargo carrier engaged in electronic intelligence-gathering off the East Coast of the DPRK. Eight days later, the Vietnamese National Liberation Front launched its Tet Offensive against South Vietnamese and American targets throughout South Vietnam. Even before Tet, the Johnson administration was convinced that the *Pueblo* incident had been coordinated between North Korea and other communist countries in order to distract American military forces from Indochina and to pressure South Korea to recall its troops from Vietnam; after Tet, it seemed certain to many of the American leaders that North Korea was trying to open up a "second front" in order to tie down American forces in both Korea and Indochina.[34] However, it appears that North Korea captured the *Pueblo* without any prior consultation, much less coordination, with any of its allies, including the Soviet Union, China, and North Vietnam. Indeed, the "fraternal" socialist allies first learned about the incident from Western newspapers, and most of these governments—especially the USSR—were none too pleased with the North Korean action.[35]

Border incidents involving the two Koreas had escalated dramatically since the full-scale American military intervention in Vietnam began in 1965. According to the State Department, North Koreans incidents across the DMZ occurred fifty times in 1966 and nearly six hundred times in 1967.[36] Some forty South Korean ships, mostly fishing vessels, were captured by North Korean coastal patrols in 1967. In October 1967, North Korean forces fired artillery against South Korean positions, the first time this had happened since the Korean War. Most spectacularly of all, in early January 1968, a team of thirty North Korean commandoes, disguised as ROK soldiers, slipped into South Korea in an attempt to assassinate Park Chung Hee, the South Korean president. The commandoes came within a few hundred yards of the presidential palace, or Blue House, before they were discovered by South Korean security forces on January 21. All but two of the commandoes were killed in the ensuing firefight. Two days later, the North Korean navy captured the *Pueblo*.

---

34. The *Pueblo* Incident has inspired several memoirs, numerous military analyses, and the first twenty minutes of the James Bond film *Die Another Day*; to date the only serious historical study of the incident (based entirely on English-language—mostly American—sources) is Mitchell B. Lerner, *The Pueblo Incident: A Spy Ship and the Failure of American Foreign Policy* (Lawrence: University Press of Kansas, 2002).

35. The Soviet were shocked and angered at the North Korean seizure of the *Pueblo*, which threatened to drag them into a war with the United States, but could do little to restrain their ally. See Radchenko, "The Soviet Union and the North Korean Seizure of the USS Pueblo."

36. Telegram from the Department of State to the Embassy in the Soviet Union, February 6, 1968. Department of State, *Foreign Relations of the United States, 1964–1968*. Vol. 29, Part 1, *Korea* (Washington: US Government Printing Office, 2000), 609. Hereafter *FRUS*.

The *Pueblo*, with a crew of eighty-three under Commander Lloyd "Pete" Bucher, left the port of Sasebo, Japan, on January 11 for the northeast coast of Korea. The ship had been outfitted with electronic intelligence gear to eavesdrop on communications from North Korea and the Soviet Far East. On January 23, the ship was discovered by North Korean coastal patrols in Wŏnsan harbor, about twenty miles from the port city of Wŏnsan and less than eight miles from the nearest North Korean island. The North Koreans ordered the *Pueblo* to surrender and be boarded. Bucher attempted to lead the ship to escape, but the North Koreans fired on the vessel, killing one of the crew and wounding four others. The *Pueblo* was commandeered by the North Koreans and the crew taken prisoner. The eighty-two surviving crewmen would endure almost a year of hardship, beating, and torture, pawns in a deadly diplomatic game between the United States and the DPRK.

The public response in the United States and South Korea was outrage; President Johnson had to deal with both belligerent South Koreans calling for reprisals against the North, and domestic attacks from prominent Republicans accusing Johnson of weakness. The Park Chung Hee government demanded that the United States support military retaliation against North Korea. California governor Ronald Reagan called the *Pueblo* incident "the most disgraceful thing to happen in my memory of America," and Senator Strom Thurmond said he had no doubt that the seizure of the *Pueblo* "was closely tied to the war in South Vietnam."[37] Johnson and his advisors weighed the options, which ranged from some form of negotiation—politically distasteful, especially in an election year—to air strikes on the DPRK, which could lead to a disastrous all-out war in Korea just as the war in Vietnam was reaching its peak.[38] The State Department notified Kosygin through the Soviet Embassy that the Soviets had better restrain their North Korean clients. Kosygin responded that the US reaction to the *Pueblo* seizure, which included dispatching aircraft carriers and other military provocations, "indicated that there were many hotheads in [the] Pentagon who needed tranquilizers."[39] In fact, the Soviets were equally if not more concerned about the "hotheads" in Pyongyang.

The day after the incident, ambassadors and acting ambassadors of Soviet-bloc allies accredited to the DPRK assembled in Pyongyang for a briefing by Kim Chae-bong, the North Korean vice foreign minister. The fraternal ambassadors had only the vaguest idea of the crisis instigated the day before. Kim announced, "I want to inform you about the armed spy ship of which you might already have

---

37. Cited in Lerner, *The Pueblo Incident*, 164, 167.
38. W. W. Rostow, "Report on Meeting of the Advisory Group," January 29, 1968. *FRUS*, 556–59.
39. Telegram from the Embassy in the Soviet Union to the Department of State. *FRUS*, 611.

read in the newspaper." He explained that the *Pueblo* "had committed acts of piracy" in violating North Korea's territorial waters, and that its crew included two "members of the notorious intelligence agency of the USA." Kim hoped "that all socialist states fully support our actions and our attitude, and condemn unanimously the serious machinations of USA imperialism." The socialist diplomats were clearly stunned. The acting ambassador of Bulgaria asked if there was a connection between the *Pueblo* incident and "the events in Seoul," referring to the commando raid on the Blue House. Kim responded that The Blue House raid had been the act of "armed partisans," and the *Pueblo* incursion was part of the American suppression of a putative South Korean partisan movement. All of this demonstrated that "USA imperialism is maximizing preparations for another war of aggression."[40]

Publicly, the USSR and its allies rallied behind the DPRK position on the *Pueblo* and deplored this act of American "aggression." Privately, socialist officials, particularly the Soviets, saw the North Korean action as excessively confrontational and ultimately counterproductive, likely to strengthen the hands of the American hawks with regard to Vietnam, not to mention bringing the United States and North Korea to the brink of open warfare.[41] Czechoslovakia and Switzerland were represented on the Neutral Nations Commission that oversaw the Korean Armistice in Panmunjŏm; via the Czechs and the Swiss, North Korean and the US officials contacted each other to establish direct talks on resolving the *Pueblo* crisis. As the Czech ambassador to the DPRK told his Polish and East German colleagues on January 28, "As long as there are talks or chances for talks, one cannot speak of an imminent outbreak of armed conflict."[42] The weeks after the *Pueblo* capture were extraordinary tense in North Korea, a country long used to military tension. The population of Pyongyang was put on highest alert on February 25, the date the Americans in Panmunjŏm demanded the return of the *Pueblo* and its crew.[43] Rumors of the imminent outbreak of war circulated in North Korea from the first day of the crisis. War with the United States could have quickly gone nuclear, as Americans had nuclear weapons stationed in South Korea (in violation of the Korean War armistice) while North Korea had mutual defense treaties with the USSR and China, both nuclear weapons states.

---

40. Embassy of the GDR in the DPRK, "Information of the Foreign Ministry of the DPRK on 24 January 1968." MfAA C 1023/73.

41. USSR Foreign Ministry, "Record of Conversation between A.A. Gromyko and Chargé d'affaires of the DPRK in the USSR, Kang Chŏl-gŭn." AVPRF, Fond 102, Opis 28, Papka 55, Delo 2.

42. Embassy of the GDR in the DPRK, "Memorandum of Conversation with the Ambassadors of the CSSR, Comrade Holub, and of the People's Republic of Poland, Comrade Naperei, on 28 January 1968." MfAA G-A 360.

43. Embassy of the GDR in the DPRK, "Information Report of 24 and 25 February 1968." MfAA C 1023/73.

All Koreans from the age of five were required to carry a backpack of emergency supplies at all times.[44]

To the relief of the world, the *Pueblo* incident did not lead to nuclear war. Rear Admiral John Smith, senior UN representative at the Military Armistice Commission (MAC) in Panmunjŏm, and DPRK major general Pak Chung-guk initiated a series of talks aimed at a peaceful resolution to the *Pueblo* crisis. The North Koreans announced that they would return the crew (but not the ship) if the United States admitted that the *Pueblo* had intruded into North Korean waters with hostile intent, gave the DPRK a "proper apology," and guaranteed against future such incidents.[45] By March, the United States was willing to go as far as to acknowledge the intelligence-gathering mission of the *Pueblo*, express "regret" at the intrusion, and promise that US ships would henceforth stay beyond twelve miles off the North Korean coast, but would not concede to North Korea's demand for an apology. The talks dragged on for nearly eleven months, as the surviving *Pueblo* crewmen languished and the American leadership resisted strong public pressure from both the United States and South Korea for military action to end the crisis.

In May, Admiral Smith's term as MAC representative expired and he was replaced by Major General Gilbert Woodward, who continued more rounds of talks with General Park. There would be twenty-nine rounds of talks in all. Finally, in December 1968, the US side offered the North Koreans a formula designed by James Leonard, the State Department country director for Korea: the United States would give the DPRK a written apology as requested, but would immediately and publicly repudiate it. Leonard had realized that North Korea wanted a formal apology not as a binding agreement, but for domestic propaganda purposes. Given the virtually absolute control the DPRK government had over foreign news reaching the North Korean public, the American repudiation would never be known by most North Koreans. Thus Kim Il Sung could declare victory against the Americans once again, and North Korea would retain its "face" against American aggression. Juche would be preserved. The Leonard proposal worked, and on December 23, Woodward and Pak Chung-guk met for the last time in Panmunjŏm. At 11:30 a.m., as the prisoners were about to be released, Woodward declared,

> The position of the United States government with regard to the *Pueblo* ... has been that the ship was not engaged in any illegal activity, that there is no convincing evidence that the ship at any time intruded

44. Embassy of the GDR in the DPRK, "Memorandum of Information of 1 February 1968." MfAA C 1023/73.

45. Memorandum from Secretary of State Rusk to President Johnson, March 14, 1968. *FRUS*, 665.

into the territorial waters claimed by North Korea, and that we could not apologize for actions which we did not believe took place. The document I am going to sign was prepared by the North Koreans and is at variance with the above position, but my signature will not and cannot alter the facts. I will sign the document to free the crew and only to free the crew.[46]

One by one, the crew of the *Pueblo* crossed the "Bridge of No Return" into South Korean territory. After Commander Bucher came two crewmen carrying the body of Duane Hodges in a wooden coffin, and then the other seventy-nine crew members in thirty-second intervals. The *Pueblo* crisis was over.

For many years, the *Pueblo* remained docked in Wŏnsan harbor, a rusting reminder of American perfidy, its deck used by local fishermen for convenient angling. In the year 2000, just as US-DPRK relations seemed finally to be making progress toward normalization in the waning months of the Clinton administration, the DPRK government had the *Pueblo* removed from Wŏnsan harbor, towed around the southern perimeter of the Korean Peninsula to the West Coast (encountering no obstacle from South Korean coastal defenses), and redocked in the Taedong River just outside of Pyongyang. The *Pueblo* was placed alongside a monument to the USS *General Sherman*, an American merchant ship whose captain had been sent to discuss the opening of Korea to Western trade in 1866. En route to Pyongyang, the Sherman ran aground on an islet in the Taedong River, and its crew was murdered by an angry mob of local residents.[47] The Sherman was taken apart, its hull burned, its cannons removed to Seoul for study, and its anchor hung on the main gate of Pyongyang as a warning to any other foreigners who would attempt to enter Korean waters uninvited. The message was clear: the Sherman and the *Pueblo* were two of a kind, American "warships" that had affronted Korean sovereignty, almost exactly a hundred years apart. Placing the *Pueblo* next to the Sherman monument would remind the people of North Korea that, despite an apparent warming in DPRK-US relations, they must maintain their vigilance against American imperialism. In April 2002, Donald Gregg, president of the Korea Society in New York and former US ambassador to Seoul, visited North Korea with a message from the citizens of Pueblo, Colorado: they would like the *Pueblo* returned to its namesake city, where it would be refurbished on dry land as a naval museum. Ambassador Gregg suggested to DPRK vice foreign

---

46. Cited in Lerner, *Pueblo Incident*, 219.

47. Beginning in the 1970s, DPRK history texts claimed that the mob who murdered the Sherman crew was led by Kim Il Sung's great-greatfather, Kim Ung-gu. *Chosŏn chŏnsa* [Complete History of Korea] vol. 13 (Modern Period, vol. 1) (Pyongyang: Kwahak-Paekkwasajon, 1980), 69–70. Earlier North Korean histories had not mentioned Kim Ung-gu's involvement.

minister Kang Sŏk-ju that returning the *Pueblo* would be an important goodwill gesture to the Bush administration and hopefully help reinvigorate US-North Korean relations, which had cooled considerably since the end of the Clinton presidency. Kang agreed. In November, Gregg returned to Pyongyang, and found that the *Pueblo* was missing. He was told that the ship was being painted and cleaned up in preparation for its return to the United States. But the *Pueblo* would not be returned. A month earlier, a crisis had erupted over American accusations that North Korea was secretly producing nuclear weapons in violation of a 1994 US–DPRK agreement. The last mission of the *Pueblo*, to be a symbol of US-North Korean reconciliation, was aborted by a crisis even more dangerous than the one the *Pueblo* itself had provoked more than three decades before.

Between "Dogmatism" and "Social Imperialism": the Sino-Soviet Conflict Deepens

Both the Chinese Cultural Revolution and the Sino-Soviet conflict reached their peak at the end of the 1960s. In the hysteria of the Cultural Revolution, even long-standing ally North Korea could become an enemy. Red Guards denounced Kim Il Sung as a "fat revisionist" and "Korea's Khrushchev."[48] Reports trickled out to the world of border clashes between the DPRK and China, while the Soviet Union and the PRC fired shots at each other in several places on their Far Eastern border. By 1968, North Korea was estranged from China yet unwilling to come fully into the Soviet camp like Eastern Europe, Mongolia, or Cuba (and as Vietnam would do in the 1970s). Pyongyang was caught in a vicious and dangerous conflict between its two most important allies, while at the same time embarking on its own "adventurism" toward South Korea and the United States—perhaps as an attempt to bring the two communist giants together in a common anti-imperialist front, hoping to reaffirm the old tripartite alliance in a new war on the Korean Peninsula. The North Koreans counted on Soviet and Chinese support in a war they saw as inevitable. After all, were not the Chinese and Soviets, despite their differences, united behind the anti-imperialist struggle in Vietnam? In 1965, Kim Il Sung remarked to the outgoing Chinese ambassador, "The political division of the Korean peninsula will not be solved without a war . . . and we will invite your army to fight with us when a war breaks out in the future!"[49]

---

48. Roderick MacFarquhar and Michael Schoenhals, *Mao's Last Revolution* (Cambridge: Belknap Press of Harvard University Press, 2006), 223.

49. Cited in Cheng Xiaohe, "The Evolution of Sino–North Korean Relations in the 1960s," *Asian Perspective* 34, no. 2 (summer 2010): 186.

While the Soviet Union accused China of "dogmatism" in its revolutionary fervor, the Chinese attacked the USSR for "great power chauvinism" or more specifically "social imperialism" (i.e., dressing naked expansionism in the hypocritical language of socialist internationalism). For the Soviets, the Cultural Revolution was dogmatism at its purest; for the Chinese, the Soviet invasion of Czechoslovakia in August 1968 to crush the "Prague Spring" exposed the harsh reality of social imperialism. The Soviet crackdown on the Budapest uprising in 1956 was a cause for concern among the leaders in Beijing and Pyongyang; among other things, the crackdown resulted, as we saw in the previous chapter, in Pyongyang withdrawing North Korea students from Hungary. But Chinese and North Korean anxiety about Soviet intervention in Eastern Europe was not expressed publicly at the time. The Soviet intervention in Czechoslovakia was another matter. Needless to say, neither China nor North Korea was in sympathy with the liberalizing goals of the Czech dissenters. Their concern was with Moscow's blatant military intervention into the affairs of a fellow socialist state. There was no longer any unified front between Moscow and Beijing behind which the Chinese were willing to hide their criticism of Soviet action, as there had been in 1956, and the Chinese media attacked the Czech invasion in the most vitriolic of language. North Korea's response was fairly mild in comparison. On August 23, *Rodong Sinmun* published an article entitled "Historical Lessons We Have Gained from the Study of Affairs in Czechoslovakia."[50] The most important "lesson" was the one North Korea had long emphasized: the inviolable right of all nations to self-determination. Juche was, as much as anything, a position of independence in the Sino-Soviet Cold War.

While China turned inward during the Cultural Revolution, alienating most of its friends in the world (with the exception of Albania, China's ever-faithful if rather useless European ally), the Soviet Union consolidated its grip on Eastern Europe, gained a new foothold in the Caribbean after the Cuban revolution, and tried to enhance its position in Asia. The latter ambition was embodied in a proposed Asian collective security system, articulated by General-Secretary Brezhnev at a speech in Almaty, Kazakhstan, in 1969. As most outside the Soviet bloc saw it, the purpose of this collective security system was to contain China, and no independent Asian country bought into the idea.[51] The North Koreans were careful to justify their lack of interest in the collective security proposal without alienating their Soviet allies. As a representative of the North Korean foreign ministry

---

50. "Historical Lessons We Have Gained from the Study of Affairs in Czechoslovakia," *Rodong Sinmun*, August 23, 1968, 3.

51. Donald Zagoria, "The Soviet Quandary in Asia," *Foreign Affairs* 56, no. 2 (January 1978): 306–23; Elizabeth Wishnick, "Soviet Collective Security Policy for Brezhnev to Gorbachev," *East Asia* 7, no. 3 (September 1988): 3–28.

explained to the Soviet ambassador to Pyongyang, the main reason the DPRK could not join in a collective security system was the state of "direct confrontation with US imperialism" on the Korean Peninsula, which meant "a policy of friendly coexistence on the Korean peninsula is impossible." An Asian collective security system in Asia would fix the territorial boundary between North and South, forgoing unification. Moreover, the DPRK had to consider "the position of China" on this matter.[52] Any marginal benefit North Korea might gain from joining a Soviet-led collective security system was not worth the cost of further alienating the Chinese.

By 1969 North Korea and China were beginning to mind fences after the rupture of the Cultural Revolution, and Moscow could no longer count on Pyongyang's unqualified support. The upswing in Pyongyang-Moscow relations that began in 1965 had been mirrored by a decline in North Korea–China relations; now, North Korea was returning to its preferred position of neutrality (or equidistance) in the Sino-Soviet dispute. When China's vice premier Li Xiannian visited Kim Il Sung in Pyongyang in December 1965, Kim had refused to be pushed into opposing the Soviets. He asked rhetorically, "The Soviet leaders are revisionists, but are they enemies?"[53] One year later, when Kim spoke to Brezhnev at a secret meeting in Vladivostok, Kim decried the Cultural Revolution as "idiocy" yet refused to publicly criticize the Chinese, even though Red Guards had begun their anti–North Korean polemics.[54]

As a classic weak state caught between major powers, North Korea benefited from competition between its two allies but not from dangerous confrontation. Sino-Soviet competition gave North Korea freedom to maneuver, playing off Moscow against Beijing and extracting maximum aid and concessions from both; neither side was willing to risk "losing" North Korea to the other, nor could the Chinese and the Soviets collude to influence Pyongyang, as they had done in the Mikoyan-Peng intervention of 1956 (and even that ultimately failed). But military confrontation between the Soviet Union and China, to say nothing of all-out war (which seemed entirely possible at the end of the 1960s) would be a disaster for the DPRK. North Korea's own tensions with China threatened to escalate into military conflict between 1966 and 1968. By 1969, however, the fervor of the Cultural Revolution had subsided, and China ceased its attacks on North Korea. Ch'oe Yong gŏn stopped in Beijing on his return from Ho Chi Minh's

---

52. GDR Ministry of Foreign Affairs, Far East Department, Korean Section. "Relations between the DPRK and Advanced Capitalist States, 1973–1975." MfAA C 297/78.

53. Chinese Embassy in the DPRK, "Minutes of Meeting between Premier Kim Il Sung and Vice-Premier Li Xiannian," December 26, 1965. CFMA, Document No. 106–01477–4.

54. Cited in Bernd Schaefer, "North Korean 'Adventurism' and China's Long Shadow, 1966–1972," Cold War International History Project Working Paper No. 44 (October 2004), 9.

funeral in September 1969, assuring Chinese leaders that the DPRK did not support Brezhnev's Asian collective security proposal.[55] Four months later DPRK foreign minister Park Sŏng-chŏl met with Zhou Enlai in Beijing, and in April 1970 Zhou traveled to Pyongyang, the first high-ranking Chinese official to visit the North Korean capital since before the Cultural Revolution.[56]

Sino–North Korean rapprochement was in full swing by the beginning of the 1970s, and while the Soviets and their allies were suspicious (as usual) of this rekindled friendship, the Soviet bloc continued its military and economic assistance to the DPRK as a counterbalance to China.[57] The Sino-Soviet conflict reached a peak of violence with bloody border clashes at Damanskii/Zhenbao Island in March 1969, and thereafter the conflict remained rhetorical rather than military.[58] Pyongyang could now maintain normal relations with both its major allies, and count on their support against the South Korean "puppets," the Japanese "militarists," and the American "imperialists." Or so it seemed. Unbeknownst to the North Koreans, the DPRK's closest ally was about to reach out to Pyongyang's greatest enemy, permanently changing the Cold War dynamic around the Korean Peninsula.

Solidarity Shattered: Sino-US Rapprochement and the North-South Accord

Just as the Sino-Soviet conflict was bringing the two communist giants to the brink of war in Asia, Sino-American relations were about to take a dramatic turn that would transform the global Cold War. Much more than US-Soviet détente, also pursued at this time, Sino-American rapprochement would have far-reaching effects on international relations in and around the Korean Peninsula. The North Korean leadership, after some initial hesitation, welcomed Sino-US rapprochement as an American capitulation to Beijing, a signal that US troops would soon leave South Korea and the peninsula would be unified in the North's favor.[59] For the same reason, the South Korean government was deeply troubled by the US overture to China. But in any case there was little Seoul or Pyongyang could do to prevent Sino-US rapprochement, and the two Koreas came together

---

55. Cheng, "Evolution of Sino–North Korean Relations," 193.
56. Schaefer, "North Korean 'Adventurism,'" 30.
57. Ibid., 31.
58. Yang Kuisong, "The Sino-Soviet Border Clash of 1969: From Zhenbao Island to Sino-American *Rapprochement*," *Cold War History* 1, no. 1 (August 2000): 21–52.
59. Bernd Schaefer, "Overconfidence Shattered: North Korean Unification Policy, 1971–1975," North Korea International Documentation Project Working Paper No. 2 (December 2010), 5–6.

through a series of secret meetings to forge a common response to the emerging geopolitical reality of Sino-American (as well as Sino-Japanese) normalization. The response was a historic, if ultimately unfulfilled, joint statement on reunification.

On July 9, 1971, Henry Kissinger, US president Richard Nixon's special advisor for national security affairs, arrived in Beijing to begin secret talks with the Chinese government on Sino-American rapprochement. Seven months later, in February 1972, Nixon himself visited Beijing and met with Mao Zedong, an event that would fundamentally transform the Great Power dynamic of the Cold War from a bipolar confrontation to a triangular relationship among the United States, the USSR, and China.[60] The two major combatants of the Korean War, bitter enemies for two decades, had also been the two closest allies of the rival Korean regimes, and the effect of Sino-American rapprochement on the two Koreas could hardly be overestimated. But Seoul and Pyongyang responded to the rapprochement between their respective patrons in very different ways.

For South Korea's president Park Chung Hee, Nixon's overture to China was yet another sign of American weakness, alongside the looming failure in Vietnam, the announcement of the "Nixon Doctrine" in 1969 that reduced the American security presence in East Asia, and the unilateral withdrawal of twenty thousand of the sixty-two thousand US troops in South Korea in early 1971.[61] As the ROK leadership saw it, America seemed willing to sacrifice its Korean ally in the game of Great Power Realpolitik, and leave it—like South Vietnam—to the mercy of the communists. As a former KCIA officer later recalled, the Park government feared that if the Americans were to normalize relations with Beijing they might "enter into détente with North Korea," or recognize as legitimate pro–North Korean groups in the South, as they would for the pro-Hanoi guerrillas in South Vietnam. Either action would destabilize the South Korean regime and play into Pyongyang's hands.[62] In retrospect, such concerns appear greatly exaggerated if not slightly paranoid: the United States was not about to recognize the DPRK without consulting Seoul, and pro–North Korea guerrilla groups in the South existed mostly in the imaginations of the South and North Korean leaders. But with Washington on the verge of abandoning its two-decade commitment to South Vietnam and ending more than four decades of hostility to China, the

---

60. The Sino-American breakthrough of 1971–73 has produced one of the largest bodies of literature of any event in the history of the Cold War; for firsthand accounts of this event, see especially Willam Burr, ed., *The Kissinger Transcripts: The Top-Secret Talks with Beijing and Moscow* (New York: The New Press, 1998), 59–123.

61. See Joo-Hong Nam, *America's Commitment to South Korea: The First Decade of the Nixon Doctrine* (Cambridge: Cambridge University Press, 1986).

62. Christian F. Ostermann and James F. Person, *The Rise and Fall of Détente on the Korean Peninsula, 1970–1974* (Washington, DC: Woodrow Wilson International Center for Scholars, 2011), 17.

previously stable realities of the Cold War were rapidly crumbling in East Asia, and almost anything seemed possible.

North Korea had two Great Power allies, rather than one, but this was small comfort, as both the USSR and China were attempting to improve their relations with the United States in the early 1970s. DPRK relations with the Soviet Union, however, had been tarnished by Soviet "revisionism"—as the North Koreans saw it—since the 1950s, and peaceful coexistence between Moscow and Washington was nothing new. Despite the strains in Sino-DPRK relations during the Cultural Revolution in the late 1960s, China at least had taken a consistently hostile position vis-à-vis the United States, putting it in the same anti-imperialist camp as North Korea. For China to welcome the American president and talk of rapprochement was much more difficult for the DPRK leadership to accept than US-Soviet détente. Nixon in China was all too reminiscent of Khrushchev in Washington more than a decade earlier. Sino-American rapprochement had troubling implications for small communist states outside the Soviet bloc, who had relied on China to stand up to the "American imperialists"; as Albania's Enver Hoxha put it in his memoirs, this development "fell like a bombshell on us Albanians, on the Vietnamese, the Koreans, not to mention the others."[63] That is not, however, the way the North Koreans expressed their view of these new developments at the time. Both publicly through its official media and privately to its socialist allies, Pyongyang presented Sino-US rapprochement as a great opportunity to advance its interest on the Korean Peninsula and beyond.

North Korean relations with both China and the Soviet Union had been on the upswing before Nixon's visit. On April 5, 1970, Chinese premier Zhou Enlai visited Pyongyang, the highest-ranking PRC official to visit North Korea since 1963.[64] Three weeks later, a Soviet military delegation led by Marshal Matvei Zakharov arrived in Pyongyang, the highest-ranking such delegation to visit North Korea since 1965. The Soviet Union and North Korea signed a new economic cooperation agreement in September 1970, and talks on Soviet-DPRK economic cooperation continued the following January.[65] While it could not match the level of Soviet economic cooperation, China gave new military equipment, including fighter planes and tanks. In the months after the Nixon visit, both China and the USSR exchanged high-level delegations with the DPRK and

---

63. Jon Halliday, ed., *The Artful Albanian: Memoirs of Enver Hoxha* (London: Chatto & Windus, 1986), 285.

64. Wayne Kiyosaki, *North Korean Foreign Relations: The Politics of Accommodation, 1945–1975* (New York: Praeger, 1976), 88; *Zhou Enlai Nianpu* [Chronological Record of Zhou Enlai], vol. 3 (Beijing: Zhongyang wenpian chubanshe, 1997), 360–61.

65. Chin O. Chung, *Pyongyang between Peking and Moscow: North Korea's Involvement in the Sino-Soviet Dispute, 1958–1975* (Tuscaloosa: University of Alabama Press, 1978), 138–39.

promised more economic and military aid. Clearly, North Korea still benefited from the competition between the Soviet Union and China, each of which feared losing influence over North Korea to its rival, the Sino-Soviet rivalry further complicated by this new US-Soviet-Chinese triangular relationship.

Although the Chinese leadership had not told the North Koreans (or any of China's allies) in advance of the Beijing-Washington talks, they assured the North Koreans that Sino-US rapprochement was an opportunity for the DPRK. In mid-July 1971, not long after meeting with Kissinger in Beijing, Zhou Enlai visited Pyongyang and discussed the US-China meetings at length.[66] Zhou had suggested to Kissinger that US troops could be withdrawn from South Korea after the end of the Indochina war and the departure of ROK troops from Vietnam.[67] The Beijing leadership was after all expecting Sino-US talks to lead to an American military withdrawal from Taiwan (which ultimately happened, albeit several years later), and US withdrawal from Indochina was on the horizon. The United States was in retreat in Asia, a development welcomed by China and North Korea alike. President Nixon, declared the DPRK, would come to Beijing waving a "white flag" of surrender.[68] And American surrender to China would mean defeat for South Korea, and final victory for the North.

It was in this context, with China reaffirming its alliance with the DPRK and raising North Korea's hopes for an American military withdrawal from the South, that Kim Il Sung publicly announced the possibility of direct North-South dialogue for the first time. The occasion was a rally in Pyongyang honoring Norodom Sihanouk, the former Cambodian head of state and a close friend of Kim's, on August 16, 1971.[69] Kim declared that the DPRK was "ready to establish contact at any time with all political parties [in South Korea], including the [ruling] Democratic Republican Party, and all social organizations and individual personages in South Korea."[70] The ROK did not respond officially,

66. Chen Jian, *Mao's China and the Cold War* (Chapel Hill: University of North Carolina Press, 2001), 269.

67. United States Department of State, *Foreign Relations of the United States, 1969–1972*, vol. 17, *China, 1969–1972* (Washington, DC: US Government Printing Office, 2006), 390. Cited in Schaefer, "Overconfidence Shattered," 6.

68. Chen, *Mao's China and the Cold War*, 275. A North Korean delegation visited Beijing in January 1972, and some officials remained in the Chinese capital during Nixon's visit in late February. Kim Il Sung himself visited Beijing secretly in early February to help finalize a common PRC-DPRK position on the Korea Question for the Chinese to present to Nixon. But while the Chinese kept the DPRK officials appraised of the Sino-US talks, North Korean delegates never met with any of Nixon's entourage. GDR Embassy to DPRK, "Note on a Conversation with the First Secretary of the USSR Embassy, Comrade Kurbatov, on 10 March 1972 in the GDR Embassy," MfAA, C 1080/78. Obtained for the North Korea International Documentation Project by Bernd Schaefer.

69. Oberdorfer, *The Two Koreas*, 12. Prince Sihanouk had been a frequent visitor to Pyongyang since the 1960s, and Kim Il Sung gave him a summer villa in North Korea which the prince (later king) used until long after Kim's death in 1994.

70. Ibid.

but a few weeks later the two sides began talks on humanitarian exchanges between North and South Korea via their respective Red Cross delegations at the truce village of Panmunjŏm. The Red Cross talks did not bear fruit with regard to their ostensible purpose, but undercover intelligence operatives of the two regimes met secretly during these talks and proposed separate talks between high-level intelligence personnel. These secret talks continued through eleven rounds, until March 1972, when the Korean Workers' Party established direct (but still secret) links to the Korean Central Intelligence Agency (KCIA), South Korea's notorious domestic security organization. The head of the KCIA, Yi Hu-rak, was a former officer in the Japanese army and the second-most powerful man in South Korea.

In early May 1972, Yi traveled to Pyongyang and met with Kim Il Sung himself. At their meeting, which began shortly after midnight on May 2 (Kim apologized for his habit of working late) the two men discussed the changing international situation, the problem of both their regimes' dependence on foreign powers, and need for the two Koreas to unite as one nation. The meeting was cordial and mutually complimentary. Yi praised Kim for his youthful patriotism as described in the anti-Japanese opera the South Koreans had seen earlier that day.[71] Kim expressed regret for the attempted assassination of Park Chung Hee in 1968, claiming that the Blue House raid "was entirely plotted by extreme leftists and did not reflect my intent or that of the Party." Kim assured his South Korean guests that the people behind the "incident" had been demoted and moved elsewhere. Kim asked Yi to convey his best wishes for President Park's health and also to convey the message that unification must be achieved peacefully, without the interference of foreign powers; that a formula for unification must be found that transcended existing ideological and social differences between North and South; and that such a formula for unification could be achieved through continued discussions.[72]

After Yi's return to the South, the North Koreans sent their deputy premier, Pak Sŏng-chŏl, to meet with President Park in Seoul. President Park greeted the DPRK official as warmly as Kim Il Sung had welcomed Yi Hu-rak and expressed his support for peaceful and independent unification. He was, however, somewhat cautious about how quickly unification could proceed. "Reunification is not a matter to rush," the president remarked. "I would like to visit Pyongyang and enjoy *naengmyŏn* [cold noodles, a northern specialty] with my family.

71. Presumably *Sea of Blood*, one of the revolutionary operas developed under the guidance of Kim Jong Il, which had just premiered the previous year.

72. Republic of Korea Foreign Ministry Archive, "Conversation with Kim Il Sung," May 4, 1972. Obtained for the North Korea International Documentation Project by Shin Jongdae and translated by Song Jihei.

However . . . desire and reality are different matters."[73] With the leaders of both Korean states communicating through intermediaries, the stage was set for the first North-South join statement on unification.

The result of these secret negotiations, like the secret overtures between China and the United States to which the Koreans were directly responding, was an agreement that surprised much of the world, including the vast majority of the people in both North and South Korea, who had been given no advanced warning: a joint statement on peaceful unification, signed by the leaders of the two Korean governments. The statement was released on July 4, 1972, a date presumably chosen to demonstrate the two Koreas' "Declaration of Independence" from the Great Powers, and from the Cold War itself. The Joint Declaration was a brief, simple statement emphasizing three principles:

1) Unification should be achieved independently, without reliance on or interference from outside forces;
2) Unification should be achieved through peaceful means, without recourse to the use of arms against the other side;
3) Korea being a homogeneous nation, great national unity should transcend differences of ideas, ideologies, and systems.

The language of the Joint Declaration largely followed the principles Kim Il Sung had outlined to Yi Hu-rak in May 1972, and the "Three Principles of National Unification" soon became a quasi-sacred text in the DPRK, attributed solely to Kim and eventually embodied in a massive concrete monument erected south of Pyongyang in 2001.[74]

The July 4 communiqué was ultimately more important for its symbolic value than any concrete results, and the initial atmosphere of euphoria about imminent unification would within a year revert to one of mutual suspicion, acrimony, and disillusionment. After just a half-dozen meetings of the new South-North Coordinating Committee the two sides reached an impasse. The talks were downgraded to vice chairman level in August 1973 and suspended altogether in 1975. Unlike the two Germanies, which sustained wide-ranging contacts and communication from the early 1970s onward, the two Koreas made virtually no progress in their relationship following the 1972 declaration. It would take another two decades, and an even more astonishing change in the international system—the collapse of the Soviet Union and the end of the Cold War—before North-South relations would make another significant breakthrough.

---

73. Republic of Korea Foreign Ministry Archive, "Conversation between Park Chung Hee and Pak Sŏng-ch'ŏl," May 31, 1972. Obtained for the North Korea International Documentation Project by Shin Jongdae and translated by Song Jihei.

74. See the official DPRK website, http://www.korea-dpr.com/reunification.html.

Seoul and Pyongyang entered into their historic negotiations proclaiming mutual respect and peaceful coexistence, but without relinquishing the game of competitive legitimation they had been playing since 1948. The South Korean government approached the talks from a position of greater vulnerability, no longer certain that the United States would guarantee South Korea's security and seeking a modus vivendi with Pyongyang out of necessity for survival. The North Koreans entered inter-Korean talks confident that history and their allies were on their side, closely coordinating their actions and statements with China.[75] The Chinese had expressed support for North Korea's eight-point program for Korean unification, and for the abolition of the UN Commission for the Unification and Rehabilitation of Korea (UNCURK), in the US-PRC Shanghai communiqué.[76] The Americans made no reciprocal remark supporting a South Korean position. A partial US troop withdrawal from Korea was imminent, and a complete withdrawal could eventually follow. American defeat in Indochina was all but declared. If, as the North Koreans argued, South Korea were an artificial nation propped up by the United States, the removal of American support would mean the end of South Korea. The "revolutionary base" in the North would finally claim the victory denied it by the Americans in 1950.

When Yi Hu-rak visited Pyongyang again in November 1972, Kim Il Sung assured him that the two Koreas were not in a state of mutual confrontation. "Confrontation means to compete with one another," Kim said. "Competition results in winners and losers. We shouldn't win or lose, don't you think?"[77] But Kim told his socialist allies a very different story, one that portrayed the North as the inevitable victor on the Korean Peninsula. When Romanian leader Nicolae Ceausescu visited Pyongyang in June 1971, Kim reminded Ceausescu that North Korea was the "liberated half of the country, but the other half is under still under occupation." Nevertheless, in South Korea "the intelligentsia is carrying out revolutionary activities" and creating a common front with the North, leading toward unification.[78] Two weeks after the North-South communiqué was announced, DPRK vice foreign minister Lee Man-sŏk briefed the Soviet-bloc ambassadors

75. The DPRK informed Beijing about the North-South secret visits and the text of the July 4 Declaration well before they told the Soviets and East Europeans, who did not receive confirmation of the inter-Korean talks until July 3, 1972. Schaefer, "Overconfidence Shattered," 11

76. United States Department of State, *FRUS 1969–1976*, Vol. 17, *China, 1969–1972, Document 203*. Available at http://history.state.gov/historicaldocuments/frus1969–76v17/d203. UNCURK was abolished in 1973 after the two Koreas were each given observer status at the United Nations.

77. Republic of Korea Foreign Ministry Archive, "Conversation with Kim Il Sung," November 3, 1972. Obtained for the North Korea International Documentation Project by Shin Jongdae, translated by Song Jihei.

78. Archives of the Central Committee of the Romanian Communist Party, "Minutes of Conversation on the Occasion of the Party and Government Delegation on Behalf of the Romanian Socialist Republic to the Democratic People's Republic of Korea," June 10, 1971. Obtained and translated for the North Korea International Documentation Project by Eliza Gheorghe.

in Pyongyang about the state of inter-Korean affairs. Repeating Kim Il Sung's statements at the Fourth Plenum of the Korean Worker's Party, Lee predicted that "when the South Korean clique receives no more aid from the United States and Japan, it will turn to us, the DPRK." He implored the fraternal socialist countries both to support the North-South dialogue and to "further isolat[e] the South Korean puppets."[79] Even after inter-Korean talks had broken down in 1973, Kim Il Sung assured Bulgarian leader Todor Zhivkov that the DPRK would continue to push for confederation, not because he believed long-term coexistence was possible but because if the South Koreans "listen to us and a confederation is established, South Korea will be done with."[80] With the Americans gone and the South Korean military reduced in a confederal system, Kim argued, the South Korean people would rise up against their oppressors and embrace the DPRK.

At the end of 1972, both the Republic of Korea and the Democratic People's Republic of Korea adopted new constitutions that seemed designed to move the regimes farther apart rather than closer together. Both constitutions consolidated more power in the hands of the top leader. Both modified the organization of the legislature. The North Korean constitution acknowledged for the first time that Pyongyang, not Seoul, was the capital of the DRPK and characterized the country as "socialist." In short, the regimes in both South and North Korea were reaffirming their distinct identities at the same time that they were discussing unification, indicating again that North-South relations were characterized more by competitive legitimation than by compromise. Both regimes wanted to deal with each other from a position of strength. But while constitutional revision occurred in both Koreas at the same time, in the midst of the same shifts in regional geopolitics, the domestic circumstances giving rise to these constitutional changes were utterly different. The Park Chung Hee regime in the South was under great strain by the early 1970s, facing a determined opposition led by Kim Dae Jung, who won over 45 percent of the vote in the presidential election of April 1971 despite the enormous financial and coercive advantages of the Park campaign. The National Assembly election of May 1971, which saw decisive opposition victories in the major cities, was an even greater setback for the Park regime.[81]

---

79. GDR Embassy to DPRK, "Note on Information from DPRK Deputy Foreign Minister, Comrade Lee Man-sok, on 17 July 1972 between 16:40 and 18:00 in the Foreign Ministry," 20 July 1972. MfAA C 951/76. Obtained for North Korea International Documentation Project by Bernd Schaefer and translated by Karen Riechert.

80. "Memorandum of Conversation between Todor Zhivkov, First Secretary of the Central Committee of the Bulgarian Communist Party and Chairman of the State Council of Bulgaria, and Kim Il Sung, President and Secretary General of the North Korean Workers' Party," 20 October 1973. Translated and reproduced in Ostermann and Person, *Rise and Fall of Détente*, 259.

81. Hyug Baeg Im, "The Origins of the *Yushin* Regime: Machiavelli Unveiled," in Byung-kook Kim and Ezra F. Vogel, eds., *The Park Chung Hee Era: The Transformation of South Korea* (Cambridge: Harvard University Press, 2011), 245.

Park's unprecedented vulnerability on the home front was exacerbated by America's military retreat in Asia and overtures toward China, which undermined South Korea's defense from external threats—above all North Korea. In part at least, Park's aggrandizement of power in 1972 was an attempt to strengthen his regime against the militarized and unified North and the dictatorial leadership of Kim Il Sung. Yi Hu-rak himself was tasked in early 1972 with finding suitable models of stable authoritarian rule, sending study missions to Taiwan, Spain, Argentina, and other "constitutional dictatorships" that could offer useful lessons for President Park.[82] If North Korea described itself at the time as "monolithic" (*yuil*), South Korea under Park would be "revitalized" (*yushin*). Park had long been an unabashed of admirer of Meiji Japan (1868–1912), and applied the same term the Japanese had used for the Meiji "Restoration" (pronounced *ishin* in Japanese, *yushin* in Korean) to his own dictatorial regime. Park declared martial law in December 1971, dissolved the National Assembly and suspended the constitution in October 1972, and promulgated the Yushin Constitution—and with it, the Fourth Republic of Korea—on November 21. The new constitution granted the president power to appoint a large part of the National Assembly and effectively enabled him to stay in office indefinitely. The two Koreas would now face each other on a more equal footing, at least until Park was assassinated in 1979 by his own chief of intelligence. South Korea may have become a dictatorship, but it was much less "monolithic" and stable than the North.

Equality with its Korean opposite number may have been one motivation for North Korea's constitutional change, but probably not a major one. Promulgated in December 1972, the new DPRK constitution gave Kim Il Sung a new title, "president" (*Chusŏk*), a term different from but equal in status to the South Korean term for president (*Taet'ongyŏng*).[83] Although Kim remained general-secretary of the party, he would henceforth be referred to in official communications mainly as president, and in popular parlance as *Suryŏng*: supreme leader or chief. Unlike Park Chung Hee, Kim Il Sung did not consolidate his constitutional power in 1972 out of a sense of insecurity. On the contrary, Kim's power was unassailable and had been since at least 1967, when the last major leadership purge took place. The DPRK "Socialist" Constitution, unlike the South Korean "Yushin" Constitution, did not announce a new regime but articulated the principles of a regime firmly in place. Kim's personal rule and North Korea's "monolithic system" faced no significant internal threats, and North Korea could count on the

---

82. Ostermann and Person, *Rise and Fall of Détente*, 82.

83. Sŏ Tae-suk [Dae-Sook Suh], *Puk Han munhŏn yŏngu: munhŏn kwa haeje* [A Study of North Korean Documents: Documents and Analysis], vol. 6, *Society and Law* (Seoul: Institute for Far Eastern Studies, Kyungnam University, 2004), 386–87.

support of its major allies in dealing with the challenges of a rapidly changing regional environment. Circumstances on the Korean Peninsula, in eastern Asia, and in the world as a whole seemed to reflect the declining fortunes of "American imperialism" and the advance of a broad (if not always unified) anti-imperialist front. Riding what looked to be an unstoppable wave of history, a newly confident DPRK was ready to break out into the world.

BREAKING OUT

Engaging the First and Third Worlds, 1972–79

> **One thing the United States lacks is a unified national will, defined, analyzed, formulated, and articulated by a leader of genius. Such a leader is Comrade Kim Il Sung.**
>
> —Eldridge Cleaver, 1972

> **The Non-Alignment Movement is a mighty anti-imperialist revolutionary force of our times.**
>
> —Kim Il Sung, December 1975

The 1970s were a decade of unprecedented outward expansion for North Korea. Admission to several UN bodies, active lobbying at the UN General Assembly, a successful diplomatic offensive in the Third World, and new economic and political ties to advanced capitalist countries all reflected a new global presence for the DPRK. Long a partisan of the socialist side in the global Cold War, Kim Il Sung presented his country in this decade as "nonaligned," and a model for postcolonial nation-building. North Korea broke out into the world in the 1970s, and in a sense, this breakout was its pursuit of what later would be called "globalization," foreshadowing South Korea's globalization, or *segyewha* policy, of the early 1990s. But it was a peculiar and limited kind of globalization. The ultimate failure of North Korea's pursuit of globalization *avant la lettre* was perhaps inevitable, reflecting the contradiction between North Korea's stated policy of Juche and the necessary requirements for active engagement in the international system, particularly the global economy. International engagement without significant internal reform or opening had some success until about the mid-1970s, especially in North Korea's Third World diplomacy, but North Korea's rise in the world would sputter out in the early 1980s, before crashing spectacularly at the end of the decade.

The Search for Capital

Amidst a thawing Cold War divide and changing domestic economic priorities, North Korea turned to advanced capitalist countries for trade and investment.

North Korea's commitment to the struggle against imperialism never officially wavered, but as the DPRK tried to develop its economy beyond the initial postwar reconstruction stage of the late 1950s and early 1960s, fellow socialist nations were unable to offer North Korea the capital and advanced technology it desired. Until the 1970s, the vast majority of North Korea's foreign trade—nearly 90 percent in 1966, according to the CIA—was with other communist countries. China and the USSR alone comprised nearly three-quarters of North Korea's total trade in the late 1960s.[1] But from about 1962, following the conclusion of postwar reconstruction and the sharp drop in developmental assistance from the USSR and the East bloc, North Korean trade with noncommunist countries steadily increased. The first capitalist country North Korea turned to for trade and investment was its former colonizer, Japan.[2] This may not be as paradoxical as it seems. Japan's proximity, its wealth and technological sophistication, and the presence of a large community of ethnic Korean sympathizers to act as intermediaries, made Japan a more desirable economic partner than any other capitalist state, and certainly much more than archrival South Korea, still lagging behind the North economically in the 1960s. Despite lack of diplomatic relations and ongoing North Korean propaganda about the threat of Japanese "militarism," Japan soon became North Korea's most important noncommunist trading partner. Trade with Japan constituted almost one-half of North Korea's trade with the noncommunist world in the mid-1960s, and Japan would remain North Korea's largest capitalist trading partner for decades to come, until South Korea surpassed it in the 2000s.[3]

North Korean trade with the "Free World" rose dramatically with the relaxation of Cold War hostilities in the early 1970s. Having mended fences with China after the easing of the Cultural Revolution in that country, and enjoying a period of good relations with the USSR at the same time, the DPRK appears

The epigraphs are from Eldridge Cleaver, forward to *Juche! The Speeches and Writings of Kim Il Sung*, edited and introduce by Li Yuk-Sa (New York: Grossman Publishers, 1972), ix–x; and "The Non-Alignment Movement is a Mighty Anti-Imperialist Revolutionary Force of Our Times," *Guidebook to the Third World* (Argentina, 16 December 1975); reprinted in Kim Il Sung, *The Non-Alignment Movement is a Mighty Anti-Imperialist Revolutionary Force of Our Times* (Pyongyang: Foreign Languages Publishing House, 1976), 317–22.

1. Central Intelligence Agency, Directorate of Intelligence, Memorandum: "North Korea's Foreign Trade," 26 January 1968, 1. CIA Records Search Tool (CREST), CIA-RDP85T00875R001500220012–5. Washington, DC: National Archives and Records Administration.

2. North Korea first began to trade with Japan through the Bank of China (BOC) in the late 1950s. The BOC also facilitated North Korean trade with Britain and France beginning in 1957, and with West Germany and Switzerland in 1958. Direct trade with Japan and Western Europe was not established until the mid-1960s. Natalia Bazhanova, *Kiroe sŏn Puk Han kyŏngje* [North Korean Economy at the Crossroads], trans. Yang Chun-yong (Seoul: Korea Economic Daily, 1992), 247–49.

3. CIA, "North Korea's Foreign Trade," 3. In the first decade of the twenty-first century, South Korea became North Korea's second-largest trading partner after China.

to have felt secure enough to pursue its own version of détente with the West in an atmosphere of a global reduction in East-West tensions. While North Korea sent some feelers to the United States on reducing mutual hostilities in the early 1970s, and signed an unprecedented joint communiqué with South Korea in July 1972, the main focus of its new First World diplomacy was to establish and expand economic ties with Western Europe and Japan.[4]

Kim Il Sung claimed at this time that the DPRK was willing to engage with "all countries," implicitly including its chief adversary the United States. In 1972, Kim Il Sung granted his first interview with American journalists at major US newspapers, Harrison Salisbury of the *New York Times* and Selig Harrison of the *Washington Post*.[5] In his lengthy and wide-ranging discussion with Salisbury, excerpted in the *Times*, Kim Il Sung criticized America's "unfriendly attitude" toward the DPRK and called repeatedly for the withdrawal of US forces from the South and the dissolution of the UN Command.[6] As Kim put it, in a phrase that would be used almost verbatim in North Korean talks with the United States over the next several decades, "If the United States government stops its unfriendly attitude toward us and stops obstructing the unification of our country, then there is no reason why we should have hostile attitudes toward the United States." Kim also stressed the threat of Japan and the US-Japan alliance to the security of the DPRK. He had nothing good to say about the government in South Korea, although he did not attack the Park Chung Hee regime in the colorful language of contemporary DPRK propaganda. Above all, Kim stressed the need for the peaceful and independent unification of Korea. Even China and the Soviet Union had no direct role to play in this process, Kim said. The Korean question "must be left to the Koreans to solve for themselves without any interference by outside forces on the basis of national self-determination." This too was a recurrent refrain of the DPRK that would long outlive the Cold War.

---

4. North Korea had its own idiosyncratic take on the division of the world's countries into "First" (advanced capitalist) "Second" (Marxist-Leninist socialist) and "Third" (developing) worlds, which reversed the usual order of first and second worlds. As the DPRK understood it, the First World was the socialist states, the Second World consisted of the imperialist and advanced capitalist states, and the Third World was the developing nations. GDR Embassy in DPRK, 29 July 1977. "Notes on Conversation with chargé d'affaires of the People's Republic of Bulgaria, Comrade Apostolov, on 27 July 1977 in the Embassy of the GDR." Apostolov is reporting the words of one Kil Chŏn-ch'ŭl of the KWP Central Committee. MfAA C6854. This was different in turn from Mao Zedong's Three Worlds theory, which placed both superpowers in the First World, Soviet and American allies in the Second World, and nonaligned nations in the Third World. See Ministry of Foreign Affairs of the People's Republic of China, "Chairman Mao Zedong's Theory on the Division of the Three World and the Strategy of Forming an Alliance against an Opponent." Available at http://www.fmprc.gov.cn/eng/ziliao/3602/3604/t18008.htm.

5. See "Talk with Journalists of the US Newspaper, *New York Times*," in Kim Il Sung, *For the Independent Peaceful Reunification of Korea* (New York: International Publishers, 1975), 157–72.

6. "Excerpts from Interview with North Korea Premier on Policy towards US," *New York Times*, May 31, 1972.

This was the only interview Kim would give to the *Times*, but not the only North Korean contribution to the newspaper. In 1973 the DPRK began paying for full-page advertisements in the *New York Times*, something it would continue to do on occasion until the 1990s. The effect of these very expensive advertisements on American public opinion was probably negligible, but if nothing else they provided good material for internal DPRK propaganda. The North Korean letters to the *New York Times* were permanently displayed in the International Friendship Exhibition Hall north of Pyongyang, as a sign that even America respected Great Leader Kim Il Sung. The fact that these were advertisements paid for by the DPRK was not mentioned. More concretely, the Americans began to respond to North Korea's call for direct contacts, in consultation with their allies in Seoul, and North Korean diplomats met with their American counterparts at the US Liaison Office in Beijing on at least one occasion.[7] The Nixon administration anticipated dramatically new diplomatic and security arrangements on the Korean Peninsula, and in March 1974 the president decided to seek the abolition of the UN Command and its replacement with US and South Korean military commanders, enabling direct North-South military negotiations through the Military Armistice Commission; a "Shanghai-type communiqué" leading to the complete withdrawal of US forces from Korea; and a nonaggression pact between the two Koreas.[8]

As it turned out, hopes for US-North Korean rapprochement were short-lived. After a brief thaw in US-DPRK relations in the early 1970s, rapprochement was soon lost in the renewed hostility between North and South, the American commitment to the deepening dictatorship in Seoul, and the resurgent military buildup in North Korea.[9] By the middle of the decade, Seoul-Pyongyang relations had shifted again to confrontation, while US-DPRK tensions reached new heights. This process culminated in the most dangerous US-DPRK confrontation since the *Pueblo* Incident in 1968: the DMZ "axe-murder incident" of August 1976, a grim example of how a minor disagreement in a highly volatile environment can bring countries to the brink of war.[10]

---

7. Telegram from Ambassador Habib to Henry Kissinger, "US-North Korean Contacts," 24 August 1973. Reproduced in Christian F. Ostermann and James F. Person, eds., *After Détente: The Korean Peninsula, 1973–1976* (Washington, DC: North Korea International Documentation Project, Woodrow Wilson International Center for Scholars, 2011), 71. See also Christian F. Ostermann and James F. Person, *The Rise and Fall of Détente on the Korean Peninsula, 1970–1974* (Washington, DC: Woodrow Wilson International Center for Scholars, 2011), 37.

8. Nixon Presidential Library, National Security Council Institutional Files: National Security Study Memorandums: Diplomatic Initiatives in Korea, box H-201, Folder NSSM 190.

9. Citing a retrospective US military study, Don Oberdorfer suggests that the 1972–77 period saw the greatest growth in the North Korean armed forces since the Korean War. Oberdorfer, *The Two Koreas: A Contemporary History* (New York: Basic Books, 1997), 59.

10. Adrian Buzo, *Guerrilla Dynasty: Politics and Leadership in North Korea* (Boulder, CO: Westview Press, 1999), 99.

On August 18, a mixed team of American and South Korean military personnel attempted to trim a large poplar standing in the Joint Security Area in the DMZ, which blocked the view between two of their guard posts. A group of North Korean soldiers came upon the scene and asked them to stop. The Americans and South Koreans refused. Tempers escalated, words leading to threats leading to blows, and in the ensuing melee the senior American officer, Captain Arthur Bonifas, was beaten to death by North Korean soldiers with iron clubs and an axe. The US platoon commander in the area, Lieutenant Mark Barett, was also killed, and several other Americans and South Koreans present were injured.

North Korean media claimed that the DMZ clash was provoked by the Americans as part of their plan to "start a new war of aggression in Korea." The DPRK declared a state of emergency (as did South Korea) and practically defied the United States to attack, vowing to "crush the aggressor" if war came.[11] News of the "Panmunjŏm axe murder incident" evoked immediate outrage in Washington. National Security Advisor Henry Kissinger convened a Washington Special Actions Group meeting in the White House Situation Room to discuss possible US responses, from laying mines to dropping bombs to seizing a North Korean naval vessel. Although the group was leery of taking direct military action lest the situation escalate to a full-scale war, Kissinger and company wanted to send a message to Pyongyang that such atrocities would not be tolerated, to punish North Korea in some way, and "to return to [the] area of incident and chop down the goddamned tree."[12] The White House ordered the raising of US and ROK alert status, and deployed fighter planes, bombers, and the aircraft carrier *Midway* to Korea. In the end military action was averted, and on August 21 the United States ordered "Operation Paul Bunyan" to remove the offending poplar once and for all.[13] By early September, after several discussions between American and North Korean officials under the auspices of the UN Military Armistice Commission in Panmunjŏm, the North Koreans had satisfied the Americans by expressing "regret" for the incident, guaranteeing the safety of US personnel, and offering to withdraw four guard posts from the area.[14]

---

11. Korean Central New Agency, "US, DPRK DMZ Guards Clash at Panmunjom, 18 August 1976 "; Archives of the Romanian Ministry of Foreign Affairs, "Telegram from Pyongyang to Bucharest, SECRET, Urgent, No. 067.212," 21 August 1974. Obtained by Izador Urian and translated for the North Korea International Documentation Project by Eliza Gheorghe. Reproduced in Ostermann and Person, eds., *After Détente*, 662, 701.

12. Washington Special Actions Group Meeting, "Korea," 18 August 1976; Memorandum for Brent Scowcroft from W. G. Hyland, "WSAG Meeting," 18 August 1976. Reproduced in Ostermann and Person, eds., *After Détente*, 663–74.

13. Oberdorfer, *The Two Koreas*, 74–83.

14. Memorandum for President Ford from William G. Hyland, "Revision of the Korean DMZ Agreement," 5 September 1976. Reproduced in Ostermann and Person, eds., *After Détente*, 737–38.

In retrospect it seems bizarre, and somewhat darkly comical, that a tree-trimming venture could almost trigger a second Korean War. But in the context of a deepening crisis between the two Koreas and a renewed US military commitment to the South, both sides were on edge over the military balance on the peninsula. Just a few months earlier, the United States and ROK had jointly staged the first Team Spirit exercises, a massive set of military maneuvers that have continued regularly since that time, and that Pyongyang has consistently denounced as a needlessly provocative rehearsal for an invasion of North Korea. The furor over the August Incident soon died down, but it had effectively scuttled any remaining hopes that US-DPRK relations would lead to a breakthrough anytime soon.

Among the "Anglo-Saxon" countries (the United States, United Kingdom, Canada, Australia, and New Zealand), Australia was the only country to establish full diplomatic relations with the DPRK before the late 1990s.[15] But Canberra-Pyongyang relations were very short-lived indeed, lasting less then a year, from December 1974 to October 1975. Australia and North Korea had long been on sharply opposed sides in the Cold War conflict. Australia had contributed seventeen thousand troops to the UN side in the Korean War, including its air force, and had also been the only Western ally to send combat troops to help the Americans in Vietnam. Australia was furthermore allied to the United States and New Zealand (and indirectly to South Korea and Japan) through the anticommunist ANZUS treaty, signed in 1951. But with the withdrawal of Australian troops from Vietnam in late 1971 and the election of a Labour government in 1972, Australian relations with its Asian communist neighbors changed significantly. Canberra normalized relations with the People's Republic of China in 1972, and in July 1974 Australia signed an agreement on diplomatic normalization with North Korea as well. The DPRK opened its embassy in Canberra in December 1974, and Australia reciprocated in April 1975. Six months later, on October 30, 1975, North Korea suddenly closed its embassy in Australia. Six days after that, Pyongyang expelled the Australian diplomats from the DPRK.[16]

The reasons for the sudden breakdown in relations remain something of a mystery. Speculation and rumor abounded, ranging from unflattering photographs of North Korean children taken by members of the Australian embassy staff in Pyongyang to Canberra's continued support for Seoul in the UN General Assembly. Whatever the causes may have been, the sudden collapse of relations with Australia meant the end of Pyongyang's only diplomatic success in the

---

15. By the early 2000s, the United States was the only member of this group *not* to have diplomatic relations with the DPRK.

16. Leonid A. Petrov, "Australia and the DPRK: A Sixty-Year Relationship," *Pacific Focus* 23, no. 3 (December 2008): 318–20.

Anglo-Saxon world during the Cold War period, and Australia and the DPRK would not resume diplomatic relations again until the summer of 2000.

Beyond North America and Australia, relations with advanced capitalist states, which North Korea idiosyncratically—but understandably, given its history—labeled the "Second World," showed some promise in the first half of the decade. Between 1970 and 1975, North Korea signed nearly $600 million dollars' worth of contracts with Japanese and West European companies.[17] The breakthrough year for DPRK contact with the West was 1972. Among European countries, France initially seemed the most promising trade partner, although among all capitalist states, West Germany came third in volume of trade with North Korea, after Japan and France.[18] Just as it had done with Soviet-bloc states in Europe, North Korea exported raw materials, especially metals (magnesite, copper, zinc, silver, etc.) to West Germany, and imported manufactured goods, machines, and chemical works. Indeed West Germany filled some of the same industrial niches East Germany had done fifteen years earlier: for example, a West German–Austrian joint venture established a chemical fertilizer plant in Hamhŭng, a city reconstructed by East German technicians after the Korean War, and where Japanese private capital had established Korea's largest chemical fertilizer plant during the colonial period. In effect, West German companies like Siemans, Mannesmann-Export AG, and Gute-Hoffnungshuette in the 1970s were updating North Korean industries originally built by the Japanese in the 1930s and rebuilt by the East Germans in the 1950s.

But it was France that played the role most analogous to East Germany in the post–Korean War period; or at least that was the French and North Korean intention. In 1972, the DPRK and French firms negotiated the construction of a chemical works in North Korea, worth 400 million francs, to be built between 1974 and 1979. When completed, the factory was expected to produce thirty thousand tons of polyethylene per year. Much like the East German specialists during the Hamhŭng project in the 1950s, some two hundred French technicians and their families were to come to North Korea during this period, and the North Koreans promised the French "good living conditions" while they resided and worked in the DPRK. The site of these negotiations, and of the proposed chemical works, was Hamhŭng.[19] Unlike the East German

---

17. Central Intelligence Agency Memorandum, "North Korean Payments Problem with the West," June 1975. CREST, CIA-RDP86T00608R000600050021–9. Washington, DC: National Archives and Records Administration.

18. GDR Embassy in Pyongyang, Political Section. "Information on Contact between the DPRK and FRG," 28 May 1973. MfAA C/297/78.

19. GDR Embassy in DPRK, Political Section. "Excerpt from Conversation with Comrade Gula, Third Secretary of the CSSR," 21 December 1972. MfAA C/297/78.

project, however, it seems that the North Korean–French partnership never achieved concrete results.[20]

As DPRK vice foreign minister Shim Tong-hae explained in a briefing to Soviet diplomats, North Korean trade with France had been publicly inaugurated at the end of 1972.[21] In November of that year, politicians from the foreign affairs commission of the French National Assembly were invited to North Korea, in order to negotiate the opening of trade offices in each others' countries. Economic relations with Switzerland and Austria were also developing, Shim said, and a trade office would soon open in Vienna. The DPRK was negotiating a trade deal with Italy through the two countries' embassies in Beijing. However, although North Korea was willing to "establish relations with those capitalist countries which request friendly relations with the DPRK," there were limits. Certain Western countries (e.g. Britain, Greece, Canada, etc.) maintained an "aggressive" policy toward the DPRK and supported the South. In such cases, trade ties were not likely to develop.

Shim stressed that, despite the expansion of economic ties with the West, the DPRK would not compromise on a number of political points. First, Pyongyang insisted that the DPRK was the sole legitimate government "representing the will of the Korean people." Second, North Korea would continue to denounce "the puppet government of South Korea, maintained by the bayonets and guns of the USA." Third, the DPRK would ceaselessly insist that US troops must be removed from the Korean Peninsula and that the UN command must be abolished. Finally, the DPRK was ready "to establish friendly relations with all countries on the basis of the five principles of peaceful co-existence."[22]

The amount of trade between the DPRK and Western Europe was small relative to the overall trade of the European countries, but it was large by North Korean standards, and growing. Pyongyang's allies noted that by 1973, North Korean trade with members of the European Economic Community exceeded its trade with all other socialist countries, excluding the Soviet Union and China.[23] Japan, though, was by far North Korea's most important capitalist economic partner. North Korean trade with Japan alone was comparable to or greater than

---

20. A Soviet report from early 1973 mentions "180 French specialists in Wŏnsan" on the East Coast of North Korea, but it is not clear how long they were there or what they accomplished. GDR Ministry of Foreign Affairs, Far East Section, 27 February 1973. "Excerpt from Briefing on Conversation with Envoy of the Embassy of the USSR, Comrade Denisov, 22 January 1973 in the Embassy of the USSR." MfAA C 297/78.

21. GDR Embassy in DPRK, 9 February 1973. "Notes on Conversation with Sim Tong-hae, Vice-Minister of Foreign Affairs." MfAA C/297/78.

22. Ibid.

23. GDR Embassy in DPRK, Political Section. 12 September 1973. "Notes on Conversation with Counselor of the USSR Embassy, Comrade Denisov, 30 August 1973 in the Embassy of the USSR." MfAA C 297/78.

its trade with all of Western Europe. Moreover, North Korea's relations with Japan were more multifaceted, including political relations with parties, particularly the Japan Socialist Party; scientific and technical relations; and culture and art exchanges. Not least, Japan and North Korea were linked by the hundreds of thousands of ethnic Koreans in Japan, many of whom were politically supportive of the DPRK, and the tens of thousands of Korean-Japanese who had immigrated to North Korea since 1959.

As we saw in chapter 3, ethnic Korean "repatriation" to the DPRK had been negotiated through the two countries' Red Cross organizations, not their governments. Japan and North Korea remained on opposite sides of the Cold War divide, but made considerable progress in political relations in the early 1970s, reflecting the changing constellation of Cold War forces in Asia. In November 1971, Diet member Kenji Chuji of the ruling Liberal Democratic Party formed a "Dietman's League for the Promotion of Friendship between Japan and North Korea," and headed a goodwill mission to Pyongyang in 1972. The group helped to conclude a bilateral trade agreement and called for the "early removal of abnormal relations between Japan and North Korea."[24] But when North Korea called for an "equidistant" Japanese policy toward South and North Korea, Prime Minister Tanaka refused. Japan was also deepening its economic presence in South Korea at this time, and maintained that the defense of South Korea was still essential to Japan's own security. North Korea, for its part, said that it would normalize relations with Japan only if Tokyo changed its "hostile policy toward the DPRK" and was willing to establish "friendly" relations. Japan did not have to break its ties with the South, Pyongyang argued, but it would have to treat both states on the Korean Peninsula equally. Moreover, as much as North Korea desired economic ties and diplomatic normalization with Japan, it would not engage in "beggar diplomacy." Economic benefit was secondary to mutual respect.[25]

On the diplomatic front, North Korea had some success in normalizing relations with states in Northern and Western Europe in the early 1970s, including Austria, Finland, Iceland, Lichtenstein, Norway, Portugal, Sweden, and Switzerland. At the same time, the DPRK (or more precisely, the Korean Workers' Party) maintained and tried to expand relations with socialist, communist, and other left-leaning parties in the West, including those in countries with which it lacked other official ties. For example, the East Germans observed that the DPRK had

24. Hung Hyun Shin, "North Korea's Relations with Japan: The Possibilities for Bilateral Reconciliation," in Robert Scalapino and Hongkoo Lee, *North Korea in a Regional and Global Context* (Berkeley: University of California Press, 1986), 250–51.

25. GDR Ministry of Foreign Affairs, Far East Section, 27 February 1973. "Excerpt from Briefing on Conversation with Envoy of the Embassy of the USSR, Comrade Denisov, 22 January 1973 in the Embassy of the USSR." MfAA C 297/78.

"contact with Maoist and Trotskyite groups in the FRG and West Berlin" in the early 1970s, although the exact nature and extent of that contact was not specified.[26] In the autumn of 1976, the Belgian Communist Party, the Socialist Party of France, and other Western parties sponsored a pro-North Korea conference in Brussels.[27] North Korea held a certain allure for radicals in the United States as well. Eldridge Cleaver, the minister of information for the Black Panther Party, took time from his exile in Algeria, where he had fled to escape arrest on murder charges in the United States, to reside briefly in North Korea. There his wife gave birth to daughter whom they named "Joju Younghi"; the child's middle name was allegedly chosen by Kim Il Sung himself.[28] At one point a group in Cambridge, Massachusetts, called itself the "Juche Collective."[29]

Still, North Korea never held the attraction for First World "revolutionaries" that Mao's China, Ho Chi Minh's Vietnam, or Fidel Castro's (or perhaps more accurately Che Guevara's) Cuba did.[30] Perhaps Kim Il Sung did not cut as romantic a figure as Ho Chi Minh resisting the Americans, or Che Guevara martyred in Bolivia for the cause of global revolution. Perhaps the history of the DPRK was too ambiguous—neither a Soviet "satellite" nor a clear-cut case of indigenous revolution—to appeal to the far-left vanguard of the West. For the DPRK, political ties with marginal groups and parties in the West had limited value except for internal North Korean propaganda. North Korea was primarily interested in capitalist countries for one thing: capital. The problem was that such countries were not going to give North Korea the economic benefits it craved on generous terms and with no strings attached, as the Soviet-bloc states and China were willing to do after the Korean War. If even the Soviets were becoming frustrated with North Korea's growing indebtedness in the 1970s, as we will see shortly, Western banks and companies were hardly going to give the DPRK a free ride.

Unfortunately for North Korea, the timing of its outward economic expansion was not good, coming just before the OPEC oil shock of 1973 and the resulting global downturn. Soon North Korea was having difficulty repaying its loans from Japanese and European banks and firms. By mid-1975, according to US intelligence estimates, North Korea was some $200–$300 million in arrears; the DPRK

---

26. GDR Embassy in the DPRK, 28 May 1973. "Information on relations and contacts between the DPRK and the FRG," 28 May 1973. MfAA C 297/78.

27. GDR Embassy in the DPRK, "Notes on Conversation between Comrade Janda, First Secretary of the Embassy of the GDR in the DPRK, and Comrade Nanu, chargé d'affaires of the DPR in the DPRK," 2 February 1977. MfAA C6854.

28. See Cleaver's forward to *Juche! The Speeches and Writings of Kim Il Sung*, footnote 1 above.

29. Author's personal communication with a former member of the Cambridge Juche Collective.

30. Max Elbaum, *Revolution in the Air: Sixties Radicals Turn to Lenin, Mao, and Che* (London: Verso, 2002). Note the absence of Kim's name in the subtitle; Elbaum's book, a largely sympathetic and perhaps definitive history of the subject, does not even include Kim Il Sung in the index.

soon had the dubious distinction of being the first communist country to default on its debts to the West.[31] In May 1975, with North Korea more than $100 million behind in its debt repayment, Japan's Export-Import Bank denied further loans to the DPRK. Japan and North Korea renegotiated a repayment schedule in 1976, 1979, and 1983, but the DPRK unilaterally terminated the final agreement in 1984, still owing Japan $600 million.[32] Having little in the way of currency or goods to repay its debts, North Korea soon found more creative ways to earn foreign exchange. In the fall of 1976, North Korean diplomats in several Scandinavian countries were accused of smuggling ginseng, liquor, cigarettes, industrial goods, and—according to some reports—illicit drugs.[33] Several diplomats were expelled.[34] As a result of its debt defaults and illegal smuggling activities, North Korea achieved a kind of pariah status vis-à-vis Western financial institutions, governments, and potential trading partners and investors that would inhibit economic relations with Western countries for decades to come.

Nonalignment

If North Korea's First World economic diplomacy had fizzled out by the late 1970s, its Third World diplomacy was somewhat more enduring, although this too would reach its limits within a couple of decades. North Korea's pursuit of economic and political ties in the Third World began in the 1960s, as we have seen in the previous chapter, but it was in the 1970s that North Korea presented itself enthusiastically as a model for Third World development. This self-promotion was paradoxical: how could North Korea be both unique and a model? After all, few countries in the world have emphasized their distinctiveness and independence as much as North Korea. Juche from its first articulation in the mid-1950s stressed its uniquely Korean characteristics, and few could dispute North Korea's distinctive circumstances and development path. On the other hand, the notion of "self-reliance" embodied in Juche did seem to jibe with a certain Zeitgeist in the 1960s and 1970s. For many countries, especially those freed from colonial domination in the first few decades after World War II, the idea of self-reliance—and North Korea's apparent success at self-reliant development—held a powerful

31. CIA, "North Korean Payments Problem."

32. Hong Nack Kim, "Japan and North Korea: Normalizing Talks between Pyongyang and Tokyo," in Young Whan Kihl, ed., *Korea and the World: Beyond the Cold War* (Boulder, CO: Westview Press, 1994), 113.

33. Bazhanova, North Korea's Economy, 255. See also Sheena Chestnut, "Illicit Activity and Proliferation in North Korean Smuggling Networks," *International Security* 32, no. 1 (summer 2007): 80–111.

34. "Swedes Convinced North Korea Directed Smuggling," *New York Times,* October 22, 1976, 6.

allure. For a time, North Korea's leaders seemed genuinely to believe their country was an example for the Third World worthy of emulation, and Kim Il Sung tried with some success to present himself as a leader of the nonaligned Third World. Several Third World governments, particular in Africa, found aspects of the North Korean model both relevant and attractive. Yet the contradiction remained: how could something "uniquely Korean" also be a model for export to far-flung parts of the world, from Asia to Africa to Latin America?

Rivalry with the South was one important component of North Korea's Third World diplomacy. For the first fifteen years or so after the two Korean states were established, North Korea had almost no diplomatic ties outside the socialist bloc and was well behind Seoul in the number of countries recognizing its legitimacy. In the 1960s, as noted in the previous chapter, North Korea opened diplomatic relations with dozens of new countries, mostly in the Middle East and Africa. But South Korea did the same and remained ahead of the North in the diplomatic game. In the 1970s, North Korea apparently decided it would try to close the gap and soon reached parity with the South in terms of numbers of countries with which it had diplomatic relations (see table 5.1).

As the table below demonstrates, among the countries with which the DPRK established diplomatic relations in the 1970s, eleven were in Europe, ten in Latin America and the Caribbean, three in the Middle East, thirteen in the Asia-Pacific, and twenty-seven in Africa. The 1970s represent the peak of North Korean Third World diplomacy and the promotion of Juche as a model. Yet by the mid-1980s, North Korea's image in the developing world had sharply declined, and many Third World countries shifted their diplomacy more in favor of South Korea, whose economic development program by then seemed much more promising.

TABLE 5.1 DPRK establishment of diplomatic relations, 1971–80

1971	Yugoslavia, Syria, Malta
1972	Cameroon, Rwanda, Chile, Uganda, Senegal, Upper Volta, Pakistan, Madagascar, Zaire
1973	Togo, Benin, Gambia, Mauritius, Sweden, Iran, Argentina, Finland, Norway, Malaysia, Denmark, Iceland, Bangladesh, India, Afghanistan, Angola
1974	Libya, Gabon, Costa Rica, Guinea-Bissau, Nepal, Ghana, Laos, Australia, Jordan, Niger, Jamaica, Venezuela, Botswana, Austria, Switzerland
1975	Fiji, Portugal, Thailand, Kenya, Burma, Ethiopia, Mozambique, Tunisia, Sao Tome-Principe, Cape Verde, Singapore
1976	Nigeria, Papua New Guinea, Seychelles
1977	Barbados
1978	Western Samoa
1979	Grenada, Nicaragua, St. Lucia, Dominican Republic
1980	Zimbabwe, Lesotho, Mexico

Source: Byung-Chul Koh, *The Foreign Policy Systems of North and South Korea* (Berkeley: University of California Press, 1984), 11.

Partly out of rivalry with South, partly to win votes at the United Nations, and partly for its own internal propaganda, North Korea energetically pursued economic and diplomatic ties among the "nonaligned" nations of the Third World. In April 1975, as Phnom Penh and Saigon were falling to the revolutionary forces of the Khmer Rouge and North Vietnamese respectively, Kim gave a triumphant speech in Beijing, in which he declared Asia to be on a "high tide of revolution." If a revolutionary war were to break out in Korea, Kim said, "We will only lose the Military Demarcation Line and will gain the country's reunification."[35] From Beijing, Kim went on to Algeria, Mauritania, Romania, Bulgaria, and finally to Yugoslavia, where he met with President Tito in Belgrade on June 6. Tito had co-founded the nonaligned movement (NAM) in the late 1950s, along with Indian prime minister Jawaharlal Nehru, and the year 1975 marked the high point of North Korea's diplomatic offensive in the Third World, and toward the nonaligned countries in particular.[36] In August 1975, the foreign ministers of the member countries of the nonaligned movement agreed to admit the DPRK as a member, while rejecting Seoul's application to join. This was, of course, a victory in North Korea's competition with the South, but Pyongyang's courting of NAM also represented a shift away from radical regimes and movements to the more moderate countries of the Third World as a whole. These countries in turn responded with initially strong support for North Korea's position in North-South rivalry and the United Nations.[37]

The Soviet-aligned countries of Eastern Europe viewed Kim's Third World offensive with caution and some unease. They were skeptical of the very idea of the Third World, a term diplomatic correspondence often put in quotation marks, as it suggested that the USSR and its allies were not the only viable alternative to US-led "imperialism." But the Third World held great promise for the expansion of Soviet influence as well. From the 1950s onward, the "darker nations" of Asia, Africa, and Latin America comprised a vast area of opportunity for the USSR and a zone of competition not only with the United States, but also with China.[38] The Soviet Union and its allies put enormous resources—economic, military, cultural, and not least in clandestine intelligence activities—into winning political support among developing and newly independent nations in the 1960s and

---

35. *Nodong Sinmun*, 20 April 1975, 1.

36. Samuel S. Kim, "Pyongyang, the Third World and Global Politics," in Tae-Hwan Kwak et al., eds., *The Two Koreas in World Politics* (Boulder, CO: Westview, 1984), 73.

37. Kim, *The Non-Alignment Movement*.

38. For a wide-ranging "Third-Worldist" perspective on this competition, see Vijay Prashad, *The Darker Nations: A People's History of the Third World* (New York: The New Press, 2007).

1970s.[39] The Soviet-bloc governments were unsure whether Kim Il Sung's Third World diplomacy helped or hindered their cause. Discussing North Korea with the East German ambassador to Moscow in April 1976, a Soviet Foreign Ministry official stressed the need to "move the DPRK towards the socialist community of nations" in its relations with the Third World. While North Korea's position was close to the Soviet bloc in some respects, the problem was lack of coordination: the DPRK "does not act jointly with the other socialist states, but proceeds in parallel to them." Pyongyang had joined the nonaligned movement without prior consultation with the USSR and its allies, and in general "conducts its foreign policy activities based on purely pragmatic considerations." The Soviets had long complained that North Korea was too independent, acting in what it perceived to be its own interest rather than as part of a Moscow-led "socialist community." North Korea was now assiduously cultivating economic and diplomatic ties outside the socialist bloc, and there was little the Soviet-aligned states could do to influence this diplomatic offensive for their own advantage.[40]

Kim's 1975 tour, book-ended by visits to Moscow's two main socialist rivals, China and Yugoslavia, demonstrated more independence than the Soviets and their allies would have liked. According to correspondence among Soviet-bloc officials, Kim had intended to visit Moscow and Prague on this tour, but the dates he proposed did not suit the Soviet or Czech leaders. The Hungarian embassy in the DPRK seemed to reflect the general view of the Soviet bloc on this matter: "[Kim's] intention to visit Moscow is an important political fact for two reasons. On the one hand, it shows that the DPRK continues to pursue a so-called policy of maintaining a balance of power between the Chinese party and our parties; on the other hand, we should take this into consideration while evaluating his trips to China, Europe, and Africa."[41] Of course, from Moscow's perspective "maintaining a balance of power" between the Chinese and Soviet sides was an illusion—only the USSR represented "true socialism"—and the Hungarian report noted with some concern that Kim's visits to China and Yugoslavia had important military implications, with Beijing being a major supplier of military equipment and technology and Belgrade helping North Korea's naval forces. The

39. On the latter, see especially Christopher Andrew and Vasili Mitrokhin, *The World Was Going Our Way: The KGB and the Battle for the Third World* (New York: Basic Books, 2005).

40. Report from the GDR Embassy in the USSR, "Note about a Conversation between Comrade Bauer and Comrade Basmanov, Deputy Head of the First Far Eastern Department of the USSR Foreign Ministry, on 10 May 1976," 13 May 1976. MfAA, C6857. Translated for the North Korea International Documentation Project by Bernd Schaefer.

41. Report, Embassy of Hungary in the DPRK to the Hungarian Foreign Ministry, 30 July 1975. XIX-J-1-j Korea, 1975m 83. doboz, 81–10, 002835/8/1975. Translated by Balázs Szalontai for the Cold War International History Project.

Hungarians feared North Korea might even be asking China for tactical nuclear weapons to offset the US nuclear forces in South Korea. As for the Third World and the nonaligned movement generally, Kim's new visibility there could easily become an asset for China (and Yugoslavia) and a detriment to Soviet influence.

While Pyongyang gained new visibility in the Third World in the 1970s, the nonaligned movement soon proved to be less than unified over the Korea question. Differences over Korea came out in the open at the NAM Summit Conference in Colombo, Sri Lanka, in August 1976. The Colombo Conference was the first attended by the DPRK after its admission to NAM the previous year. Although the conference passed two resolutions supporting North Korea's position on the Korea question, many of the delegates expressed reservations about their support for the DPRK, and North Korea's high-pressure tactics alienated many of the participants.[42] Even Yugoslavia, whom Pyongyang could usually rely on for support, was not enthusiastic about the DPRK position. North Korea's reputation was also damaged by the Panmunjŏm axe-murder incident, which occurred during the time of the Colombo conference. As the Vietnamese ambassador to Pyongyang explained in private conversation with his East German counterpart, the axe-murder incident severely damaged North Korea's international image. The Socialist Republic of Vietnam remained a staunch supporter of Pyongyang, but in the Third World as a whole "the DPRK has lost many friends."[43]

Inevitably, the Sino-Soviet Cold War affected NAM as well: at the Sixth NAM Summit, held in Havana in 1979, the Cubans sharply criticized both the United States and China, and tried to push NAM in a more pro-Soviet direction, with North Korea caught in the middle.[44] North Korea tried to keep remain neutral in this dispute, stressing independence; this moderation was effective, and Pyongyang was admitted to the Coordinating Bureau of the NAM that year. But North Korea never achieved the kind of leadership status in NAM that Kim Il Sung had clearly desired.

Such problems aside, global events in the mid-1970s seemed to prove Kim's Beijing speech to be correct: there appeared to be a "high tide of revolution" not just in Asia, but in the Third World as a whole, and in Africa in particular. It was, in retrospect, a Pyrrhic victory. The blooming of diverse "people's democracies" in the period dating roughly from the fall of Saigon in the spring of 1975 to the

42. Dae-sook Suh, *Kim Il Sung, the North Korean Leader* (New York: Columbia University Press, 1988), 265–6; Buzo, *Guerrilla Dynasty*, 99.

43. GDR Embassy in Pyongyang, 23 September 1976. "Notes on a conversation of the Ambassador of the GDR in the DPRK, comrade Franz Everhartz, with the Ambassador of the Socialist Republic of Vietnam, comrade Le Tung Nam, on 22 September 1976 in the residence of the Ambassador of the GDR," 2. MfAA C6854.

44. Kim, "Pyongyang, the Third World and Global Politics," 78.

Soviet invasion of Afghanistan in December 1979 would prove to be the last advance of Marxist-Leninist socialism before its ignominious fall into the dustbin of history. It is however worth remembering how remarkable this mid-1970s transformation was: in a period of some eighteen months in 1974 and 1975, for example, self-professed Marxist-Leninist leaders came to power in Angola, Mozambique, Madagascar, and Ethiopia, while all three Indochinese states fell to communist rule. Congo had been the first African state to declare itself a "people's republic," as early as 1969—the same year Mohamed Siad Barre took power in Somalia and began to move his country closer to the Soviets. Somalia signed the first treaty between of friendship between a sub-Saharan state and the Soviet Union in 1974.[45] By the end of the decade, in the eyes of Moscow, a dozen states in Africa could be considered Marxist-Leninist or at least "socialist-oriented."[46] While people's democracies were less common in the Middle East and Latin America, the communist coup in Afghanistan in 1978 and the Sandinista victory in Nicaragua in July 1979 were also gains for Marxism-Leninism in the Third World.

Claims to socialist status did not reflect common interests or mutual agreement among these states. A coherent "Red Africa" existed only in the Cold War imagination of certain Washington policy planners, if even there. The Moscow-Beijing alliance had fallen apart a decade or more before Marxist-Leninists took power in sub-Saharan Africa, and by the late 1970s the socialist world had long ceased to be unified, or even particularly civil among its members. The Sino-Soviet Cold War belatedly played itself out in Africa, where there was fierce intercommunist rivalry, as well as various forms of cooperation, among Soviet, Chinese, East European, Cuban, and North Korean aid programs and advisors. Bedfellows could be strange. For example, in Angola, the Soviets supported the People's Movement for the Liberation of Angola (MPLA), while the Chinese, Romanians, and North Koreans sided with the rival National Front for the Liberation of Angola (FNLA), which was also supported by the United States. Chinese instructors based in Zaire used American supplies to arm and train FNLA guerrillas, and brought in Romanian and North Korean assistants. While there appears to have been no direct cooperation between American CIA operatives in Zaire and the communist supporters of the FNLA, in effect North Korea was siding with the United States against the Soviet Union.[47]

45. Marina and David Ottaway, *Afro-Communism*, 2d ed. (New York: Africana, 1981), 5.

46. Ibid., 164.

47. Odd Arne Westad, *The Global Cold War: Third World Interventions and the Making of Our Times* (Cambridge, UK: Cambridge University Press, 2005), 226–27.

North Korea did not focus its assistance only on "socialist-oriented" African countries. Indeed Pyongyang did not always display much ideological discrimination with the African regimes it supported. The DPRK assisted such unsavory and arguably rightwing dictators as Mobutu Sese Seko in Zaire, Idi Amin of Uganda, and Jean-Bédel Bokassa, the self-styled emperor of the Central African Republic. Bokassa's first state visit after proclaiming himself emperor in 1976 was to Pyongyang. North Korean engineers also built a presidential palace for Jean-Baptiste Bagaza, military president of Burundi, in the late 1970s.[48]

The one area of the Third World where North Korea had little profile was Latin America, still overwhelmingly dominated by pro-US governments. Cuba, of course, was the notable exception, and the DPRK often expressed its support for Cuba and for the Cuban revolutionary influence in Latin America more broadly. Kim Il Sung reportedly told the outgoing Cuban ambassador to Pyongyang in 1967 that the views of the KWP and the Cuban Communist Party were "completely identical," and that North Korea "supported only those Latin American revolutionary movements which the Cubans also agreed with and which they supported."[49] In 1975, Kim called the Cuban revolution "the continuation of the October revolution on the South American continent [sic]," and an example for the whole world.[50] Although Pyongyang's direct support for Latin American revolution beyond Cuba was generally more symbolic than real, there were some indirect signs of North Korean involvement in Latin American affairs. In 1971, for example, Mexican authorities arrested nineteen Mexicans who had allegedly received guerrilla training and financial support from North Korea. As Mexico had no diplomatic relations with North Korea, five Soviet diplomats were expelled because of alleged Soviet complicity in the affair.[51]

North Korea and Cuba had ideological affinities as well as complementary economies, although the great distance between the two countries may have limited their economic interaction. Cuba sent an economic delegation to Pyongyang in 1976 to negotiate cooperation in areas ranging from the production of automobile tires to chemical fertilizer and oil refining. The Cuban side asked for the DPRK to sent machinists to train Cuban technicians, a proposal the North Koreans promised to "examine."[52] Elsewhere in the Caribbean

---

48. Jon Halliday, "The North Korean Enigma," *New Left Review* 1, no. 127 (May–June 1981): 49.

49. Report, Embassy of Hungary in North Korea to the Hungarian Foreign Ministry, 9 March 1967. MOL, XIX-J-l-j Korea, 1967, 61. doboz, 1, 002130/1967. Translated by Balázs Szalontai for the Cold War International History Project.

50. GDR Embassy in Pyongyang, "Notes on a conversation with the Cuban ambassador, comrade Dr. Forras Morena, 19 March 1975 in the Soviet Embassy."

51. CIA Intelligence Memorandum, "North Korean Subversive Diplomacy," June 1971. CIA-RDP79–01194A000300090001–4.

52. GDR Embassy in DPRK, 29 December 1976. "Notes on Conversation with Envoy of Cuban Embassy, Comrade Nunez, 20 December 1976, in Embassy of GDR." MfAA C6854.

region, North Korea's one notable diplomatic success was with the South American nation of Guyana. Prime Minister Forbes Burnham, who declared Guyana a "Cooperative Republic" in 1970, advocated national self-reliance (under the name "cooperative socialism") and saw a kindred ideology in North Korean Juche. The DPRK established diplomatic relations with Guyana in May 1974, and after Guyana fell out with the Soviet Union and Cuba in 1976, North Korea became the country's major source of assistance in industry, agriculture, education, and military equipment. Guyana, in turn, became an outspoken advocate of North Korea's unification policy on the international stage, and in January 1979 hosted the first Latin American-Caribbean Conference for the Independent and Peaceful Reunification of Korea.[53] Like Mengistu Haile Mariam of Ethiopia, to be discussed below, Forbes Burnham greatly admired the discipline of North Korean society under the leadership of Kim Il Sung and sought to replicate elements of Kim's cult of personality.[54] However, DPRK-Guyana relations did not long survive Burnham's death in 1985, by which time North Korea had lost most of its attraction as a model for Third World development.

In the Middle East and North Africa, North Korea built on its successes of the 1960s. Algeria was the first country in the region to establish relations with North Korea and remained a strong supporter of Pyongyang on the Korean question. Syria was an especially important partner,[55] and the DPRK and Syria continued trade and technical cooperation long after the end of the Cold War—by which point, North Korea's exports of missile and nuclear technology was causing much anxiety in Washington. North Korea developed good relations with Iraq under the Ba'ath Party and made contact with Iran under the Shah. In 1974, Iran discussed exporting oil to the DPRK in exchange for North Korean minerals. The staunchly pro-US Iranian government assured the DPRK that Tehran supported Korean unification "without outside influences."[56] After the Iranian revolution in 1979, North Korea expressed strong support for Ayatollah Khomeini's Islamic Republic, perhaps more for its anti-Americanism than out of any genuine sense of ideological solidarity.[57] If nothing else, North Korea's outspoken criticism of

---

53. Moe Taylor, "One Hand Can't Clap: Guyana and North Korea, 1974–1985," unpublished paper. I am grateful to the author for sharing his paper with me.

54. Probably North Korea's most notorious admirer in Guyana was the cult leader Jim Jones, who led his followers to collective suicide in in Jonestown, Guyana in 1978. Jones often extolled North Korea's achievements in his nightly radio broadcasts and screened North Korean films for his cult members. Taylor, "One Hand Can't Clap," 12–13.

55. GDR Embassy in DPRK, Political Section. "Notes on Conversation with Mr. Omani, Counselor of Syrian embassy in DPRK, 12 March 1974." MfAA C6854.

56. GDR Embassy in Beijing, 23 April 1974. "Notes on Conversation with Iranian Ambassador, Mr. Abbas Ahram, in Embassy of GDR." MfAA C6854.

57. Halliday, "North Korean Model," 49.

Israel since the Six-Day War in 1967 helped keep it on good terms with most Arab and Muslim states, whether conservative or radical.[58]

Closer to home—both geographically and ideologically—the acrimony among communist states over Vietnam and Cambodia in the late 1970s put North Korea in a very awkward position. In the end, Pyongyang emerged from this conflict relatively unscathed, but it took considerable diplomatic skill for the DPRK to navigate the complex dynamics of cooperation and conflict among China, the USSR, Vietnam, and Democratic Kampuchea (as Cambodia under the Khmer Rouge renamed itself). The fall of Phnom Penh, Saigon, and Vientiane to communist-led forces in 1975 was greeted euphorically from Moscow to Beijing to Pyongyang, not to mention in many other parts of the world. In short order tensions between the erstwhile communist brothers ruling Hanoi and Phnom Penh escalated into propaganda wars, internal purges of alleged agents of the other side, and border clashes. Moscow and Beijing, as the main backers of Vietnam and Cambodia respectively, were soon drawn into these disputes, and the Sino-Soviet Cold War erupted into open military conflict in Indochina. Any remaining illusions of socialist solidarity in the region went up in flames with the Vietnamese invasion of Cambodia in 1978 and the subsequent Sino-Vietnamese border war. While Marxist-Leninist regimes had faced a number of intramural conflicts since Tito's falling-out with Stalin in the late 1940s, the Third Indochina War among Cambodia, Vietnam, and China was the first large-scale military clash among communist states.

North Korea, as we have seen, had been a keen supporter of North Vietnam and the South Vietnamese National Liberation Front in their struggle against the US-backed regime in Saigon, and praised Hanoi's victory in 1975 as loudly as anyone. These two relatively small divided countries on the rim of Asia had much in common, not least their dependence on both China and the USSR for political, military, and economic support. North Vietnam, like the DPRK, had tried to remain equidistant in the Sino-Soviet dispute. But well before the unification of Vietnam, as early as 1970 according to one careful study of the Soviet archives, Hanoi had been "tilting" toward Moscow.[59] Meanwhile, China had long been an enthusiastic backer of the Khmer Rouge movement of the 1960s and early 1970s. Pol Pot, Khieu Samphan, Ieng Sary, and other Khmer Rouge leaders were warmly welcomed in Beijing well before the fall of Phnom Penh in April 1975.[60]

---

58. In 1973, Kim Il Sung told Arab diplomats in Pyongyang, "The DPRK supports the Arab countries in their struggle against Israeli aggression." GDR Embassy in Pyongyang, Political Section. "Notes on conversation with chargé d'affaires of Iraqi Embassy, Ghasu Fatah, 9 November 1973." MfAA C6854.

59. Stephen J. Morris, *Why Vietnam Invaded Cambodia: Political Culture and the Causes of War* (Stanford: Stanford University Press, 1999), 197–215.

60. Zhai Qiang, "China and the Cambodian Conflict, 1970–1975," in Priscilla Roberts, ed., *Behind the Bamboo Curtain: China, Vietnam, and the World beyond Asia* (Stanford: Stanford University Press, 2006), 391.

In the Vietnam-Cambodia clash of the late 1970s, the USSR backed Vietnam and China supported the Khmer Rouge, despite the fact that the Vietnamese had not even informed Moscow in advance of their plans to invade Cambodia.[61] The United States also supported the anti-Vietnam forces, meaning that Washington indirectly supported the Khmer Rouge as well. North Korea's official position on this dispute was to talk about the "victory of socialism" in Indochina in the most general terms and to stay out of the dispute as much as possible.

The ever-mercurial Prince Norodom Sihanouk of Cambodia embodied the diplomatic complexities surrounding Indochina, especially for North Korea. On the one hand, North Korea had initially supported the Khmer Rouge, and Pol Pot (like Ethiopia's Mengistu, another overseer of "red terror" in the 1970s) saw Kim Il Sung as something of a role model. North Korea was the first country after China to give aid and send advisors to the Khmer Rouge after the latter took power in the spring of 1975. A song and dance troupe from Pyongyang was the first arts delegation to visit Democratic Kampuchea, in November 1976.[62] According to Vietnamese reports, there were North Korean advisors in Cambodia until at least 1977. The Koreans were mostly assisting with the agricultural economy (clearly they did not help much, given the famine unfolding there), and although North Koreans were much less numerous than Chinese advisors, Cambodia was probably Pyongyang's largest aid mission in Asia.[63]

In the mid-1970s, Beijing, Pyongyang, and Phnom Penh formed a triangle of mutual support and praise. Pol Pot received a hero's welcome when he visited Beijing in September 1977, his second visit to China following his seizure of power, and from there he traveled to Pyongyang where he was greeted enthusiastically by Kim Il Sung and received promises of North Korean military aid.[64] On the other hand, the deposed Prince Sihanouk, who fell out with the Khmer Rouge shortly after the latter came to power, was a personal friend of Kim Il Sung's and a frequent visitor to Pyongyang. In 1974 Kim built the prince a lavish summer residence, reportedly modeled on one of the Great Leader's own palaces, on the

61. Stephen J. Morris, "The Soviet-Chinese-Vietnamese Triangle in the 1970s: The View from Moscow," Cold War International History Project Working Paper No. 25 (April 1999).

62. Ben Kiernan, *The Pol Pot Regime: Race, Power, and Genocide in Cambodia under the Khmer Rouge, 1975–1979* (New Haven: Yale University Press, 1996), 131–32.

63. GDR Embassy in Pyongyang, 9 February 1977. "Notes on a conversation of the GDR Ambassador in the DPRK, Comrade Franz Everhartz, and the SRV Ambassador in the DPRK, Comrade Le Trung Nam, on 2 February 1977, in the GDR Embassy," 2–3. MfAA C6854. The Soviets estimated that some 2,500 Chinese advisors were in Cambodia as of July 1977. North Korean advisors probably numbered a few hundred at most. GDR Embassy in DPRK, "Notes on conversations with Comrade Pimenov, chargé d'affaires of USSR, 15 July and 25 July 1977." MfAA C6584.

64. David P. Chandler, *Brother Number One: A Political Biography of Pol Pot* (Boulder, CO: Westview Press, 1992), 145–47; Zhai Qiang, "China and the Cambodian Conflict," 393.

outskirts of Pyongyang.[65] Sihanouk also spent a good deal of time in Beijing, and as far as Moscow and its allies were concerned, the prince was not much of a friend to the Soviet bloc. The East Germans relied on the Indian embassy to Pyongyang to convey to them Sihanouk's message to the Indians in April 1974. According to the Indian chargé d'affaires, Sihanouk thanked the Indians for their support of his position against the US-backed Lon Nol government in Phnom Penh, and thanked the Chinese and North Koreans for their financial assistance to his government-in-exile—annual support amounting to $5 million dollars from China and $1 million dollars from North Korea. As the GDR embassy glumly noted, "The S[oviet] U[nion] and other socialist states were not mentioned in [Sihanouk's] speech."[66]

In general, relations among communist states in the 1970s were far looser and more volatile than in previous decades, giving the DPRK more room for maneuver between the Soviet Union and China. Needless to say, North Korea's lack of commitment in the Sino-Soviet dispute pleased neither Moscow nor Beijing. In early 1974, the Soviet ambassador to Pyongyang discussed with his East German counterpart the upcoming World Conference of Communist and Workers' Parties, noting that the DPRK had played little role in these conferences in the past. As the Soviet envoy remarked, "The DPRK does not participate in collective consultations of this kind and prefers bilateral contact and consultation."[67] He blamed "Juche" for such uncooperative attitudes, noting also that overreliance on independent development and ideological incentives were not succeeding in developing North Korea's economy. Motivating workers with ideological exhortations might have worked in the past, but was no longer effective. Yet rather than change course, the DPRK was trying to intensify its ideological program, with counterproductive results. "The emergence of dullness and apathy [among North Korean workers] is not to be overlooked."[68]

North Korea's relations with China were generally good throughout the 1970s. Following Zhou Enlai's visit to Pyongyang in 1970, the DPRK and PRC maintained a steady rate of cultural, political, and military exchanges. By 1973 China had replaced the Soviet Union as the leading supplier of weaponry to North Korea.[69] Unlike in the past, improvement in DPRK-PRC relations did

65. Chris Springer, *Pyongyang: The Hidden History of the North Korean Capital* (Budapest: Entente, Bt. 2003), 142–143.

66. GDR Embassy in Pyongyang, Political Section. "Notes on a conversation with Mr. Kumar, chargé d'affaires of the Republic of India in the DPRK, 23 April 1974," 2. MfAA C6854.

67. GDR Embassy in Pyongyang, Political Section. "Notes on a conversation with Comrade Pimenov, envoy of the USSR Embassy,"2 March 1974, 2. MfAA C6854. Of course, "multilateral consultation" at such conferences was largely dominated by Moscow, as the North Koreans knew well.

68. Ibid.

69. Buzo, *Guerrilla Dynasty*, 98.

not correspond to a weakening of DPRK-Soviet ties.[70] North Korea's relations with China and the Soviet Union were relatively balanced, and on the whole cordial, during the 1970s. To be sure, the Pyongyang leadership could not help but be concerned over the developing strategic alignment between China and the United States after Nixon's visit to Beijing. Nor was the DPRK willing to subscribe to China's virulent anti-Soviet position. China, for its part, was none too pleased with what Beijing saw as needlessly provocative acts against the United States, such as the *Pueblo* incident in 1968 and the axe-murder incident of 1976.[71] But these mutual reservations were kept quiet by both sides. On the surface, the DPRK-PRC alliance was stronger than it had been in almost two decades.

Under the surface there were tensions in the Soviet-DPRK relationship as well, over issues ranging from the DMZ axe-murder incident to the deepening North Korean debt to the USSR. The latter was a source of growing Soviet frustration. A Soviet embassy official in Pyongyang recounted in detail to the East German ambassador the hundreds of millions of rubles owed them for North Korean projects, including the construction of a nuclear power plant; the continuing demands the North Koreans made of them; and the unlikelihood that these debts would be paid until 1990 or so (a particularly inauspicious date, as it turned out).[72] When a North Korean delegation visited Moscow to ask for help in the development of the Kim Ch'aek iron and steel works and a power station at Pukch'ŏng, Prime Minister Kosygin's response was "unusually negative."[73] At a time when the Soviet economy itself was under increasing strain, North Korea's requests for further assistance and credit were not welcome.

As usual, the Soviets' greatest concern was a potential North Korean "tilt" toward China. Attempting to assuage his Soviet-bloc comrades, DPRK foreign minister Hŏ Dam gave a lengthy speech at the Hungarian embassy in 1976 explaining his country's views of the Soviet Union and China. Hŏ wanted to answer directly the question, he said, often asked of him: which side is North Korea on? To begin with, Hŏ stated that North Korea had "old historical, friendly relations

70. Yi Chong-sŏk, *Puk Han-Chungguk kwanggye, 1945–2000* [North Korea-China Relations, 1945–2000] (Seoul: Chungim, 2001), 260.

71. Bernd Schaefer, "North Korean 'Adventurism' and China's Long Shadow, 1966–1972," Cold War International History Project Working Paper No. 44 (October 2004); Ch'oe Myŏng-hae, "Chungguk-Pukhan tongmaeng yŏn'gu: Yangguk tongmaengŭi kiwŏn kwa yŏkdongjŏk palgae kwajŏng" [The China-North Korea Alliance: The Origins and Development Process of a Bilateral Alliance], Ph.D. diss., Korea University, 2007, 257–59.

72. GDR Embassy in DPRK, "Notes on Conversation of Comrade Steinhoffer, Ambassador, with envoy of embassy of USSR, Comrade Pimenov, 10 February 1976." MfAA C6584.

73. GDR Embassy in DPRK, "Notes on conversation with chargé d'affaires of embassy of USSR in DPRK, Comrade Pimenov, 16 November 1976. MfAA C6854. The Soviets noted at the time that North Korea's factories in its East Coast industrial belt were suffering from a shortage of energy and not working at full capacity. Much worse, of course, was yet to come.

with the Soviet Union." Kim Il Sung had fought the Korean War in part "to safe-guard the Soviet Union," the fatherland of world revolution, and Moscow had given a great deal of material aid to the DPRK after the war, for which the North Koreans would be eternally grateful. China, for its part, also had long historical ties to Korea, and had sent its People's Volunteers to help the North during the war, something the Koreans could never forget. Although there was "a period of cool relations" between Pyongyang and Beijing during the Chinese Cultural Revolution, Sino–North Korean relations had since become normal, and there were no particular problems between the two countries. But the Chinese did not interfere in North Korea's internal affairs. As for China's domestic matters, "they do not inform us and we do not ask."[74]

Soviet-bloc anxiety over Chinese–North Korean relations went beyond political and military matters; it also had much to do with North Korea's cultural politics, which seemed to the Soviets and their allies as dangerously "Maoist." Maoism in the decade of the Cultural Revolution meant, among other things, the state's relationship to domestic intellectuals. As we have seen, North Korea viewed the Chinese Cultural Revolution with considerable ambivalence. Astute Soviet bloc observers were aware of the similarities and differences in between Chinese and North Korean approaches to culture, which they naturally viewed through the lens of what they considered more "objective" and "scientific" Marxism-Leninism. As a Bulgarian diplomat put it, both China and North Korea extolled their respective cults of personality and were dangerously "subjectivist," rather than following the "scientific ideology of the working class and Marxist-Leninist politics" as proscribed by Soviet orthodoxy.[75] The works of Kim Il Sung in North Korea, like the writings of Mao Zedong in China, had by the 1970s become almost the sole scripture read by the party, eclipsing the work of Marx, Lenin, and Stalin. Reading Kim Il Sung was a quantitative task for party members, the intellectual equivalent of mass industrial production. For example, in preparation for the thirtieth anniversary of the establishment of the Korean Workers' Party in 1975, KWP members were required to study ten thousand pages of Kim Il Sung's works.[76] The North Koreans, as the Soviets saw, were pursuing their own version of a Great Proletarian Cultural Revolution. But this did not mean the two

74. GDR Embassy in DPRK, "Notes on conversation of Hungarian Ambassador, Comrade Sabo, on 8 May 1976 in the Bulgarian Embassy." MfAA C6854.

75. GDR Embassy in Pyongyang, 19 September 1975. "Notes on a conversation between Comrade Tuparov, attaché of the Embassy of the PRB, and Comrade Stark, Second Secretary of the Embassy of the GDR, on 29 August 1975 in the Embassy of the GDR," 2. MfAA C6854.

76. GDR Embassy in Pyongyang, 20 October 1975. "Notes on a conversation between Comrade Irgabaev, First Secretary of the Embassy of the USSR, and Comrade Stark, Second Secretary of the Embassy of the GDR, on 16 October 1975 in the Embassy of the GDR." MfA C6854.

Cultural Revolutions were identical. For one thing, the North Korean "Cultural Revolution" (a term the North Koreans used much less often than did the Chinese) was not nearly as violent or socially disruptive as its Chinese counterpart. For another, intellectuals as a class were not attacked in North Korea. Rather, North Korea emphasized the cultivation of "correct" intellectuals.

In September 1975, First Secretary Irgabaev of the Soviet Embassy in Pyongyang gave a brief history lesson to East German officials about North Korea's policy toward intellectuals. As Irgabaev outlined, there were two periods of evolution in DPRK policy toward intellectuals. The first, "correct one," lasted from liberation until the Korean War. North Korea benefited from the presence of the Soviet advisors, the study of Marxism-Leninism in the Soviet Union and other socialist countries, and the education of Korean youth in proletarian internationalism. The second (presumably "incorrect") phase began in the Korean War but became noticeably more pronounced in the postwar period. North Korean cultural life was dominated by the Juche ideology and the fantastic personality cult of Kim Il Sung. Over the long term, Irgabaev noted, North Korean ideology developed the following characteristics: the struggle against dogmatism and flunkeyism (*sadaechuйi*); the struggle against revisionism and for the establishment of Juche: and the arming of the whole society with the ideas of Kim Il Sung. As a result of this practice, North Korean intellectuals had become largely isolated from outside influences.

However, as Irgabaev was quick to point out, this was not the same as the Maoist policy toward intellectuals in China. In the DPRK, unlike in China, there had been no attempt to liquidate intellectuals as a group or force them to do physical labor only. One reason for this difference, Irgabaev observed, was that "the DPRK must also take into consideration the struggle of South Korean intellectuals. For this reason they cannot carry out measures that would repel South Korean intellectuals."[77] In other words, North Korea was trying to appeal to South Korean intellectuals in support of a revolutionary uprising in the South.

Was South Korea really "ripe for revolution"? Or rather, did the DPRK leadership believe this to be so? Comparisons to Vietnam were self-serving and not always sincere. The North Koreans were particularly frank with their Vietnamese counterparts about their hopes for a "Vietnam solution" to Korea's division, as well as their understanding of the considerable differences between the two situations. But if revolution in the South was a distant possibility at best, this did not mean that the North Korean side seriously entertained the idea of North and

---

77. GDR Embassy in Pyongyang, 6 June 1975. "Notes on a conversation between Comrade Irgabaev, First Secretary of the Embassy of the USSR, and Comrade Stark, Second Secretary of the Embassy of the GDR, on 6 April 1975 in the Embassy of the GDR," 3. MfAA C6854.

South unifying under their current systems—contrary to official DPRK propaganda about "Confederation." In early September 1975, just over four months after the fall of Saigon, a Vietnamese diplomat in Pyongyang summarized the North Korean position as follows:

> Unification between the DPRK and the Park Chung Hee regime on the basis of the joint communiqué of 1972 is not possible. The negotiations have definitely failed. . . . A peaceful democratic unification requires a revolution in South Korea, for which there is at present no indication. The most important prerequisite for a revolution in South Korea is the withdrawal of US troops. The DPRK is well aware of this, and struggles persistently for withdrawal.[78]

By contrast, the unification of Vietnam was essentially complete, although there remained some differences between North and South Vietnam to be resolved. The Workers' Party of Vietnam was "the leading party in all of Vietnam," having led the struggle against "US imperialism and the Thieu clique." The Korean Workers' Party could only envy such a state of affairs.[79]

Juche in Africa

Africa was the great prize for North Korea's Third World diplomacy, both because of the continent's large number of newly independent countries that might be persuaded to confer diplomatic recognition to the DPRK and support North Korea's positions in the United Nations, as well as its potential as a site for demonstrating North Korea's successful development strategy. Similar to China at the time, North Korea gave economic aid to several African countries on very generous terms.[80] It is debatable how seriously North Korea's development model was considered worth emulating in African countries, whose colonial experience, resource endowments, and cultural backgrounds were vastly different from those of the DPRK. Kim Il Sung certainly did not portray his country's experience as anything like a blueprint for postcolonial nations in Africa, although he did not shy from presenting the DPRK as an inspiration for successful

---

78. GDR Embassy in Pyongyang, "Notes on a Conversation of the counselor of the Embassy of the GDR, Comrade Steinhofer, with chargé d'affaires of the Embassy of the DRV, Comrade Ho Kong Khieu, 2 September 1975," 2. MfAA C6854.

79. Ibid.

80. For Chinese aid to Africa in the Maoist period, see Philip Snow, *The Star Raft: China's Encounter with Africa* (London: Weidenfeld and Nicolson, 1988), 144–85.

independent development. As he told the president of the Front for the Liberation of Mozambique (FRELIMO) in May 1975, shortly after the country had gained its independence from Portugal: "Now I am going to talk about our experience in building a new country. . . . Our experience may not suit the conditions in Mozambique. So I hope that you will take it, to all intents and purposes, as a reference in your construction of a new society."[81] Most of Kim's speech was a recapitulation of North Korean history in the early postliberation years. The main lessons he offered his Mozambican guests were the need to create a broad-based political party and affiliated mass organizations, instigate "democratic" reforms such as land redistribution, and above all to make sure that the economy was entirely under the command of the state. Following his brief history lesson, Kim offered assistance to Mozambique in areas such as irrigation, farming technology, and the construction of "small local industry factories." Although Kim admitted that "the quality of our goods is still not so high," he offered free aid, including food.[82]

No doubt, for the new and underdeveloped African regimes, North Korea's success at rapid industrialization, without dependence on Western capital, was impressive. As one pro-Juche African scholar put it, in a book published in the DPRK, "In the period of industrialization which lasted less than 20 years, a country which had been backward like today's Africa was totally transformed and has been converted into a powerful, independent industrial country which calls forth the admiration of the people of the world."[83] It is unlikely, however, that the specifics of North Korea's industrialization held much relevance for the postcolonial states of sub-Saharan Africa. Few if any African states had anything like the industrial infrastructure built in Korea during the Japanese colonial period or the level of assistance North Korea received from the socialist countries in the post–Korean War reconstruction period, to say nothing of the linguistic and cultural unity or strong and effective state that helped enable North Korea's collective economic endeavors. Be that as it may, North Korea put a great deal of energy and resources into demonstrating its popularity as a political and economic model among developing nations. Numerous International Seminars

81. Kim Il Sung, "Talk to the President of the Liberation Front of Mozambique," *Works*, vol. 30 (Pyongyang: Foreign Languages Publishing House, 1987), 119.

82. Ibid., 139–40.

83. Huber Mono Ndkana, *Revolution and Creation: A Treatise on the Juche Philosophy* (Pyongyang: Foreign Language Publishing House), 229. In the 1970s Pyongyang sponsored a great many books by Third World authors praising the North Korean system and Kim Il Sung's genius behind it. See for example *Comrade Kim Il Sung, an Ingenious Thinker and Theoretician* (Pyongyang: Foreign Languages Publishing House, 1975); and Muhammad al Missuri, *Kim Il Sungism: Theory and Practice* (Pyongyang: Foreign Languages Publishing House, 1978).

on the Juche Idea were held in various locations around the world, fully underwritten by the DPRK, and whose purpose seemed to be at least as much for internal North Korean propaganda as advancing "science" abroad. For example, a Scientific Seminar of the Middle East, Near East and African Countries on the Great Idea of Juche was held in Mogadishu, Somalia, in November 1973.[84] Three years later another Scientific Seminar on the Juche Idea was held in Madagascar, presided over by President Didier Ratsiraka himself.[85] All publications regarding these seminars showed attendees unequivocally praising the achievements of the DPRK and eagerly reading the works of Kim Il Sung.

Other than the rather abstract notion of "self-reliance," what seemed to be most appealing for several African governments was concrete assistance from the DPRK, which often meant military assistance. Much of North Korea's aid to Africa appears to have been in the form of military equipment and training—although here the figures, mostly from South Korean intelligence sources, must be treated with some caution. According to one estimate, there were eight thousand North Korean military personnel sent to thirty-eight countries between 1966 and 1983, while in the same period North Korea provided training for some seven thousand military personnel from thirty countries.[86] The London-based International Institute for Strategic Studies reported in 1985 the presence of a thousand North Korean military personnel in Angola, one hundred in Madagascar, forty in Seychelles, twenty in Uganda, and "unspecified numbers in seven other African countries," as well as three hundred in Iran.[87] In 1973, Mobutu Sese Seko of Zaire replaced his Israeli military advisors with North Koreans to train his elite military division, and was himself warmly welcomed in Pyongyang in December 1974.[88] North Korean military aid to Robert Mugabe of Zimbabwe was instrumental in the consolidation of his regime, in particular Mugabe's ability to crush the resistance in Matabeleland between 1982 and 1985. This aid did not lead to formal "alliances," as the only country other than the USSR and China with which North Korea ever signed a mutual defense treaty was Libya in 1982. But North Korean aid to Africa was not only military: between 1957 and 1982, 57 percent of North

---

84. *The Third World Marches Forward to Independence and Self-Reliance: Documents of the Scientific Seminar of the Middle East, Near East and African Countries on the JUCHE Idea* (Beirut: dar Al-Talie, 1975). Two years later Somalia would switch to a pro-Western position and North Korea would become an ally of Somalia's archrival, Ethiopia.

85. *Juche: The Banner of Independence* (Pyongyang: Foreign Languages Publishing House, 1977).

86. Young C. Kim, "North Korea and the Third World," in Scalapino and Lee, eds., *North Korea in a Regional and Global Context*, 338.

87. Cited in Ralph N. Clough, *Embattled Korea: The Rivalry for International Support* (Boulder, CO: Westview Pres, 1987), 296.

88. Piero Gleijeses, *Conflicting Missions: Havana, Washington, and Africa, 1959–1976* (Chapel Hill, NC: University of North Carolina Press, 2002), 187, 477 n.76.

Korea's trade agreements were signed with African countries. North Korea had become, relative to the size of its own economy, a rather substantial contributor to African development.[89]

North Koreans in Ethiopia

Ethiopia under Mengistu Haile Mariam was one of the most significant of the Marxist-Leninist experiments in Africa and one of North Korea's most active African partners in the late 1970s and early 1980s. North Korea's newfound friendship with Ethiopia was rather ironic, as Ethiopia under the old regime had participated in the Korean War on the *South* Korean side, and Ethiopia maintained diplomatic relation with both Seoul and Pyongyang during Mengistu's reign. After the 1974 overthrow of Emperor Haile Sellassi, Mengistu approached the Americans for support. Rebuffed, he turned to Moscow in January 1975. The Soviets gave generously: Ethiopia became the most important Soviet-led intervention outside Europe (until Afghanistan in 1979), the largest foreign assistance program the USSR had undertaken since China in the 1950s, and the largest socialist multilateral aid project since the reconstruction of North Korea after the Korean War. China itself was conspicuously absent in Ethiopia, as Beijing's African aid program focused on other parts of the continent and left the reconstruction of Ethiopia to the USSR and its allies. Cuba played a particularly active role, sending 11,600 soldiers and 1,000 advisors.[90] East Germany was also a leading source of military and economic aid to the Mengistu regime.[91] North Korean aid to Ethiopia probably came in fourth after that of the USSR, Cuba, and East Germany, but was applied to a number of high-profile projects both in the capital Addis Ababa, and in the countryside.

Kim Il Sung commented to GDR leader Erich Honecker in 1984 that "we have agricultural specialists in nearly all African countries," and that "Ethiopia has obviously achieved the highest level of consolidation of a Marxist party" in Africa.[92] North Korea's decision to send military advisors, engineers, and agricultural experts to Ethiopia was almost a mirror-image of North Korea's role as an aid recipient after the Korean War, and perhaps that was a conscious motivation. Just

---

89. Chongwook Chung, "North Korea and the International Community: The Search for Legitimacy in the United Nations and Elsewhere," in Scalapino and Lee, *North Korea in a Regional and Global Context*, 359.

90. Westad, *Global Cold War*, 277, 279.

91. Benno-Eide Siebs, *Die Aussenpolitik der DDR 1976–1989: Strategien und Grenzen* (Paderborn, Germany: Schoningh, 1999), 211–12.

92. Central Committee, German Socialist Unity Party, "Memorandum of Conversation between Erich Honecker and Kim Il Sung," 1 June 1984. SAPMO-BA, DY 30, 2460.

as the Soviets helped rebuild Pyongyang and the East Germans Hamhŭng, so the North Koreans helped to reconstruct Addis Ababa as a "socialist" city. One unique skill the North Koreans had was in staging parades and "mass games," which they taught the Ethiopians to perform for the celebration of the tenth anniversary of the Revolution in September 1984.[93] Another of their projects was the Tiglachin Monument in front of the main hospital in Addis Ababa, which North Korean engineers helped build to commemorate Ethiopia's success (with considerable Cuban help) in its war against Somalia. The monument is an enormous obelisk with a red star on top and revolutionary figures carved on the bottom pedestal. Aside from the African features of the carved figures, the monument would have looked completely at home in Pyongyang.

North Korea sent several hundred advisors to Ethiopia from 1977, mostly in the military field to train the Ethiopian army in antiguerrilla tactics and for fighting in Somalia (which by now had switched to a pro-American position). North Korean civil engineers helped to rebuild the Addis Ababa sewage system, and agricultural advisors tried to plant rice in the south of the country, an experiment that utterly failed. Mengistu visited Pyongyang twice and was deeply impressed by what he saw there, so much so that he made his citizens sport North Korean-style uniforms after returning from one of his visits.[94]

According to my interviews with Assefe Medhanie, formerly in charge of foreign affairs for the Ethiopian Workers' Party, the Mengistu regime sought "loose solidarity under the umbrella of the Soviet Union," and turned to several socialist countries for support. The Chinese were not forthcoming with the kind of weaponry and aid they wanted, and the Chinese presence in Ethiopia was minimal. But the North Koreans gave more of what the new Ethiopian regime desired and were active in several areas in addition to military assistance, including small-scale construction, agriculture, and organizing parades (the latter which particularly impressed the Ethiopians). North Korea built two large ammunitions factories in the country and supported Ethiopians' ambitions to produce their own weapons. There was some competition between the Cubans and North Koreans, and Koreans also helped in the war against Somalia, although not on the scale of the Cubans. Assefe had the sense that the North Koreans liked Mengistu, a take-charge "big man" who seemed like a Kim Il Sung in the making.

Nevertheless, despite the mutual admiration that existed between the two governments, Juche never really took root in Ethiopia. According to my informant,

---

93. Donald L. Donham, *Marxist Modern: An Ethnographic History of the Ethiopian Revolution* (Berkeley: University of California Press, 1999), 14. Donham remarks that the Mengistu regime spent US $50 million on the anniversary celebration just as the historic Ethiopian famine was reaching a point of catastrophe.

94. Author's interview with Dr. Min Chul Yoo, Addis Ababa, Ethiopia, November 30, 2004.

a few university professors were invited to Pyongyang to study Juche and "came back running." Some students went to study Taekwondo, but many more students went to Eastern Europe to study modern administration and science; a group of North Korean students also came to study in Addis Ababa. Party relations were good, with members attending each others' party congresses. But the deeper lessons of the North Korean experience did not seem particularly applicable to the Ethiopian environment. Juche, the Ethiopians felt, was not translatable.[95]

"Victory" at the United Nations and the North-South Impasse

North Korea's Third World offensive helped secure the DPRK's first "victory" at the UN General Assembly (UNGA) in October 1975. In the early 1970s, North Korea dropped its hostile position toward the United Nations. North Korea and China had after all ostensibly fought a war against the international body, even though the Korean War enemy was usually portrayed as the "American imperialists." But now the PRC had finally taken Taiwan's seat at the UN Security Council (UNSC), joining the Soviet Union as one of the Permanent Five UNSC members. The UN Commission for the Unification and Rehabilitation of Korea was dissolved, and the DPRK joined the World Health Organization in 1973, the first of several UN bodies Pyongyang would join in the 1970s. The DPRK refused to join the United Nations itself alongside South Korea, although this had been proposed by the Soviet Union as early as 1956.[96] Only after the collapse of the USSR in 1991 and the recognition of South Korea by both Russia and China in 1992 would the two Koreas join the international body.

At the Thirtieth UN General Assembly in 1975, a DPRK proposal on the Korean Question was adopted for debate by the UNGA for the first time. North Korea's proposal called for the withdrawal of all foreign forces from the Korean Peninsula (meaning, essentially, US forces from South Korea) and the dissolution of the UN Command. The United States and other supporters of South Korea submitted a rival resolution that would allow the maintenance of US troops while the UN Command was officially dissolved. The two draft resolutions were taken up for debate by the full UNGA in October 1975. The pro-DPRK resolution passed with considerable support from Third World countries, particularly in Africa. This has been portrayed in North Korean propaganda ever since as a

95. Author's interview with Assefe Medhanie, Addis Ababa, Ethiopia. December 1, 2004.

96. Gills, *Korea versus Korea: A Case of Contested Legitimacy.* (London: Routledge, 1996), 73.

resounding victory for the DPRK and a sign of its deep global support.[97] However, the pro-ROK resolution also passed shortly thereafter. In the end, nothing changed on the Korean Peninsula. Contrary to DPRK official accounts, North-South rivalry at the United Nations in the mid-1970s resulted not in a North Korean victory, but a stalemate. For the remainder of the decade, there would be no movement in inter-Korean relations.

Inter-Korean relations had reached a new impasse barely a year after the July 4, 1972, agreement was signed. By the time North-South talks broke down in the latter part of 1973, peaceful coexistence between the two Koreas—much less unification—appeared as distant as ever. In August 1973, North Korea canceled scheduled inter-Korean talks in protest against the kidnapping of opposition leader Kim Dae Jung, who had been abducted from a Tokyo hotel room on August 8 by South Korean intelligence agents. A few days later Kim was released, and North-South talks resumed in December, but only at lower-level meetings in Panmunjŏm rather than high-level meetings in Seoul and Pyongyang. Inter-Korean meetings finally ended altogether in March 1975.[98] In the meantime, clashes occurred between North and South Korean naval vessels in the West Sea around the so-called Northern Limit Line (NLL), the maritime boundary drawn unilaterally by the UN Command after the Korean War that gave South Korea control of territorial waters hugging the coastline of the DPRK. The North Koreans had not disputed the maritime boundary for the past twenty years, but in October 1973 the DPRK began to claim jurisdiction over five islands on the southern side of the NLL, and sent naval patrols into the area to back up their claim. At a MAC meeting in December, the North Koreans demanded that all foreign or South Korean vessels receive prior permission from the DPRK authorities before traveling to or landing on the islands, even though they were currently occupied by South Korean military and civilian personnel.[99]

The Americans speculated that North Korea's provocations in the West Sea were intended to push out the UN Command, destabilize South Korea, and shake South Korea's confidence in the American security umbrella just as the Korean Question was coming before the United Nations.[100] While North Korea's demands were not met, neither did the maritime clashes escalate into a broader military

---

97. *Chosŏn Chungang Nyŏngam* [Korean Annual], 1976, 500–501. See also Gills, *Korea versus Korea*, 141–3.

98. Bernd Schaefer, "Overconfidence Shattered: North Korean Unification Policy, 1971–1975," North Korea International Documentation Project Working Paper No. 2 (December 2010), 23.

99. Central Intelligence Agency, Directorate of Intelligence, "The West Coast Korean Islands," January 1974. Reproduced in Ostermann and Person, eds., *After Détente*, 143.

100. Washington Special Action Group. Working Group Meeting, "North Korea," December 4, 1973. Reproduced in Ostermann and Person, eds., *After Détente*, 130.

confrontation. The NLL, patrolled by the navies of both Koreas, remained a point of contention thereafter. In 1975, the South Korean navy sank two North Korean vessels in the area, and the militaries of both sides went on high alert.[101] By that time, the hopes for inter-Korean peace raised by the July 4 Joint Statement were a distant memory.

On June 23, 1973, the Park Chung Hee government in Seoul announced a Seven-Point Declaration for Peace and Unification, and for the first time proposed the simultaneous admission of the ROK and DPRK to the United Nations.[102] The following day, North Korea rejected out of hand Seoul's proposal for joint entry to the UN—although the Soviets had proposed this, with DPRK support, in the late 1950s.[103] The North Koreans argued that joining the United Nations as separate states would perpetuate the division of Korea indefinitely. Instead, Pyongyang offered a Five-Point Program for Independent Peaceful Unification, which Kim explained at some length in a letter to his comrade Erich Honecker. These points included a proposal for a confederation of North and South to be called the Federal Republic of Koryŏ (the name of the penultimate dynasty of premodern Korea), a formula Pyongyang would return to repeatedly over the next twenty years. Seoul never warmed to the Koryŏ idea for both political and logistical reasons (how such radically different systems could become "confederated" as a single state, Pyongyang never fully explained). It didn't help that the capital of Koryŏ had been Kaesŏng, currently in North Korea, and that Koryŏ had been a northern-oriented dynasty—thus giving the North a symbolic edge over the South. Kim insisted to Honecker that if joining the United Nations was a goal for Korea, it could not occur until Korea entered as a single nation under the name Federal Republic of Koryŏ. This did not, however, preclude the DPRK (and the Seoul government as well) from joining individual UN agencies.[104]

The Soviets publicly supported the North on the Korean question, of course, but privately felt the North Koreans were exploiting inter-Korean conflict for their own purposes and didn't really want a peace agreement with the South. The Soviet ambassador to Pyongyang told a visitor from the East German embassy in January 1974 that "the Korean comrades increasingly believe that they can get effective support from the PR China and the S[oviet] U[nion] and the other

101. Archives of the Romanian Ministry of Foreign Affairs, "Telegram from Pyongyang to Bucharest, SECRET, No. 059.057, 27 February 1975." Translated and reproduced in Ostermann and Person, eds., *After Détente*, 311.

102. Ostermann and Person, *Rise and Fall of Détente*, 105.

103. Chong-sik Lee, "The Evolution of North-South Korean Relations," in Scalapino and Lee, eds., *North Korea in a Regional and Global Context*, 119–120.

104. GDR Department of Internal Affairs, Berlin, 3 August 1973. Letter to Erich Honecker from Kim Il Sung. SAPMO-BA, DY 30, 2460. Translated by Grace Leonard for the Cold War International History Project.

fraternal states" to obtain the withdrawal of US troops from South Korea via the United Nations. The North Koreans exploited controversies such as the North-South dispute over islands in the West Sea, in order to paint the Park Chung Hee regime as aggressive.[105] As DPRK leaders' statements to both their allies and the international media made clear, North Korea did not plan to invade the South. But that did not mean North Korea had ruled out a military unification of the peninsula. The North Koreans understood their military weakness relative to South Korea, much less the United States; as Kim Il Sung told a Japanese parliamentarian in August 1974, "from the point of view of numbers and from the size of their air force, they are superior to us. What we excel in is the moral aspect."[106] It was this "moral aspect," the North Koreans had long argued, that would make the South Korean people support the DPRK. Kim went on to say, "We will not advance South. . . . However, as for a revolution that arises naturally, we can't guarantee it won't take place. This is because, where there is suppression, revolutions arise."[107] It was only the US military presence and American support for the South Korean dictatorship that kept this revolution from arising.

Few if any of North Korea's allies agreed with Kim Il Sung's prognosis for a South Korean revolution. The Vietnamese, who knew something about supporting revolution in a divided country, were particularly skeptical. Le Dong, the North Vietnamese ambassador to the DPRK, told his East German counterpart that the DPRK leaders did not understand "the real situation in the ROK." Le believed that some members of the North Korean military, nervous about North-South détente, "prefer, in light of their existing incorrect perception of the enemy, to solve the reunification issue by military means."[108] The Vietnamese had the impression that the North Koreans expected to receive "arms from the Soviet Union and soldiers from the PR China" in case of renewed military conflict with South Korea, just as they had received during the Korean War.[109] A Romanian Foreign Ministry report surmised that economic difficulties in the DPRK, "combined with an inaccurate understanding of the situation in South Korea," were behind North Korea's provocations toward the South: the DPRK leadership aggravated

---

105. GDR Embassy in Pyongyang, "Report on Courtesy Visit of Comrade Steinhofer, First Secretary, from the envoy of the Soviet Ambassador, Comrade Pimenow, 24 January 1974." MfAA C6854.

106. "Details of the Meetings between President Kim Il Sung and Representative Tokuma Utsunomiya," in Ostermann and Person, eds., *After Détente*, 213

107. Ibid., 217.

108. GDR Embassy to the DPRK, "Conversation with the Ambassador of the Democratic Republic of Vietnam," 31 October 1973. MfAA, G-A 352. Translated for the North Korea International Documentation Project by Bernd Schaefer.

109. GDR Embassy to the DPRK, "Note about Conversation with the Ambassador of the Democratic Republic of Vietnam, Comrade Le Quang Khai, on 5 May 1976 at the GDR Embassy," 6 May 1976. MfAA, C6857. Translated for the North Korea International Documentation Project by Bernd Schaefer.

North-South tensions both to keep their own people distracted from problems at home and to exploit instability in the South, leading to a collapse of the Park regime and unification on Pyongyang's terms.[110] In his conversation with Representative Utsunomiya of Japan on August 9, 1974, Kim Il Sung insisted that North Korea no longer engaged in provocative acts toward the South and in fact "I have had the persons who made these mistakes punished."[111] Six days later, a Korean-Japanese gunman associated with the pro-DPRK General Association of Korean Residents in Japan (known as Chōsen Sōren in Japanese) tried to kill the South Korean president.

On August 15, 1974, an ethnic Korean from Japan named Mun Se-gwang attempted to assassinate Park Chung Hee at a Korean Independence Day celebration in Seoul. Mun, who came out of the pro–North Korea Japanese residents' association in Osaka, missed his intended target but managed to shoot and kill the president's wife on the stage of the auditorium.[112] South Korea immediately accused Pyongyang of responsibility for the attempted assassination; North Korea denied any connection to the shooting and blamed the "South Korean puppet clique" and the "Japanese reactionaries" for staging the incident themselves in order to discredit the DPRK and Chōsen Sōren.[113] While North Korea may not have been directly linked to the attempted assassination of Park Chung Hee, we can assume that the DPRK leadership had hoped Park's death would create instability in South Korea and open the door to unification on North Korea's terms. That had been North Korea's motivation for the Blue House raid in 1968. Mun Se-gwang's assassination attempt failed, but we will never know whether a successful assassination at that time would have destabilized the South for the benefit of the North. Five years later Park was assassinated by his own chief of intelligence, leading to a period of instability and ultimately a second military coup, but North-South unification did not advance in the least. The effect of the 1974 assassination attempt was to heighten tensions between the North and the South, as well as between South Korea and Japan, and to further harden the Park dictatorship.

Shortly after the attempt on Park's life, South Korean soldiers discovered tunnels dug under the DMZ by the North Koreans, in order to infiltrate troops into the South. Although the South Koreans had long suspected the North of

---

110. Archives of the Romanian Ministry of Foreign Affairs, "Telegram from Washington to Bucharest, SECRET, Regular, No. 83.895," 14 April 1976. Obtained by Izador Urian and translated for the North Korea International Documentation Project by Eliza Gheorghe.

111. Ostermann and Person, eds., *After Détente*, 213.

112. Oberdorfer, *The Two Koreas*, 51–2.

113. Korean Central News Agency, "Foreign Ministry Comments on Assassination Attempt," 19 August 1974. Reproduced in Ostermann and Person, eds., *After Détente*, 233.

burrowing clandestinely under the DMZ, the first confirmed tunnel was inter-cepted in November 1974, and a second in February 1975. The United States and ROK estimated that thousands of soldiers per hour could have been put through these tunnels, to emerge well within South Korean territory. Another two tunnels were later discovered, in 1978 and 1990, although many more were suspected. The North Koreans had world-beating experience in building military and industrial facilities underground, going back to the Korean War, but tun-neling under the DMZ to infiltrate South Korea was something new. A Korean Workers' Party official from Kaesŏng, who defected to the South in September 1974, claimed that orders to build the tunnels came from the highest levels of the DPRK leadership in late 1972.[114] According to an East German military official formerly posted to North Korea, the North Koreans may have been inspired by an East German film of the late 1960s called *For Your Eyes Only* (no relation to the James Bond film of the same name), which featured tunnels for East Ger-man infiltration into West Germany. The official recalled that his North Korean counterparts asked in detail how these tunnels had been built—not deterred by the fact that they were entirely fictional.[115]

In August 1973, Kim Yŏng-ju, member of the KWP Politburo and Kim Il Sung's younger brother, told Soviet officials in Pyongyang that North Korea's unification policy was in "crisis." The younger Kim, who had led the DPRK delegation in North-South talks, said that Pyongyang had made a number of errors in its ap-proach to the South. First, the North Koreans had overestimated their influence in South Korea. Second, they had not taken into sufficient account the differences in the two social systems. Third, the North had underestimated the strength of the Park Chung Hee regime both in terms of its military power and its political stability.[116] In other words, the North Koreans had been counting on a popular advantage in the South, but they had badly miscalculated. Kim Yŏng-ju, who was at this time a strong contender for successor to his brother, would soon disappear from the party leadership for several years while his nephew Kim Jong Il was el-evated to heir apparent. Whether the failure of Kim Yŏng-ju's unification strategy had anything to do with his disappearance and demotion, we may never know.

One very worrisome development in South Korea was Seoul's attempt to develop nuclear weapons. North Korea itself had sought nuclear training and

114. Ibid., 56–59.

115. Author's interview with former East German military attaché in North Korea, Vienna, Aus-tria, June 8, 2006.

116. GDR Embassy in DPRK, Political Section. "Notes on Conversation with Counselor of the Embassy of the USSR, comrade Denisov, 30 August 1974 in the Embassy of the USSR." MfAA C 297/78.

technology from the USSR since the end of the 1950s, but the Soviets had been circumspect in their nuclear aid, bringing some North Korean scientists to the USSR and building a small reactor in Yŏngbyŏn, north of Pyongyang. South Korea, on the other hand, pursued an aggressive nuclear weapons development program in response to the reduction of America's security commitment in 1972. In 1975, Park Chung Hee openly stated in the US media that South Korea would defend itself with its own nuclear weapons if necessary, should the US nuclear umbrella be withdrawn.[117] Despite strong US objections, the South Koreans continued to work on a nuclear weapons program until the end of the Park regime in 1979. Not to be outdone, the North Koreans claimed to the Hungarian ambassador in 1976 that the DPRK had its own nuclear-tipped missiles.[118] This was certainly a bluff; North Korea would not successfully test a nuclear device, much less place one on a missile, until thirty years later. But North Korea's nuclear braggadocio reflected the severity of tensions on the Korean Peninsula in the mid-1970s, and the North Korean understanding that, one way or another, a new military clash on the peninsula would likely involve nuclear warfare.

The promise of US president Jimmy Carter, elected in 1976, to withdraw all US troops from South Korea, may have given some hope to the North Koreans that unification on their terms could finally be realized. It certainly created high anxiety among the South Korean leadership.[119] The DPRK attached "great meaning" to Carter's withdrawal plan, according to the North Korean conversations with their East European allies, and was pleased with the restrained US response to the downing of an American helicopter in July 1977, as compared to the near-catastrophe over the axe-murder incident a year earlier. From the end of 1976 to the middle of 1977 North Korea toned down its usually shrill anti-American rhetoric and refrained from attacking Carter personally. Still, as the East Europeans understood, North Korea's restraint "did not reflect a change of strategic orientation of the DPRK, but was tactical in nature. . . . The DPRK holds no illusion about the Carter administration."[120] The United States maintained a nuclear umbrella over the ROK and continued to pour resources into modernizing the South Korean military. If anything, the North Koreans feared that the South

---

117. Seung-young Kim, "Security, Nationalism, and the Pursuit of Nuclear Weapons and Missiles: The South Korean Case, 1970–82," *Diplomacy and Statecraft* 12, no. 4 (December 2001): 65.

118. Balázs Szalontai and Sergey Radchenko, "North Korea's Efforts to Acquire Nuclear Technology and Nuclear Weapons: Evidence from Russian and Hungarian Archives," Cold International History Project Working Paper No. 53 (August 2006), 56.

119. See William H. Gleysteen Jr., *Massive Entanglement, Marginal Influence: Carter and Korea in Crisis* (Washington, DC: Brookings Institution, 1999), 20–30. Gleysteen was Carter's ambassador to Seoul.

120. GDR Foreign Ministry, Far East Section, "Analysis of the GDR Embassy in DPRK on the Question of the Withdrawal of US Troops from South Korea." MfAA C6874.

was getting politically and militarily stronger, regardless of the American troop presence. Furthermore, Japan was taking an increasing role in developing South Korea as US land forces were reduced. The removal of US troops from the ROK (a decision which Carter ultimately reversed) did not necessarily throw open a window for a North Korean victory over the South.

Despite such short-term pessimism, overall the DPRK in the mid- to late-1970s saw history on its side. Following the communist victories in Indochina, North Korea looked forward to a "Vietnam solution" to Korean division: a revolutionary uprising in the South, supported by military assistance from the North, which would lead to unification on Pyongyang's terms. The protests against the Park Chung Hee dictatorship in Seoul, and the existence of some pro-Pyongyang elements in South Korea, apparently led Kim to believe that such a solution was a real possibility. The Chinese were not thrilled with North Korea's militaristic approach to Korean unification and strongly discouraged Kim from taking that approach during his visit to Beijing. Kim did not appear to be dissuaded, insisting that the DPRK "could not remain indifferent" "if a revolution flared up in South Korea." But in the end Kim did not push for a military solution to Korean unification, at least in part because the Chinese stated clearly that they would not support it.[121] In June 1975, two months after his visit to Beijing, Kim told Todor Zhivkov of Bulgaria "the DPRK does not favor a military method to solve the unification problem," although "this does not mean the DPRK will be unable to defend its achievements if attacked."[122] Always suspicious of Chinese motives, the Soviet-bloc states saw Chinese discouragement of North Korean militarism as a way to help the Americans. As a Hungarian embassy report put it, "China holds back and opposes any kind of armed struggle that might shake the position of the USA in Asia."[123]

The Limits of North Korea's "Globalization"

Despite North Korea's initially successful diplomatic offensive in the Third World, Juche was never much of a development model, for several reasons. First, at the most general level there is probably no readily transferable model of

121. Bernd Schaefer, "Overconfidence Shattered," 26

122. GDR Embassy to the People's Republic of Bulgaria, "Information on the Talks between Kim Il Sung and Todor Zhivkov," 18 June 1975. MfAA C 294/78. Obtained and Translated for the North Korea International Documentation Project by Bernd Schaefer.

123. Report, Embassy of Hungary in North Korea to the Hungarian Foreign Ministry, 9 March 1967. MOL, XIX-J-l-j Korea, 1967, 61. doboz, 1, 002130/1967. Translated by Balázs Szalontai for the Cold War International History Project.

development, including that of South Korea, and North Korea's conditions are truly unique in the world. Second, of course, North Korea's development path has been a failure by almost any measure, as was beginning to become evident in the 1980s (especially in contrast to South Korea), and no sensible Third World government would have wanted to emulate it. Third, even at the height of North Korea's Third World activism, Juche diplomacy was useful more for domestic propaganda and diplomatic rivalry with South Korea than as a genuine blueprint for developmental assistance, although there were no doubt some true believers on both sides. Ironically perhaps, North Korea's economic involution since the early 1990s has reduced the DPRK to a level of poverty more typical of the poorer states of southern Asia and sub-Saharan Africa than of the advanced economies of East Asia. In that sense, in its very failure, North Korea has been a more typical example of a Third World state than it once appeared.

As for the First World, North Korea's attempts at economic engagement with advanced capitalist countries in the 1970s did not result in deep and long-term linkages between North Korea and the West, nor did they give much long-term benefit to either side. North Korea managed to establish diplomatic relations with a number of countries in Northern and Western Europe, but the expansion of ties with the First World reached a plateau in the mid-1970s that the DPRK would not move beyond until the late 1990s, when under very different circumstances (and with the encouragement of South Korea) North Korea launched an unprecedented diplomatic offensive in Europe, the Americas, and the Asia-Pacific. Most important, North Korea's initial turn to advanced capitalist countries for trade and economic assistance ended badly, with massive unpaid debts and diplomats expelled for smuggling. North Korea had hoped that engagement with the West would bring in the necessary capital and technology to help fulfill its ambitious Six-Year Economic Plan (1971–76), much as assistance from the Soviet Union, China, and Eastern Europe had enabled North Korea's post–Korean War development program.[124] Such hopes, and with them the goals of the Six-Year Plan, remained unfulfilled in the late 1970s, and North Korea's industrialization efforts were frustrated at the very moment when the South Korean economy was about to move into heavy industry and visibly surpass the North in economic development.

Finally, notwithstanding its new relationships with Western and nonaligned nations, the DPRK remained closely tied to the Soviet bloc and China. The USSR and China still accounted for nearly half of North Korea's trade in the late 1970s. Trade with the Third World comprised another 25 percent of North

---

124. Kim Kisu, "North Korea's Foreign Economic Policy," in Yang Sŏngch'ŏl and Kang Sŏnghak, eds., *Puk Han wegyo chŏngch'aek* [The Foreign Relations of North Korea] (Seoul: Seoul Press, 1995), 119.

Korea's overall trade, and Eastern Europe, Japan, and a few West European nations comprised most of the rest.[125] While North Korea sought imports and investment from the West, few outside of the communist bloc and the poorer nations of the Third World were interested in North Korea's exports.[126] As Kim Il Sung remarked to Erich Honecker during the latter's official visit to North Korea in December 1977, the DPRK was first and foremost a socialist nation. The Korean Workers' Party advocated the "joining of all revolutionary forces, especially those of socialist countries, 'Third World' countries, the nonaligned nations, the international workers movement, and the national liberation movement." Despite "difficulties in joining the forces of Socialist nations" due to the friction between the USSR and China, both were "comrades in arms of the DPRK."[127] Pyongyang's official foreign policy priority remained the "all-round victory of socialism," and North Korea's solidarity with the Third World and opportunistic engagement with capitalist nations were supposed to be means to that end.[128]

The last European holdout of hard-line Stalinism in the 1970s, Enver Hoxha of Albania, thought little of North Korea's overtures to the capitalist nations and its pretensions to Third World leadership. Of course, Albania under Hoxha barely even attempted industrialization, and Hoxha was a bitter enemy of Tito, the self-appointed leader of the nonaligned movement. Still, Hoxha's cynical critique of Kim Il Sung's goals held some insight. Commenting in 1977 on the eve of Tito's official visit to the DPRK, Hoxha wrote in his memoirs that

> Tito is going to Korea to carry out negotiations on behalf of American imperialism with Kim Il Sung and not to get [financial] credits.... Korea is so deeply in debt itself that it is unable to meet repayments.... In regard to the "third world," Kim Il Sung pretends to be not only a member, but possibly, also its leader. He also has pretensions that the "Juche" ideas, i.e., Kim Il Sung thought, should be spread throughout the world with great speed. All these pretensions do not upset Tito who, as we know, poses as the leader of the "nonaligned world.[129]

125. Ibid., 121.

126. Joseph S. Chung, "Foreign Trade of North Korea: Performance, Policy and Prospect," in Scalapino and Lee, eds., *North Korea in a Regional and Global Context*, 107.

127. Central Committee, German Socialist Unity Party, "Report on the Official Friendship Visit to the DPRK by the Party and State Delegation of the GDR, Led by Com. Erich Honecker, 8–11 December 1977." Translated by Grace Leonard. *Cold War International History Project Bulletin* 14/15 (winter 2003–spring 2004): 51.

128. For example, an official history of DPRK foreign relations, published in the late 1980s, stressed that the period since the beginning of the 1970s was "the era of advancing the all-round victory of socialism." Pak T'ae-ho, *Chŏson Minjujuŭi Inmin Konghwaguk taeoe kwangyesa* [History of DPRK Foreign Relations] (Pyongyang: Sahe kwahak ch'ulp'ansa, 1987), 85.

129. Jon Halliday, ed., *The Artful Albanian: Memoirs of Enver Hoxha* (London: Chatto & Windus, 1986), 314.

Hoxha's answer to the dangerously revisionist tendencies he saw in the DPRK was to keep his country poor, isolated, and unreformed. But Kim Il Sung had bigger ambitions for North Korea, and sought in the 1970s to deepen his country's industrialization through ties with the capitalist nations, and make North Korea more visible globally through greater contact with the Third Word.

In terms of actual economic reform, however, Kim was unwilling to go much farther than Albania. This created a contradiction that undermined North Korea's outward-oriented foreign policy of the 1970s. Engagement with the world soon gave way to retreat from the world, or at least from Western countries and global markets. The contrast with China, whose outward turn in the late 1970s followed the North Korean path begun a few years earlier, is striking. By the end of the decade, China was embarking on market-oriented reforms that would soon reap enormous economic benefits, as well as far-reaching social changes, for the PRC. North Korea had neither the political will nor, as the leadership perceived it, the favorable international environment that would allow the DPRK to take such bold steps. A closed-door, command-economy nation such as North Korea could only engage comfortably with the wider world while the socialist community of nations provided it with guaranteed markets and military and political support. With the collapse of that socialist universe at the end of the 1980s, North Korea's globalization would come to an abrupt end as well, and the DPRK would have to practice a grim, genuine "self-reliance" for the first time.

A NEW GENERATION AND A NEW COLD WAR, 1980–84

> The Party's cause continues from generation to generation, and it must preserve its revolutionary character until it fulfils its mission.
>
> —Kim Jong Il, 1982

> We are of the same opinion that the present international situation which has become aggravated owing to the manoeuvres for confrontation and armament expansion by the most aggressive forces of imperialism, the US in particular, requires more urgently than ever the people rise in the struggle for peace.
>
> —Erich Honecker, 1984

The Rise of Kim Jong Il

In the late 1970s, Deng Xiaoping emerged as China's supreme leader out of the succession struggles that had followed Mao Zedong's death in 1976. Deng proceeded to take China on a path of economic modernization that would in time utterly transform the country. Twenty years earlier, Khrushchev had denounced his predecessor Stalin and instituted a liberalizing campaign in the USSR that would reverberate throughout the communist world. Kim Il Sung abhorred any such destabilizing changes in the DPRK. As the 1980s began, Kim's eldest son Kim Jong Il was officially anointed successor to his father. This generational succession ensured that, unlike the Soviet Union after Stalin and China after Mao, North Korea would not take a radically new course after Kim Il Sung's death.

Kim Jong Il literally embodied continuity in the North Korean system. He was the biological son of the Great Leader, and beneath his revolutionary and quasi-socialist rhetoric, what was most evident in Kim Jong Il's words and deeds was the time-honored Korean value of filial piety. Far from making a generational break with the past, the "Dear Leader"—as Kim Jong Il was called in the 1980s—would carry on and amplify the policies of his father.[1] While China and some

---

The epigraphs are from Kim Jong Il, "The Workers' Party of Korea is a Juche-type Revolutionary Party which Inherited the Glorious Tradition of the DIU," October 17, 1982, published in Kim Jong Il, *On Enhancing the Party's Leading Role* (Pyongyang: Foreign Languages Publishing House, 1992), 101;

of the East European states experimented with market incentives and varying degrees of political openness, North Korea reemphasized centralized, personalized leadership and moral and ideological exhortation. North Korea would not totally abandon attempts at economic reform, but by and large the DPRK in the early 1980s retreated from the Third World and First World activism of the previous decade while trying to deepen its ties to China and the Soviet Union. In the same period, South Korea came under new military leadership and began to pull decisively ahead of the North in economic development and international recognition. Meanwhile the United States, under the conservative presidency of Ronald Reagan, went on a counteroffensive against global communism—or rather, against the Soviet Union and its real or perceived influence in the world. North Korea therefore found itself in the difficult position of maneuvering among a pro-American China, a more assertive United States, an increasingly defensive USSR, and a newly confident South Korea. It was in this uncertain environment, at the dawn of what would be the final decade of global communism, that Kim Jong Il took the reins of power from his father.

Although being the son of the Great Leader gave Kim Jong Il privileges far surpassing those of ordinary North Koreans, including other members of the elite, leadership succession in the DPRK was not based on hereditary privilege alone. Kim Jong Il's rise to the top of North Korea's power structure was not ordained from birth. The younger Kim had to prove his ability and his loyalty, and to compete with other contenders for the throne from within the Kim family.[2] Kim Jong Il seems to have gained the support of his father for succession in the early 1970s, when he was just over thirty years old, roughly the same age the elder Kim was when he became North Korea's leader.

If Kim Jong Il's upbringing was much more comfortable than that of his father, it was also more circumscribed. Unlike Kim Il Sung, who had spent most of his adolescence and early adulthood in Manchuria and Russia among poor immigrants and guerrilla fighters, Kim Jong Il grew up almost entirely in Korea,

---

and "Speech of Comrade Erich Honecker at the Banquet Given by Comrade Kim Il Sung," in *Everlasting Fraternal Friendship: The Great Leader Comrade Kim Il Sung's Official Goodwill Visits to the Soviet Union and Other European Socialist Countries* (Pyongyang: Foreign Languages Publishing House, 1984), 66.

1. After Kim Il Sung's death in 1994, North Korean media began calling Kim Jong Il "Great Leader" (*widaehan chidoja*) instead of "Dear Leader" (*ch'inaehanŭn chidoja*), but using a less elevated term for "leader" than "Suryŏng," which remained exclusive to the elder Kim posthumously as it was during his lifetime. Kim Jong Il's most common appellation became *Changgunnim* ("The Respected General").

2. Kim Jong Il is the only surviving son of Kim Il Sung from his first wife, Kim Chŏng-suk. His brother died in a swimming accident in 1947 and his mother died in childbirth in 1949, leaving Jong Il and his sister Kim Kyŏng-hŭi. Kim Il Sung remarried in 1952 and had several children, including at least two sons, with his second wife, Kim Sŏng-ae.

the sheltered son of an absolute ruler. Kim Jong Il spent part of his childhood in China during the Korean War but appears not to have learned Chinese; in his late teens he traveled once to the Soviet Union, accompanying his father to the Twenty-First Congress of the Soviet Communist Party, but turned down the opportunity to go to a Soviet or East European university.[3] Instead, Kim Jong Il attended Kim Il Sung University, North Korea's leading institution of higher learning. Kim Jong Il's official biographies claim that he had turned down the opportunity to study abroad out of patriotism and loyalty to his father. Whatever his reasons for choosing Kim Il Sung University, it comes as no surprise that the Great Leader's eldest son had an exemplary academic record—or at least, that was the official line after he had been named successor. It would of course have been extremely unwise for an instructor to give young Kim anything but the highest marks, but later North Korean publications extolled Kim Jong Il's academic performance to the skies and beyond. Majoring in political economy, Kim allegedly surpassed his own professors with his amazing knowledge and analytical ability. Kim's undergraduate thesis, "The Place and Role of the County in the Building of Socialism," was published immediately as an "immortal work."[4] In the hagiography surrounding Kim Jong Il, his university record became the functional equivalent of his father's anti-Japanese guerrilla struggle: the youthful experience that qualified him to be the nation's leader, "a brilliant chapter in the history of the country and the glorious annals of the Workers' Party of Korea and the Korean people."[5]

This awe-inspiring academic performance was made public only after the younger Kim came out as the heir apparent in the early 1980s. In the meantime, he moved rapidly up the ranks of the Korean Workers' Party. In September 1964, not long after graduating from Kim Il Sung University, Kim Jong Il became head of personnel guidance in the Organization and Guidance Department of the KWP. In February 1966 he moved to the Propaganda and Agitation Department, a field he seems to have had a particular fondness for, and soon became director of the Motion Picture and Arts Division; in October 1970 he became deputy director in charge of culture and the arts.[6] At this stage Kim's work focused largely

---

3. Bradley Martin, *Under the Loving Care of the Fatherly Leader: North Korea and the Kim Dynasty* (New York: Thomas Dunne Books, 2004), 216; Hwang Chang-yŏp, *Nanŭn yŏksa chillirŭl poatta: Hwang Chang-yŏp hoegorok* [I Have Seen the Truth of History: Memoirs of Hwang Chang-yŏp] (Seoul: Hanul, 1999), 360.

4. Choe In Su, *Kim Jong Il, The People's Leader* (Pyongyang: Foreign Languages Publishing House, 1983), 1:344.

5. Ibid., 256.

6. Sung Chull Kim, *North Korea under Kim Jong Il: From Consolidation to Systemic Dissonance* (Albany: State University of New York Press, 2006), 39. See also Dae-sook Suh, *Kim Il Sung, The North Korean Leader* (New York: Columbia University Press, 1988), 276–77.

on film and the performing arts. In a country where propaganda played such a central role in politics, this was not an insignificant post. But Kim took North Korean arts in a direction that seemed specifically designed to ensure his father's favor: under his guidance, new films and operas focused as never before on the anti-Japanese guerrilla struggle of Kim Il Sung and his comrades in Manchuria during the 1930s.

In July 1971 Kim Jong Il founded the P'ibada Opera Group which produced five major "revolutionary operas." The most important was *P'ibada* (Sea of Blood), which dealt with Japanese atrocities during the colonial period and the anti-Japanese resistance led by Kim Il Sung. *P'ibada* later became a film, unofficially directed by Kim Jong Il himself, and both the play and the film were shown regularly in North Korea well into the twenty-first century. Not by accident, the opera *P'ibada* was produced to coincide with Kim Il Sung's sixtieth birthday in April 1972.[7] The sixtieth birthday, or *hwan'gap*, is one of the most important milestones in Korean culture; nothing could be more filial than to revere one's father's achievements for the whole country to see at the time of his sixtieth birthday.

The year 1973 was a turning point, after which Kim Jong Il's path to leadership succession was assured. Up until that time it appears that Kim Jong Il had serious competition from his uncle, Kim Il Sung's younger brother Kim Yŏng-ju. According to Soviet observers, Kim Jong Il and Kim Yŏng-ju continued their rivalry at least until 1976.[8] But the nephew's star had by then decisively eclipsed the uncle's. Kim Yŏng-ju disappeared from public view from 1975 until 1993, when he re-emerged as a full member of the Politburo and vice president of the state, helping North Korea through its severe post–Cold War crisis.[9] The rivalry between Kim Jong Il and his uncle was merely the most important conflict in a complex intrafamily dynamic at the apex of the North Korean leadership system.[10] By the 1970s, North Korea had become a family state unlike any other in the communist world. The DPRK in this respect was more like Saudi Arabia or a Gulf Emirate state than East Germany or Vietnam. Closer to home geographically if not ideologically, Taiwan and Singapore both saw transfers of power from their

---

7. Kang Myŏng-do, *P'yŏngyangŭn mangmyŏngŭl kkum kkunda* [Pyongyang Dreams of Defection] (Seoul: Chosŏn Ilbosa, 1995), 65.

8. GDR Embassy in Japan, 28 September 1976. "Notes on Conversation with Counselor of the USSR Embassy, Komaravsky, 23 September 1976." MfAA C6854.

9. Hwang, Truth of History, 173–74.

10. Relatives and in-laws of Kim Il Sung had positions in the regime from the beginning, but began to dominate the political system in the late 1960s and continue to do so. As the identities and backgrounds of North Korea's leadership are not often made public, much of what we know of this comes from the testimonies of high-level defectors. See for example Hwang, Truth of History, 150–51; and Kang, Pyongyang Dreams of Defection.

founding leaders to their sons in the 1980s and 1990s. But among communist states, which generally decried hereditary succession as "feudal" (as did North Korea itself until hereditary succession became official policy),[11] the Kim family's intergenerational power transfer was unique. Perhaps the Ceausescu family of Romania came close to such a monopoly of power toward the end of the communist regime there—Elena Ceausescu was allegedly slated to succeed her husband before their execution in 1989—but Nicolae Ceausescu had long been inspired by Kim Il Sung's leadership style, not excluding familial rule.[12]

Although such a move was unprecedented in the communist world, selecting Kim Il Sung's eldest son to succeed him fit logically with North Korea's evolving political culture, which had moved increasingly away from communist orthodoxy since the 1950s. Or to put it another way, the underlying layer of Korean Confucian familism was increasingly revealing itself through the palimpsest of communist ideology. Even in the earliest years of the regime, North Korean propaganda noted Kim Il Sung's "revolutionary lineage" (*hyŏngmyŏngjŏk kagye*) as one of his qualifications for his leadership.[13] Kim, in contrast to Stalin or Mao, did not become a revolutionary out of rebellion against his father but carried on his father's own revolutionary (that is, nationalist and anti-Japanese) worldview and activities. Beginning with the example of the Great Leader, North Korean propaganda increasingly stressed filial piety as a key virtue. Korean culture—even (perhaps especially) in North Korea—has long placed a supreme value on filial piety and obedience to elders.[14] Unlike in China during the Cultural Revolution, North Korean ideology simply had no place for rebellion against one's parents. The other side of filial piety is the belief that parents' values will inevitably pass down to the next generation, for good or ill. Thus children and grandchildren of landlords and pro–South Korean collaborators still face discrimination in the DPRK, and conversely descendents of revolutionaries and Korean War heroes are held to be politically and even morally superior. Given this logic, Kim Il Sung's family was the ultimate "good" family, and being raised in the bosom of the Great Leader gave Kim Jong Il the ideal background for leadership himself. As the cult of Kim Il Sung and his family became ever more entrenched in the

---

11. In the 1970 edition of its *Dictionary of Political Terminology*, the DPRK Academy of Social Sciences defined hereditary succession as "a reactionary custom of exploitative societies." The 1972 edition contained no such reference. Cited in Kongdan Oh and Ralph C. Hassig, *North Korea through the Looking Glass* (Washington, DC: Brookings Institution Press, 2000), 87.

12. Ceausescu visited North Korea in 1971 and began to institute his own version of Juche after his return to Romania.

13. Charles K. Armstrong, *The North Korean Revolution, 1945–1950* (Ithaca, NY: Cornell University Press, 2003), 226.

14. Han S. Park, *North Korea: The Politics of Unconventional Wisdom* (Boulder, CO: Lynne Reiner, 2002), 10–13.

DPRK, it became increasingly unlikely that anyone would question Kim Jong Il's right to succeed his father once the Great Leader had put his imprimatur on it. In his own way, Kim Il Sung had solved the problem of political instability that had plagued other communist states following the demise of their founding leaders. Post–Kim Il Sung North Korea was to have many profound problems, but unstable leadership succession was not among them.

A list of blood relatives and in-laws of the Kim family, compiled by the Soviet embassy in January 1974, gives a sense of the "Kim family regime" already in place in the early 1970s: in addition to Kim Jong Il and Kim Yŏng-ju, there was Kang Yang-uk, the Protestant minister related to Kim Il Sung's mother, who was vice president of the DPRK; Kim's second wife, a member of the KWP Central Committee; and Foreign Minister Hŏ Dam, the husband of Kim Il Sung's cousin. Another cousin was the vice president of the Academy of Social Sciences, Kim's brother-in-law was second secretary of the State Party Committee of Pyongyang, and several others family members occupied leading positions in the party and state.[15] The one area of leadership where Kim's relatives were conspicuously aspect was the military, but that sector was dominated by Kim Il Sung's old comrades-in-arms from his Manchurian guerrilla days, who were "blood brothers" if not biologically related.[16]

From his position in the party, Kim Jong Il was assigned to direct the Three Revolution Team Movement, a kind of more systematic and less violent version of China's Cultural Revolution. Launched in 1973, the new movement sent groups of twenty-five to fifty university-age youth to factories and collective farms around the country, tasked with raising political consciousness and economic production. The three revolutions were ideological, technical, and cultural; clearly the emphasis was more on the spiritual than the material side of things. In terms of leadership transition, the important point of the Three Revolution Team Movement was that its cadres were explicitly carrying out the orders of Kim Jong Il and pledging loyalty to him.[17] The team cadres, like Kim Jong Il, represented a new revolutionary generation, carrying on the spirit of the elders with the energy of youth. In its emphasis on revolutionary continuity rather than rupture, it was exactly the opposite of the Chinese Cultural Revolution: conservative, not radical. At this point Kim Jong Il was still working mostly behind the

---

15. GDR Embassy in DPRK, 28 January 1974. "Notes on Conversation with Comrade Samilov, Second Secretary of the Embassy of the USSR, 22 January 1974." MfAA C6954.

16. Their blood-cemented friendship with Kim Il Sung did not prevent a group of Manchuria guerrilla veterans being purged in the late 1960s, however. By some accounts the purge was directed by Kim Jong Il himself, although that has been disputed. See Hwang, Truth of History, 172–23, and Suh, *Kim Il Sung*, 239–42.

17. Kim Sung Chull, *North Korea under Kim Jong Il*, 44; Suh, *Kim Il Sung*, 277–8.

scenes, as he gradually emerged into the public spotlight. Around 1974, according to testimonies of defectors, songs about Kim Jong Il began to proliferate on the radio, surpassing even songs about Kim Il Sung.[18] In the fall of 1975, North Korean media began referring to a mysterious "Party Center" (*Tang Chungang*), apparently a person, who was issuing important directives. It soon became apparent that the Party Center was Kim Jong Il.[19]

There were and continue to be many criticisms in foreign media about Kim Jong Il's qualifications for leadership, most based on scanty information or none at all. Rumors in the West about Kim Jong Il have ranged from insanity to alcoholism to a speech impediment and debilitating illnesses. The Soviets knew Kim Jong Il better than most, and although publicly not opposed to family succession in the DPRK, privately Soviet officials did not have a particularly high opinion of Kim's character. The Soviet evaluation of Kim Jong Il is a useful corrective to the outrageous North Korean propaganda on the one hand, and the Western media's specious denigrations on the other. In January 1976, a Soviet diplomat in Pyongyang reported to an East German colleague that Kim Jong Il's university record had been distinguished not so much by "particular talents or accomplishments," as by a good deal of consorting with female classmates. In fact, the younger Kim had hardly studied at all and barely passed his course. Nevertheless, the Soviets were certain that by 1975 Kim Jong Il had already been chosen as Kim Il Sung's successor. Although the younger Kim was not yet in authority, there was really no other competition after the elimination of his uncle Kim Yŏng-ju, nor anyone with the equivalent experience in the party and state apparatus. A few aging comrades such as Ch'oe Yong-gŏn, Kim Il, and Ch'oe Hyŏn commanded the necessary respect to be Kim Il Sung's successor, but were too physically or mentally infirm to carry out such work. The military might have opposed Kim Jong Il, who had no military experience to speak of, but Kim Jong Il was already taking steps to replace key members of the military old guard with his own followers.[20] Kim Jong Il may not have been an intellectual giant, but he had a consummate talent for ruthless political maneuvering. In this respect he was very much like his father, who had maneuvered his way to leadership under the Soviet occupation thirty years before.

---

18. Author's interview with former Korean People's Army officer, New York, October 1999.

19. Morgan E. Clippinger, "Kim Chong-il in the North Korean Mass Media: A Survey of Semi-Esoteric Communication," *Asian Survey* 21, no. 3 (March 1981): 289–309. Some eyewitnesses tell of references to the "Party Center" as early as the mid-1960s (author's interview with former East European diplomat, Vienna, July 8, 2006).

20. GDR Embassy in DPRK, 3 February 1976. "Notes on Conversation of Comrade Joachim Pohl, Third Secretary of the GDR Embassy, with Second Secretary of the USSR Embassy in the DPRK, Comrade Victor Alexandrovich Tibunsky, 20 January 1976." MfAA C6854.

Kim's final step toward official succession was receiving the Order of Kim Il Sung in 1979. Like the Order of Lenin in the USSR, the Order of Kim Il Sung was the highest award granted in the DPRK. It was established in April 1972 on Kim Il Sung's sixtieth birthday, under the auspices of the Central Committee of the Korean Workers' Party. According to Kim Jong Il's 1985 biography, the Central Committee "in compliance with the unanimous wish of the Workers' Party of Korea and the Korean people" wanted to give the first award to Kim Jong Il. The young Kim modestly declined, and the decoration remained unawarded for seven years. Finally, in April 1979 Kim Jong Il accepted the award.[21]

Whether or not it is true that the Central Committee's insisted on giving Kim Jong Il the Order of Kim Il Sung and that he coyly refused for a quasi-biblical seven years, the period 1972–79 was precisely the time during which Kim was actively groomed for succession. The following year Kim Jong Il's rise to leadership went public at the Sixth Congress of the Korean Workers' Party, convened October 10–14, 1980.[22] The younger Kim was appointed to the second-highest rank in the Secretariat after his father, the third-highest rank in the Military Commission, and the fourth-highest rank in the Politburo. No North Korean leader other than Kim Il Sung had achieved such high positions in all three organizations simultaneously.[23] Kim Jong Il was now the number-two person in the entire North Korean leadership system and the unassailable heir to the throne.

As befitting a filial son, Kim Jong Il marked Kim Il Sung's seventieth birthday in 1982 with even greater reverence than he had the sixtieth. That year, Kim Jong Il unveiled some of North Korea's most grandiose monuments, including the Juche Tower and the Kaesŏn Mun, or Gate of Triumphant Return. The latter, also known as North Korea's Arc de Triomphe, celebrated Kim's return to North Korea in 1945 after his Manchurian exile and is slightly larger than the original arch in Paris. The former, of course, celebrated the ruling North Korean ideology that was now firmly under the guidance of Kim Jong Il, even as Juche became indistinguishable from the Thought of Kim Il Sung (*Kim Ilsŏng sasang*), or what was now officially called "Kim Il Sung-ism" (*Kim Ilsŏngchuŭi*).

Kim Jong Il himself made "Kim Il Sung-ism," as opposed to merely Juche, into North Korea's ruling ideology. In this way, he placed his father's thought in the direct line of communist "isms"—Marxism, Leninism, Stalinism, Maoism, Kim

21. Choe, *Kim Jong Il* 2:375–9.

22. The Communist Party of the Soviet Union began the practice of regularly convening party congresses, as often as once a year in the early USSR. The Korean Workers' Party held its first congress in August 1946, its second in March 1948, its third in April 1956, its fourth in September 1961, and its fifth in November 1970. Nearly a decade passed between the Fifth and Sixth Congresses, and as of this writing the KWP has yet to convene its Seventh Congress.

23. Suh, *Kim Il Sung*, 281; *Rodong Sinmun*, October 15, 1980, 1.

Il Sung-ism. Needless to say, Kim Jong Il argued that Kim Il Sung-ism surpassed all of its predecessors in brilliance and effectiveness. Kim Jong Il's main public role in the early 1980s was interpreting the regime's ruling ideology; he became something like the high priest of the Korean Workers' Party. Not by coincidence, the Three Revolution Team Movement led by Kim Jong Il in the early 1970s placed ideology first. Under Kim Jong Il, ideology became the centerpiece of the North Korean system as never before, and ideology was now indistinguishable from the person of his father. In other words, according to Kim Jong Il's ideological interpretation, Kim Il Sung didn't merely *convey* truth, as other leaders before him had done. Kim Il Sung *was* the Truth, and only his son could interpret this Truth to the masses.

The term *Kim Il Sung-ism* was first mentioned in a speech "On Some Problems of the Party's Task to Convert All Society into a Kimilsungism-Oriented One," given by Kim Jong Il at a KWP forum on February 19, 1974.[24] He elaborated on this concept in a March 1982 article entitled "On the Juche Idea" (*Chuch'e sasang wihayŏ*), which was the most extensive articulation to date of North Korea's official ideology.[25] The article was submitted to the National Seminar on the Juche Idea marking Kim Il Sung's seventieth birthday. Kim Jong Il's lengthy treatise (more than twenty thousand words in its English translation) was at its core an elaboration of his father's 1965 speech in Indonesia, in which Kim Il Sung had laid out the four guiding principles of Juche: Juche in ideology, independence in politics, self-sufficiency in the economy, self-reliance in self-defense. But two aspects of the younger Kim's treatise are especially striking. One is its emphasis on ideology and "consciousness" (*ŭisiksŏng*), and the other is its emphasis on the "leader" (*Suryŏngnim*). The two concepts are often linked, for example, in the statement "How the masses are awakened to consciousness and organized in a revolutionary way, and how they perform their revolutionary duties and historical mission, depend on whether or not they are given correct leadership by the party and the leader."[26]

Philosophically, Kim Jong Il's new interpretation of Juche was an idealist (as opposed to materialist) inversion of Marxism: ideas, not material conditions, drive history. Ironically perhaps, Kim traces this back to Marx himself, stating "the history of the communist movement spanning a hundred and scores of

---

24. Cited in Ilpyong J. Kim, *Historical Dictionary of North Korea* (Lanham, MD: Scarecrow Press, 2003), 74.

25. "On the Juche Idea," in *On Carrying Forward the Juche Idea* (Pyongyang: Foreign Languages Publishing House, 1995), 7–78. In Korean, see "Chuch'e sasang wihayŏ," in Suh Dae-Sook, ed., *Puk Han munhŏn yŏn'gu: munhŏn kwa haeje* [Research on North Korean Documents: Documents and Introduction], vol. 3 (Seoul: Kyungnam University Institute for Far Eastern Affairs, 2004), 191.

26. "On the Juche Idea," 31.

years is *a history of working-class leaders creating revolutionary ideas, a history in which these ideas have been applied to transform the world.*[27] Every age and place had its own "guiding idea of revolution," and Kim Il Sung had created Juche as the perfect guide for Korea. Politically, the message of "On the Juche Idea" appears straightforward: regardless of material circumstances, the masses owe unquestioning obedience to the Great Leader, who alone can bring the masses to consciousness. This message would be extremely useful for the North Korean state in the difficult years ahead.

Kim Jong Il's next major treatise on ideology was published on October 17, 1982. Bearing the ungainly title "The Workers' Party of Korea Is a Juche-type Revolutionary Party which Inherited the Glorious Tradition of the DIU," Kim's paper was another paean to his father, emphasizing Kim Il Sung's anti-Japanese guerrilla struggle and his alleged founding of the Down with Imperialism Union (DIU) as a fourteen-year-old student in China.[28] Unlike in the more abstract "On the Juche Idea," here Kim Jong Il grounded Juche specifically in the history of his father's guerrilla experiences, with which the younger Kim became increasingly associated. In the early 1980s, North Korean propaganda placed Kim Jong Ils' birth in a Lincolnesque log cabin at a guerrilla base camp on the slopes of Mount Paektu, Korea's largest mountain straddling the border with China. As his official biography notes, "The son of the General [Kim Il Sung] . . . was born and grew on Mount Paektu, on the field of battle against the Japanese imperialists."[29] Historically, the above statement is doubly false: Kim Il Sung did not operate at a base on Mount Paektu, and he and Kim Jong Il's mother were nowhere near the Korean border when their son was born. The younger Kim was born in 1942 at a military camp near Khabarovsk in Russia, where his father and the remnants of his Manchurian guerrilla group (including Kim Jong Il's mother, Kim Chŏng-suk) spent the final years of World War II in a special reconnaissance unit of the Soviet Far Eastern Army.[30] Nevertheless, North Korean media duly produced "evidence" of Kim Il

---

27. Ibid., 9. Emphasis added.

28. The speech appeared in the KWP theoretical journal *Kŭlloja* [The Worker] 487 (November 1982): 3–25. English translations may be found in Kim Jong Il, *On Enhancing the Party's Leading Role*, 87–123, and *Carrying Forward the Juche Idea*, 79–141. It should be noted that early North Korean speeches by and biographies of Kim Il Sung make no mention of the DIU, and no independent evidence from North Korea or China has ever been produced to support the claim that he founded such an organization.

29. Choe, *Kim Jong Il*, 1:1.

30. Soviet and Japanese records establish Kim Il Sung at a Soviet base during the time of Kim Jong Il's birth. See Chung'ang Ilbo, *Pirok: Chosŏn Minjujŭi Inmin Konghwaguk* [Secret Record: The Democratic People's Republic of Korea], vol. 1 (Seoul: Chung'ang ilbosa, 1991); and Wada Haruki, *Kin Nichisei to Manshû kônichi sensô* [Kim Il Sung and the Anti-Japanese War in Manchuria] (Tokyo: Heibonsha, 1992). Kim Il Sung's activities in the Russian Far East were acknowledged in early North Korean publications, but the "secret guerrilla camp" on Mt. Paektu and Kim Jong Il's birth there began appearing in North Korean propaganda in the 1970s, when Kim's succession was established.

Sung's base camp, including falsified revolutionary graffiti scratched into local trees, and Kim Jong Il's log cabin "birthplace" became a site of political pilgrimage.

By the 1980s the cult of the Kim family extended back several generations through both paternal and maternal lines. Kim Il Sung's great-grandfather Kim Ung U was alleged to have led the attack on the USS *General Sherman*, an American merchant ship that had the misfortune of running aground near Pyongyang in 1866.[31] Kim Jong Il's mother Kim Chŏng-suk gained a substantial personality cult of her own. The birthplace of Kim Il Sung in Mangyŏngdae outside of Pyongyang became a shrine to the Great Leader's family, which in a revolutionary twist on Confucian tradition was said to have "educated their children in the high spirits of patriotism and revolution" from generation to generation.[32] Clearly the regime was attempting to mobilize familial emotions to elicit citizen loyalty, with a certain implicit division of emotional identification. Whereas Kim Il Sung became identified with paternal imagery, referred to increasingly as "father" (*abŏji*) by the 1970s,[33] Kim Jong Il was associated with more maternal images of tenderness, intimacy, and love. He became the "Beloved" or "Dear" Leader, the center of the "Mother Party" (*ŏmŏnidang*). The sentiment this imagery is apparently expected to inspire is not obedience to the stern authority of the father, but spontaneous love for the motherly party-state, represented by Kim Jong Il. Love for parents and love for nation were said to be inseparable. According to a biography of Kim Il Sung's mother, Kang Pan-sŏk: "Indeed, there cannot be a patriot, who would not love and respect his parents. Any patriot loves his parents, wife and children above all. These feelings are not only connected with the persons near and dear, they are closely bound up with the motherland's destiny."[34]

North Korea became a full-fledged family state in the 1980s not only in the sense of one-family rule, but in the self-image of the whole society as a nuclear family. The "familization" of North Korea represented by Kim Jong Il's succession was a further step in the increasingly inward-looking, nationalistic path North Korea had pursued since the 1950s. Henceforth the DPRK would give little more than lip service to Marxism-Leninism or proletarian internationalism.[35] North Korean

31. Choe, *Kim Jong Il*, 1:18.

32. Ibid., 1:16.

33. Thomas Hosuck Kang, "Changes in the North Korean Personality from Confucian to Communist," in Jae Kyu Park and Jung Gun Kim, eds., *The Politics of North Korea* (Seoul: Kyungnam University Institute for Far Eastern Studies, 1979), 93

34. *The Mother of Korea: Biographical Novel* (Pyongyang: Foreign Languages Publishing House, 1978), 108.

35. After the collapse of the Soviet Union, the revised DPRK Constitution of 1992 dropped all references to Marxism-Leninism, declaring Juche to be the "guiding principle" of North Korean politics. See Christopher Hale, "Multifunctional Juche: A Study of the Changing Dynamic between Juche and the State Constitution in North Korea," *Korea Journal* 42, no. 3 (autumn 2002): 283–308.

publications continued to speak of the "working class," but the main emphasis in North Korea propaganda was not on class conflict, but on the conflict between the Korean nation (represented by Kim Il Sung) against aggressive and hostile outside forces. The nation was a family, Kim Il Sung was the father, the party was the mother, and all foreigners were outside the boundaries of understanding and intimacy. Communist or capitalist, developed or undeveloped, other countries had nothing to teach the Kims' Korea, which would go its own unique way. Politically and economically, North Korea may have looked like the most unreformed of communist states in the early 1980s. Ideologically however, North Korea was already becoming postcommunist.

The Changing Correlation of Forces

The Soviet invasion of Afghanistan in December 1979 and the election of the hawkish Ronald Reagan to the American presidency in November 1980 marked a period of renewed Soviet-American tensions that some have called the "Second Cold War."[36] Strictly speaking, the Cold War between the US-aligned nations on the one hand, and the Soviet Union and its allies on the other, continued uninterrupted from the late 1940s until the collapse of the Soviet Union in 1991. But at the end of the 1970s, the overall relaxation in East-West tensions embodied in US-Soviet détente gave way to a more confrontational relationship between Washington and Moscow. The geopolitics of the new Cold War was not the same as that of the pre-détente period, which had reflected a bipolar, communist ver sus anticommunist global conflict. In fact, "East-West" conflict had not been a bipolar confrontation since the early 1960s, but rather a three-cornered struggle among the United States, the USSR, and China. In its final decade of existence, the Soviet Union was very much the odd man out in this triangle, facing fierce criticism and opposition from both the United States and China.[37]

President Ronald Reagan led the attack, famously calling the Soviet Union an "evil empire." But the United States would not engage in the kind of direct military confrontation with communist forces that had led to the Cuban Missile Crisis and ignominious American defeat in Indochina. After the debacle of Vietnam, American policy toward communism shifted to "low-intensity conflict"

---

36. As Fred Halliday wrote at the time, "If the First Cold War was clearly anticommunist, this Second Cold War was more specifically directed against the USSR." Halliday, *The Making of the Second Cold War* (London: Verso, 1983). This hawkish and anti-Soviet turn in American foreign policy began in the last two years of the Carter administration, even before the invasion of Afghanistan, but the Soviet invasion and Reagan's election consolidated it.

37. Ibid. 20.

through proxy forces in places like southern Africa, Central America, and Afghanistan.[38] Despite the anticommunist rhetoric, American actions were driven more by power politics than ideology, and the once-demonized "Red China" was a convenient partner against the Soviet enemy. While denouncing communism more harshly and directly than at any time since the 1960s, the United States drew increasingly close to the People's Republic of China, with which it had established full diplomatic relations on January 1, 1979. In short, the "Second Cold War" was between the United States and USSR, and Great Power politics in the 1970s and 1980s were dominated by a strategic triangle among Washington, Moscow, and Beijing with much of the Third World as a proxy battleground. For North Korea, reform within socialist countries and the confrontation between the Soviet Union and the United States changed very little. But the increasingly warm relationship between the United States and China, and the unrelenting hostility between Beijing and Moscow, were troubling.

The End of Anti-Imperialist Solidarity

Kim Il Sung's major foreign policy statement at the Sixth Party Congress was entitled "Let Us Strengthen the Unity of the Anti-Imperialist, Independent Forces."[39] By 1980 such sentiments already sounded jarringly out of date, compared to the global situation of just a few years earlier. Kim appealed in particular to the unity of the socialist countries and of the nonaligned and developing nations, two groups that were becoming increasingly fragmented. Acknowledging the Sino-Soviet confrontation, albeit without naming any countries specifically, Kim noted that "at present, because of differences of opinion the socialist countries and the Communist and Workers' Parties fail to achieve unity and solidarity and play the role they should play in world revolution. The differences among fraternal parties and solidarity of the socialist forces and the international communist movement must be achieved as soon as possible."[40] The Sino-Soviet split was old news, of course, even if the growing ties between China and the United States added another troubling dimension to the rift. But the Third World solidarity embodied in the 1955 Bandung Conference, the nonaligned movement (NAM), and opposition to the Vietnam War was rapidly fraying as the 1980s

---

38. Mahmood Mamjani, *Good Muslim, Bad Muslim: America, the Cold War, and the Roots of Terror* (New York: Pantheon, 2004), 95–100. The Afghan case would create a major "blowback," in the form of a US-armed anti-Soviet Mujahideen that would later became the source of terrorist attacks against the United States itself.

39. Kim, *Report to the Sixth Congress of the Workers' Party of Korea on the Work of the Central Committee* (Pyongyang: Foreign Languages Publishing House, 1980), 82–96.

40. Ibid., 91–92.

began. By the middle of the decade, many Third World countries had rejected the revolutionary model represented by Cuba, North Korea, and Vietnam and turned for inspiration to the East Asian "miracle" economies of South Korea, Taiwan, Singapore, and Hong Kong. As the historian Vijay Prashad aptly summarized, the 1983 NAM summit meeting in New Delhi "allows us to write the obituary of the Third World."[41]

Despite (or because of) these realities, Kim called for unity among developing countries as well as within the socialist bloc. According to Kim, the common enemy of all of them—the socialist countries, nonaligned countries, and newly emerging nations—was a relentless global imperialism led by the United States. "We must not have any illusions about imperialism," Kim declared. "Its aggressive nature will never change."[42] Only its "methods of aggression" would change, not its intent. Therefore there could be no "unprincipled compromises" with the imperialists. Kim's stated view of the world in 1980 remained as rigidly binary as it had been thirty years before: "imperialists" (Western capitalist countries, led by the United States) versus everyone else.

However, presumably without making any "unprincipled compromises," North Korea continued to reach out to the United States for improving relations between the two countries. Representative Stephen Solarz of Brooklyn, New York, visited the DPRK in July 1980, the first American congressman to do so. Solarz was received by Kim Il Sung, and the two met for a series of conversations over three days. Among other initiatives, Kim proposed dropping preconditions for North-South humanitarian discussions and having cultural exchanges between the DPRK and the United States.[43] In addition to such rare direct talks, North Korea also sent messages to the United States through intermediaries. For example, in April 1983 President Hosni Mubarak of Egypt visited Pyongyang, where DPRK officials asked him to convey to Washington North Korea's desire for bilateral talks leading to diplomatic normalization.[44]

Because of its historic friendship with the DPRK and its growing closeness to the United States, China became the most important intermediary between North Korea and the United States at this time, a role China would continue to play in the decades ahead. With Chinese support, Pyongyang shifted its position

---

41. Vijay Prashad, *The Darker Nations: A People's History of the Third World* (New York: New Press, 2007), 209.

42. Kim, *Report to the Sixth Congress*, 88.

43. Henry Scott Stokes, "President of North Korea Drops a Condition for Talks with South," *New York Times*, July 19, 1980, 1; "Solarz Says North Koreans Want Cultural Exchanges," *New York Times*, July 21, 1980, A7.

44. Samuel S. Kim, *The Two Koreas and the Great Powers* (Cambridge: Cambridge University Press, 2006), 243.

from bilateral talks with the United States alone to tripartite talks among North Korea, South Korea, and the United States. The United States had long demanded South Korean participation in any talks with the DPRK and had conveyed that demand to the Chinese for the past decade.[45] North Korea now responded in kind, first proposing trilateral talks to the United States via China in October 1983. In April 1984, Zhao Ziyang and Hu Yaobang brought up tripartite talks again in discussion with Ronald Reagan.[46] But North Korea's overtures to the United States were more than offset by fears of Reagan's military buildup in South Korea, which Pyongyang attacked vociferously. The Korean Peninsula was the application point for the Reagan administration's new Airland Battle doctrine, which called for swift military strikes deep within North Korean territory in the event of hostilities. South Korea was on the front line against the global communist threat ("freedom's frontier" as the US military called it), and the Reagan administration aggressively modernized and expanded its military assistance to the ROK, including deliveries to South Korea of America's most advanced fighter jet, the F-16. Central to new US military thinking on Korea was the use of nuclear weapons. The United States had placed nuclear weapons in South Korea since 1958, but the majority of these weapons had been removed under President Carter. The Reagan administration reversed this, increasing the number of American nuclear weapons from about twenty into the hundreds.[47] The Korean Peninsula had been a potential nuclear flashpoint since the Korean War. Under the Reagan buildup, the danger of nuclear war in Korea reached unprecedented heights.

North Korea was not alone in condemning the US conventional and nuclear buildup in Korea, which paralleled American and NATO military buildup in Europe. North Korea especially attacked the US-ROK joint "Team Spirit" military exercises. These exercises had begun in 1976, and it was in part North Korea's response to Team Spirit that led to the DMZ axe murder incident that year. By 1983 Team Spirit was the largest US-led multilateral military exercise in the world, involving nearly 200,000 troops, nuclear-capable B-52 bombers, and mock incursions into North Korean territory.[48] North Korea condemned Team Spirit in

---

45. For example, when Henry Kissinger met with Deng Xiaoping in Beijing in 1975, he started the discussion on Korea by stating, "We have said that we are prepared to talk to North Korea, in any forum that includes South Korea." Gerald R. Ford Library, Memorandum of Conversation, Deng Xiaoping [Teng Hsiao-p'ing] and Henry A. Kissinger," 22 October 1975. Reproduced in Christian F. Ostermann and James F. Person, eds., *After Détente: The Korean Peninsula, 1973–1976* (Washington, DC: North Korea International Documentation Project, Woodrow Wilson International Center for Scholars, 2011), 567.

46. Byung-joon Ahn, "North Korea and the United States in Global and Regional Perspective," in Robert Scalapino and Hongkoo Lee, *North Korea in a Regional and Global Context* (Berkeley: University of California Press, 1986), 291.

47. Peter Hayes, *Pacific Powderkeg: American Nuclear Dilemmas in Korea* (Lexington, MA: Lexington Books, 1991), 89, 84.

48. Ibid., 93.

no uncertain terms, calling the exercises practice invasions of the DPRK (which, of course, they were).[49] If North Korea was the perfect embodiment of the "communist menace" in Reagan's new Cold War, the Reagan administration nakedly exposed "American imperialism" for the DPRK. The KWP journal *Kŭlloja* in July 1983 published an article entitled "The Reagan Administration Is the Most Bellicose of All Past Administrations that Have Made a Profession Out of Aggression and War."[50] Not surprisingly then, North Korea looked for greater support from America's main enemy, the Soviet Union.

Leaning Toward Moscow

North Korea and China may have spoken loudly of their mutual friendship, but when it came to confronting a newly assertive United States, North Korea's position was much closer to that of the Soviets. While attempting to maintain good relations with both Beijing and Moscow, in some respects North Korea began "leaning toward" the USSR in the 1980s. This was especially true in the area of military assistance. Pyongyang and Moscow signed new economic and military agreements in the mid-1980s that brought the two countries closer together than they had been in decades.[51] Both sides had reservations about this newfound intimacy: the Soviets were far from enthusiastic about the Kim cult, family succession, and North Korea's ideological atavism in general, while the North Koreans were wary of Soviet heavy-handedness in Eastern Europe, Afghanistan, and Indochina. North Korea did not join the Soviet-led Council on Mutual Economic Assistance (Comecon), as Vietnam had done in 1978, but it refrained from joining China in denouncing Soviet "social imperialism." This was not the old ideological solidarity of the 1950s. North Korea needed the USSR materially, while the Soviet Union needed North Korea strategically. Moscow-Pyongyang reconciliation was in turn part of a broader reconfiguring of relations in the communist world of the late Cold War.

The "high tide of revolution" Kim Il Sung had declared in Beijing in 1975 had begun rapidly receding by the end of the decade. The relationship between the Soviet Union and its ostensible allies, to say nothing of rival China, had become immensely more complicated in just two short years between 1978 and 1980. The Soviet invasion of Afghanistan in December 1979 was followed eight months later by labor unrest in Gdansk, Poland, leading to the worst crisis in the Warsaw

---

49. Pak T'ae-ho, *Chosŏn Minjujŭi Inmin Konghwaguk taeoe kwangyesa* [History of DPRK Foreign Relations] (Pyongyang: Sahe kwahak ch'ulp'ansa, 1987), 269.

50. *Kŭlloja* 495 (July 1983): 28–37.

51. Dmitri Volkogonov, *Autopsy for an Empire: The Seven Leaders Who Built the Soviet Regime*, ed. and trans. Harold Shiman (New York: The Free Press, 1999), 418–19.

Pact since the Prague Spring of 1968. In December 1981 General Wojciech Jaruzelski declared martial law in Poland, temporarily defusing the crisis. But the price to the Soviets was very high, both economically—some 1.5 billion dollars in aid to Poland in 1981 alone—and politically, as the Polish crisis marked in retrospect the beginning of the unraveling of the entire Soviet bloc.[52]

The situation in Indochina was even more complex. One month after signing a Treaty of Friendship and Cooperation with the USSR, Vietnam invaded Cambodia in December 1978, apparently without informing the Soviets in advance of their invasion plans.[53] Vietnam removed the Khmer Rouge from power, installed a pro-Hanoi government in Phnom Penh, and maintained a military presence in Cambodia until 1989. China, the most important backer of the Khmer Rouge, engaged Vietnam in a brief border war in early 1979. Although Chinese forces were pushed back, China continued to support the Khmer Rouge in exile, joining a de facto anti-Vietnamese alliance with the United States, which also supported Cambodia's coalition government in exile—although the United States did not in theory support the Khmer Rouge directly.[54] North Korea, as we have seen in the previous chapter, had been at times a strong supporter of both North Vietnam and the Khmer Rouge, and tried to stay out of this dispute as much as possible.[55] For the Soviet Union, the upshot of this unrest in Eastern Europe, Southeast Asia, and Central Asia, as well ongoing support for pro-Soviet regimes in Africa, the Middle East and Cuba (and, after 1979, Nicaragua), was continued economic outlay and confrontation with American and Chinese proxies. Like virtually every other Soviet ally in the 1980s, North Korea was a strategic asset and an economic liability. But for now at least, the Kremlin thought North Korea important enough to accede to its requests for increased aid.

Most of the new Soviet economic and military aid to North Korea came after Kim Il Sung's visit to the USSR in May 1984, which will be covered later in this chapter. Overall, Soviet-DPRK economic relations had increased dramatically since the mid-1970s. According to Soviet records, for example, North Korean exports to the USSR were relatively flat between 1970 and 1975, then nearly doubled

---

52. Vladslov M. Zubok, *A Failed Empire: The Soviet Union in the Cold War from Stalin to Gorbachev* (Chapel Hill: University of North Carolina Press, 2007), 270.

53. Stephen J. Morris, "The Soviet-Chinese-Vietnamese Triangle in the 1970s," in Priscilla Roberts, ed., *Behind the Bamboo Curtain: China, Vietnam, and the World Beyond Asia* (Stanford: Stanford University Press, 2006), 425, and *Why Vietnam Invaded Cambodia: Political Culture and the Causes of War* (Stanford: Stanford University Press, 1999), 215.

54. Edwin A. Martini, *Invisible Enemies: The American War on Vietnam, 1975–2000* (Amherst: University of Massachusetts Press, 2007), 83–114.

55. North Korea continued to host the exiled Cambodian Prince Norodom Sihanouk, who called Kim Il Sung his "best friend." Henry Scott Stokes, "A President and a Prince Live the Good Life in Korea," *New York Times*, July 22, 1980.

between 1975 and 1980, and increased by almost 50 percent again between 1980 and 1986.[56] North Korean requests for Soviet economic assistance also increased in the early 1980s. A KWP delegation led by Premier Yi Chŏng-ok, attending the Twenty-sixth CPSU Congress in Moscow in 1981, met with Soviet Premier Nikolai Tikhonov mainly to discuss economic issues. The North Koreans asked for the Soviets to accelerate and expand the development of the Kim Ch'aek metal works, already the largest iron and steel combine in the country. The DPRK hoped to quadruple steel production there by 1985. The Soviets agreed to consider it, meanwhile promising to defer repayment of 400 million of the 700 million rubles currently owed by the North Koreans and due in 1985. However, Tikhonov emphasized that after 1985 interest on the repayment would increase from 2 to 4 percent, something that "surprised" the North Koreans. Russian largesse, the North Koreans would soon learn, was not inexhaustible. The two sides also agreed on continued North Korean participation in coal mining and lumbering in Siberia.[57]

The North Koreans were especially keen on aid for their nuclear program. Yi Chŏng-ok's delegation brought up the question of the USSR building North Korea a nuclear power plant, which the Soviets explained was a "complicated request belonging to the category of long-term planning" and would require North Korea's own financial investment, as the Czechs and others were doing in similar ventures with the USSR. The North Koreans had no answer to this; apparently they were hoping the Soviets would give them the technology for free, as in the heyday of post–Korean War reconstruction.[58] Around this time North Korean delegations also visited technical universities and colleges in Czechoslovakia and East Germany, where training and assistance in their nuclear program was at the top of their wish list.[59] But, in addition to lack of resources and trained personnel, one significant obstacle to nuclear cooperation for the DPRK was North Korea's hesitance to join the Nuclear Non-Proliferation Treaty (NPT). The Soviets and their East European allies urged North Korea to join the NPT, but North Korea put it off until 1985, citing the presence of US nuclear weapons in South Korea as one of the reasons for not joining.[60]

56. Natalia Bazhanova, *Kiroe sŏn Puk Han kyŏngje* [North Korean Economy at the Crossroads], trans. Yang Chun-yong (Seoul: Hanguk kyŏngje sinmunsa, 1992), 119.

57. Report, Embassy of Hungary in North Korea to the Hungarian Foreign Ministry, 12 March 1981. XIX-J-1-j Korea, 1981, 86. doboz, 103, 002477/1981. Obtained and translated for the Cold War International History Project by Balázs Szalontai.

58. Ibid.

59. Report, Embassy of Hungary in North Korea to the Hungarian Foreign Ministry, 30 April 1981. XIX-J-1-j Korea, 1981, 86. doboz. 72, 003729/1981. Obtained and translated for the Cold War International History Project by Balázs Szalontai.

60. Report, Embassy of Hungary in North Korea to the Hungarian Foreign Ministry, 4 August 1983. XIX-J-1-j Korea, 1983, 78. doboz. 81–40, 004628/1983. Obtained and translated for the Cold War International History Project by Balázs Szalontai.

Of course, DPRK-Soviet cooperation on nuclear technology had a long history, as we have seen in previous chapters. The first nuclear research center in North Korea was built in Yŏngbyŏn with Soviet assistance in the 1960s. Again with Soviet assistance, North Korea began construction of a five-megawatt reactor at Yŏngbyŏn in 1980, and the reactor first went critical in 1985. Russian scientists and officials have long insisted that Soviet policy forbade any exchange of nuclear weapons technology with the DPRK, or any export of excessive supplies of nuclear fuel that could be used for weapons.[61] But in the face of an expanding American nuclear presence in South Korea, as well as South Korea's own recent history of nuclear weapons development, an independent nuclear deterrent could not have been far from the minds of North Korea's leaders in the early 1980s. In the event, North Korea was well positioned to build its own nuclear weapons when the Soviet nuclear umbrella disappeared ten years later.

The escalating superpower tensions of the Second Cold War reached a climax with the Korean Airline (KAL) incident of September 1, 1983. When KAL 007, a South Korea-based commercial airline, crossed inadvertently into Soviet airspace off Sakhalin Island, Soviet air defenses misidentified the craft as an American warplane and shot it down. All 269 passengers were killed. The Soviet authorities first denied the incident, and later insisted the incursion into Soviet airspace had been a deliberate American provocation. Post-Soviet revelations have shown that the act was the result of errors and miscalculations, not a deliberate attack on innocent civilians.[62] Nevertheless, the KAL 007 incident was another blow to the Soviet reputation, and the shoot-down was angrily condemned in the United States, Western Europe, Japan, and South Korea. Although North Korea was not involved in the KAL 007 tragedy and had little to say about it, the incident compounded Soviet-American tensions on a global level and over Korea in particular—and gave an ominous foretaste of North Korea's attacks on South Korean officials and civilians shortly to follow.

Friendship with China

While North Korea and the Soviet Union drew closer together, China took pains to reassure North Korea of Beijing's continued support, including support for North Korea's hereditary leadership succession, a subject on which the Soviets had been largely silent. Mutual visits, whether of high officials or civil organizations,

---

61. Valery I. Denisov, "Nuclear Institutions and Organizations in North Korea," in James Clay Moltz and Alexandre Y. Mansourov, eds., *The North Korean Nuclear Program: Security Strategy and New Perspectives from Russia* (London: Routledge, 2000), 21.

62. Volkogonov, *Autopsy for an Empire*, 269; Zubok, *Failed Empire*, 272.

public or secret, were much more frequent between North Korea and China than between North Korea and the Soviet Union. And unlike the Soviets, the Chinese were willing to meet with Kim Jong Il and acknowledge the younger Kim's new position in the DPRK hierarchy. Chinese leaders Deng Xiaoping and Hu Yaobang visited North Korea secretly in April 1982, where they met with Kim Jong Il; Hu also visited North Korea in 1985, meeting both the elder and younger Kims. Kim Jong Il, accompanied by Defense Minister O Chin-u, secretly visited China in June 1983 and met with top leaders there, followed by Kim Il Sung's meeting with Deng Xiaoping in the Northeast Chinese city of Dalian two months later.[63]

China's alliance with the DPRK was a crucial pillar of its security in eastern Asia. North Korea was the last socialist state in the region over which China still held influence. Mongolia had been in the Soviet camp from the beginning, and Vietnam, Laos, and Cambodia were all firmly pro-Moscow. It would be a nightmare for Beijing if the Soviets were to establish a naval presence in North Korea, as they had at Cam Ranh Bay in southern Vietnam after the Americans left.[64] Pyongyang's leaders were well aware of this, and tried to exploit their importance to Chinese security by asking for military assistance and advanced weaponry from the PRC. Although China could not compete with the USSR in this arena, they did supply items such as the F-7 fighter jet, the Chinese version of the MiG-21, some forty of which they delivered to North Korea in 1982.[65] But Beijing's main support was political and diplomatic. China consistently backed Pyongyang's demand for the complete withdrawal of US troops from South Korea and recognized the DPRK as the sole legitimate government on the Korean Peninsula. China's leaders and state media referred often to the "fraternal" and "blood-cemented friendship" between the China and North Korea, and the memories of shared sacrifice in the Korean War were still strong among the Chinese military leadership, many of whom were veterans of the conflict.

In the economic realm, Sino–North Korean relations remained close, but here also China could not compete at the level of the Soviet Union. In the 1970s and 1980s trade with China comprised about 20 percent of North Korea's overall trade, significantly less than the 30 percent that North Korea traded with the USSR. The two counties engaged in extensive cross-border trade along the Yalu and Tumen rivers, and as with the USSR, North Korea's overall trade with China

63. Deng Xiaoping, *Deng Xiaoping Nianpu: 1975–1997*, vol. 2 (Beijing: Zhongyang wenxian chubanshe, 2005), 817; Yi Chong-sŏk, *Puk Han-Chungguk kwangye, 1945–2000* [North-Korean China Relations, 1945–2000] (Seoul: Jungshim, 2000), 262–63; Pak, History of DPRK Foreign Relations, 203–10.

64. Chae-Jin Lee, *China and Korea: Dynamic Relations* (Stanford: Hoover Institution Press, 1996), 70.

65. Ibid., 72.

expanded considerably in the late 1970s, although by a much smaller propor-tion.[66] North Korea received more advanced technology and manufactured goods from the Soviet Union, but China stepped up its economic aid to North Korea at this time, and crucially supplied the DPRK with oil—at cut-rate "friend-ship" prices—from the Daqing oil fields in Northeast China via the China-Korea Friendship Pipeline, completed in 1976.[67]

China at this time was embarking on Deng Xiaoping's wide-ranging eco-nomic reform program under the slogan of "The Four Modernizations" (agri-culture, industry, technology, and defense). In retrospect, the divergence between China's market-oriented path and North Korea's Stakhanovite conservatism ap-pears enormous, but at the time the two countries were not dissimilar in their approach to economic development. Despite North Korea's emphasis on self-reliance, which the Chinese abandoned early on in the reform process, the DPRK was willing to entertain the possibility of limited economic reform, albeit more cautiously than China. Kim Jong Il's extensive tour of China in June 1983, which included visits to some of China's new foreign-investment sites, may have in-fluenced North Korea's decision to set up a new law on foreign investment the following year.

On the surface, North Korea tried to demonstrate a policy of equidistance, or more accurately equal friendship, toward both China and the USSR. The twen-tieth anniversaries of North Korea's mutual security treaties with Moscow and Beijing in 1981 were covered with equal fanfare in the North Korean media.[68] The DPRK refused to side with the Soviets in condemning China's "hegemonic aspi-rations" in Southeast Asia, just as they refused to join China in attacking Soviet interventions in Eastern Europe and Central Asia.[69] As ever, North Korea played the two communist Great Powers against each other. The early 1980s were a par-ticularly fruitful time for North Korea to play this game, as each side was willing to offer North Korea substantial economic, military, and political support to keep Pyongyang in its orbit. At a global level, the Soviet Union was the odd man out in the Moscow-Beijing-Washington triangle, but within the communist world, the balance of power was tilted heavily toward the Soviet Union. After Nixon's visit to

---

66. Bazhanova, North Korean Economy, 221. Total trade between the PRC and DPRK increased from $481.8 million in 1975 to $677.5 million in 1980. There was a much bigger leap in the first half of the 1970s, from $155 million to $481.8 million.

67. GDR Embassy to the DPRK, "Note About a Conversation with the Soviet Ambassador, Com-rade Kryulin, on 5 May 1976 in his Residence," 6 May 1976. MfAA C6854. Translated for the North Korea International Documentation Project by Bernd Schaefer.

68. *Nodong Sinmun*, July 5, 1981 and July 11, 1981. The nuance however was slightly different: the headline on the Korea-Soviet treaty referred to it simply as a "treaty of cooperation and mutual as-sistance," whereas the treaty with China was called a "fraternal treaty of friendship and cooperation."

69. Embassy of Hungary Report, 12 March 1981.

China in 1972, the PRC had lost its one friend in Eastern Europe, Enver Hoxha's Albania. By the end of the 1980s, all the smaller communist states in Asia except the DPRK were firmly in the Soviet camp. China, despite its alignment with the United States, needed to strengthen ties with North Korea to avoid isolation in communist Eurasia. Thus China embraced North Korea more warmly than did the USSR, but North Korea relied more on the Soviets and their allies for material benefits.

South Korea in Transition

Like the DPRK, South Korea also underwent a change of leadership in the early 1980s, but much more violently than the North. President Park Chung Hee's deepening "Yushin" dictatorship was brought to an abrupt end by his assassination, at the hand of his own chief of intelligence, on October 26, 1979. Less then two months later, on December 12, Major General Chun Doo-hwan took over the South Korean military with the backing of other members of his eleventh class of the ROK Military Academy. In a pattern reminiscent of the tumult between Syngman Rhee's resignation in April 1960 and Park's own coup in May 1961, there followed a period of political uncertainty and high hopes for democratic change. But these hopes were dashed in April 1980, when Chun declared himself head of the Korean Central Intelligence Agency, Park's most notorious instrument of coercion and social control, and moved the country toward martial law. Protests erupted throughout the country, especially on university campuses in Seoul and in the southwestern provincial capital of Kwangju, hometown of longtime opposition leader Kim Dae Jung.[70] On May 17 Chun declared martial law, and the following day the protests in Kwangju were brutally put down by Special Forces paratroopers. The crackdown led to a popular local response that became a full-scale insurrection, and for a few days the city of Kwangju was ruled by local citizens' councils, beyond the reach of the central government. On May 27, the army moved in. The result was a massacre that killed hundreds of Kwangju citizens.[71] The bloody suppression in Kwangju would haunt Chun's entire presidency, until he was forced to step down amidst nationwide protests in 1987.

---

70. Kim Dae Jung was arrested and sentenced to death for inciting the protests in Kwangju. His death sentence was later commuted, under strong pressure by the United States, and Kim became president himself in 1998.

71. See, among others, Gi-wook Shin and Kyung Moon Hwang, eds., *Contentious Kwangju: The May 18th Uprising in Korea's Past and Present* (Lanham, MD: Rowman & Littlefield, 2003). For the then US ambassador's perspective on this event, see William H. Gleysteen Jr., *Massive Entanglement, Marginal Influence: Carter and Korea in Crisis* (Washington, DC: Brookings Institution Press, 1999), 127–43.

Similar to the 1960 "Student Revolution" in Seoul, the tumult surrounding Chun's coup and the Kwangju Incident offered North Korea a potential opening for political gains in the South, and may have even raised hopes once again for a collapse of the South Korean government and unification on the North's terms. Certainly North Korea tried to get the maximum possible political gain from denouncing Chun's "fascist coup" and the suppression of popular protest. But Pyongyang's approach to South Korea's internal affairs was a cautious one. As Kim Il Sung put it, two days after Park's assassination, "We must wait and see what change this will bring about in the revolutionary situation in South Korea."[72] The latter half of the 1970s was probably the last point at which the DPRK held any serious hope of a military solution that would unify Korea in the North's favor. As we have seen in the previous chapter, the North Vietnamese conquest of the South in April 1975 might have suggested that Korean unification would follow suit, an idea reinforced by US presidential candidate Jimmy Carter's campaign promise the following year to pull American troops out of Korea, signaling a reduced American military commitment to the ROK.[73] But the Carter administration reversed itself on the troop withdrawal in 1979, and if there had been any chance that chaos in the ROK would invite a North Korean intervention, the establishment of Chun's iron-fisted rule in 1980 and Reagan's declaration of unqualified commitment to the ROK's defense in 1981 soon closed that window of opportunity.[74] Thereafter, even the military balance shifted away from the North, the economic gap grew increasingly in the South's favor, and the DPRK and ROK experienced a "diplomatic reversal"—analogous to the "economic reversal" that had begun in the late 1960s—with more and more countries recognizing the South at the expense of the North.[75]

In the abstract, North Korea never gave up on the idea that South Korea would one day undergo a socialist revolution and join the North under a single revolutionary government. But in concrete terms, by the 1980s it was clear to North Korea's leaders that the balance of forces on the Korean Peninsula had shifted toward the South, military and economically if not politically, and that unification on

72. Cited in Oberdorfer, *The Two Korea: A Contemporary History*, rev. ed. (New York: Basic Books, 2001), 116.

73. Nicholas Eberstadt, "North Korea's Unification Policy, 1948–1996," in Samuel S. Kim, ed., *North Korean Foreign Relations in the Post-Cold War Era* (Hong Kong: Oxford University Press, 1998), 242; Oberdorfer, *The Two Koreas*, 84.

74. Chun Doo Hwan was the first foreign head of state to visit the White House after Ronald Reagan's inauguration in January 1981, and Reagan rapidly expanded and modernized US military assistance to the ROK. See Peter Hayes, *Pacific Powderkeg*, 89–103.

75. Barry K. Gills, *Korea versus Korea: A Case of Contested Legitimacy* (London: Routledge, 1996), 190.

Pyongyang's term was not likely to happen any time soon. Reflecting recognition of these new realities, North Korea's policy toward South Korea changed in 1980 from a "revolutionary strategy" to a "federation strategy," emphasizing collaboration between two distinct entities rather than—or as an important step toward—full-scale unification. This amalgamation policy was encapsulated in the term "Democratic Confederal Republic of Koryŏ" (DCRK), which would be a central theme in North Korea's unification proposals to the South for the next two decades.[76] While Kim had proposed the DCRK a number of times before, the confederal idea became central to North Korea's unification strategy (at least rhetorically) from the 1980s onward.

At the Sixth Party Congress in October 1980, Kim Il Sung laid out a ten-point political program for national unity centered on the proposed Confederal Republic.[77] Kim had talked about a "Federation System" (yŏnbangche) as a way to overcome North-South division since 1960, but this was the first time he had outlined a detailed plan.[78] Kim claimed his policy was founded "on the lofty ideas and principles laid down in the July 4 [1972] North-South Joint Statement," explaining that "our Party considers that the most realistic and reasonable way to reunify the country independently, peacefully and on the principle of great national unity is to bring the north and the south together into a confederal state, leaving the ideas and social systems existing in north and south as they are."[79] Some of the ten points would have seemed reasonable to many South Koreans, including economic cooperation, scientific and cultural exchange, reopening of transport and communication lines, and friendly relations with all neighboring countries. Other points were more problematic, such as forming a unified national army and protecting the rights and interests of overseas Koreans. And some of the points were open to sharply contesting views, including Kim's call for the DCRK to "effect democracy throughout the country" and "ensure a stable livelihood for the entire people including the workers, peasants and other working masses and promote their welfare systematically." Furthermore, Kim proposed an administrative formula that was sure to be rejected by the South, namely, that the DCRK "supreme national confederal assembly" should have "an equal number of representatives from north and south." Outnumbering the North two to one in population, South Korea was unlikely to give up its demographic advantage this

76. Ko Yu-hwan, "The Basis and Development of North Korea's Policy toward South Korea and Unification," in Puk Han yŏngu hakhoe, ed., Puk Hanŭi t'ongil waegyo [North Korea's Unification and Foreign Policy] (Seoul: Kyŏngin munhwasa, 2006), 27.

77. Kim Il Sung, Report to the Sixth Congress, 69–81.

78. Yun Hwang, "North Korea's Federation Formula," in Puk Hanŭi t'ongil waegyo, 110–11.

79. Kim Il Sung, Report to the Sixth Congress, 69.

way. Indeed, as North Korea was calling for the overthrow of the Chun government at the time, it is easy to dismiss the DCRK proposal as mere propaganda.[80]

By 1983, the Chun regime had stabilized, and the North Korean government
seemed more serious about dealing directly with the South Korean republic. A
second wave of North-South exchanges, the first since the historic opening of
1972–73, ensued. After a five-year hiatus following the collapse of North-South
talks in 1975, inter-Korean dialogue moved forward again in 1980, with ten "preliminary" meeting between February and August that year—that is, prior to the
Sixth Party Congress. For the first time, the two governments referred to each
other by their official names, the Republic of Korea and Democratic People's
Republic of Korea.[81] The following year, high-level contacts between Seoul and
Pyongyang resumed, facilitated through the Red Cross organizations of the two
countries. In November 1984, the two sides met to discuss economic cooperation. In July 1985, members of the South Korean National Assembly and the
DPRK Supreme People's Assembly met for the first time. Two months later, the
first meeting of divided family members took place, followed by discussions of
sport cooperation. Cultural troupes from the two sides visited each other's capitals in 1985 as well.[82] South Korea even agreed to accept rice, cement, and other
material assistance from DPRK to deal with severe flooding in 1984. This was the
first and last time economic aid would flow from North to South, rather than in
the other direction.

At the beginning of this new round of North-South exchanges, Pyongyang
may have assumed it had the upper hand in terms of world opinion. The end of
the Park era and beginning of the Chun regime was one of the lowest points for
South Korea's global reputation. The severe repression of human rights of the
Yushin era, the kidnapping of Kim Dae Jung by South Korean agents in Tokyo in
1973, the "Koreagate" scandal surrounding South Korean attempts to bribe US
congressmen in the late 1970s, and the massacre in Kwangju in 1980 added up to
a very unsavory international image. Furthermore, the South Korean economic
"miracle" of the late 1960s and 1970s was hurt by the 1979–80 global recession,
and South Korea's economy contracted slightly in 1980. But the Chun Doo Hwan
administration reversed this situation with remarkable speed. South Korea's
economy rapidly revived, the new administration of Ronald Reagan gave Chun
its blessing, and the conservative Japanese government of Yasuhiro Nakasone

---

80. B. C. Koh, "A Comparison of Unification Policies," in Young Whan Kihl, ed., *Korea and the World: Beyond the Cold War* (Boulder, CO: Westview Press, 1994), 156.

81. Chong-Sik Lee, "The Evolution of North-South Korean Relations," in Scalapino and Lee, *North Korea in a Regional and Global Context*, 122.

82. Ko, "Basis and Development," 27.

gave both economic and political support to the new South Korean administration.[83] South Korea benefited from the conservative turn among its major allies, the United States and Japan, for whom Chun's poor record on human rights was less important than his country's robust anticommunism and economic growth.

The situation in the North was almost exactly the opposite, and North Korea continued to lose ground to the South as the 1980s progressed. Despite its upbeat propaganda about economic output, North Korea's difficulties were becoming increasingly obvious: the 1971–76 Six-Year Plan was extended for one year, having failed to meet its goals; a second Seven-Year Plan was launched in 1978, but even the DPRK admitted that it had only "partly attained" its goals by the time the plan concluded in 1984.[84] During this time South Korea's explosive economic growth became world-renown as the "Miracle on the River Han." South Korea proved adept at translating its newfound economic prowess into diplomatic gains, upstaging the DPRK in diplomatic recognition and as a site for high-profile international events. Seoul gained the right to host the 1986 Asian Games and was named host city of the 1988 Summer Olympics by the International Olympic Committee in November 1981. As one of its first major multilateral events, a reflection of how far and how quickly South Korea had moved from its near-pariah status in the 1970s, Seoul hosted the Inter-parliamentary Union (IPU) in 1983. Seoul's overshadowing of Pyongyang on the international stage was made all the more dramatic by an event that happened just before the IPU opened. On October 9, 1983, four members of Chun Doo Hwan's cabinet, along with seventeen others, were killed by a bomb in Rangoon during an ROK state visit to Burma, in a failed attempt to kill the South Korean president. Three North Korean agents were convicted of the bombing by Burmese authorities. The Rangoon bombing, about which more will be said below, dealt a severe blow to North Korea's relations with Seoul in particular and the rest of the world in general.

The First and Third Worlds

As North Korea turned toward the Soviet bloc for assistance, it put less emphasis on relations with the nonsocialist developing world and Western developed countries. North Korea retained most of the economic and political ties it had established in the great breakout of the 1970s, but the gains proved to be more short-lived and less important than they had appeared at the time. Japan remained North Korea's largest trading partner among advanced capitalist counties,

---

83. Gills, *Korea vs. Korea*, 203.
84. Marcus Noland, *Avoiding the Apocalypse: The Future of the Two Koreas* (Washington, DC: Institute for International Economics, 2000), 67–68.

but wary of North Korea's poor debt repayment record, the West Europeans were no longer beating a path to Pyongyang's door. Nor was there much progress on diplomatic normalization between Japan and the DPRK. Like the Europeans, the Japanese were unhappy about the huge financial debt North Korea owed their banks and firms, and acts of terrorism sponsored by North Korea against South Korean targets in the 1980s did not help matters.[85]

Overall, North Korean trade outside of the socialist bloc declined in the early 1980s, due both to North Korea's internal economic difficulties and its relative retreat from economic engagement with the First and Third Worlds.[86] Of course, the Third World had been at least as important for North Korea politically as economically, but despite public enthusiasm for "South-South Cooperation" and the nonaligned movement, Kim Il Sung expressed private disillusionment with Third World solidarity to his socialist allies. In a conversation with East Germany's Erich Honecker on June 1, 1984, Kim told Honecker "we no longer belong to the [nonaligned] movement."[87] This is a puzzling remark that does not seem to be supported by the facts, as North Korea continued to participate in NAM summits well into the twenty-first century. Pyongyang had recently hosted a series of high-profile NAM meetings, including a food and agriculture conference in August 1981 and an education and culture conference in March 1983.[88] At the latter, Kim greeted delegates with a lengthy speech entitled "Let Us Uphold the Banner of Autonomy and Independence for Nonaligned and Developing Countries," a speech published in its entirety in the journal *Kŭlloja*.[89] Nevertheless, as Kim explained to Honecker, the nonaligned movement

> set forth good solutions but is not in a position to resolve the basic issues. Above all it is not in a position to realize the requirement for a new economic order. The states that belong to it are politically independent, but they do not have independent national economies. This is why the danger of expanding neo-colonialism is growing. . . . The problems of the developing countries cannot be solved simply by cooperation among themselves. . . . The best solution would be close ties between the socialist market and the market of the developing lands.[90]

---

85. Kim, *The Two Koreas and the Great Powers*, 175.

86. Joseph S. Chung, "Foreign Trade of North Korea: Performance, Policy and Prospects," in Scalapino and Lee, *North Korea in a Regional and Global Context*, 92.

87. "Memorandum of Conversation between Erich Honecker and Kim Il Sung, 1 June 1984." SAPMO-BA, DY 30, 2460. Translated by Grace Leonard for the North Korea International Documentation Project.

88. Pak, History of DPRK Foreign Relations, 241–45.

89. Kim Il Sung, "Let Us Uphold the Banner of Autonomy and Independence for Non-Aligned and Developing Countries," *Kŭlloja* 499 (November 1983), 2–9.

90. "Memorandum of Conversation between Erich Honecker and Kim Il Sung."

Kim's remarks were no doubt intended to flatter the East German leader about the importance of socialist countries like his own and allay his fears of North Korea becoming too "nonaligned." But they seem also to reflect North Korea's realization of the limits of economic ties with developing countries.

While direct trade with advanced capitalist countries was constrained by North Korea's debt problems and poor international reputation, the DPRK also sought economic ties with the West through other means. In 1981 the United Nations Development Programme (UNDP) opened an office in Pyongyang, the first UN program to establish a resident presence there. The UNDP channeled some Western aid money to the DPRK but would not play a major role in the North Korean economy until the famine of the 1990s. More promising at the time was North Korea's first-ever foreign joint venture law announced September 8, 1984. Apparently modeled on similar laws in China, the joint-venture law invited international cooperation in a wide range of fields, from technology to tourism.[91] However, the law failed to attract much attention in the West for a variety of reasons, not least because North Korea's reputation for violent and erratic behavior reached new heights in the mid-1980s.

The Turn to Terror

The "Second Cold War" came to a peak in 1983 with Reagan's first reference to the Soviet Union as an "evil empire" in March, the Soviet shooting of KAL 007, and the American invasion of Granada. On the Korean Peninsula, the United States announced the introduction of a much more aggressive Airland Battle doctrine and increased its support for the South Korean military as well as its own nuclear presence. North Korea, finding itself in a weak and deeply insecure position, apparently deployed its forces farther south toward the DMZ at this time, inviting criticism from the Americans and South Koreans that the North was positioning itself to attack the South.[92] North Korea's "forward deployment" would long remain a contentious issue with the United States and ROK. Conventional force redeployment was not North Korea's only novel tactic. The DPRK also turned to unconventional warfare against South Korean officials and ordinary citizens, acts which swiftly evoked the opprobrium of Western countries and the label of a "terrorist state." Such terrorism (the appropriateness of this term for North Korean actions may be debatable) was a longstanding tactic of the weak that North Korea had engaged in before, but never to the degree that it did in the 1980s.

---

91. Chung, "Foreign Trade of North Korea," 111.
92. Hayes, *Pacific Powderkeg*, 138.

After the failure of North Korean commandoes to assassinate Park Chung Hee in 1968, direct action by military forces gave way to terrorist tactics by North Korean agents, or at least those claiming to act in the name of the DPRK. In some cases the connection between terrorists act and the DPRK could not be proved, and in all cases North Korea denied responsibility. In 1974 an ethnic Korean from Japan attempted to assassinate Park Chung Hee but failed, shooting and killing Park's wife instead; in 1983, North Korean agents attempted to kill ROK president Chun in Rangoon, killing several members of his cabinet; and in 1987, North Korean spies planted a bomb that killed more than a hundred passengers on a South Korean airliner. These acts, as well as numerous kidnappings from Japan, Hong Kong, and even Europe, did little to advance North Korea's agenda on the Korean Peninsula, much less engender sympathy in South Korea or any-where else. On the contrary, North Korea's actions did enormous damage to its reputation abroad. The world increasingly saw the DPRK less as an eccentric communist state and more as an international pariah.

Did North Korea's actions qualify as terrorism? The political scientist David Whittaker defines terrorism as "the deliberate creation or exploitation of fear through violence or the threat of violence in the pursuit of political change."[93] By this definition most of North Korea's unconventional foreign policy behavior, while at times illegal and deplorable, has not been terrorism. Almost from the beginning North Korea was something of a "rogue state" even with respect to its allies, much less its enemies. But a deliberate turn toward state terrorism appears to have been relatively brief, roughly a ten-year period from the late 1970s to the late 1980s, reaching a peak in two spectacular acts of bombing in 1983 and 1987. North Korea's more extreme foreign policy tactics were driven by weakness rather than confidence, and it is not surprising that the DPRK turned to terror precisely when the correlation of forces appeared to turn sharply against it, at least in regard to South Korea, but still before the situation deteriorated to the point of economic catastrophe. It is in this window between the sharp decline of the DPRK's position vis-à-vis South Korea in the early 1980s and the near-death experience of communist collapse at the turn of the 1990s that terror tactics ap-pear to have been a favored option.

Until the 1987 bombing of a South Korean passenger plane, to be covered in the next chapter, the DPRK did not engage in random violence toward civilians in order to terrorize the population, but rather targeted political leaders for assas-sination.[94] This was consistent with the North Korean belief that the people and

---

93. David J. Whittaker, *The Terrorism Reader*, 2d ed. (London: Routledge, 2007), 9.
94. David Kang, "North Korea's Military and Security Strategy," in Kim, ed., *North Korean Foreign Relations*, 177–79.

government in South Korea could be separated, and that eliminating unpopular South Korean leaders would create a favorable image of North Korea among the oppressed South Korean civilian population. On the other hand, North Korea seemed to have had little compunction about kidnapping. The DPRK may have kidnapped hundreds of South Koreans, including many unlucky fishermen who strayed into North Korean waters, after the Korean War. But it was the abduction of Japanese citizens, almost all taken from Japan to North Korea between 1977 and 1983, that was to create the greatest international outcry. More than a dozen Japanese were abducted at this time, the first being one Kume Yutaka, a fifty-two-year-old security guard, who disappeared along the coast of Ishikawa Prefecture in September 1977. Most of the kidnap victims were truly random, including two young couples taken by North Korean agents during a romantic stroll on the beach. The motivations for these kidnappings were not always clear; some were taken to teach Japanese language and custom to North Korean spies, others in order for spies to steal their identities. Long denied by the DPRK and dismissed as a wacky conspiracy theory by many Japanese, the abductions became an enormous media cause célèbre in Japan and a major impediment to improving Japan-North Korea relations after Kim Jong Il admitted North Korea's responsibility for (some of) the kidnappings in 2002.[95]

Among the South Koreans kidnapped to the North, by far the highest-profile victims of the late 1970s and 1980s were the ex-husband and wife team of film director Shin Sang-ok and actress Ch'oe Ŭn-hŭi.[96] According to the couple's account, shortly after their divorce, Ch'oe was kidnapped by North Korean agents while vacationing in Hong Kong in 1978. When she failed to return to South Korea, Shin went to Hong Kong to find her and was also kidnapped and brought to North Korea. The two were confined separately, neither knowing the other was in North Korea, until 1983, when they were brought to a dinner party hosted by Kim Jong Il. Apparently, Kim had brought Shin and Ch'oe through these rather unorthodox methods in order for them to help reinvigorate North Korea's moribund film industry.[97] Film, as we have seen, was a driving passion for the Dear

95. Tessa Morris-Suzuki, "Refugees, Abductees, 'Returnees': Human Rights in Japan-North Korean Relations," in Sonia Ryang, ed., *North Korea: Toward a Better Understanding* (Lexington, MA: Lexington Books, 2009), 129–56.

96. After escaping the DPRK the couple wrote a memoir of their experience, which became a bestseller in South Korea. See Ch'oe Ŭn-hŭi and Sin Sang-ok, *Kim Chŏng-il Wangguk* [The Kim Jong Il Kingdom] (Seoul: Donga Ilbosa, 1988).

97. In August 1984 the *Rodong Sinmun* announced that Sin and Ch'oe had been granted an audience with Kim Jong Il. This was both the first time the couple's presence in the DPRK was made public, and the first time the highly elevated term "granted an audience" (chŏpgyŏn) was used in reference to Kim Jong Il, rather than his father. "Kim Jong Il Receives South Korean Film Director Couple Sin Sang-ok and Ch'oe Ŭn-hŭi," *Rodong Sinmun*, August 4, 1984, 1.

Leader, and he wanted to bring his country's movies up to world standards with the assistance of his favorite South Korean director.[98] Shin was hardly in a position to refuse, and over the next three years directed seven films in North Korea, with Kim Jong Il as de facto executive producer. Shin and Ch'oe also remarried each other following Kim's suggestion.

In 1986, while the two were in Vienna on a business trip, they escaped from their North Korean minders and sought political asylum in the US embassy. Shin settled in the United States for a number of years and worked as a producer in Hollywood, before returning to South Korea, where he died in 2004. After Shin's escape, North Korea denied the allegations of kidnapping and detention, claiming that Shin had voluntarily defected to North Korea and left with a good deal of North Korean money. Many of the details of Shin and Ch'oe's account are impossible to verify. But the couple's kidnapping story is consistent with the tactics used at this time by North Korea to gain valuable knowledge from abroad, such as Japanese language skills. Perhaps Kim Jong Il had watched too many spy movies and was attempting to make them into reality.

If the Shin/Ch'oe kidnapping was merely bizarre, the Rangoon bombing incident was a violent and bloody act of terror. On October 9, 1983, while on a state visit to Burma, Chun Doo Hwan was scheduled to visit the Martyrs Memorial in Rangoon. As several members of Chun's cabinet and staff, along with other guests, assembled at the memorial, a bomb concealed in the roof exploded, killing seventeen South Koreans and four Burmese. Among the Koreans killed were Foreign Minister Lee Bum Suk, Deputy Prime Minister Suh Suk Joo, and Presidential Secretary Kim Jae Ik, a key figure in designing South Korea's rapid economic development program.[99] Chun himself, not yet having arrived at the memorial, escaped injury. The Burmese authorities arrested three North Korean army officers in connection to the incident. One of them, Captain Kang Min-chŏl, confessed that the bombing had been planned by the North Korean government.

North Korea denied all responsibility, both publicly and to its socialist allies. The DPRK ambassador in East Berlin, for example, stated categorically "the DPRK rejects any authorship of this incident."[100] But in much of the world, and not only in the West, the Rangoon bombing damaged North Korea's standing enormously. Burma, previously a close friend of the DPRK, cut off diplomatic relations with

---

98. John Gorenfeld, "The Producer from Hell," *The Guardian*, 4 April 2003. Available at http://www.guardian.co.uk/film/2003/apr/04/artsfeatures1.

99. Oberdorfer, *The Two Koreas*, 140–41.

100. GDR Ministry of Foreign Affairs, Information Section. Confidential Report No. 48/XII, 8 December 1983. "Position of the DPRK on the Bomb Explosion in Rangoon." STASI Files, North Korea International Documentation Project, Woodrow Wilson Center, Washington, DC.

North Korea for the next fourteen years. Ronald Reagan, at a speech to the South Korean National Assembly November 12, 1983, deplored "the despicable North Korean attack in Rangoon."[101] Coming just one month after the KAL 007 incident, the Rangoon bombing seemed to confirm (at least to South Koreans and Americans) that North Korea and the Soviet Union shared a callous disregard for human life. As the Second Cold War peaked, their escalating confrontation with the United States pushed North Korea and the USSR closer together. And in the appropriately Orwellian year of 1984, Kim Il Sung took one last "friendship tour" of the Soviet Union and Eastern Europe.

"Everlasting Fraternal Friendship"

North Korea entered the decade of the 1980s reaffirming its identity as a socialist country. Kim Il Sung declared that the KWP was based on the "principles of independence and proletarian internationalism" and that the DPRK would "ceaselessly strive for strengthening unity and developing friendly relations with the socialist countries."[102] But for all these claims of "friendship," North Korea kept its people almost as isolated from contact with citizens of fellow socialist countries as from capitalist and "imperialist" ones. This had been the case since the Hungarian uprising of 1956, when most of the North Korean students were recalled from Eastern Europe for fear of ideological contamination. Afterward student exchanges were resumed, but even in as politically orthodox a country as East Germany, North Korean students kept themselves aloof. Those who managed to study in Eastern Europe were carefully chosen elites. For example, Kim Yŏng-il, a son of Kim Il Sung by his second wife, studied electronics at Dresden in East Germany and went on to obtain a Ph.D. at Humboldt University in Berlin. In May 1984, the East German Ministry of State Security (Stasi) issued a report on Yŏng-il—at that time a research assistant (*Aspirant*) at Humboldt—and other North Korean students in the GDR. There were a grand total of fifty-nine students from the DPRK in East Germany, of whom the largest number (twenty) was studying at Karl Marx University in Leipzig. As the East Germans saw it, the North Koreans were an ideologically retrograde and deeply suspicious group: "They maintain that Marxism-Leninism is outdated and that their country has introduced a higher ideology than Marxism-Leninism. They see Kim Il Sung as

---

101. Cited in Byung-joon Ahn, "North Korea and the United States in Global and Regional Perspective," in Scalapino and Lee, *North Korea in a Regional and Global Context*, 304.

102. Kim Il Sung, *Collected Works,* vol. 36 (Pyongyang: Foreign Languages Press, 1980), 266.

the greatest Party leader of the international workers' movement. . . . The students are therefore careful to make no contact with other foreigners. Related to this, political operatives never leave the Korean students."[103] In other words, the North Korean students were the perfect products of North Korea's inward-looking, highly nationalistic, and Kim Il Sung–centered ideological system. Even the Stasi, no slouches when it came to repression and surveillance, found the political restrictions on the North Korean students to be remarkable.

On May 16, 1984, Kim Il Sung boarded a special train at the North Korean port city of Ch'ŏngjin for a six-week series of state visits to the Soviet Union and Eastern Europe.[104] It was Kim's most extensive and high-profile tour of the region in twenty-eight years, since the summer of 1956. At that time, a conspiracy of Kim's rivals attempted to replace him during his absence. Now, Kim's leadership faced not the remotest threat. His succession was assured, and Kim could confidently leave the country in the hands of his son, who was already running day-to-day political affairs in the DPRK. Kim's itinerary passed through Northeast China, where Kim sent a message of thanks to the PRC leadership. A day or so after crossing into Russia, Kim made his first stop in Krasnoyarsk, where he visited a hydraulic power station and was greeted by representatives of the local Communist Party and Soviet of People's Deputies. On May 23, Kim and his entourage arrived in Moscow. According to Dmitri Volkogonov, then head of political administration for the Soviet army, Kim Il Sung "was given the full red-carpet treatment, a guard of honour, a state dinner and a residence."[105] Kim met with General Secretary Konstantin Chernenko, who had recently taken over from Yuri Andropov, who died in February after just fifteen months in office. Chernenko, visibly ailing, would spend an even shorter time as general-secretary—just under thirteen months, until his death on March 1985. In their photographs together, Chernenko looks like a wax figure, while the seventy-year-old Kim appears the embodiment of health and vigor.

Kim's main request from the Soviet Union was for weapons and other military supplies. In an hour-long speech to Chernenko, Kim stressed the growth of South Korean militarization, rising American aggression in East Asia, and the common threat the USSR and North Korea faced in the struggle against imperialism. Chernenko listened patiently, and in the end granted Kim everything he requested.[106]

---

103. GDR Ministry of State Security, "Information on the situation of the students from the DPRK," 25 May 1984. North Korean International Documentation Project, Woodrow Wilson Center, Washington, DC.

104. For a detailed itinerary, including maps, photos, and Kim's speeches and those of his counterparts in the countries he visited, see *Everlasting Fraternal Friendship*.

105. Volkogonov, *Autopsy for an Empire*, 418.

106. Ibid.

From the Soviet Union, Kim went on to meet General Wojciech Jaruzelski in Poland, Erich Honecker in East Germany, Gustav Husak of Czechoslovakia, Janos Kadar of Hungary, Dragaslav Markovic of Yugoslavia (Kim's old friend Josef Broz Tito had died four years earlier), Todor Zhivkov of Bulgaria, and finally his sometime protégé Nicolae Ceausescu of Romania. Kim and his entourage then crossed back into the Soviet Union, traveled northeast through Kiev back to Moscow, and took the long trans-Siberian route across Russia through Khabarovsk—this time without passing through China—and disembarked at Chŏngjin.

Looking at Kim's East bloc tour from the vantage point of the twenty-first century, it seems like a journey through an ancient civilization on the brink of collapse. None of the leaders Kim met would be in power six years later; two would be dead. All of the ruling parties would soon fall, and three of the countries (the Soviet Union, the German Democratic Republic, and Yugoslavia) would cease to exist by the beginning of the 1990s. North Korea chose this unpropitious moment to turn decisively to the socialist countries of Eastern Europe for economic aid, military assistance, and political support. Kim could not see that, behind the façade of parades, folk dances, and showcase industrial projects that greeted him at every stop, his socialist allies were ailing leaders overseeing crumbling economies and disillusioned publics.

For his part, Kim Il Sung was in good health, and the North Korean people may or may not have been disillusioned. But if anything, the economy of North Korea was even more moribund than that of Eastern Europe. While nearly all the socialist countries were engaged in some kind of market-oriented reform by 1984, North Korea was still relying on old-fashioned moral exhortation and slogans such as Ch'ŏllima and the Three Revolution Red Flag movement. Rather than experiment with economic reform, North Korea took the advent of a new decade to disseminate a new Stakhanovite slogan, "The Speed of the '80s" (*P'alsimnyŏndae sokdo*).[107] It sounded much like the speed of the 1950s: economic development was still a "struggle"; the masses had to fight to build ever faster, work ever harder. This hardly seemed like a country preparing for the technological challenges of the late twentieth century.

Nor did it make a great deal of sense for the USSR and its European allies to continue giving economic assistance to North Korea when they were facing so many serious economic challenges at home. The Soviet Union in particular could ill afford such continued generosity to the DPRK. The USSR was becoming overextended in its Third-World commitments just as its own economy began grinding down. While actual aid grants were not always large, Moscow offered very

---

107. See the front pages of *Nodong Sinmun* for July 10, 13, 18 and 23, 1982, among others.

generous terms of trade, resulting in massive debts owed by Third World partners such as Cuba, Mongolia, and Vietnam.[108] Such debts, including North Korea's, would finally be called by Moscow in 1991. For the Soviet Union, North Korea was one of many Third World allies asking a high price in economic benefit for its strategic value to Moscow. Soviet generosity would not last much longer, and under Chernenko's successor Mikhail Gorbachev, Moscow would make a rapid retreat from the Third World.

Following his European tour, Kim Il Sung visited Beijing in November 1984. There he met with Deng Xiaoping, Hu Yaobang, Chen Yun, Peng Zhen, and other Chinese leaders, seeking to assure them that North Korea remained a steady ally and asking the Chinese as well for more economic support. Kim was also concerned about China-US military cooperation.[109] But Kim's low-key visit to China was completely overshadowed by his ostentatious tour through the Soviet Union and Eastern Europe. In these visits Kim Il Sung had reaffirmed his country's ties to the old Soviet bloc. It would prove to be a case of consummate bad timing. Kim turned to the Soviet bloc for help just as the Soviet economy was entering a fatal downward spiral. Soviet GDP fell significantly from 1979 onward, while military expenditure and support for socialist allies continued to grow.[110] These two contradictory tendencies could not be reconciled, and the contradiction only grew worse until Gorbachev's attempt to take the Soviet economy on a new course ultimately led to the unraveling of the entire system. Five years after Kim's "friendship" tour, North Korea found itself virtually alone and friendless on the eastern fringe of a once-great empire.

---

108. Margot Light, *Troubled Friendships: Moscow's Third World Ventures* (London: British Academic Press, 1993), 195.

109. O Chin-yong, *Kim Il-sŏng sidae ŭi Chung-So wa Nam-Buk Han* [China, the Soviet Union, and North and South Korea in the Kim Il Sung Era] (Seoul: Nanam, 2004), 150.

110. Odd Arne Westad, *The Global Cold War: Third World Interventions and the Making of Our Times* (Cambridge: Cambridge University Press, 2005), 336.

THE SUN SETS IN THE EAST, 1985–92

Our style of socialism centered on the masses is based on the Juche idea and embodies this idea; it is Juche-orientated socialism. Socialism devoid of ideological foundation and perfect guiding ideology cannot be called genuine socialism and it might be frustrated, unable to check the anti-socialist schemes of the imperialists and reactionaries. This is shown graphically by the lesson of those countries where socialism was frustrated and capitalism has been restored. Our socialism is advancing victoriously unperturbed amidst the continuing vicious moves of the imperialists and reactionaries just because it is based on the Juche idea and guided by this idea.

—Kim Jong Il, November 1992

The Beginning of the End

When he first became secretary-general of the CPSU in March 1985, Mikhail Gorbachev showed no sign of taking Soviet-Korean relations on a new course, much less setting in motion the collapse of the entire Soviet empire. On the contrary, during Gorbachev's first two years in office, Moscow-Pyongyang relations reached heights of cooperation and assistance not seen since the late 1950s. A joint Korea-Soviet communiqué signed in April 1985 envisioned a considerable expansion and deepening of the bilateral relationship.[1] On the economic front, the USSR stepped up technical assistance and trade on "friendship" (i.e., concessionary) terms. Following Premier Kang Sŏng-san's visit to Moscow in December 1985, the two countries signed an agreement for enhancing cooperation in the years to come. By 1985 the Soviet Union accounted for 43 percent of North Korea's bilateral trade, compared to 24 percent just five years earlier. Trade volume increased another 20 percent between 1985 and 1986.[2] Soviet technical assistance

---

Epigraph from Kim Jong Il, "Socialism is the Life of Our People: Talk with Senior Officials of the Central Committee of the Workers Party of Korea." Available at http://www.korea-dpr.com/lib/558.pdf.

1. For the full text of the communiqué, see *Rodong Sinmun*, April 25, 1985, 4.

2. Seung-ho Joo, *Gorbachev's Foreign Policy toward the Korean Peninsula, 1985–1991* (Lewiston, NY: Edwin Mellen Press, 2000), 131.

was especially important in the area of energy: by October 1986, according to a Soviet report, Soviet-built plants accounted for 66 percent of electricity production in the DPRK.[3] North Korea mainly exported raw materials (especially metals), agricultural goods, and fish products in exchange for Soviet-built light industrial goods. The two sides began joint production of ships, trucks, and machine tools. In the Russian Far East, North Korea provided workers for the Soviet timber industry, while the USSR supplied the machines. The Soviets also increased oil shipments to the DPRK, and the two sides expanded cross-border trade by rail transport. Not since the early years of Khrushchev's rule had Soviet-North Korean economic relations been so active.

Military cooperation was, if anything, even more robust than economic relations. The USSR supplied North Korea with new shipments of attack aircraft, helicopter gunships, surface-to-air missiles, and MiG-29 fighter jets. This was the first time the USSR had sent advanced military equipment to the DPRK since the early 1970s. The two sides began joint naval exercises in the fall of 1985, and for the first time since the Korean War, Soviet warships docked at North Korean ports. Soviet military aircraft were allowed flyover rights in North Korean airspace.[4] In May 1985, a squadron of North Korean MiG-21 fighters flew to Vladivostok to join in the celebration of the fortieth anniversary of the Soviet victory in World War II. The Soviets in turn sent MiG-23s to Hwangju Air Base in North Korea for a reciprocal friendship visit.[5] Ships of the Soviet Pacific Fleet arrived in North Korea on August 12 for the fortieth anniversary of Korea's liberation, a visit covered extensively in the North Korean media. Two days later, a military delegation from the USSR was given a similar large and warm welcome in Pyongyang.[6] Military cooperation reflected a strong convergence of views about the strategic environment, both globally and in East Asia. The USSR and North Korea were, on the surface at least, in perfect agreement over the common threat of US imperialism, allied in East Asia with South Korean and Japanese militarism. From the North Korean perspective, the Soviets—unlike the fickle Chinese—stood firmly against the Americans and their "puppets" in East Asia. China's economic relations with South Korea were beginning to take off in the mid-1980s, while Chinese aid to North Korea had been reduced. Soviet assistance was therefore necessary for the North to offset the economic and military advantages of the South. Both the Soviets and the North Koreans saw enhanced security cooperation as essential to restoring a military balance on the Korean

---

3. Ibid., 132.

4. Peggy Falkenheim Meyer, "Gorbachev and Post-Gorbachev Policy toward the Korean Peninsula: The Impact of Changing Russian Perceptions," *Asian Survey* 32, no. 8 (August 1992): 758.

5. Joo, *Gorbachev's Foreign Policy*, 119.

6. *Rodong Sinmun*, August 12, 1985, 2, and August 14, 1985, 3.

Peninsula. For the Soviets, North Korea also offered a valuable strategic asset in Northeast Asia to complement their new military presence in Indochina.[7]

The symbolic high point of this renewed friendship was Soviet participation in North Korea's fortieth-anniversary Liberation Day celebrations in August 1985. The Soviets sent their highest-level delegation to Pyongyang in two decades, headed by First Vice Premier Gaidar Aliyev and Marshal Vasily Petrov, first deputy minister of defense. All of the visiting Soviet groups, including the Pacific Fleet and military delegations mentioned above, as well as industrial and cultural delegation, received huge welcoming rallies. The Soviet delegates' activities were closely followed in the North Korean press. North Korea, which had for decades downplayed the role of the USSR in Korea's liberation from Japan, found a new enthusiasm for commemorating this role, even if the actual extent of Soviet involvement (or rather, Kim Il Sung's lack of involvement) in Korea's liberation was left somewhat vague. The emphasis here was on the strength of Soviet-Korean relations in the present, anchored in a solid forty-year history of unbroken friendship. As one example of this, the journal *Korean-Soviet Friendship* (*Cho-Sso Ch'insŏn*), which had maintained a low profile since the 1960s, published a special issue on the event.[8]

Dmitri Volkogonov traveled with Marshal Petrov's entourage for the Liberation Day commemoration. Several years later Volkogonov described his negative impression of Kim Il Sung (whom he had met the previous year in Moscow) and of North Korea in general. Kim "referred several times to the promises Chernenko and Ustinov had made to modernize the North Korean Army," Volkogonov recalled. Sounding exactly like Park Hŏn-yŏng when he requested military aid from Stalin on the eve of the Korean War, Kim asserted that if South Korea attacked, "a mighty partisan army will rise up in the south."[9] Volkogonov remarks, "It was if they had learnt nothing from the experience of 1950–1953. The appalling poverty of the country, its high degree of regimentation and the fanatical faith shown by the people in their leader convinced me that North Korea had come closest to the model of barracks Communism. They still revered Stalin, as no one in the USSR did, and seemed happy that they still had an earthly god."[10] This is of course the recollection of a Soviet hardliner-turned-liberal reformer,

---

7. In 1979 the Soviets had signed a twenty-five-year lease agreement for the use of Cam Ranh Bay, the former US naval center in South Vietnam, and had substantially expanded the facilities there by the mid-1980s. Flyover rights in North Korea allowed Soviet aircraft to travel from Vladivostok to Danang and Cam Ranh Bay in less time than before, while avoiding South Korean and American intelligence. It also helped Soviet reconnaissance against China.

8. *Rodong Sinmun*, August 1, 1985, 1.

9. See chapter 1 in this volume. It may be recalled that Pak's unrealized prediction of a partisan uprising in the South was one of the main charges against him in his show trial of 1955.

10. Dmitri Volkogonov, *Autopsy for an Empire: The Seven Leaders Who Built the Soviet Regime*, ed. and trans. Harold Shukman (New York: Free Press, 1998), 418–19.

with a deep revulsion for anything reminiscent the bad old days of the USSR. But his impression of North Korea in the mid-1980s was essentially accurate.

Soviet aid and cooperation in nuclear energy development were near the top of North Korea's wish list. As we have seen, North Korea had sought Soviet nuclear assistance since the 1960s. North Korea's industrial ambitions had long outpaced the country's ability to supply adequate electrical power. Although the DPRK was a net exporter of electricity in the late 1940s, thanks to the abundance of hydroelectric power generation bequeathed by Japanese colonial industrialization, by the 1960s energy shortages had become acute. Nuclear energy, aggressively being pursued by Japan and South Korea during the same period, seemed the logical answer to North Korea's energy needs—especially since North Korea was endowed with ample deposits of natural uranium. The North Korean leadership decided to promote nuclear research and technological development at this time, establishing new laboratories and research institutes throughout the country. More than three hundred North Korean nuclear specialists were trained in the Soviet Union. But Moscow had been reluctant to export advanced nuclear technologies and large amounts of fuel to the DPRK, presumably fearing that North Korea might divert such goods to weapons development, and kept close supervision over North Korea's nuclear installations and fuel supplies. Soviet specialists left the DPRK after building much of the Yŏngbyŏn nuclear research facility in 1965. Twenty years later, the Soviets were back.

In February 1985, a delegation of the Soviet National Planning Office (GOS-PLAN) visited the DPRK to negotiate the construction of a nuclear power plant. Premier Kang Sŏng-san told his guests that the project was important politically as well as economically: a nuclear power plant was already operating in South Korea, and a plant in the North would enhance the DPRK's international prestige.[11] The Soviets had already built such a plant in Cuba. The two sides approached agreement on planning, construction, and payment, and began investigating appropriate sites. The area around Hamhŭng on the East Coast seemed the most likely location for the new plant. The North Koreans agreed to abide by the standards of the International Atomic Energy Agency (IAEA) and allow IAEA inspections. Under strong Soviet pressure, the DPRK signed the nuclear Non-Proliferation Treaty on December 12, 1985. On December 26, the USSR and North Korea finally signed an agreement on economic and technical cooperation for the construction of a nuclear power plant in the DPRK.[12] The Soviets estimated it would

11. Report, Embassy of Hungary in North Korea to the Hungarian Foreign Ministry, 9 March 1985. XIX-J-1-k Korea, 1985, 76. Doboz, 81–532, 2745/1985. Obtained and translated for the Cold War International History Project by Balázs Szalontai.

12. Georgiy Kaurov, "A Technical History of Soviet–North Korean Nuclear Relations," in James Clay Moltz and Alexander Y. Mansourov, eds., The North Korean Nuclear Program: Security, Strategy, and New Perspectives from Russia (London: Routledge, 2000), 18.

take ten to twelve years to build the plant; the North Koreans wanted it in five. The Soviet collapse in 1991 meant the plant would never be built, but it was no coincidence that when the Americans agreed to help North Korea build a reactor in 1994, the site was the same one chosen by the Soviets nine years earlier.

Despite growing differences within the Soviet leadership over such open-ended support for the DPRK, the Soviets took pains to reassure their Korean allies that they would support Pyongyang's position on Korean Peninsula issues and would not interfere in North Korea's internal affairs. Soon, however, political and economic changes within the Soviet Union—encapsulated by Gorbachev in the term *perestroika* ("restructuring") at the Twenty-seventh CPSU conference in early 1986—would have far-reaching effects on Moscow's relations with allies and adversaries alike. This shift in foreign policy had already been prefigured in July 1985, by the resignation of Andrei Gromyko after twenty-eight years as foreign minister, and his replacement by the relatively young and inexperienced Eduard Shevardnadze. At first, Shevardnadze—like Gorbachev—seemed to represent continuity rather than change in the Soviet–North Korean relationship. Shevardnadze traveled to Pyongyang for a four-day "friendship visit" in January 1986, the first Soviet foreign minister to visit the DPRK in almost two decades. In his joint communiqué with DPRK foreign minister Kim Yŏng-nam, Shevardnadze expressed Moscow's full support for North Korea's positions on Korean unification, the US military presence in South Korea, and North-South joint hosting of the 1988 Olympics.[13]

Upon returning to Moscow, Shevardnadze reported to the Soviet Politburo that his trip had reinforced the Soviet position in the Far East by cementing Moscow's alliance with the DPRK. Shevardnadze pointed out that North Korea was important for the USSR, first, because of its firm anti-American stance and its efforts to weaken the US position in East Asia; and second, North Korea was a valuable channel for communication with Beijing, so that good ties with Kim Il Sung could influence the Chinese position to Moscow's advantage. Thus, whatever reservations the Soviet leaders might have about North Korea's dynastic socialism, it was vital to continue to work closely with Kim Il Sung and Kim Jong Il.[14]

This reaffirmation of the Moscow-Pyongyang alliance was soon followed by strong hints of a shift in Moscow's overall Far Eastern policy. In July 1986, at the Pacific port city of Vladivostok, Gorbachev gave one of the most important speeches on Soviet Asian policy in the history of the USSR.[15] The occasion of Gorbachev's speech was the presentation of the Order of Lenin to the city of

---

13. *Rodong Sinmun*, January 24, 1986, 4; Joo, *Gorbachev's Foreign Policy toward the Korean Peninsula*, 39

14. Minutes of CPSU Central Committee Politburo Meeting, January 30, 1986. Cited in Sergey Radchenko, "Russia and North Korea, from the 1960s to the 1990s," unpublished ms., 4.

15. Elizabeth Wishnick, "Soviet Asian Collective Security Policy from Brezhnev to Gorbachev," *Journal of Northeast Asian Studies* 7, no. 3 (September 1988): 3.

Vladivostok, and the first half of the speech focused on the development of the Soviet Far East. But it was the second half of the speech, on foreign affairs and Asia-Pacific security, which caught the attention of foreign observers across the region and beyond. In some ways Gorbachev was reiterating Brezhnev's 1969 call for collective security in Asia, an appeal that had fallen mostly on deaf ears at the time. But as Gorbachev acknowledged, the Asia-Pacific region—and East Asia in particular—was a very different place almost two decades after Brezhnev's failed proposal. Above all, it was a region of great economic dynamism, in which "Japan has turned into a power of front-rank significance," and other Pacific Rim economies were emerging into the spotlight.[16] "The Soviet Union is also an Asian-Pacific country," Gorbachev declared, and while the USSR was actively involved in the Helsinki peace process in Europe, no such dialogue was taking place in Asia. The main barrier to peace, as usual, was American imperialism, including the increasingly militarized "Washington-Tokyo-Seoul triangle."[17] This anti-American position was hardly new. What was new, however, was a set of positive and rather specific proposals for changing the Soviet position in the region. This included withdrawing "a considerable number of Soviet troops" from Mongolia; expanding ties with the members of the Association of Southeast Asian Nations (ASEAN); reconciling with China; intensifying cooperation with Japan; promoting "peaceful, good neighbourly relations with the USA"; ending the arms race in the Pacific; and reducing nuclear, naval, and ground forces of all countries in the region.

The *Rodong Sinmun* excerpted part of Gorbachev's Vladivostok speech with little comment.[18] Individually, no item in Gorbachev's speech was a radical departure from earlier Soviet positions on security, economic cooperation, and peaceful coexistence. Gorbachev's statements about the Korean Peninsula were in fact a stronger affirmation of Soviet support for the DPRK than the North Koreans had seen in some time. But taken as a whole, the Vladivostok speech represented a bold, proactive, and wide-ranging new approach to the Asia-Pacific that would enmesh the USSR into growing linkages of economic, political, and security cooperation in the region. In short, Gorbachev was approaching Asia as he and his predecessors had dealt with Europe since the Helsinki Accord of 1975: accepting existing boundaries, promoting economic cooperation and growth, and reducing military confrontation. This approach implied a long-term acceptance of the status quo in East Asia, and on the Korean Peninsula in particular,

---

16. "Appendix: Text of Speech by Mikhail Gorbachev in Vladivostok, 28 July 1986," in Ramesh Thakur and Carlyle A. Thayer, eds., *The Soviet Union as an Asian Pacific Power: Implications of Gorbachev's 1986 Vladivostok Initiative* (Boulder, CO: Westview Press, 1987), 216.

17. Ibid., 218.

18. See *Rodong Sinmin*, July 30, 1986.

which ran counter to the fundamental priority of the DPRK on unification. North Korea could accept a divided Germany, as East Germany was a necessary outpost of socialism in Europe. But Korea was one nation, and an overly cooperative and conciliatory Soviet attitude to the West could undermine the ultimate dream of Korean unity.[19]

Kim Il Sung visited Moscow again in late October 1986, his second trip there in less than two years. This time Kim traveled with much less fanfare and stayed just five days. His primary purpose was to pay a call on the new leader of the USSR. Kim met with Gorbachev shortly after the Soviet leader's historic summit meeting with Ronald Reagan in Rekjavik, Iceland. According to the recollections of Vadim Medvedev, then Central Committee secretary in charge of relations with fellow socialist countries, Kim praised Gorbachev's outreach to the United States and reassured him that improved US-Soviet relations "would also help resolve the Korea problem."[20] But he emphasized repeatedly that Korean division must not be made permanent, and that the South Korean people were ready to unite with the North on their own, if only the United States did not stand in the way. North Korea had no intention of attacking the South, Kim said, both because such an attack would be suicidal given the American nuclear presence on the peninsula, and because the South was well on its way to a revolution from within. As Kim put it, "The people of South Korea would support socialism, though this would meet with resistance in the West. There is a large movement for socialism in the South; work is being carried out to create a national front. One-third of South Korean parliamentarians support the North. Many people, not just students, are now speaking out against the American presence."[21] The key to unification, Kim suggested, was to pressure the United States to withdraw its forces from South Korea. Without the American military presence, the "puppet government" in the South would lose its legitimacy and the South Korean people would freely embrace their northern brethren. Gorbachev may not have been aware, as Kim surely was, that Stalin had suggested something similar almost four decades ago, when Kim and Pak Hŏn-yŏng met the Soviet leader in February 1949. Although a year later Stalin would support a North Korean invasion, at the time he opposed direct military action and encouraged North Korean promotion

---

19. Since the early 1970s East Germany had accepted two German states as a long-term prospect, a position the North Koreans officially supported while insisting that the Korean situation was quite different. Dr. Hans Maretzki, the last East German ambassador to the DPRK, has called the different policies "separation and cooperation" (Germany) as opposed to "unification without contact" (Korea). Author's interview with Hans Maretzki, Postdam, Germany, 29 July 2002. See also Maretzki, "Probleme koreanischer Wiedervereinigung aus deutscher Sicht," *WeltTrends* 5 (1999): 123–39.

20. Vadim A. Medvedev, *Raspad: kak on nazreval v "mirovoi sisteme sotzializma"* [Collapse: How It Happened in the "World Socialist System"] (Moscow: Mezhdunarodnye Otnosheniia, 1994), 324.

21. Ibid., 325.

of internal subversion in the South, which would lead quickly to a South Korean collapse after the United States withdrew its forces. Kim tried to assure Gorbachev that this strategy would lead to unification in the 1980s, but Gorbachev did not seem convinced. Nor did he agree with Kim's vehement opposition to "cross-recognition"—diplomatic normalization between North Korea and the United States and Japan, on the one hand, and South Korea with the USSR and China, on the other—and simultaneous entry of the two Koreas into the United Nations. Furthermore, Gorbachev criticized Kim for the failure of the North Korean economy and the misappropriation of Soviet aid.[22] Such an attitude must have shocked and insulted Kim, who had been expecting the kind of blank check he had enjoyed from Chernenko. Gorbachev was less of a Stalin and more of a Khrushchev, it appeared.

None of these differences came out in public at the time, of course. At the state banquet held for Kim on October 24, Gorbachev emphasized the unity of purpose and reciprocity of interests between the USSR and the DPRK, and the evils of South Korean reaction and US imperialism in keeping Korea divided. He suggested again that an emerging Washington-Seoul-Tokyo axis was "the real threat to the USSR, DPRK, to many other countries, and to peace in the world."[23] Adopting the North Korean lexicon, Gorbachev called this triple alliance "a kind of Eastern NATO." This public display of lockstep unity submerged differences of policy and ideology between the two countries that would soon come to the surface. For Gorbachev, Kim represented precisely the kind of unreformed Leninism that the Soviet Union had to overcome. For Kim, Gorbachev was uncomfortably reminiscent of the liberalizing, meddling, and arrogant Khrushchev.

If the North Korean–Soviet relationship reflected strategic commonality and growing ideological divergence, North Korea's relationship with China in the mid-1980s was the opposite: the personal and historic ties of "blood-cemented friendship" were still strong, but China's strategic interests were converging with the United States in a way deeply troubling to the DPRK leadership. The higher Soviet profile in North Korea corresponded with a downgrade in the Chinese profile, at least temporarily. In striking contrast to the strong Soviet presence, China did not send a delegation to the Liberation Day commemorations in 1985, and references to Sino-DPRK relations largely disappeared from the North Korean media. But much was going on behind the scenes in China-DPRK relations. In November 1984 Kim Il Sung secretly visited China, where he discussed North-South Korean

22. Joo, *Gorbachev*, 130.
23. *Pravda*, 25 October 1986. Cited in Eugene Bazhanov, "Soviet Policy towards South Korea under Gorbachev," in Il Young Chung, ed., *Korea and Russia: Toward the 21st Century* (Seoul: The Sejong Institute, 1992), 71.

relations and other issues with Hu Yaobang, general secretary of the Chinese Communist Party.[24] In May 1985 Hu in turn made a secret visit to the North Korean border city of Sinŭiju, meeting with Kim Il Sung, Kim Jong Il, and Defense Minister Oh Chin-u over a period of three days.[25] According to Chinese sources, Kim assured Hu that despite warm relations with the Soviet Union, Korea's "blood alliance with China has not changed one bit." Hu responded, "We welcome the fact that you receive help from the Soviets that we cannot give."[26] Kim expressed concern about the growing economic ties between China and South Korea. Hu assured him that, although China was now accepting investment from all countries to help in its modernization program, relations with South Korea would go no further than practical economic ties. In October 1985, commemorating the thirty-fifth anniversary of China's entry into the Korean War, Vice-Premier Li Peng led a Chinese delegation to North Korea. It was the first time in twenty years this event had been commemorated in the DPRK.[27] North Korea once again emphasized its friendship with China, balancing its partnership with the USSR.

Still, all the reassuring words among leaders and the pomp and ceremony in Pyongyang could not disguise the deep and growing strategic divergence between the DPRK and China. The two differed fundamentally in their views of the countries that mattered most to North Korea: South Korea, Japan, the United States, and the Soviet Union. For China, the USSR was a strategic adversary, while for North Korea the Soviet Union was its principal military partner. As the main global adversary of the USSR, the United States was for China a de facto strategic partner, if still an ideological foe, and American forces in Asia were a useful counterbalance to the growing Soviet military presence in the region. Even in Korea, where China publicly supported Pyongyang's call for the withdrawal of US forces from the peninsula, it was not clear that China was enthusiastic about North Korea's insistence on the *immediate* withdrawal of US forces, so long as China faced a powerful Soviet threat on its borders.[28] The heightened military cooperation between Moscow and North Korea must have worried the Chinese, already facing pro-Soviet states in Mongolia, Vietnam, and Afghanistan, not to mention Soviet weapons and troops amassed along the 4,500-mile Soviet-Chinese border. As for the other two members of the potential "eastern NATO," Japan and South Korea were welcome economic partners for China, and Beijing's criticisms of the right-wing

---

24. O Chin-yong, *Kim Ilsŏng sidae ŭi Chung-So wa Nam-Buk Han* [China, the Soviet Union, and North and South Korea in the Kim Il Sung Era] (Seoul: Nanam, 2004), 178.

25. Hu Yaobang, *Hu Yaobang nianpu ziliao changbian* [Materials for a Chronological Record of Hu Yaobang's Life], vol. 2 (Hong Kong: Shidai guoji chuban youxian gongsi, 2005), 1022–3.

26. Cited in Oh, China–Soviet Union and North-South Korea, 185.

27. See *Rodong Sinmun*, October 22–28, 1985.

28. Chae-jin Lee, *China and Korea: Dynamic Relations* (Stanford: Hoover Institution Press, 1996), 82.

governments in Tokyo and Seoul were far more muted than Pyongyang's regular anti-Nakasone and anti-Chun diatribes.

In the domestic area as well, the two were starting to diverge more sharply. In the early 1980s, the two countries appeared to be on parallel paths: engaging in localized experiments in market economics, while the state remained in firm control of the overall economy, and the party remained in control of the state. North Korea promoted a new independent enterprise accounting system (*tongnip ch'aesangje*) in March 1984, and in September promulgated a new law on foreign investment that was strongly influenced by China's outward-oriented development strategy. But in the second half of the 1980s, China pushed energetically for greater opening and modernization in its economy, a move that Pyongyang was reluctant to follow. China had already opened fourteen cities and three regions to foreign investment by 1984. It had experimented with Special Economic Zones from the late 1970s onward, decollectivized agriculture, and officially declared "market-oriented socialism." In short, China by the mid-1980s had already gone far beyond North Korea in economic reform and opening. In the latter part of the decade, China would begin to privatize state-owned enterprises, deregulate the economy, and lift price controls. Economically China began to look much more like South Korea than North Korea.

China in the late 1980s remained a mixed state-market economy, far from the quasi-capitalist economy it would become in subsequent decades. Increasingly, however, South Korea's impressive economic growth since the 1960s—itself directed in large part by the state—was an inspiration for China's modernization program, and South Korea's economy was much more complementary to China's than was the autarkic, defense-heavy North Korean economy. For China's modernizing leaders, high-growth, export-oriented, and politically authoritarian South Korea was their country's hoped-for future, while North Korea looked increasingly like the past China was struggling to escape. In 1985 China's indirect trade with South Korea exceeded its trade with North Korea for the first time.[29] Sino–South Korean trade would soon dwarf Sino–North Korean trade, and the gap would only widen over time.

The mid-1980s were a pivotal time for the North Korean economy. The DPRK was having increasing difficulty even maintaining the illusion of sustained economic growth, much less demonstrating it concretely. In February 1985 the *Rodong Sinmun* announced the completion of North Korea's Second Seven-Year Economic Plan (1978–84) with relatively muted fanfare compared to earlier plans.[30] The regime claimed the economy had grown at an annual rate of 8.8 percent during the plan

29. Ibid., 139.

30. Ri Chong-ok, "Report on the Fulfillment of the Second Seven-Year Plan," *Rodong Sinmun*, February 17, 1985. Reprinted in Sö Tae-suk [Dae-Sook Suh], *Puk Han munhŏn yŏngu: munhŏn kwa haeje* [A Study of North Korean Documents: Documents and Analysis], vol. 5 (Seoul: Institute for Far Eastern Studies, Kyungnam University, 2004), 621–30.

period, somewhat short of the 9.6 percent projected at the outset of the plan but certainly impressive by world standards and comparable to the South Korean growth rate at the time. Of course, North Korea's economic growth statistics had been vague and unreliable since at least the 1960s; more revealing was the fact that, by the regime's own admission, "ten long-term goals" had only been partially fulfilled. The plan was not declared complete until 1985, a year behind schedule, and a further year was set aside to prepare for the new plan.[31] The Third Seven-Year Plan (1987–93) was finally launched in April 1987, with the ambitious and very specific goals of increasing national income 1.7 times, industrial output 1.9 times, grain output 1.4 times, and foreign trade volume 3.4 times.[32] As it turned out, none of these goals would be fulfilled, both because of North Korea's long-term structural problems and the collapse of the socialist international system just two years later. Far from clambering up to the dizzying heights of newfound affluence, North Korea was about to plunge into the abyss of famine. The Third Seven-Year Plan was the last multiyear economic plan North Korean would produce.

Although South Korea may have surpassed North Korea in per capita income as early as 1969, the two Korean economies did not diverge dramatically until several years afterward. By the mid-1980s, the South Korean per capita income was two and a half times that of the North, and the South was much more technologically advanced.[33] North Korea refused to acknowledge its loss of economic primacy to the South, much less concede that its rigid ideology of self-reliance might have had something to do with its economic difficulties. Indeed, ideological emphasis seemed to grow in inverse proportion to the economy, and the North Korean family cult was becoming ever more peculiar. In 1988, for example, the DPRK announced that a Japanese botanist had developed a "Kim Jong Il flower" (*Kim Chŏngil kkot*, or Kimjongilia) as a token of Japanese-Korean friendship.[34] A variety of begonia, the Kimjongilia was supposedly designed to bloom every year at the time of Kim Jong Il's birthday in mid-February.[35] The flower took pride of place beside (or rather, with proper filial deference, below) the Kimilsungia, a variety of orchid allegedly developed by an Indonesian botanist after Kim Il Sung's visit to that country in 1965.

---

31. Marcus Noland, *Avoiding the Apocalypse: The Future of the Two Koreas* (Washington, DC: Institute for International Economics, 2000), 67.

32. Ri Kŭn-mo, "On the Third Seven-Year Plan (1987–1994) for People's Economic Development of the DPRK," Report to the Second Meeting of the 8th Supreme People's Assembly," *Rodong Sinmun* April 22, 1987. Reprinted in Suh, Study of North Korean Documents, vol. 5, 631–59.

33. Károly Fendler, "Economic Problems of the Democratic People's Republic of Korea in the 1980s," *Information Service on the Unification Question of the Korean Peninsula* (Seoul: National Unification Board of Korea, 1991), 32.

34. See Pang Hwan Ju, *Kimjongilia* (Pyongyang: Foreign Languages Publishing House, n.d.)

35. Glyn Ford and Soyoung Kwon, *North Korea on the Brink: Struggle for Survival* (London: Pluto Press, 2008), 98

While North and South Korea continued to diverge economically and ideologically, the two sides reached a new level of rapprochement in the mid-1980s. The
October 1983 Rangoon bombing had dealt a severe blow to North-South relations, which only began to recover almost a year later, when the North Korean
Red Cross sent emergency rice, cement, clothing, and medical supplies to flood
victims in South Korea. This disaster relief opened the door to new North-South
contacts, and 1985 turned out to be the most important year for inter-Korean relations since the July 4 communiqué in 1972. Two interparliamentary meetings were
held between members of the South Korean National Assembly and the DPRK
Supreme People's Assembly, the first such meetings since the two states were established in 1948. Even more groundbreaking were the first-ever exchange of cultural
troupes—including dancers, singers, and other performers—and the first officially
sanctioned reunions of separated families. Some ninety people separated by Korea's division were briefly united with relatives they had not seen since the Korean
War, or even earlier. These family reunions made a big splash in the international
media, and in South Korea the tearful, almost unbearably emotional family meetings were covered in great detail, especially on television. But in the North, these
reunions were given very little media attention, mentioned only in short, matter-
of-fact articles in the *Rodong Sinmun* and elsewhere. Television images of weeping
family members meeting their long-lost kin, ubiquitous in the South on these occasions, were nowhere to be seen in the North. Instead, North Korean media used
these occasions to highlight the allegedly miserable, "nightmarish" conditions of
the US-occupied capitalist South Korea compared to the free and affluent North.[36]
Whether or not the people of North Korea believed these terms of comparison,
elsewhere in the world it was becoming increasingly clear that it was the South, not
the North, that was ahead in living standards and international prestige.

Internationally South Korea's star continued to rise at the expense of the
North's, but there was one place where North Korea's reputation was rapidly
growing: among the antigovernment dissidents, especially university students, in
South Korea. In the late 1980s, while much of the world (and much of the South
Korean population) celebrated the Seoul Olympics as South Korea's "coming-out
party" and a decisive propaganda victory over Pyongyang, the South Korean dissident movement was dominated by the pro-North Korean Juche Ideology Faction
(*Chuch'e sasang p'a*, or *Chusap'a* for short), dominance never achieved before or
since.[37] For the first time since the Korean War, North Korea had a small but vocal
and influential group of sympathizers among the antigovernment opposition in

---

36. See *Rodong Sinmun* September 20 and 22, 1985.
37. Namhee Lee, *The Making of Minjung: Democracy and the Politics of Representation in South
Korea* (Ithaca: Cornell University Press, 2007), 139. The activists interviewed by Lee estimated that 80–90
percent of the student and labor movement participants were Chusap'a followers in the late 1980s.

the South. This had less to do with North Korean agitation (although Pyongyang was happy to take the credit) than with developments in South Korea's economy and society: the explosive growth of the university-educated population and the blue-collar workforce; the heavy-handed and widely despised authoritarianism of Chun Doo Hwan; and the search among dissident intellectuals for an ideology that combined anticapitalism, anti-imperialism, and Korean nationalism. Juche, as these intellectuals understood it, seemed to fit the bill perfectly.

It is debatable how much the Pyongyang government influenced, or even understood, the South Korean movement carried out in the name of North Korea's official ruling ideology. Of course, South Korean leaders since founding president Syngman Rhee had attacked any antigovernment dissent as communist and pro-North Korean. Many cases of alleged pro-Pyongyang espionage and agitation in the 1960s and 1970s were clearly fabrications of the Korean Central Intelligence Agency intended to suppress criticism of the dictatorship. Sometimes espionage circles would be "discovered" around election time in the South, thus underscoring the government's message about the continuous threat of subversion from the North and the need for vigilance and authoritarian rule in the South. In perhaps the most notorious spy case, several South Korean citizens residing in West Germany were accused of contacting North Korean agents in East Berlin and, after an "extraordinary rendition" back to South Korea courtesy of the KCIA, were tried for espionage. One of the accused was Yun I-sang, Korea's leading modern composer. Yun was sentenced to life imprisonment but was released in 1969 under intense pressure from Western governments and prominent musicians from around the world, including Igor Stravinsky. On his release Yun returned to Berlin, where he died in 1995. Although he subsequently visited North Korea several times, he was never again able to return to the South as he had wished.[38]

The so-called East Berlin Incident was a major embarrassment for the KCIA and nearly led to a diplomatic breakdown between Seoul and the German Federal Republic. Whether or not any of those accused in the incident had even contacted North Koreans, much less spied for Pyongyang, could not be confirmed for many years.[39] But in at least once case, a South Korean underground group

---

38. The Yun I-sang Music Institute opened in Pyongyang in 1984. Yun is lionized in North Korea for his dedication to unification. Whether his modernist, often atonal music is appreciated there is another question.

39. German government archives suggest that several of the so-called spies had been approached by North Koreans in East Berlin but were not engaged in espionage themselves. On the other hand, a South Korean truth commission concluded in 2006 that the KCIA did not merely concoct the story to distract attention from the disputed election of 1967, as some critics thought at the time. This was, rather, a case of intelligence agents overreaching their jurisdiction by kidnapping citizens from abroad—not the last time the KCIA (or its American namesake) would do so. See *Hangyore Sinmun*, October 29, 2004, and *Tonga Ilbo*, January 27, 2006.

seems to have received contact and direction from the DPRK. This was the so-called Revolutionary Party for Unification (T'ongil Hyŏngmyŏngdang or RPU) organized in 1964.[40] Several of its leaders visited the DPRK, received funding from the North, and even met with Kim Il Sung.[41] According to the South Korean government, which arrested several alleged RPU leaders in 1968 and sentenced four to death in 1974, the organization had studied Marxist-Leninist ideology and guerrilla tactics and had established a number of front organizations, planning a violent overthrow of the ROK regime and unification with the North. But the RPU was never more than a small club of students and activists, with no effective widespread network or mass following. It was hardly the Korean equivalent of the South Vietnamese National Liberation Front, although both the South and North Korean governments had a stake in playing up the significance of the RPU. For the Seoul government, uncovering the RPU showed that North Korea was still bent on subverting and "communizing" the South through underground organizations. Indeed, the RPU was probably the only "pro-North Korean group" of the many alleged cases in the 1960s and 1970s that had genuine ties to the DPRK.[42]

For the North, too, the RPU was unique: the one organization in the South openly sympathetic to North Korean interests. Not surprisingly, DPRK propaganda greatly exaggerated the RPU's popularity and significance. Kim Il Sung referred to the RPU at length in his report to the Fifth Congress of the Korean Workers' Party in 1970. "With its emergence," Kim said, "broad masses of the oppressed and exploited people in south Korea have acquired a genuine defender of their class and national interests."[43] Throughout the 1970s and into the 1980s, DPRK media portrayed the RPU as a major opposition force in the South. In August 1984, for example, the *Rodong Sinmun* reprinted in its entirety the RPU's denunciation of Chun Doo Hwan's visit to Japan, declaring that the organization spoke "in the name of the whole [South Korean] people."[44]

---

40. According to the organization's own history, a preparatory committee was formed in 1964 and the RPU was officially launched in 1969. In 1985 the group was renamed the Korean National Democratic Front (Hanguk Minjok Minju Chŏnsŏn), and since 2005 it has been the Anti-Imperialist National Democratic Front (Panje Minjok Minju Chŏnsŏn). See the Front's website, http://ndfsk.dyndns.org/.

41. Lee, *Making of Minjung*, 97. Lee relies extensively on recent South Korean scholarship on the underground opposition movements on the 1960s and 1970s. See ibid., n.113.

42. Ibid., 96.

43. Kim Il Sung, "Report to the Fifth Congress of the Workers' Party of Korea on the Work of the Central Committee," in *Independent Peaceful Unification of Korea* (New York: International Publishers, 1975), 131.

44. "Declaration of the Central Committee of the Revolutionary Party for Unification," *Rodong Sinmun,* August 10, 1984.

In reality, overtly pro-Pyongyang sentiments, much less a political movement with close ties to the DPRK, were thoroughly suppressed in South Korea from the Korean War until the mid-1980s. It is debatable whether the RPU even existed outside North Korean propaganda after its leaders were arrested in the late 1960s; radio transmissions allegedly broadcast by an underground RPU station in South Korea have been traced to Hwanghae Province in the North. Anticommunism penetrated deeply into postwar South Korean society, where attempts at organizing workers independently of the government, or use of socialist-sounding language, were punishable offenses until the late 1980s. South Korea's "red complex" was one of the severest in the world. Even after democratization and the end of the Cold War, positive statements about North Korea could land one afoul of the National Security Law. The writings of Marx and Lenin, to say nothing of Kim Il Sung and Kim Jong Il, were absolutely forbidden for a generation after the Korean War. Partly for this reason, the antigovernment opposition movement of the 1970s and early 1980s articulated itself not in the international traditions of socialism or communism, but predominantly as a home-grown movement of the *minjung,* or popular masses.[45]

The emergence of Chusap'a as the dominant force in the South Korean dissident movement was therefore a significant departure from the anticommunist, anti–North Korean opposition of the previous three decades. But Juche ideology was attractive to these activists less because it was communist than because it was nationalist. The rise of Chusap'a coincided with the rise of anti-Americanism, emerging in the aftermath of the Kwangju massacre.[46] General Chun Doo Hwan's brutal crackdown on protesters in the southwest city of Kwangju in May 1980, an atrocity for which many South Koreans held the United States culpable, led to a radicalization of the dissident movement. Until that point, South Korean protest movements had appealed to Western notions of democracy and upheld the United States as a model. Now the United States was seen increasingly as the source of South Korea's problems, through propping up military dictatorships and bringing a rapacious capitalism to Korea. Antigovernment students and intellectuals quickly turned against the United States, targeting the symbols of American culture in particular. In March 1982, the United States Information Service (USIS) building in Pusan was firebombed. In May 1985, students occupied the USIS building in Seoul for seventy-two hours. Beyond these acts

---

45. Kang Man-gil, "Contemporary Nationalist Movements and the Minjung," in Kenneth Wells, ed., *South Korea's Minjung Movement: The Culture and Politics of Dissidence* (Honolulu: University of Hawai'i Press, 1995), 31–60.

46. Gi-wook Shin, "Marxism, Anti-Americanism, and Democracy in South Korea: An Examination of Nationalist Intellectual Discourse," *Positions: East Asia Cultures Critique* 3, no. 2 (1995): 510–36.

of protest, the new anti-Americanism inspired a thorough reconsideration of Korea's modern history, especially the South Korean regime's roots in pro-Japanese colonial collaboration, American responsibility for Korea's division, and the history of North Korea.[47] Younger South Korean activists sought to escape from the reflexive anticommunism of the previous forty years, turning their parents' ideology upside-down. For many, the American savior and the North Korean demon switched places.

The Revolutionary Party for Unification reemerged as the Korean National Democratic Front (Hanguk minjok minju chŏnsŏn, KNDF) on July 27, 1985. Ten months later, Seoul National University students announced on a campus wall poster that they had been listening to KNDF radio broadcasts.[48] Such blatant defiance of the National Security Law signified a new stage in the South Korean student movement, one in which consumption of North Korean and pro–North Korean books, pamphlets, and radio broadcasts became de rigueur among a significant segment of the movement.[49] Somewhat like radical intellectuals of Western Europe in the 1940s and 1950s, South Korean movement activists, disgusted with the system under which they lived, saw a superior system on the other side of the Cold War divide and were willing to overlook the latter's severe shortcomings.[50] Unlike the Europeans, however, what motivated the Chusap'a was not so much an abstract ideology of communism but a sense of aggrieved nationalism that they saw as embodied in the North Korean system and its leader. As the historian Namhee Lee puts it, Juche ideology "had become for the *chusap'a* an empty vessel into which all of their own aspirations, past failures, disappointments, and future hopes were placed."[51] North Korea's claim to be a "People's Democracy," in contrast to the sham democracy of South Korea, was taken at face value. Like the postwar West European left, which had a peculiar blind spot for the problems of Eastern Europe, the pro-Pyongyang activists in

---

47. These new intellectual trends focused especially on the "liberation space" between the end of Japanese colonial rule and the Korean War. The representative text, bringing together many of the leading progressive scholars of the period, is *Haebang chŏnhusa ŭi insik* [Perspectives on Pre-and Post-Liberation History], published in six volumes between 1979 and 1987. Perhaps the most important external intervention in this debate, a text which catalyzed revisionist scholarship in South Korea, was Bruce Cumings's *Origins of the Korean War*, published the United States in 1981 and circulated underground in South Korea in the early 1980s.

48. Lee, *Making of Minjung*, 127–29.

49. Like many opposition movements of the radical Left, the South Korean movement in the 1980s was deeply and often bitterly divided. A major split in the student movement was between the more class-focused, orthodox Leninist "People's Democracy" group and the more nationalistic and Third World-oriented "National Liberation" group. The Chusap'a overlapped mostly with the latter, but was not identical to it.

50. Tony Judt, *Past Imperfect: French Intellectuals, 1944–1956* (Berkeley: University of California Press, 1992), 168–86.

51. Lee, *Making of Minjung*, 143.

South Korea refused to criticize the DPRK in any way or to find common cause with antiauthoritarian movements within Communist countries, including the prodemocracy movement then emerging in China.

As it turned out, enthusiasm for Juche ideology among South Korean dissidents could not survive South Korea's successful democratization, the collapse of communism in Eastern Europe, and the economic implosion of North Korea itself. By the early 1990s many of these activists had become utterly disillusioned with the North Korean system. Many abandoned politics altogether; some went into the moderate civil society movements then proliferating in the South; yet others made a complete 180-degree turn and become rightists. One of the original Chusap'a leaders, Kim Yŏng-hwan, confessed in 1999 that he had been actively recruited by the DPRK intelligence service in 1989 and secretly trained in Pyongyang.[52] If this story is true, the disintegration of the Chusap'a a few years latter suggests that North Korea's resources were not well spent.

The Seoul Olympics and the Pyongyang Alternative

In September 1981, the International Olympic Committee (IOC) awarded the 1988 summer games to the city of Seoul. The effect of this on North Korea was twofold. First, the Seoul Olympics shone the international spotlight on the rival Korean capital as never before, and despite Pyongyang's efforts the North was unable to share this spotlight with Seoul. More than any other single event, the 1988 Olympics demonstrated South Korea's eclipse of the North in international prestige. Second, the Seoul Olympics created a rift between the DPRK and its major allies. After attempts at sharing the Olympics between Seoul and Pyongyang failed, fellow socialist countries refused to join North Korea in boycotting the Seoul Olympics. In fact, the 1988 Olympics facilitated unprecedented contact between socialist countries and South Korea, and accelerated the process of normalization between Seoul and North Korea's allies. Trying to make the best of a bad situation, Pyongyang hosted its own international sporting event in 1989, the Thirteenth World Festival of Youth and Students (WFYS). But the WFYS, a sort of left-wing alternative Olympics, could not begin to compete with the Seoul Olympics in international visibility and prestige. The expense of hosting the Festival only added to North Korea's growing economic difficulties, helping to bring about the catastrophe of the 1990s.

---

52. Martin Bradley, *Under the Loving Care of the Fatherly Leader: North Korea and the Kim Dynasty* (New York: St. Martin's Griffin, 2006), 646.

South Korea lobbied hard to bring the Olympics to Seoul. The city was not an obvious choice to host the Olympics: the capital of half a divided nation still technically at war, just thirty miles from one of the most militarized and dangerous boundaries in the world, in a country run by a military-led authoritarian regime, Seoul hardly reflected the peace and stability that were the Olympic ideal. But the Olympics themselves had lost some of their luster in recent years. The previous four summer games had all been marred by serious problems: Mexico City in 1968 saw the gunning down of student protesters, Munich in 1972 was remembered mostly for the murder of Israeli athletes by Palestinian terrorists, the Montreal Olympics in 1976 were a huge financial flop, and the 1980 Moscow Olympics were boycotted by the United States and its allies protesting the Soviet invasion of Afghanistan. Any country willing to host the Olympics would have to be prepared to take enormous political and financial risks. South Korea was not only willing to take these risks, but did so with unfettered energy and enthusiasm. South Korea's political and business leaders hoped the 1988 Olympics would be for their country what the 1964 Tokyo Olympics had been for Japan: the symbol of a poor, war-ravaged country coming of age and establishing its place in the sun as a strong, affluent member of the international community. Led by Chung Ju Young, chairman of the Hyundai Group, the Seoul Olympic Committee tirelessly lobbied the IOC, foreign diplomats at the UN, and countries all over the world to bring the Olympics to Seoul. When the final vote was held in Baden-Baden, West Germany, Seoul won over its nearest rival—the Japanese city of Nagoya—by a margin of two to one.[53]

North Korea did not respond immediately to the choice of Seoul as the site for the 1988 Olympics. Toward the end of 1981, the *Rodong Sinmun* mentioned for the first time that the games "are said to be going to be held in Seoul in 1988," ridiculing the "fascist" leaders of South Korea who hoped the Olympics would bring international recognition to their so-called "state."[54] At first, the North Korean media seemed unable to acknowledge that the choice of the Olympic venue was final. As it became clear that the Olympics really would take place in Seoul, North Korea tried to persuade the IOC to change its mind. President Fidel Castro of Cuba took it on himself to champion Pyongyang's cause. In November 1984, Castro wrote a letter to IOC president Juan Antonio Samaranch criticizing the choice of Seoul to host the Olympics (as Samaranch was a native of Barcelona, the two corresponded in Spanish).[55] Olympic host nations, Castro argued,

53. Don Oberdorfer, *The Two Koreas: A Contemporary History*, rev. ed. (New York: Basic Books, 2001), 180–81.

54. Ibid., 181.

55. Castro and Samaranch shared a native language but politically they could not have been farther apart: as a youth in Franco's Spain, Samaranch had been a member of the fascist Falange movement.

should "respect the freedom and the social and human rights of their people." Alluding to the 1980 Kwangju massacre, Castro wrote "The bloodshed in Korea is still fresh in the memory of humanity." He continued, "The Olympic games in Seoul, in the form they are designed, do not contribute to the unity of the Korean nation, do not help heal the wounds of war, do not really promote peace, harmony, cooperation and friendship between peoples." Given these problems, and especially after the socialist countries' boycott of the Los Angeles Olympics in 1984, Castro suggested that the IOC choose another site for the 1988 games.[56]

Samaranch replied politely that the IOC was committed to hosting the 1988 games in Seoul. "I sincerely thank you for your advice," Samaranch wrote, "and I can assure you that the IOC is willing to chair a meeting between the two parts of Korea, as long as the two voluntarily agree to attend it with the commitment that no time must be addressed to any political issues." The safety of participating athletes would be assured. Hosting the Olympics in Seoul would not violate Olympic principles nor pose a problem for the participants.[57] Not to be deterred, Castro took up the case with the Western media. In March 1985, Castro gave an interview in New York with American academic Jeffrey Elliot and Congressman Mervyn Dymally of California. After repeating almost verbatim some of the concerns he had expressed to Samaranch, Castro proposed a new idea: sharing the Olympics between South and North Korea. "I think we must avoid the catastrophe which the choice of Seoul alone implies and share the Olympics" by giving part of the games to Pyongyang, Castro declared. The DPRK was prepared to do this, and Third World leaders supported the idea. Otherwise, the Olympic movement would continue lurching from crisis to crisis: "crisis in Moscow, crisis in Los Angeles and crisis, without any doubt, at the point things have reached, in Seoul."[58]

While Castro was the first to propose a shared Olympics to the international media, the North Koreans had begun several months earlier pressuring Samaranch to concede part of the games to Pyongyang. In September 1984, the head of the DPRK Olympic Committee, Kim Yu-sŏn, met with Samaranch at the Hotel Prague in Moscow. The Olympics cannot be held in half a country at war, Kim implored. In the interest of peace, North Korea must co-host the games. But Samaranch was unmoved, saying curtly, "In 1981 Seoul was chosen to celebrate the Games. That decision is final." Nevertheless, Samaranch conceded that it might

56. Letter from Fidel Castro to Jan Antonio Samaranch, 29 November 1984, IOC Archives. Obtained by the Cold War International History Project, Woodrow Wilson Center, Washington, DC.

57. Letter from Juan Antonio Samaranch to Fidel Castro, 4 December 1984, IOC Archives. Obtained by the Cold War International History Project, Woodrow Wilson Center, Washington, DC.

58. Interview with Fidel Castro, 25 July 1985, IOC Archives. Obtained by the Cold War International History Project, Woodrow Wilson Center, Washington, DC.

be possible to hold some games in the North.[59] Kim Yu-sŏn met Samaranch again in July 1985 with more specific proposals. Kim suggested that seven or eight events be held in North Korea, and that the games be called the "Korean Olympic Games" rather than the "Seoul Olympic Games." In order to facilitate this, the DPRK and South Korea would form a joint Olympic committee. Unfortunately, Kim said, he had met with the South Koreans three times already without coming to an agreement.[60]

Around the same time, IOC vice president Ashwini Kumar, a native of India, visited the DPRK to discuss this issue with North Korean sports and government officials. Kumar arrived in Pyongyang via Moscow and Beijing on July 16, 1985 ("Pyongyang is a very difficult capital to reach," he noted). He assured his hosts that North Korean participants would have sufficient security for "peaceful participation in the games" and that the North Korean athletes could march right after the South Koreans in the opening ceremony, but a unified North-South team was not feasible. The North Koreans reminded Kumar of Fidel Castro's suggestion for a unified North-South Olympic Committee and an equal sharing of the games. Kumar replied that "the contract with Seoul City was sacrosanct and could not be violated." DPRK vice president Park Sŏng-chŏl then showed Kumar the proposal North Korea had already distributed around the world, which included (1) a unified Korean organization for the Olympics, (2) equal sharing of the events by both sides, and (3) naming the games "Korea Pyongyang Seoul Olympic Games." Kumar did not think any of this was feasible, although he hoped that North and South Korea could work out some sort of mutual agreement for North Korean participation in the games. In his notes to the IOC, Kumar remarked, "It need hardly be commented upon that the conditions set forth in this manifesto are repugnant to the [Olympic] Charter and our contract with the Seoul authorities. The only way in which North Korea could be given a face saving device is to agree to symbolic unity."[61] In the end South Korea and the IOC could not offer the North even a symbolic role in the games that the DPRK authorities found satisfactory. Like the UN-sponsored 1948 elections that created the Republic of Korea, the 1988 Olympic Games would take place in the South alone.

---

59. Notes on meeting in Hotel Prague, Moscow, 21 September 1984, IOC Archives. Obtained by the Cold War International History Project, Woodrow Wilson Center, Washington, DC. The meeting notes are in French, although it is not clear whether both sides spoke in French or through interpreters.

60. Notes on meeting between Juan Antonio Samaranch and Yu Sun Kim, Moscow, 28 July 1985, IOC Archives. Obtained by the Cold War International History Project, Woodrow Wilson Center, Washington, DC.

61. Report by Mr. Ashwini Kumar, IOC Vice President, on his trip to North Korea, 16 July 1985, IOC Archives. Obtained by the Cold War International History Project, Woodrow Wilson Center, Washington, DC.

Park Sŏng-chŏl concluded his remarks to Kumar with a warning that hosting the games in Seoul alone was a recipe for violence. This had become a standard theme in North Korea's (and Castro's) criticism of the Seoul Olympics. "In the present atmosphere," Park said, "there would be widespread violence and unrest in South Korea." Kumar noted that Park "ominously declared that the course of events would definitely take a violent turn in case the situation was not diffused."[62] Kumar's sense of foreboding was more prescient that he knew. North Korea itself would ensure that events leading up to the Olympics would "take a violent turn."

Hwang Chang-yŏp, secretary of the Central Committee of the Korean Workers' Party, was the main person to communicate North Korea's position on the Olympics to other socialist countries. In June 1985 Hwang spoke to his counterpart in the East German Socialist Unity Party, Hermann Axen, harshly condemning the Seoul Olympiad as a tool of the American imperialists and their South Korean puppets intended to shore up the crumbling Seoul regime. "This is part of their divisive politics and their anti-communist campaign to create 'two Koreas,' against socialism and for the defense of capitalism," Hwang declared. He insisted that the 1988 Olympics be renamed the "Korean Olympics" or the "Seoul-Pyongyang Olympic Games" and that the games be split evenly between North and South Korea.[63] When Hwang met with Soviet Central Committee secretary A. N. Yakovlev eleven months later, he had softened his demands somewhat. This time, Hwang asked only for three or four events to be held in the North. He reminded his Soviet comrades that Castro promised Cuba would not participate in the games if they were not shared between Seoul and Pyongyang. This was a matter of critical importance to all socialist and nonaligned nations. "In order to ensure peace in Korea and its peaceful unification," Hwang said, "we must disrupt the enemy's intention to hold the Olympics in Seoul." Yakovlev called Hwang's proposals "reasonable" and duly promised Soviet support.[64]

Although the DPRK pushed for cohosting the Olympics until the very last moment, the proposal ultimately failed. South Korea and the IOC were never very enthusiastic about the idea to begin with, and North Korea never convinced the IOC that Pyongyang could overcome the technical obstacles that joint hosting

---

62. Ibid.

63. Letter from Hwang Dschang Job [Hwang Chang-yŏp], Secretary of the Central Committee of the Korean Workers' Party, to Comrade Hermann Axen, Secretary of the Central Committee of the German Socialist Unity Party, 19 June 1985. NKIDP, Stasi Documents, 10041042. Twelve years later Hwang became the highest-level North Korean official to defect to the South.

64. A Conversation with KWP CC Secretary, Comrade Hwang Chang-yŏp. GARF, fond 10063, opis 2, delo 55, listy 1–8. Obtained for the North Korea International Documentation Project by Sergey Radchenko and translated by Gary Goldberg.

would face. On September 8, 1988, just nine days before the Olympic opening ceremonies, Samaranch wrote a telegram to DPRK Olympic Committee president Kim Yu-sŏn, asking North Korea to send even a symbolic representation to the games, which would benefit "the noble cause of the reunification of Korea."[65] But North Korea refused to participate in any form. By this time the North Koreans were aware that most of their allies would not join them in sitting out the Seoul Olympics. Despite their initial support for a North-South shared Olympics, the USSR, the East European socialist countries, and China would not follow Pyongyang in boycotting the games. After the US boycott of the 1980 Moscow Olympics and the Soviet bloc's reciprocal boycott of the 1984 Olympics in Los Angeles, the socialist sports powerhouses were not willing to forego the opportunity to compete against the West for a third time in a row. In the end all of North Korea's socialist allies except Cuba and Ethiopia attended the Seoul Olympics. For North Korea, China's position was probably the most disappointing. China had refused to go along with the Soviet boycott of the Los Angeles Olympics in 1984 and had joined the 1986 Asian Games in Seoul, the first major international sports event in South Korea attended by the PRC. North Korea ended up almost completely isolated in its opposition to the Seoul Games.

As Pak Sŏng-chŏl warned IOC vice president Kumar in 1985, events did indeed take a violent turn in the run-up to the Olympics. Part of this was the mounting antigovernment protests in South Korea, which forced Chun Doo Hwan to step down in 1987. But the most significant act of violence against civilian targets was perpetrated by North Korea itself. North Korean terrorism, discussed in the previous chapter, reached a peak in 1987 through one last, spectacular act of carnage. On November 29, all 115 passengers on a Korean Airlines were killed when their flight en route from Baghdad to Seoul exploded over Southeast Asia. The cause of the explosion was a bomb planted by two North Korean agents, one of whom—a young woman named Kim Hyŏn-hŭi—survived and became a celebrity in South Korea. According to Kim, the purpose of the bombing was to sow fear in South Korea and the international community, and thereby to undermine the Seoul regime and to disrupt or block altogether the Seoul Olympics.[66] Once the United States was satisfied with the accuracy of Kim's confession, it placed North Korea on its list of states that sponsor terrorism, where it would remain for the next twenty years. The Seoul Games, on the other hand, proceeded as scheduled and turned out to be one of the most successful Olympiads in recent history.

---

65. Letter from the President of the IOC to the DPRK's National Olympic Committee representative, IOC Archives. Obtained by the Cold War International History Project, Woodrow Wilson Center, Washington, DC.

66. Oberdorfer, *The Two Koreas*, 183.

Astonishingly, South Korea came in fourth in the medal count, after the global sports giants of the USSR, East Germany, and the United States. South Korea, it seemed, had truly found its place in the sun and left North Korea in the shade.

Unable to share or prevent the Seoul Olympics, Pyongyang staged its own international games the following year. The Thirteenth World Festival of Youth and Students (WFYS) opened in Pyongyang on July 1, 1989. More than just a sporting event and much more politically partisan than the Olympics, the WFYS included art exhibits and workshops with explicitly political themes. The WFYS had been sponsored by the World Federation of Democratic Youth and the International Union of Students since 1947, when the first festival was held in Prague. The event was held irregularly in East Bloc capitals or neutral nations such as Austria or Finland; the largest attendance was at the Moscow WFYS in 1957, where thirty-four thousand people participated. Moscow played host again in 1985, for the Twelfth WFYS. As was the case for the Tenth, Eleventh, Twelfth, and Fourteenth festivals, the official theme of the Thirteenth WFYS in Pyongyang was "For Anti-Imperialist Solidarity, Peace and Friendship."

The DPRK applied all possible financial, human, and propaganda resources to the success of the Thirteenth WFYS. The first time the festival had been held in Asia, the Pyongyang WFYS was attended by the largest number of countries in the history of the event, 177 nations in all. Pyongyang allegedly spent over $4 billion on the WFYS, including $33 million in grants from Moscow.[67] The North pulled out all the stops: Pyongyang's already impeccable streets were cleaned further, clothing factories produced colorful traditional clothing for the city's residents and department stores were stocked with goods—in fact, an entire department store, Kwangbok (Liberation) Department Store, was built especially for the event.[68] The presence of Western foreigners in Pyongyang was unprecedented, at least since the Korean War. Some one hundred American delegates attended, and more than twenty American journalists were admitted to Pyongyang to cover the festival.[69] Yet the event was largely ignored in the Western press, and was completely overshadowed by the Seoul Olympics.

The one delegate whose presence did make waves in the Western and South Korean media was Im Su-gyŏng, a fourth-year undergraduate French major at the Hanguk Foreign Language University in Seoul, who traveled secretly and illegally

67. Kongdan Oh, "North Korea in 1989: Touched by Winds of Change?" *Asian Survey* 30, no. 1 (Jan. 1990): 74.

68. Sheryl Wu Dunn, "Reporter's Notebook: In Pyongyang, Pro-American and Anti-U.S.," *New York Times*, July 2, 1989.

69. Nicholas Kristoff, "Change Comes to North Korea, Ever so Reluctantly," *New York Times*, July 19, 1989.

to North Korea to attend the festival.[70] Im was sent by the National Council of Student Representatives (Chŏnguk Taehaksaeng Taep'yoja Hyŏbŭihoe, or Chŏndaehyŏp), an umbrella organization formed in August 1987, representing some 1 million South Korean university students.[71] In emotion-choked press conferences, Im brought Chŏndaehyŏp's anti-ROK government, prounification message to Pyongyang, becoming an instant celebrity in the North and a highly divisive figure in the South. The Pyongyang media called Im "The Flower of Unification" (*T'ongil ŭi kkot*) and television cameras followed the smiling, often dazed-looking South Korean student ceaselessly for her entire week-long stay in North Korea.[72] Her every word and gesture in the streets and sports stands was captured in photographs and on film. The DPRK even published an Im Su-gyŏng calendar, complete with a photo of her in Pyongyang for every month of the year. Even if the WFYS was a huge financial drain on the DPRK and achieved less publicity than the North Korean authorities hoped, Im's visit scored big points for Pyongyang in its propaganda war with the South.

Part of that propaganda war for the DPRK (and Chŏndaehyŏp) was to provoke the South Korean government into punishing Im for her unauthorized visit to the North, thus showing that Seoul was opposed to unification. The South Korean authorities duly complied, arresting Im Su-gyŏng as soon as she crossed back into the South and placing her in jail for three years.[73] However, the propaganda effect of Im Su-gyŏng's visit may not have been entirely what the North Korean authorities expected. According to North Korean defectors interviewed by the American journalist Bradley Martin, Im Su-gyong's physical appearance and treatment in the South created doubts about their own government's official position, and especially what they had been told about life in South Korea. One defector recalled, "After Im Su-gyŏng's visit, people's thought changed. They figured North Korea couldn't feed them but South Korea was better off. It was seeing her appearance—she seemed well off, acted free and confident." After seeing the arrest of Im and the Reverend Mun Ik-hwan, who also traveled illegally to the North, another defector recounted, "But when they came we could see they were well fed. Then she got out of jail, after only three years, and had a child. I thought

---

70. See for example David Holley, "Student Flies to N. Korea to Attend Event: S. Korea Dissident Defies Festival Ban," *Los Angeles Times*, July 1, 1989.

71. Chŏndaehyŏp dominated the student movement in the late 1980s. In 1993 it was replaced by the Korean Federation of General Student Councils (Hanchongnyŏn).

72. Im Su-gyŏng published a lengthy account of her visit shortly after her return to the South, entitled *Ŏmŏni, hana toen choguk e salgo sip'ŏyo: Im Su-gyŏng okchung pangbuk paeksŏ* [Mother, I Want to Live in a Unified Fatherland: White Paper of Im Su-gyŏng's Visit to the North] (Seoul: Tolbegae, 1990).

73. An oil painting depicting Im's arrest, entitled "The Apprehension of Im Su-gyŏng," currently hangs in the Mansudae Art Gallery in Pyongyang.

they must have a lot of freedom in South Korea—only three years, then marriage and a child." Nor did television images of political demonstrations in South Korea necessarily convince North Koreans of the Seoul government's brutality. On the contrary, the same defector recalled asking himself, "If they have that kind of freedom to fight the police, what's the rest of society like?"[74] Apparently reflecting the government's fear of subversive bourgeois influences from the foreigners descending on Pyongyang for the World Festival of Youth and Students, on July 6, 1989, the *Rodong Sinmun* took the unusual step of publishing a full-page article extolling the superiority of the socialist system and the need for continued ideological vigilance.[75]

"Socialism Betrayed"

The North Korean leadership had good reason to fear the corrupting influence of the capitalist world, and especially South Korea, in the late 1980s. Under President Roh Tae-woo, South Korea had launched an aggressive policy to develop economic and political relations with communist countries, which the ROK called its "Northern Policy" (*Pukbang chŏngch'aek*)—often translated as *Nordpolitik*, an allusion to West Germany's *Ostpolitik* toward communist Eastern Europe.[76] The Nordpolitik strategy was first articulated in 1983 by ROK foreign minister Yi Pŏm-sŏk, who proposed that Seoul normalize relations with the USSR and China in order to isolate North Korea from its major allies.[77] Yi was killed a few months later in Rangoon, but his idea was revived by President Roh Tae-woo, who gave it more of an economic emphasis and sought to incorporate North Korea into this engagement strategy. Roh officially launched the Northern Policy in a declaration "to all sixty million Korean people" (i.e., North and South Koreans) on July 7, 1988. He offered trade and full diplomatic normalization with communist countries, and invited North Korea to expand economic and cultural exchanges with the South, and for the leaders of the two Koreas to hold a summit meeting.[78] North Korea's leaders viewed Roh's invitation with suspicion and hostility, telling a visiting East German delegation in 1988 that Nordpolitik was designed "to

74. Bradley, *Under the Loving Care of the Fatherly Leader*, 608, 625.

75. *Rodong Sinmun*, August 6, 1989.

76. For an early overview of the policy's motivations and successes, see Charles K. Armstrong, "South Korea's Northern Policy," *Pacific Review* 3, no. 1 (1990): 35–45.

77. Oberdorfer, *The Two Koreas*, 187. The origin of Roh's Northern Policy can be traced back a decade further to Park Chung Hee's "June 23 Declaration" of 1973, when the ROK announced it would seek diplomatic relations with countries of different ideologies or social systems.

78. Barry K. Gills, *Korea versus Korea: A Case of Contested Legitimacy* (London: Routledge, 1996), 222.

permanently split the country."[79] Many of North Korea's socialist allies, on the other hand, saw this as an irresistible economic opportunity.

The timing of Roh's Nordpolitik was fortuitous. By the late 1980s, the combination of South Korea's impressive export-oriented growth and market reforms in several communist countries had made natural economic partners of South Korea and these countries—including China and the Soviet Union. Hungary was the farthest along in this reform process, having pursued since the 1960s a so-called "goulash communism" that mixed state planning and private incentives, and Hungary was the first East Bloc country to develop economic—and then political—relations with South Korea.[80] In December 1984, Daewoo chairman Kim Woo-chung, whose company was at the forefront of South Korea's business expansion into the East Bloc, made a secret trip to Budapest to negotiate trade between Hungary and the ROK. Bilateral economic relations rapidly expanded thereafter, accompanied by secret diplomatic negotiations led by Roh Tae-woo's nephew Pak Chŏl-un, later to be ROK minister of sports.[81] On September 13, 1988—four days before the start of the Seoul Olympics—South Korea and Hungary announced that they would establish full diplomatic relations, which came into effect on February 1, 1989.

The North Korean official media responded with unrestrained anger, calling Hungary's recognition of Seoul a "betrayal of socialism" and "a treacherous and grave act against the principles of Marxism-Leninism and the revolutionary cause of the working class."[82] This was especially embarrassing as Kim Il Sung's younger son, Kim Jong Il's half-brother Kim Pyŏng-il, had just been appointed ambassador to Budapest. Pyongyang downgraded its diplomatic relations with Hungary to the level of chargé d'affaires, and transferred Kim Pyŏng-il to Bulgaria. But the diplomatic rush to Seoul could not be stopped. Yugoslavia was the next socialist (or, as they soon would be, postsocialist) country to normalize relations with South Korea, followed by Poland, Czechoslovakia, Romania, Bulgaria, and Albania. If by "socialism" the DPRK meant following Pyongyang's line in shunning South Korea, all of Eastern Europe had "betrayed socialism" by the beginning of the 1990s.

One loyal friend remained in Eastern Europe, however: the German Democratic Republic, led by Kim Il Sung's "younger brother" Erich Honecker.[83] The last East German ambassador to the DPRK, Dr. Hans Meretzki, has suggested

79. Oberdorfer, *The Two Koreas*, 189.

80. Susan Chira, "South Korea Woos Communists; Moves to Full Ties with Hungary," *New York Times*, September 14, 1988.

81. "Hungary Fetes 20-Year Ties with Korea," *Korea Times*, February 1, 2009. Available at http://www.koreatimes.co.kr/www/news/special/2009/08/176_38755.html.

82. Gills, *Korea versus Korea*, 223.

83. Honecker was four months younger than Kim, both born in 1912 (Kim in April and Honecker in August). As it turned out, the two men would die within two months of each other in 1994, Honecker in May and Kim in July.

that the GDR was "100 percent in the Soviet camp" until 1985. Deeply uneasy with the changes instituted in the Soviet bloc under Gorbachev, Honecker and other East German hard-liners tilted away from the USSR and toward North Korea.[84] For the last five years of its existence, East Germany was an outpost of old-fashioned socialist solidarity with North Korea in Eastern Europe, fighting a losing battle against history.

During Kim's visit to the GDR in 1984, Honecker had promised a reciprocal visit to the DPRK. As a preliminary step to that visit, East German official Manfred Gerlach paid a call on Kim Il Sung in May 1986. Gerlach was the leader of the Liberal Democratic Party, one of the so-called "bloc parties" aligned with the ruling German Socialist Unity Party, and future chairman of the State Council (Staatsratsvorsitzender) from December 1989 to April 1990, the last person to hold this post. According to the Foreign Ministry report to Honecker, Kim greeted Gerlach warmly and repeatedly interrupted Gerlach's remarks with enthusiastic assenting comments. Kim told his East German visitor that he would never forget his 1984 visit to the GDR and the time he spent with Honecker, "his best friend and comrade-in-arms." Kim said that "he waited every day for news that Erich Honecker is coming to the DPRK," and that if Honecker came, the people of North Korea would welcome him with enthusiasm, and Kim would show Honecker the great progress the DPRK had made in the nearly ten years since Honecker's last visit (in 1977). The warm relationship between the GDR and the DPRK, as shown by the jubilant greeting Kim received in his 1984 visit to East Germany, "is truly a strong force that can withstand even its greatest foes."[85]

Six months later Honecker and his entourage came to the DPRK. He received the enthusiastic welcome Kim had promised, with 100,000 North Koreans coming out to greet him in the streets of Pyongyang.[86] Honecker and his group visited the sights of the capital, Kim Il Sung's birthplace-cum-museum in Mangyŏngdae, the model Taean heavy machinery complex, and Kim's proudest industrial achievement, the gigantic West Sea barrage near Nampo City. Everything the East Germans witnessed was on an enormous scale, from an artistic display involving 150,000 participants, to the "mass games" utilizing 50,000 athletes "which took the form of a political manifestation of the close and friendly relations between the two Parties, nations and people."[87]

84. Author's interview with Ambassador Hans Meretzki, Postdam, Germany, 29 July 2002.

85. "Report on Conversation between Professor Manfred Gerlach and Kim Il Sung," 26 May 1986. SAPMO-BA, DY 30, 2460. Translated by Grace Leonard for the Cold War International History Project.

86. *Rodong Sinmun*, October 21, 1986, 1.

87. "Report on the Visit by Erich Honecker to the DPRK, 18–21 October 1986." SAPMO-BA, DY 30, 2460.

The Great Leader and his brotherly comrade from Germany met in private for more than four hours.[88] The two began with pro forma remarks on the great achievements in building socialism in their respective countries, followed by the usual denunciations of US imperialism, NATO, and South Korea. Honecker praised Gorbachev's proposals for peace in his recent meeting with Ronald Reagan in Reykjavik and encouraged North Korea's efforts to create a nuclear-free peace zone on the Korean Peninsula. Kim expressed support for Gorbachev's initiatives in Vladivostok and Reykjavic as well, noting that improved US-USSR relations would help resolve the Korean problem.[89] The two leaders "praised the excellent state of fraternal relations between the two Parties, states, and peoples" which had reached a new level since they had signed a Treaty of Friendship and Cooperation with one another in 1984. Honecker invited Kim to visit the GDR again, and Kim "accepted with great joy and sincere thanks."

On the subject of South Korea, Kim told his visitor that the DPRK had no intention or ability to attack the South. More than a thousand American nuclear weapons were maintained in South Korea, he claimed, and it would take only two such weapons to destroy North Korea. In his earlier meeting with Manfred Gerlach, Kim had suggested that the South Korean dictatorship was crumbling from within, faced with an emerging oppositional "united front" of students and a broad range of social forces. While North Korea continued to build socialism, the South Korean people were waging a struggle against military dictatorship and US occupation, a struggle they would inevitably win without any intervention from the North.[90]

A good part of Kim's discussion focused on economic issues. North Korea was preparing to launch its Third Seven-Year Economic Plan in a few months. It had been two years since the completion of the Second Seven-Year Plan (1978–84), an unusually long time lag between plans, and although officially the plan was declared a success, in reality—as we have seen above—the North Korean economy was facing serious difficulties. An admission of North Korea's economic troubles lay not far beneath the surface of the optimistic and upbeat tone of Kim's remarks to Honecker. The focus of the 1987–93 plan, Kim explained, was to "resolve the food problem and to provide residential living space and adequate clothing" for the North Korean people. This would be done by a vast expansion of irrigated

---

88. The record of the meeting appears in the above document. I have supplemented this record with some additional details and interpretations of the meeting based on the recollections of Honecker's Korean-language interpreter, Helga Picht, whom I interviewed in Berlin on August 1, 2002.

89. In their off-the-record conversation, according to the recollection of Honecker's interpreter, Honecker and Kim indirectly criticized Gorbachev, agreeing with each other that "every socialist country takes its own path."

90. "Report on Conversation between Professor Manfred Gerlach and Kim Il Sung."

farmland, building 150,000–200,000 residential units per year, and creating new production facilities for making synthetic fibers from local materials such as limestone and anthracite—North Korea's famous "vinalon." Technological modernization was the key, and in this context, cooperation with East Germany was crucial, especially in the area of scientific and technical training and advice. The future, as always, was rosy. Affluence was just around the corner, and East Germany would help North Korea achieve it, as the GDR had done since the 1950s. And yet, one wonders if Honecker or any of his colleagues considered that by Kim's own admission, after forty years of "building socialism" North Korea could not adequately feed, house, or clothe its people.

In May 1988, a delegation from the Berlin District of the Socialist Unity Party (SED), led by Politburo member Guenter Schabowski, visited Pyongyang as part of an Asian tour that included Beijing and Ulan Bator.[91] When Schabowski met with Kim Il Sung on May 10, Kim immediately inquired about Honecker's health and asked that his warm regards be conveyed to his "friend and brother."[92] On the question of GDR-DPRK economic cooperation, Kim admitted that North Korea had fallen behind on its trade obligations, due in part to severe flooding in 1986 and 1987—a natural disaster that had not been revealed to the international community. The flooding had caused a halt in the production of magnesite, one of North Korea's major export commodities. Despite the economic setback, Kim said, the whole North Korean population was focused on preparing the country for the Thirteenth World Festival of Youth and Students. In particular, the army was building up constructions sites in Pyongyang, which would be completed in a "200-day speed battle."

The last GDR official visit to the DPRK was a military delegation in July 1988, led by East Germany's minister of defense, army general Heinz Kessler. The North Korean host was Defense Minister O Chin-u, who accompanied the delegation to various sites, including a vigorous hike up Mount Paektu on the Sino-Korean border. The group met Kim Il Sung on July 21, and once again Kim's first question was "How is my brother and my best friend, Erich Honecker?"[93] On inter-Korean relations, Kim said the situation was "still tense." Without mentioning the dramatic prodemocracy breakthrough of the previous year in Seoul,

---

91. Schabowski was First Secretary of the Berlin chapter of the SED. On November 9, 1989, he famously gave a wrong answer at a press conference, declaring that restrictions on East Germans travelling to the west would be lifted "immediately." Hordes of East Germans headed for the border, and the Berlin Wall came down that night. See Andreas Herbst et al., *Die SED: Geschichte, Organisation, Politik—Ein Handbuch* (Berlin: Dietz Verlag, 1997), 1065.

92. "Report on a Trip to the DPRK by a Delegation for the GDR, 16 May 1988." SAPMO-BA, DY 30, 2205.

93. "Report on Visit of GDR Military Delegation to DPRK, July 1988." SAPMO-BA, DY 30, 2508.

Kim called South Korea's leaders "puppets" and—while praising the mass protests led by young people in the South—blamed the United States for blocking North Korea's peace overtures. On the economic front, Kim drew attention to North Korea's current "massive campaign for building socialism," involving new plants and mines and a "200-day battle" leading up to the fortieth anniversary of the founding of the DPRK in September. Finally, Kim expressed his gratitude for East German military assistance, and as a parting gesture awarded General Kessler with the Order of the State Banner (First Class). Other members of the delegation also received awards, and the two sides signed an agreement on future military cooperation. In the end, little of this cooperation materialized, and Kim never took up Honecker's invitation for a return visit to the GDR. Two years after the East German military delegation visited North Korea, the GDR was gone, and Kim Il Sung's "brother and best friend" was an international fugitive.

Gorbachev and the Two Koreas

It was bad enough for North Korea that Hungary and other East European socialist states recognized Seoul at the end of the 1980s. Far worse was when the Soviet Union, North Korea's most important patron since the DPRK was founded in the 1940s, normalized relations with the Republic of Korea in September 1990. Within a few short years Soviet-DPRK relations plunged from the heights of economic and military cooperation to the depths of mutual criticism and acrimony. But what seemed to North Korea's leaders a sudden and unprovoked betrayal by Moscow had been under discussion in the USSR for several years. Even before the ascension of Gorbachev, the possibility of improving relations with South Korea had been a subject of secret debate within Soviet academic and policy circles. At a meeting of the International Department of the CPSU Central Committee on August 14–15, 1984 (coinciding with the thirty-sixth anniversary of Korean liberation), one G. Kim of the Oriental Institute of the Soviet Academy of Sciences asserted, "It is high time that the tail stops telling the dog what do. Why should we look at South Korea through Pyongyang's eyes? . . . To respond positively to Seoul's overtures correlates with the USSR national interest." Kim's proposal was quickly shot down by conservative members of the CPSU Central Committee, one of whom defended Moscow's alignment with the idiosyncratic DPRK by stating, "North Korea, for all the peculiarities of Kim Il Sung, is the most important bastion in the Far East of our struggle against American and Japanese imperialism and Chinese revisionism."[94] The North Korean tail continued to wag the Soviet dog in the first two years of Gorbachev's rule. But in the latter half of

---

94. Quoted in Eugene Bazhanov, "Soviet Policy towards South Korea under Gorbachev," 65, fn.

1987, after having reflexively supported Pyongyang's positions (despite private reservations) for nearly four decades, the Soviet leadership began seriously to reassess Moscow's relations with the Korean Peninsula.

When Kim Il Sung visited Moscow in 1986, Gorbachev had refused to support Kim in categorically opposing cross-recognition and joint entry of North and South Korea into the UN. Gorbachev later recalled that he even suggested that such moves would be "reasonable," a position which greatly disappointed Kim.[95] Thereafter the USSR and North Korea increasingly diverged in their domestic and foreign policy. The Soviets, as always, presented themselves as an example for the North Koreans to follow, but Gorbachev's "New Thinking" and "restructuring," to say nothing of glasnost ("openness") were repellent to North Korea's hard-line leaders. Still, so long as the USSR respected "non-interference in the internal affairs of fraternal socialist countries," North Korea's standard principle about such matters, Pyongyang's leaders could tolerate Gorbachev's reforms, however distasteful they found them. Although CPSU secretary Adim Medvedev later suggested that it was Pyongyang's failure to follow the Soviet path of reform that led to the rift with Moscow,[96] it was Moscow's emerging relationship to South Korea that most alarmed the North. In October 1988, KWP secretary Hwang Chang-yŏp met with Alexander Yakovlev, senior advisor to Gorbachev on foreign policy. Hwang expressed concern about a statement Gorbachev had made in his speech at Krasnoyarsk the previous month. Gorbachev had suggested that "in the context of a general amelioration of the situation on the Korean Peninsula, opportunities can also be opened up for arranging economic ties with South Korea." Presumably speaking for Kim Il Sung, Hwang warned Yakovlev that the USSR could not warm up to Seoul so long as the South Korean dictatorship remained in power and American troops were stationed there.[97] It was a warning the Soviets would not heed. Yakovlev himself was a strong advocate of freeing Moscow from the "dogmatic" Pyongyang line and pursuing independent relations with South Korea. By early 1988 the Soviet leadership had decided it was in their country's economic, political, and security interests to normalize relations with Seoul, regardless of what their North Korean allies wanted.

Over the next two years, the Soviet Union assiduously cultivated relations with South Korea while reducing its commitments to Pyongyang. Foreign economic and military assistance was eating away at the Soviet economy—defense

95. Cited in Kim Hakjoon, "The Process Leading to the Establishment of Diplomatic Relation between South Korea and the Soviet Union," Asian Survey 37, no. 7 (July 1997): 642.

96. Sergey Radchenko, "Building Bridges, Burning Bridges: Soviet Moves in Korea, 1988–1991," International Workshop on Foreign Relations of the Two Koreas during the Cold War Era (Seoul: Institute for Far Eastern Studies, Kyungnam University, 2006), 121; Medvedev, Raspad, 327–8.

97. Radchenko, "Russia and North Korea," n.p.

expenditures, long kept secret even from much of the Politburo until the Gorbachev era, took up an astonishing 40 percent of the Soviet budget—and clients such as North Korea, Vietnam, Cuba, Syria, and Iraq had to be cut loose in order to save the Soviet economy.[98] Beyond the economic cost of Soviet military outlays to the DPRK, Gorbachev and his advisors had come to the conclusion that adhering to the rigid Pyongyang position in East Asia inhibited Soviet security goals in the region and prevented Moscow from mending fences with Japan, South Korea, and the United States. The USSR reduced military aid to North Korea in 1988 and thereafter refused Pyongyang's requests for new military assistance.[99] At the same time, Soviet-South Korean contacts took off, much as Hungarian-South Korean relations had a few years earlier. In January 1989, Hyundai founder Chung Ju-yung traveled to Moscow, just as Daewoo's Kim Woo-jung had gone to Budapest in 1984, to discuss bilateral economic cooperation. In April the USSR opened a Soviet Chamber of Commerce and Industry office in Seoul, and in July the South Korean Trade Promotion Corporation (KOTRA) opened an office in Moscow.

The South Koreans pressed for Moscow to open diplomatic and not just economic relations with Seoul. The Koreans argued that this was to better facilitate direct trade, but the political benefits for South Korea in its competition with the North were obvious. In 1989 both the two leading South Korean opposition leaders, Kim Dae Jung and Kim Young Sam, made high-profile visits to Moscow. In June 1990, Gorbachev held a summit meeting with Roh Tae-woo in San Francisco. That the Soviet leader would meet with the South Korean president, in the United States no less, may have been a good reflection of Gorbachev's vision of a cooperative Asia-Pacific but was a bitter pill for the North Koreans to swallow. It was especially insulting after Gorbachev had failed to visit Pyongyang at the time of his summit with Deng Xiaoping in May 1989, contrary to North Korean expectations. To the North Koreans, this was an unhappy replay of Khrushchev's no-show in 1958. Gorbachev was after all another Khrushchev, perhaps even worse.

Still, the Soviets did not want to abandon North Korea altogether. In September 1990, Shevardnadze traveled to Pyongyang in order to assure the North Koreans that the USSR was still their faithful ally. The North Koreans were deeply skeptical of Shevardnadze's message and harshly attacked recent Soviet behavior toward the Korean Peninsula. Shevardnadze gave DPRK foreign minister Kim Yŏng-nam his word "as a Party member" that the USSR had no intention of normalizing relations with Seoul.[100] It turned out that a Communist's promise did

---

98. Vladislav M. Zubok, *A Failed Empire: The Soviet Union in the Cold War from Stalin to Gorbachev* (Chapel Hill, NC: University of North Carolina Press, 2007), 299.

99. Bazhanov, "Soviet Policy toward South Korea," 86.

100. Oberdorfer, *The Two Koreas*, 204.

not count for much. Shevardnadze's rude treatment by his North Korean hosts contributed to his decision to push for an accelerated timetable for Soviet–South Korean normalization. Instead of normalizing relations on January 1, 1991 as the Soviets had originally planned, Seoul and Moscow normalized relations that very month—September 30, 1990. The North Korean media reacted with even more vitriol than they had when Hungary normalized relations with South Korea nineteen months earlier, attacking the Soviets for submitting to ugly "dollar diplomacy" and selling their socialist souls for filthy South Korean lucre.[101] This time, there was a tinge of desperation in North Korea's anger. A political earthquake was spreading across socialist Eurasia, and one ruling party after another was teetering on the brink of collapse. China itself had faced its most alarming political challenge in forty years of communist rule, and the future of communism as a political system was seriously in question. Within a year of Moscow's normalization of relations with South Korea there was no Soviet Union for North Korea to criticize, and the new Russian leader Boris Yeltsin made life even more difficult for the DPRK than had Gorbachev.

The Communist Collapse

In 1988 the USSR officially let go of its "satellites," renouncing the Brezhnev Doctrine established in the aftermath of the Soviet invasion of Czechoslovakia in 1968, and allowing each Soviet ally in Eastern Europe to go its own way (a policy dubbed "the Sinatra Doctrine" by Gorbachev's foreign ministry spokesman Gennadi Gerasimov). While pulling back from Eastern Europe, the USSR drastically reduced its economic and military aid to non-European allies, and repudiated its support for Third World revolution. Gorbachev visited Cuba in April 1989, where he formally renounced the "export of revolution or counter-revolution."[102] Following an agreement with the United States that they would both refrain from interfering in Afghanistan, Moscow began withdrawing its troops from that war-ravaged country in the spring of 1988 and removed all troops by mid-February 1989. Moscow's ally Vietnam did the same in Cambodia, which Hanoi had occupied since 1978. Vietnamese troop withdrawal began in April 1989 and was completed by the end of September.

The Soviet withdrawal from Afghanistan and Vietnamese withdrawal from Cambodia eliminated two of the "three obstacles" Beijing had insisted stood in the way of improved Sino-Soviet relations. Soviet troop reductions in Mongolia and

101. *Rodong Sinmun*, October 5, 1990.

102. Christopher Andrew and Vasili Mitrokhin, *The World Was Going our Way: The KGB and the Battle for the Third World* (New York: Basic Books, 2005), 477.

along the Chinese border eliminated the third, and by the spring of 1989 China and the USSR were moving rapidly toward ending their thirty-year schism.[103] In May 1989 Gorbachev went to Beijing to meet with the Chinese leadership and finalize the Sino-Soviet rapprochement. Gorbachev was the first top Soviet leader to make an official visit to China since Khrushchev in 1959. But his visit was completely overshadowed by massive political demonstrations in the Chinese capital. To avoid the tens of thousands of demonstrators protesting the Chinese communist regime, Gorbachev had to be smuggled through tunnels under Tiananmen Square to meet with Chinese leaders.[104] Three weeks after Gorbachev's visit to Beijing, the People's Liberation Army moved in on the Tiananmen Square protestors. The resulting bloodbath of June 4, 1989, shocked much of the world and caused many Western countries, including the United States, to ostracize China for a time. But the incident actually helped solidify the revived Sino-Soviet friendship, as Moscow continued to expand economic and even military ties to the PRC. From the vantage point of Pyongyang, the Sino-Soviet rapprochement was a mixed blessing at best. The reduction of tension between the two nuclear-armed communist giants made the situation in continental East Asia more secure, but it also eliminated the leverage Pyongyang had used so successfully to extract maximum concessions from China and the Soviet Union for thirty years. North Korea could no longer play off Moscow and Beijing against each other, but perhaps even more troubling was that China and the Soviet Union would no longer accuse the other of betraying North Korea by improving relations with the South. After May 1989, first the USSR and then China moved inexorably toward normalizing relations with Seoul.

Whether the Tiananmen Massacre was a failed popular uprising or, as the Beijing and Pyongyang authorities saw it, the successful suppression of counterrevolution, it was a disturbing sign of a communist government's weakening control. But events in Eastern Europe were far more shocking. On June 4, the day of the Tiananmen crackdown, Poland held its first democratic elections since the assertion of Communist Party rule, and the communists lost to the opposition Solidarity Party by a huge margin. Hungary followed, dissolving its Communist Party and declaring the end of the People's Republic in October. The Communist Party of Czechoslovakia relinquished power in November 1989, and Bulgaria's communists were ousted in early 1990. Albania's communists followed suit the next year, while Yugoslavia devolved into warring ethnic republics.

---

103. Qian Qichen, *Waijiao shiji* [Ten Episodes in Diplomacy] (Hong Kong: Sanlian shudian youxian gongsi, 2004), 24–29. Qian was foreign minister at the time.

104. Zhang Liang (comp.) and Andrew J. Nathan and Perry Link, eds., *The Tiananmen Papers* (New York: Public Affairs, 2001), 173; Zhao Ziyang, *Prisoner of the State: The Secret Journal of Premier Zhao Ziyang* (New York: Simon and Schuster, 2009), 25.

Two events in particular were chilling precedents for North Korea. One was the collapse of East Germany and its absorption into the West, which took effect in October 1990. Despite the differences between the two, both East Germany and North Korea had seen themselves playing similar roles as divided nations at the forefront of the struggle against imperialism in Europe and East Asia, respectively. East Germany's bloodless surrender to the West was the exact opposite of North Vietnam's military victory over Saigon fifteen years earlier. If Hanoi's success in unifying Vietnam on its own terms had made Kim Il Sung hopeful, even cocky, about North Korea's prospects vis-à-vis Seoul in the 1970s, East Germany's absorption into the German Federal Republic must have gravely worried Kim and the rest of the North Korean leadership. But even the North Koreans understood East Germany to be an artificial state propped up by Soviet arms and could argue that the DPRK had greater legitimacy and a more powerful nationalist base. More disturbing were the case of Romania and especially the fate of its leader Nicolae Ceausescu, one of Kim Il Sung's great admirers. Romania was no compliant Soviet "satellite" like East Germany. Ceausescu's Romania, like Kim's North Korea, was a state that espoused Marxist-Leninist socialism but preferred to follow its own course, independent of the USSR. Neither Romania nor North Korea had pursued "de-Stalinization" in the 1950s, and both emphasized an assertive nationalism (albeit complicated in Romania's case by its multiethnic society). And like Kim, Ceausescu had embarked on a kind of "dynastic socialism," placing his family members, including his wife Elena, in high political positions. Amidst the chaos of the disintegrating Romanian government, Nicolae and Elena Ceausescu were executed by members of their own security forces on Christmas Day 1989. Television footage of the Ceausescus' trial and of the couple's corpses were broadcast throughout the world—although not, of course, in North Korea.

The shock waves from Eastern Europe reached as far as the Mongolian People's Republic (MPR), the second oldest Marxist-Leninist state in the world after the Soviet Union and a country long close to the DPRK. The first peaceful protests against the communist-led regime took place in Ulan Bator on December 10, 1989. Three months later, after widespread antigovernment demonstrations and the emergence of new and vocal opposition parties, the ruling Mongolian People's Revolutionary Party resigned on March 9, 1990.[105] The new postcommunist Mongolian government normalized relations with Seoul on March 26, the same month Czechoslovakia, Romania, and Bulgaria established diplomatic relations with South Korea. Although it took another two years for the Mongolian

---

105. Morris Rossabi, *Modern Mongolia: From Khans to Commissars to Capitalists* (Berkeley: University of California Press, 2005), 1–29.

Republic to drop the word *People's* from its name, any socialist solidarity with North Korea had disappeared with Ulan Bator's recognition of the ROK.

Finally, even North Korea's closest ally China "betrayed socialism" by recognizing the Seoul government in 1992. Hu Yaobang's promise in 1985 that the PRC would not normalize relations with South Korea turned out to be as empty as Shevardnadze's word "as a Communist" in 1989. However, unlike the USSR, China attempted to mollify the North in the process and cushioned the blow to some extent. For example, as Moscow was turning openly toward diplomatic relations with Seoul in 1990, Beijing was careful to stress its militant solidarity and "blood-cemented friendship" with North Korea in its official media and in several exchanges of military delegations. China did not turn its back on its ally as completely as the Soviet Union had done, and partly as a result, Sino–North Korean relations remained relatively close after the end of the Cold War, avoiding the deep acrimony that colored relations between North Korea and Yeltsin's Russia in the 1990s. But in the end, China followed the Soviet path and normalized relations with Seoul on August 24, 1992. The Pyongyang regime was devastated. Its two major allies had recognized its archenemy, while the DPRK remained estranged from the United States and Japan.[106]

In the meantime the Soviet Union itself had disintegrated at the end of 1991, but not before Gorbachev cut off aid to North Korea and demanded payments for oil and other goods in hard currency at world market prices. Gorbachev's successor Yeltsin continued to take a hard line on North Korea and, while not cutting off diplomatic ties with Pyongyang altogether, essentially abandoned the North for deepening relations with the South. By the end of 1992 even socialist Vietnam, which North Korea had once seen as a kind of mirror of itself in Southeast Asia, had established diplomatic relations with Seoul. Except for a few distant friends such as Fidel Castro's Cuba—itself on the verge of economic collapse after the loss of Soviet aid—the old world of anti-imperialist socialist solidarity in which North Korea had been embedded for decades, however idiosyncratically, was now gone. North Korea was alone in the world, truly "self-reliant" for the first time.

North Korea with and against the World

"Our-Style Socialism"

The seemingly overnight collapse of Marxist-Leninist socialism, except for a few outposts in eastern Asia (China, North Korea, Vietnam, and Laos) and

---

106. Washington made some modest attempts at reaching out to North Korea in the late 1980s, and with Chinese encouragement American diplomats even began to meet with their North Korean counterparts in Beijing. But these initiatives did not get very far and were soon sidelined by American concerns over North Korea's nuclear program in the early 1990s. Oberdorfer, *The Two Koreas*, 192–96.

one in the Caribbean (Cuba) did not lead the North Korean regime to abandon its commitment to "socialism." On the contrary, North Korea declared its commitment to socialism stronger than ever. It merely defined its own type of socialism as uniquely Korean, not at all the same as the failed socialism in Eastern Europe. The DPRK therefore coined the phrase "our-style socialism" or "socialism of our style" (*urisik sahoechuŭi*) to define its political-ideological system in the early 1990s.[107] This was very different from Deng Xiaoping's "socialism with Chinese characteristics," which was a kind of de facto authoritarian capitalism. "Korean-style socialism" was almost the opposite: it totally rejected capitalist economic methods but emphasized social solidarity embedded in a fervent Korean nationalism. North Korean publications began to refer increasingly to the Korean "nation" or "race" (*minjok*, similar to the German *Volk*) as the basis of state legitimacy. This was not entirely new; North Korea had long claimed to be the true representative of the Korean *minjok*, in contrast to the American-loving traitors in the South. But the degree of emphasis on the *minjok*, and the disappearance of the old socialist term *people* (*inmin*), was a striking departure for North Korean propaganda and reinforced the idea of Juche, or self-reliance.

At the same time, the military appeared to rise in social prominence and political power. As the Hungarian Korea expert Karoly Fendler has observed, North Korea became more of a *yangban* society, to use the word for the traditional Korean elite: not in the Chosŏn meaning of an educated aristocracy, but in the original Koryŏ sense of "two groups" (*yang ban*) of leadership, civilian and military.[108] North Korea had been a militarized society from the beginning of the regime, but the newly isolated and defensive DPRK became militarized as never before. This military emphasis was reflected in new titles for North Korea's top two leaders. In December 1991 Kim Jong Il assumed North Korea's top military position as head of Korean People's Army, and on April 20, 1992, he was named "marshal" (*Wŏnsu*).[109] Kim Il Sung had been named "generalissimo" (*Taewŏnsu*) one week earlier, on April 13. The leadership succession to Kim Jong Il was fully consolidated by April 1992, and the younger Kim—despite his lack of any real military experience—would henceforth be known primarily by his military titles: as commander-in-chief (*Ch'oego saryŏnggwan*) in North Korean state media, in popular parlance simply "the general" (*Changgunnim*).

---

107. See Charles K. Armstrong, "'A Socialism of Our Style': North Korean Ideology in a Post-Communist Era," in Samuel S. Kim, ed., *North Korean Foreign Relations in the Post-Cold War Era* (New York: Oxford University Press, 1998), 41–43.

108. Author's interview with Karoly Fendler, Budapest, Hungary, July 2002.

109. *Rodong Sinmun*, April 21, 1992, 1.

Rejoining the World

North Korea had never been as isolated as many in the West believe, and even after its abandonment by Russia and the loss of its socialist allies in Eastern Europe, North Korea tried to make the best of a bad situation by rapidly normalizing relations with post-Soviet successor states and cultivating relations with Japan and the United States. Indeed Foreign Minister Kim Yŏng-nam had threatened Shevardnadze with recognizing the Soviet republics as independent in 1990, hoping that this threat would deter Soviet recognition of Seoul. Kim had even threatened Shevardnadze that North Korea would turn to Japan out of "racial solidarity" now that Moscow had abandoned "class solidarity"![110] Whether or not North Korea was serious about playing the "race card," Pyongyang did try to improve relations with Japan at the beginning of the 1990s. Liberal Democratic Party godfather Shin Kanemaru led the highest-profile group of Japanese Diet members ever to visit North Korea in a delegation to Pyongyang in September 1990, and for a time it looked like Tokyo would normalize relations with the DPRK, perhaps as a precursor for the United States to do likewise—just as Japan had normalized relations with Beijing in 1972 and the United States followed suit in 1978. North Korea seems to have made a strategic decision to improve ties with the United States around 1991, when it became clear that it could no longer rely on China and Russia for security.[111] But neither of these initiatives went very far: Japan-DPRK relations soon fell out over the issue of Korean "comfort women" in World War II and renewed North Korean fears of a revived Japanese militarism, while any prospect for improved relations with the United States was sidelined by emerging American suspicions that North Korea was attempting to develop nuclear weapons.

There was, however, positive movement in Pyongyang's relations with South Korea. Like 1972 and 1985, 1991 was a breakthrough year in North-South relations. In December 1991, at the end of the fifth in a series of high-level inter-Korean talks that had begun in 1990, Seoul and Pyongyang issued a "Basic Agreement on Reconciliation, Non-aggression, and Exchanges and Cooperation."[112] The "Basic Agreement" was the most important declaration of North-South cooperation and coexistence since the 1972 Joint Communiqué, and was far more detailed than the 1972 agreement had been. It was followed in February 1992 by a joint "Declaration of the Denuclearization of the Korean Peninsula."

---

110. Radchenko, "Russia and North Korea."

111. Selig S. Harrison, *Korean Endgame: A Strategy for Reunification and US Disengagement* (Princeton: Princeton University Press, 2002), inter alia.

112. Tae Hwan Kwak, "The United Nations and Reunification," in Young Whan Kihl, ed., *Korea and the World: Beyond the Cold War* (Boulder, CO: Westview Press, 1994), 306–7.

As part of the process of denuclearizing the Korean Peninsula, the United States withdrew its tactical nuclear weapons from South Korea. Even more dramatically, Pyongyang finally dropped its longstanding opposition to North and South Korea joining the United Nations as two separate states. North Korea had little choice in the matter. The ROK had told the North in 1990 that if Pyongyang did not agree with both Koreas joining the UN, Seoul would apply for membership on its own, and given the shift of world opinion to its favor South Korea's UN membership would probably be approved, leaving North Korea even more isolated. By the spring of 1991, the Soviet Union and China had declared their support for South Korea's entry into the UN. On May 27, the DPRK announced its reluctant agreement to join the United Nations as a separate state from the South. On September 17, 1991, the DPRK was admitted to the United Nations alongside the ROK.[113] Forty years after fighting a brutal war against the international body, North Korea had become a member of it. North Korea had symbolically joined the world. But in the aftermath of the communist collapse in Eastern Europe, amid growing signs of impeding economic crisis in the DPRK, while a potential confrontation with the United States over North Korea's nuclear program quietly brewed, it was not at all certain that North Korea could continue to exist much longer in the post–Cold War world.

---

113. Young Whan Kihl, "The Politics of Inter-Korean Relations: Coexistence or Reunification," in Kihl, *Korea and the World*, 135.

TYRANNY OF THE WEAK, TYRANNY OF THE STRONG

To be sure, in our world, there remain outposts of tyranny, and America stands with oppressed people on every continent, in Cuba, and Burma, and North Korea, and Iran, and Belarus, and Zimbabwe.

—Condoleezza Rice, 2005

The first post–Cold War decade was an unmitigated disaster for North Korea. Politically, the regime was isolated as never before. The Soviet Union was gone, and Boris Yeltin's Russia turned its back on North Korea as it sought closer relations with South Korea. China appeared more balanced in its relations with the two Korean regimes, but its interests had become increasingly congruent with Seoul and divergent from Pyongyang. Diplomatically, North Korea soon found itself at odds with the United States and the International Atomic Energy Agency over its nuclear program; by the spring of 1993 disagreements had become acute, and in the summer of 1994 the US and North Korea came to the brink of war over Pyongyang's nuclear activities.[1] Although the US–North Korea confrontation ultimately led to a nuclear freeze agreement in October 1994, crisis erupted anew in 1998 over North Korean missile tests. In 2002–3, a second US-DPRK nuclear confrontation led to the collapse of the 1994 agreement. In the midst of the 1994 crisis, Kim Il Sung died, and the country entered a period of mourning that almost paralyzed the political system for the next three years. Kim's death was soon followed by economic catastrophe. In 1995–96, a series of natural disasters, amidst a general collapse of the economy, tipped the North Korean food situation

---

1. A good analysis of the first nuclear crisis and the resulting US-DPRK agreement of October 1994 is Leon V. Sigal, *Disarming Strangers: Nuclear Diplomacy with North Korea* (Princeton: Princeton University Press, 1998). More of an "insiders' perspective" can be found in Joel Wit, Daniel Poneman, and Robert L. Gallucci, *Going Critical: The First North Korean Nuclear Crisis* (Washington, DC: Brookings Institution Press, 2005).

into full-scale famine.[2] Not surprisingly, many in the outside world expected an inevitable collapse of the DPRK.

North Korea did not collapse. In 1998, Kim Jong Il was reaffirmed as North Korea's leader, and the previous three years were consigned to history as an "Arduous March" by the DPRK media. At the end of the 1990s, abetted by a new government in Seoul committed to North-South engagement, the DPRK began to come out of its diplomatic isolation, normalizing relations with nearly every country in Western Europe, Southeast Asia, and Latin America, as well as with Canada, Australia, and New Zealand. Under Vladimir Putin, Russia attempted to mend fences with the DPRK, and Kim Jong Il visited China and Russia in 2001, his first official visits abroad as North Korean leader. In June 2000, Pyongyang hosted the first summit between the leaders of North and South Korea. In September 2002, in another unprecedented move, Kim Jong Il held a summit meeting with Japanese prime minister Koizumi. Meanwhile, the DPRK appeared to be moving toward reform in its economy, initiating a set of wage and price adjustments in July 2002. The one area that hadn't changed significantly was the hostility between North Korea and the United States.

No longer tied to calculations of superpower rivalry, the US–North Korean confrontation became less inhibited and more direct in the post–Cold War period, and also more of a priority for American leaders and policymakers, who had lost their global rival. Following the Soviet collapse, American security concerns shifted toward local conflicts and so-called "rogue states." Terms such as *rogue states* or *outlaw regimes* had entered the lexicon of US foreign policy in the late 1980s and became the main focus of national security in the 1990s.[3] As the political analyst Robert Litwak has put it, rogue states—defined as regional powers with aggressive intentions to upset the status quo, in pursuit or possession of weapons of mass destruction—in the new US national security doctrine reflected "the policy preferences of the United States as the post–Cold War era's pre-eminent power."[4] In effect, rogue states were regimes that did not play by the rules of international relations as defined by the United States as the world leader; more cynically, they were simply countries the United States did not like. This

---

2. Estimates of famine–related deaths between 1995 and 1999 (a period euphemistically referred to as a "food shortage" by the DPRK) vary widely, with some suggesting as many as 3 million of North Korea's 23 million people died. The most detailed publicly available work on this subject, by two American social scientists, suggests the famine killed around 600,000 people. Stephan Haggard and Marcus Noland, *Famine in North Korea: Markets, Aid, and Reform* (New York: Columbia University Press, 2007), 7.

3. Michael Klare, *Rogue States and Nuclear Outlaws: America's Search for a New Foreign Policy* (New York: Hill and Wang, 1995), 27.

4. Robert S. Litwak, *Rogue States and U.S. Foreign Policy: Containment after the Cold War* (Washington, DC: Woodrow Wilson International Center for Scholars, 2000), 47.

rogues' gallery usually included North Korea and Iraq at the top of the list, followed by Iran, Libya, and Syria.[5] The Pentagon's "two-war strategy" of the 1990s was clearly designed to thwart Iraq and North Korea; after the defeat of Saddam Hussein in the first Gulf War of 1990–91, the dispute over North Korea's nuclear program appeared to set the stage for a war in Northeast Asia as well.

In the event, war between the United States and North Korea was averted, and the October 1994 US-DPRK agreement established a framework for lessening tension and ultimately normalizing relations between Washington and Pyongyang. After several years of relative neglect, American attention was focused again on North Korea after the DPRK fired ballistic missiles over Japan in 1998, and in the fall of 2000, the two countries exchanged visits of high-level officials for the first time in their history. Secretary of State Madeleine Albright even announced that the term *rogue states* would be dropped from the official lexicon of US foreign policy, to be replaced by the less provocative "states of concern." Against all odds North Korea had survived to the twenty-first century, and appeared to be on the verge of a breakthrough in relations with its greatest enemy. But hopes for US-DPRK normalization would soon evaporate.

If a single event marked the end of the post–Cold War period and the beginning of a new and uncertain millennium, it was the terrorist attacks of September 11, 2001. September 11 hardly "changed everything," as many in the US administration insisted at the time.[6] But it gave US foreign policy a new focus of threat, one which seemed to justify an American military power that had lacked a global enemy since the end of the Cold War: worldwide terrorism. Yet, almost immediately after the Bush administration declared its "global war on terror," the old "rogue states" of the 1990s were conflated with the new terrorist threat in a way that justified American intervention but seemed to defy logic. This rhetorical conflation was neatly captured by the phrase "Axis of Evil" in Bush's January 2002 State of the Union address. Referring to Iran, Iraq under Saddam Hussein, and North Korea, Bush declared "states like these, and their terrorist allies, constitute an axis of evil, arming to threaten the peace of the world."[7]

Theocratic Iran, Ba'athist Iraq, and Communist North Korea were radically different kinds of regimes; the first two had fought a brutal eight-year war against

---

5. Klare, *Rogue States and Nuclear Outlaws*, 132.

6. No one insisted on this more forcefully than Vice President Dick Cheney. See for example Cheney's interview on *Meet the Press* one year later, in which he says, "And in a sense, sort of the theme that comes through repeatedly for me is that 9/11 changed everything. It changed the way we think about threats to the United States. It changed about our recognition of our vulnerabilities. It changed in terms of the kind of national security strategy we need to pursue, in terms of guaranteeing the safety and security of the American people." Available at http://www.msnbc.msn.com/id/3080244/.

7. "Bush State of the Union Address," http://transcripts.cnn.com/2002/ALLPOLITICS/01/29/bush.speech.txt.

each other, and the third was an impoverished country thousands of miles away. The three countries had little trust or cooperation among each other, nor did any of them have much if anything to do with Al Qaeda, the organization behind the September 11 attacks. North Korea may have been the least likely supporter of Islamist terrorism among the three, and had never directly threatened the United States. In fact, immediately after the September 11 attacks, the official DPRK news media expressed sympathy with the US, stating, "The very regretful and tragic incident reminds [us] once again of the gravity of terrorism. As a UN member the DPRK is opposed to all forms of terrorism and whatever support to it and this stance will remain unchanged."[8] Nevertheless, the Bush administration seemed determined to exploit 9/11 in order to take the offensive against North Korea and other "rogue regimes." In retrospect, it is clear that the main target of the Bush administration offensive was Iraq, with Iran a secondary target. North Korea, while viewed with deep hostility by the Bush administration, was peripheral to the main focus of the administration's foreign policy, which was the Middle East. Nevertheless, North Korea was explicitly mentioned in the 2002 National Security Strategy report as a threat to global and US security, based on Pyongyang's development of ballistic missiles and pursuit of "weapons of mass destruction." The Defense Department's Nuclear Posture Review of late 2001 had named North Korea as a potential target of nuclear attack in the event of hostilities on the peninsula. North Korean officials and media responded harshly to what they considered new gestures of hostility. A Foreign Ministry spokesman called the 2002 State of the Union speech "little short of declaring war against the DPRK," and accused the Bush administration of "political immaturity and moral leprosy."[9] Terrorism, North Korea declared, was something the United States brought on itself by its own belligerence: "Herein lie answers to questions as to why the modern terrorism is focused on the United States alone and why it has become serious while Bush is in office."[10] Not to be outdone in slandering a foreign leader, Bush told the author Bob Woodward "I loathe Kim Jong Il!" and referred to Kim as "a pygmy."[11] What limited trust had developed in eight years of engagement between the DPRK and the United States rapidly gave way to renewed recriminations and deepening antagonism.

In October 2002, the Bush administration decided to restart diplomatic dialogue with North Korea, on hold since the end of the Clinton years, by sending

---

8. Korean Central News Agency, "DPRK Stance towards Terrorist Attacks on U.S.," September 12, 2001. Available at http://www.kcna.co.jp/index-e.htm.

9. "DPRK Denounces Bush's Charges: Statement of FM Spokesman on Bush's State of the Union Address," *People's Korea*, February 9, 2002, 1.

10. Ibid.

11. Bob Woodward, *Bush at War* (New York: Simon and Schuster, 2002), 340.

Assistant Secretary of State James Kelly to Pyongyang. But far from signaling a diplomatic breakthrough, Kelly's visit became a forum for the United States to accuse the DPRK of violating the 1994 nuclear freeze by secretly enriching uranium for weapons use.[12] North Korea responded with denials and predictable outrage, and both sides declared the 1994 Agreed Framework to be null and void. As it had in 1993, North Korea threatened to withdraw from the Nuclear Non-Proliferation Treaty, only now it carried out the threat. The DPRK ejected the International Atomic Energy Agency inspectors, restarted the Yŏngbyŏn reactor, and announced that it would start reprocessing the spent fuel. Such steps nearly led the United States and North Korea to war in the summer of 1994, and threatened to do so again in the winter of 2002–3. This time, however, the United States was focused on war elsewhere: the invasion of Iraq.

The US-led invasion of Iraq in March 2003 was intended not only to "shock and awe" the Iraqi enemy, in the famous phrase of US military planners, but equally to cow other "rogue states" into submitting before American might. "Regime change" was the term of choice for the Bush administration's goals toward Iraq, Iran, North Korea, and other regimes hostile to the United States. This is not to suggest that the United States planned a military strike against North Korea, although some in the administration may have been considering such a move, but rather that the United States expected the Kim Jong Il regime to collapse under pressure. For example, the Pentagon's new war planning for Korea—pushed by many who had advocated the war in Iraq—included "Operations Plan 5030," intended to drain North Korea's military resources through flying surveillance planes closer to North Korean territory or expanding US-led military exercises in the region. This appeared to be "a strategy to topple Kim's regime by destabilizing its military forces," supposedly without leading to all-out war.[13] The risks of provoking such a war, soberly contemplated by the Clinton administration eight years earlier, seemed to have been forgotten.[14]

If the Iraq War was intended to help facilitate an end to the North Korean regime, it obviously failed. If it was intended to force North Korea to give up weapons of mass destruction, its effect was the exact opposite. Three weeks after the invasion of Iraq, the DPRK Foreign Ministry stated that "the Iraqi war shows that to allow disarming through inspection does not help avert war but rather

12. Gavan McCormack, *Target North Korea: Pushing North Korea to the Brink of Nuclear Catastrophe* (New York: Nation Books, 2004), 161.

13. Bruce B. Auster and Kevin Whitelaw, "Upping the Ante for Kim Jong Il: Pentagon Plan 5030, A New Blueprint for Facing Down North Korea," *U.S. News and World Report*, July 21, 2003. Available at http://www.usnews.com/usnews/news/articles/030721/21korea.htm.

14. In 1994, General Gary Luck, then commander of US forces in Korea, estimated that a war between the US and North Korea could kill 1 million people. Sigal, *Disarming Strangers*, 122.

sparks it. . . . Only a physical deterrence force, a tremendous military-deterrence force powerful enough to decisively beat back an attack . . . can avert war and protect the security of the country and the nation."[15] As the rapid toppling of the Saddam Hussein regime gave way to a protracted and brutal (and apparently unanticipated) counterinsurgency war in Iraq, the United States insisted on multilateral diplomacy over North Korea. Six-Party Talks involving North and South Korea, the United States, China, Russia, and Japan began in the summer of 2003. The talks proceeded in fits and starts, with significant agreements reached in 2005 and 2007 over the cessation of North Korea's nuclear program and improvement of relations between North Korea and the United States and Japan. But at the same time, North Korea appeared determined to move forward with its "tremendous military-deterrence force." In October 2006 the DPRK announced it had exploded a nuclear device. In May 2009, North Korea detonated a second device. The nuclear line had finally been crossed, but contrary to the warnings of the previous fifteen years, this did not bring on the apocalypse. The United Nations condemned both actions, and for the first time China and Russia both supported UN Security Council sanctions against the DPRK. Yet for all the condemnatory rhetoric and strongly-worded sanctions, the effect of international approbation on North Korea's weapons development, much less on the nature of North Korean regime, was minimal. North Korea had beaten the odds yet again. In the middle of the twentieth century, the DPRK (with much Chinese help) fought the United States to a standstill. In the first decade of the twenty-first century North Korea defied the whole world, including its former allies, and the result was again a stalemate.

Korea has been a vortex for conflict among rival empires for all of the "long twentieth century," ever since an expanding Japan went to war with a defensive China in 1894. The Sino-Japanese War was followed in short order by the Russo-Japanese War of 1904–5, followed in turn by Japan's colonization of Korea in 1910. Soon after the end of Japanese colonialism in 1945, North Korea and China—backed by the Soviet Union—fought US-led UN forces in the Korean War of 1950–53, the most destructive local conflict of the entire Cold War period.[16] Since the signing of the 1953 armistice, the Korean Peninsula has existed in a state of tension just short of war, with open conflict coming close to the surface at many points—1968 (the *Pueblo* Incident), 1976 (the Panmunjŏm "axe

---

15. Cited in Yoichi Funabashi, *The Peninsula Question: A Chronicle of the Second Korean Nuclear Crisis* (Washington, DC: Brookings Institution Press, 2007), 126.

16. The Vietnam War killed more Americans (58,000 versus 34,000), but over a longer period of time than the Korean War. Korean and Vietnamese casualties were probably comparable, over 2 million for each (although estimates vary widely), and thousands of Chinese died in the Korean War, which has no equivalent in Vietnam.

murder" incident), 1994 (the first nuclear crisis), 2002 (the second nuclear crisis), and 2010 (the North Korean shelling of Yŏnpyŏng Island in South Korea), among others.

Of course, long before the twentieth century Korea had fallen victim to the imperial aggrandizement of its neighbors. Until the Korean War, the most destructive invasions on the Korean Peninsula were those of the Mongols in the thirteenth century and the Japanese at the end of the sixteenth. But these were relatively isolated events. Contrary to common wisdom, including that of many Koreans, the history of Korea is not one of constant invasion and victimization. Rather, a close examination of Korean history over the last thousand years or so reveals a remarkably stable polity with relatively unchanging boundaries, a deep-rooted cultural integrity, and until 1910, an almost unbroken record of independence. Korea's geographical position, first between continental East Asian empires and Japan, later at the confluence of Russian and American interests as well, has made it the center of regional rivalry and conflict many times in its history. On the other hand, Korea's peninsular geography and its history of largely independent development has made it very difficult to be absorbed for long into any neighboring imperial formation. This distinguishes Korea from other similar points of interimperialist conflict such as the Middle East, the Balkans, or Poland, which became fragmented or disappeared as distinct polities for long periods of time.

North Korea, like South Korea, is heir to this long history of independence and resistance to imperial incorporation. South Korea, too, has practiced at times a highly successful policy of extraction and manipulation vis-à-vis its superpower backer, the United States. Indeed, forty years of almost unqualified economic, military, and political support by the Americans of successive authoritarian regimes in the Seoul—regimes the United States often privately criticized but rarely publicly condemned—reflects in part South Korea's own "tyranny of the weak." But in the tactics of the weak manipulating the strong, North Korea had two advantages over the South. First, North Korea benefitted from the rivalry of two major supporters, the USSR and China. There was no equivalent for South Korea—Japan remained a subordinate player under American hegemony in East Asia, and unlike China kept any Great Power pretensions firmly suppressed. Second, North Korea's internal structure enabled it to insist on autonomy and resist interdependence with regional or global political economies, unless it was on its own terms. South Korea, despite deeply illiberal practices from the foundation of the republic in 1948 until the democratization of the late 1980s, could not avoid market-oriented economic interdependence or the rhetoric (and eventually the practice) of liberal democracy. North Korea faced no such constraints. The DPRK articulated a policy of Juche not long after the Korean War and made it the centerpiece of its ideology a decade later. After the collapse of North

Korea's communist allies at the end of the Cold War, "self-reliance" had to face the bitter test of reality, and hundreds of thousands of North Koreans died in the process. The world had changed radically, but North Korea refused to change with it, and insisted on following its own path: fiercely nationalist, militant, self-enclosed. What little remained of Marxism-Leninism was finally abandoned for a guiding principle of "military-first politics" (sŏn'gun chŏngch'i).[17] The death of North Korea's second leader, Kim Jong Il, in 2011 did not result in any fundamental change in the nature and leadership of the regime, and power was passed on quickly to Kim Jong Il's own son Kim Jong Un. Within months of Kim Jong Il's death, the third-generation heir to North Korea's Kim family regime appeared firmly in charge.

What can we call such a regime? North Korea no longer seems categorizable into a twentieth-century "type," whether that type be totalitarian, communist, Stalinist, or corporatist. Its peculiarities and pathologies are more deeply rooted than these now-defunct political systems. Perhaps it is worth reexamining here the notion of "tyranny," despite (or even because of) the moral and emotional connotations the term evokes. Tyranny (from the Greek tyrannos—"sovereign, master") is one of the oldest terms in Western political philosophy. Aristotle understood tyranny as "the rule of one for his own advantage or aggrandizement rather than for the common good."[18] Thucydides argued that the "tyrant's first thought was always for himself, for his own personal safety, and for the greatness of his own family."[19] North Korea, ruled by successive Kims for over sixty years, is a "family state" as Stalin's USSR and Mao's China never were. It is possible that at one time Kim Il Sung believed his rule was for the benefit of the common good; perhaps even his son believed so, and his grandson after him. But in light of the unimaginable suffering the North Korean people have endured in recent decades, it is hard to understand the actions of North Korea's core elite as being intended for anyone's benefit but their own. Despotism, defined as absolute rule by a small, close-knit elite, accurately describes the regime but seems far too mild a term.[20]

---

17. "Military-First Ideology is a Precious Sword of Sure Victory for National Sovereignty," Rodong Sinmun, April 3, 2003, 1.

18. Mark Blitz, "Tyranny, Ancient and Modern," in Toivo Koivukoski and David Edward Tabachnick, eds., Confronting Tyranny: Ancient Lessons for Global Politics (Lanham, MD: Rowman & Littlefield, 2005), 11.

19. David Edward Tabachnick, "Tyranny Bound," in Koivukoski and Tabachnick, Confronting Tyranny, 28.

20. The sociologist Daniel Chirot describes tyranny as a particularly abusive form of despotism and usefully compares North Korea and Ceausescu's Romania as two parallel Stalinist-cum-corporatist tyrannies. See Chirot, Modern Tyrants: The Power and Prevalence of Evil in Our Age (New York: Free Press, 1994), 2–9, 231–35.

In the decade after the end of World War II, the University of Chicago political scientist Leo Strauss tried to revive the analysis of tyranny. Although the study of tyranny was "as old as political science itself," Strauss argued, "when we were brought face to face with tyranny—with a kind of tyranny that surpassed the boldest imagination of the most powerful thinkers of the past—our political science failed to recognize it."[21] Strauss's target was a "value-free" social science that refused to make moral judgments on the societies it analyzed, preferring bland, neutral, and "scientific" typologies. According to Strauss, modern political science traced its origins to Machiavelli, specifically *The Prince*, which made no distinction between the king and the tyrant. Strauss decried not just the brutal tyrannies of the Nazis and the communists, but also the relativism and creeping nihilism of Western liberalism. Tyranny, Strauss seemed to suggest, is best confronted and defeated by something stronger than liberalism.

The link between Strauss and the so-called "neoconservatives" that became influential during the Bush administration—former students such as Assistant Secretary of Defense Paul Wolfowitz, and others with less direct connections to Strauss—has been the subject of considerable debate.[22] If there is such a connection, the heirs of Leo Strauss seem to have taken very seriously his admonishment to recognize tyranny. But the neoconservative solution was an absolute, black-or-white, Manichean struggle for "an end to evil," in the words of David Frum—the speechwriter who coined the term "axis of evil" for George W. Bush.[23] It was a peculiarly American crusading moralism that was far removed from Strauss's own measured philosophical inquiries. In a lengthy exchange with the French philosopher Alexandre Kojève, Strauss acknowledged that "under certain conditions the abolition of tyranny may be out of the question. The best one could hope for is that the tyranny be improved, i.e., that the tyrannical rule be exercised as little inhumanely or irrationally as possible."[24] Such nuances had little place in the assertive foreign policy of the first George W. Bush administration, and in the views of its neoconservative supporters. In the early 2000s "United States Empire" became a common phrase, especially on the American right, used positively and

---

21. Leo Strauss, *On Tyranny*, rev. ed. (New York: Free Press, 1991), 22–23.

22. See especially Anne Norton, *Leo Strauss and the Politics of American Empire* (New Haven: Yale University Press, 2004). Mark Lilla has argued that some members of the "Straussian school" of political science have indeed gravitated toward Republican politics in Washington, but primarily in the administrations Reagan and Bush Sr. rather than that of George W. Bush, and played more of a role in formulating neoconservative ideology than implementing policy. Lilla, "Leo Strauss: The European," *New York Review of Books* 51, no. 16 (October 21, 2004).

23. David Frum and Richard Perle, *An End to Evil: How to Win the War on Terror* (New York: Random House, 2003).

24. Strauss, *On Tyranny*, 187.

unironically for the first time in nearly two hundred years.[25] The United States had unprecedented power in the world, and therefore—advocates of American empire asserted—could remake the world unimpeded.[26] The neoconservative project appeared intent on putting into practice Thucydides' famous phrase that I cited in the introduction, "the strong do what they have the power to do and the weak accept what they have to accept."[27]

It might be useful at this point to remember the context of Thucydides' statement, the so-called "Melian Dialogue" in *The Peloponnesian Wars*. About midway through this conflict, the island of Melos was one of the few Aegean states not to take sides in the struggle between Athens and Sparta, although the Melians were descendents of Spartan colonizers. They resisted Athenian overtures in 426 BC, and ten years later Athens sent a multinational coalition, consisting of a fleet of some thirty ships, to force Melos into an alliance. The "dialogue" between the Athenian commanders and the leaders of Melos was not a negotiation, but a set of demands and responses to those demands. Neutrality, the Athenians insisted, was not an option—much as George W. Bush would later declare "you're either with us or against us." Given such a disparity of power, opposition was simply irrational; hence the remark about the strong and the weak. In the end, the Melians continued to refuse, and the Athenians lay siege to the city. A few successful insurgencies provoked greater reinforcements from Athens, and finally Melos surrendered unconditionally. The Athenians killed all military-age Melian males, sold off the children and women as slaves, and made Melos an Athenian colony.[28]

As the political theorist Herfried Münkel suggests, the Melian dialogue shows us the "incompatibility of an imperial logic with the expectations of a small power in relations with a larger power. Athens did not accept the wish of the Melians to be acknowledged as an equal power."[29] I have tried to show in this book that North Korea has defied all "imperial logics" since the Korean War began. Its

---

25. A veritable deluge of books critiquing "American empire" poured out in the first half of the 2000s, representing a wide swath of political views and disciplinary approaches. See among others Andrew J. Bacevich, *American Empire: The Realities and Consequences of US Diplomacy* (Cambridge: Harvard University Press, 2002); Michael Mann, *Incoherent Empire* (London: Verso, 2003); David Harvey, *The New Imperialism* (Oxford: Oxford University Press, 2003); Chalmers Johnson, *The Sorrows of Empire: Militarism, Secrecy, and the End of the Republic* (New York: Metropolitan Books, 2004); and Niall Ferguson, *Colossus: The Price of America's Empire* (New York: Penguin Press, 2004). While authors disputed the positive value of an American empire, most agreed it was unsustainable.

26. In a phrase attributed to a "senior advisor" to the President Bush, "We're an empire now, and when we act, we create our own reality." Ron Suskind, "Faith, Certainty, and the Presidency of George W. Bush," *New York Times Magazine*, October 17, 2004.

27. Thucydides, *The Peloponnesian Wars*, trans. Rex Warner (New York: Penguin Books, 1972), 402.

28. Ibid., 400–408.

29. Herfried Münkel, *Empires: The Logic of World Domination from Ancient Rome to the United States*, trans. Patrick Camiller (Cambridge, MA: Polity Press, 2007), 15.

goal has been to be "acknowledged as an equal power," whether by its communist patrons or by the United States. The core issue has been sovereignty, which the DPRK takes as absolute and indivisible. North Korea's refusal to comply with American demands demonstrates how even the most powerful nation the world has ever seen cannot shape the world entirely in its own image. This defiance has provoked condemnation not only from the Americans, but even from North Korea's former supporters in the UN Security Council. Yet, the greater danger in this conflict may come not from North Korea but from the United States. Carl Schmitt, Strauss's contemporary and sometimes debating partner,[30] believed that conflicts between nations were endemic, and that an "enemy" was both normal and necessary for the sovereign state. But he feared the global consequences of a state justifying its actions on the basis of universal principles, turning the enemy into "an outlaw of humanity." Under the guise of ridding humanity once and for all of evil, "a war waged to protect or expand economic power must, with the aid of propaganda, turn into a crusade and into the last war of humanity."[31]

The first George W. Bush administration seemed determined to carry out such a crusade and sought to remove inconvenient states like Iraq, Iran, and North Korea from the face of the earth. The realities of war in Iraq and Afghanistan, not to mention the crisis of the world financial system, were sobering lessons on the limitations of American military power to promote and maintain US global dominance. By the middle of the century's first decade, the dream of unfettered American domination over the world was already being reconsidered by some of its earlier advocates.[32] Even in the military realm, where America far outstrips any potential rival, the United States has proven vulnerable to organizations and states employing new technologies of "asymmetric warfare," from suicide bombing to improvised explosive devices. Unilateral global power is also undermined by nuclear proliferation. Once the monopoly of the strong, nuclear weapons are now increasingly the weapons of the weak as well; even puny North Korea can deter the mighty United States with a handful of bombs. This creates a grim kind of leveling of the international playing field, in which politics, not military might, must resolve outstanding problems, even between the most unequal of enemies. North Korea may indeed by an "outpost of tyranny," as Condoleezza Rice said in her 2005 inauguration as secretary of state, but it is also a country

---

30. See Leo Strauss, "Notes on Carl Schmitt, *The Concept of the Political*," in Carl Schmitt, *The Concept of the Political*, trans. and with an Introduction by George Schwab (1932; reprint Chicago: University of Chicago Pres, 1996), 97–122.

31. Schmitt, *Concept of the Political*, 79.

32. David Rieff, "The Beginning of the End of the Adventure," *New York Times Magazine*, August 6, 2006, 11–12.

with a long history of maneuvering for advantage, and even survival, in the face of overwhelming odds. Such a confrontational approach to the world may not have been in the best interest of the DPRK in the long run, and certainly has not done much to benefit the lives of ordinary people there, but North Korea—like all countries—acts on the basis of historical experience. A tyranny of the weak, like that of the strong, comes at a great cost.

ARCHIVAL SOURCES

Bauhaus Archives. Dessau, Germany.

Center for Korean Research, Columbia University. Soviet documents on Korea from the Russian Presidential Archives, Archives of the CPSU Central Committee, USSR Ministry of Foreign Affairs, General Staff of the USSR Armed Forces, and USSR Ministry of Defense, 1946–50.

Dandong Korean War Museum. Dandong, Jilin, People's Republic of China.

Federal Republic of Germany, Ministry of Foreign Affairs (MfAA). Political Archives of the German Democratic Republic. Materials on Korea, 1951–71.

Federal Republic of Germany, Federal Archives. Archives of Party and Mass Organizations of the German Democratic Republic (SAPMO-BA). Materials on Korea, 1949–90.

Foreign Policy Archive of the Russian Federation (AVPRF). Materials on Korea, 1953–73.

Hoover Institution, Stanford University. Alfred Conner Bowman Papers, box 1.

People's Republic of China, Ministry of Foreign Affairs. *Zhongguo waijiaobu jiemi dangan* (Archives of China's Ministry of Foreign Affairs, Declassified Diplomatic Files), 1949–65.

Russian State Archive of Contemporary History (RGANI). Materials on Korea, 1953–73.

United Nations Archives, New York.

United States National Archives and Records Administration. Record Group 59, "Records of the Department of State."

United States National Archives and Records Administration. Record Group 242, "National Archives Collection of Foreign Records Seized, 1941–, Records Seized by U.S. Military Forces in Korea," Shipping Advices 2005–2013.

United States National Archives and Records Administration. Record Group 497, box 464. Headquarters, 181st Counter-Intelligence Corps Detachment, 1st Marine Division, Fleet Marine Force. "Communist Indoctrination of North Korean Civilian Populace," 30 November 1950.

United States National Archives and Records Administration. United States Army, Record Group 319, *Intelligence Summaries—North Korea* (1946–51).

United States National Archives and Records Administration. United States Army, Far East Command. Allied Translator and Interpreter Section (ATIS). Korean documents, 1945–50.

PUBLISHED DOCUMENT COLLECTIONS

Nam-buk Han kwan'gye saryojip [Historical Materials on South-North Korean Relations]. 22 vols. Seoul: National Institute of Korean History, 1995.

Sŏ Tae-suk [Dae-Sook Suh]. *Puk Han munhŏn yŏngu: munhŏn kwa haeje* [A Study of North Korean Documents: Documents and Analysis], 6 vols. Seoul: Institute for Far Eastern Studies, Kyungnam University, 2004.

SECONDARY SOURCES IN WESTERN LANGUAGES

Agamben, Giorgio. *Homo Sacer: Sovereign Power and Bare Life*. Trans. Daniel Heller-Roazen. Stanford: Stanford University Press, 1998.

Andrew, Christopher, and Vasili Mitrokhin. *The World Was Going our Way: The KGB and the Battle for the Third World*. New York: Basic Books, 2005.

Appleman, Roy E. *South to the Naktong, North to the Yalu*. Washington, DC: Office of the Chief of Military History, Department of the Army, 1961.

———. *Disaster in Korea: The Chinese Confront Macarthur*. College Station, TX: Texas A&M University Press, 1989.

Armstrong, Charles K. *The North Korean Revolution, 1945–1950*. Ithaca: Cornell University Press, 2003.

Arrighi, Giovanni. *The Long Twentieth Century: Money, Power, and the Origins of Our Times*. London: Verso, 1994.

Bailey, Sidney D. *The Korean Armistice*. New York: St. Martin's 1992.

Bajanov, Evgueni. "Assessing the Politics of the Korean War, 1949–1951." *Cold War International History Project Bulletin* 6–7 (winter 1995/96): 41, 87–91.

Bartelson, Jens. *A Genealogy of Sovereignty*. Cambridge: Cambridge University Press, 1995.

Bradley, Martin. *Under the Loving Care of the Fatherly Leader: North Korea and the Kim Dynasty*. New York: St. Martin's Griffin, 2006.

Buzo, Adrian. *The Guerilla Dynasty: Politics and Leadership in North Korea*. Boulder, CO: Westview Press, 1999.

Cheong, Seong Chang. *Ideologie et systeme en Corée du nord: de Kim Il-Sông a Kim Chông-il*. Paris: L'Harmattan, 1997.

Chernov, I. F., et al., eds. *Otnosheniia Sovetskogo Soiuza s narodnoi Koreeii, 1945–1980: Dokumenty i materialy* [On the Soviet Union and People's Korea, 1945–1980: Documents and Materials]. Moscow: Nauka, 1981.

Chon, Tuk Chu. *Die Beziehungen zwischen der DDR und der Koreanischen Demokratischen Volksrepublik, 1949–1978*. Munich: Minerva, 1982.

Chung, Chin O. *Pyongyang between Peking and Moscow: North Korea's Involvement in the Sino-Soviet Dispute, 1958–1975*. Tuscaloosa: University of Alabama Press, 1978.

Chung, Joseph S. *The North Korean Economy: Structure and Development*. Stanford: Hoover Institution Press, 1974.

Clark, Mark W. *From the Danube to the Yalu*. New York: Harper, 1954.

Clough, Ralph. *Embattled Korea: The Rivalry for International Support*. Boulder, CO: Westview Press, 1987.

Crane, Conrad C. *American Airpower Strategy in Korea, 1950–1953*. Lawrence: University Press of Kansas, 2000.

Cumings, Bruce. *The Origins of the Korean War*. Vol. 2. *The Roaring of the Cataract: 1947–1950*. Princeton: Princeton University Press, 1990.

Eberstadt, Nicholas, and Judith Banister. *The Population of North Korea*. Berkeley: University of California, 1992.

Eberstadt, Nicholas, Marc Rubin, and Albina Tretyakova. "The Collapse of Soviet and Russian Trade with the DPRK, 1989–1993: Impact and Implications." *Korean Journal of National Reunification* 4 (1995) : 87–104.

Edkins, Jenny, Nalini Persram, and Veronique Pin-Fat, eds. *Sovereignty and Subjectivity*. Boulder, CO: Lynne Reiner, 1999.

Everlasting Fraternal Friendship: The Great Leader Comrade Kim Il Sung's Official Goodwill Visits to the Soviet Union and Other European Socialist Countries. Pyongyang: Foreign Languages Publishing House, 1984.

Fendler, Karoly. "Economic Assistance from Socialist Countries to North Korea in the Postwar Years, 1953–1963." In Han S. Park, ed., *North Korea: Ideology, Politics, Economy*. Englewood Cliffs, NJ: Prentice Hall, 1996.

Foot, Rosemary. *A Substitute for Victory: The Politics of Peacemaking at the Korean Armistice Talks*. Ithaca: Cornell University Press, 1990.

Fox, Annette Baker. *The Power of Small States: Diplomacy in World War II*. Chicago: University of Chicago Press, 1959.

Frank, Andre Gunder. *Reorient: Global Economy in the Asian Age*. Berkeley: University of California Press, 1998.

Frank, Ruediger. *Die DDR und Nordkorea: Der Wiederaufbau der Stadt Hamhung von 1954–1962*. Aachen: Shaker, 1996.

Futrell, Robert F. *The United States Air Force in Korea, 1950–1953*. New York: Duell, Sloan, and Pearce, 1961.

Gaddis, John Lewis. *We Now Know: Rethinking Cold War History*. Oxford: Clarendon Press, 1997.

Gills, Barry K. *Korea versus Korea: A Case of Contested Legitimacy*. London: Routledge, 1996.

Ginsburgs, George, and Roy U.T. Kim. *Calendar of Diplomatic Affairs, Democratic People's Republic of Korea, 1945–1975*. Moorestown, NJ: Symposia Press, 1977.

Goncharov, Sergei N., John W. Lewis, and Litai Xue. *Uncertain Partners: Stalin, Mao, and the Korean War*. Stanford: Stanford University Press, 1993.

Haas, Michael E. *In the Devil's Shadow: UN Special Operations during the Korean War*. Annapolis, MD: Naval Institute Press, 2000.

Halliday, Jon, ed. *The Artful Albanian: Memoirs of Enver Hoxha*. London: Chatto & Windus, 1986.

Handel, Michael I. *Weak States in the International System*. London: Frank Cass, 1981.

Hanley, Charles J. *The Bridge at No Gun Ri: A Hidden Nightmare from the Korean War*. New York: Henry Holt, 2001.

Harding, Neil. *Leninism*. Durham, NC: Duke University Press, 1996.

Harrison, Hope M. "Ulbricht and the Concrete 'Rose': New Archival Evidence on the Dynamics of Soviet–East German Relations and the Berlin Crisis, 1958–1961." *Cold War International History Project Working Paper* No. 5 (May 1993).

Harrison, Selig. *Korean Endgame: A Strategy for Reunification and U.S. Disengagement*. Princeton: Princeton University Press, 2002.

Hasegawa, Tsuyoshi, ed. *The Cold War in East Asia, 1945–1991*. Stanford: Stanford University Press, 2011.

Haslam, Jonathan. *Russia's Cold War: From the October Revolution to the Fall of the Wall*. New Haven: Yale University Press, 2011.

Hinsley, F. H. *Sovereignty*. 2d ed. Cambridge: Cambridge University Press, 1986.

Hunt, Michael. *The Genesis of Chinese Communist Foreign Policy*. New York: Columbia University Press, 1996.

Hunter, Helen-Louise. *Kim Il-song's North Korea*. Westport, CT: Praeger, 1999.

Immortal Juche Idea. Pyongyang: Foreign Languages Publishing House, 1979.

Institute of Oriental Studies, USSR Academy of Sciences. *Koreiskaia Narodno-Demokraticheskaia Respublika* [Korean People's Democratic Republic]. Moscow: USSR Academy of Sciences, 1954.

Johnston, Alastair I. *Cultural Realism: Strategic Culture and Grand Strategy in Ming China*. Princeton: Princeton University Press, 1995.

Jones, Robert A. *The Soviet Concept of "Limited Sovereignty" from Lenin to Gorbachev*. New York: St. Martin's Press, 1990.

Joy, C. Turner. *How Communists Negotiate*. Santa Monica: Fidelis, 1970.

———. *Negotiating while Fighting: The Diary of Admiral C. Turner Joy at the Korean Armistice Conference.* Stanford: Hoover Institution Press, 1978.

Kapitsa, Mikahil S. *Na Raznykh Parallelyakh: Zapiski Diplomata* [At Different Latitudes: Notes of a Diplomat]. Moscow: Kniga i biznes, 1996.

Kim, Georgii Fedorovich. *Proletarskii Internatsionalizm i Revoliutsii v stranakh Vostoka* [Proletarian Internationalism and Revolutions in the East]. Moscow: USSR Academy of Sciences, Institute of Oriental Studies, 1972.

Kim, Key-Hiuk. *The Last Phase of the East Asian World Order: Korea, Japan, and the Chinese Empire, 1860–1882.* Berkeley: University of California Press, 1980.

Kim Il Sung. *For the Independent Peaceful Reunification of Korea.* New York: International Publishers, 1975.

———. *On the Juche Idea.* New York: The Guardian, 1980.

———. *Works.* Pyongyang: Foreign Languages Publishing House, 1980.

Kim, Ilpyong J. *Historical Dictionary of North Korea.* Lanham, MD: Scarecrow Press, 2003.

Kiyosaki, Wayne. *North Korean Foreign Relations: The Politics of Accommodation, 1945–1975.* New York: Praeger, 1976.

Korea Institute of Military History. *The Korean War.* Vol. 1. Lincoln: University of Nebraska Press, 2000.

Koschmann, J. Victor. *Revolution and Subjectivity in Postwar Japan.* Chicago: University of Chicago Press, 1996.

Lankov, Andrei. *From Stalin to Kim Il Sung: The Formation of North Korea, 1945–1960.* New Brunswick, NJ: Rutgers University Press, 2002.

———. *Crisis in North Korea: The Failure of De-Stalinization, 1956.* Honolulu: University of Hawai'i Press, 2005.

Latham, Robert. *The Liberal Moment: Modernity, Security, and the Making of the Postwar International Order.* New York: Columbia University Press, 1997.

Lee, Chae-Jin. *China and Korea: Dynamic Relations.* Stanford: Hoover Institution Press, 1996.

Lee, Chong-sik. *The Politics of Korean Nationalism.* Berkeley: University of California Press, 1963.

———. *The Korean Workers' Party: A Short History.* Stanford: Hoover Institution Press, 1978.

Lee, Mun Woong. *Rural North Korea Under Communism: A Study of Sociocultural Change.* Rice University Studies in Behavioral Science. Vol. 62, no. 1. Houston: Rice University, 1976.

Leffler, Melvyn P. *A Preponderance of Power: National Security, the Truman Administration, and the Cold War.* Stanford: Stanford University Pres, 1992.

Leitenberg, Milton. "New Russian Evidence on the Korean War Biological Warfare Allegations: Background and Analysis." *Cold War International History Project Bulletin* 11 (winter 1998): 185–99.

Lerner, Mitchell B. *The Pueblo Incident: A Spy Ship and the Failure of American Foreign Policy.* Lawrence: University Press of Kansas, 2002.

Li, Xiaobing, Allan R. Millett, and Bin Yu, trans. and eds. *Mao's Generals Remember Korea.* Lawrence: University Press of Kansas, 2001.

Lim Un. *The Founding of a Dynasty in North Korea: An Authentic Biography of Kim Il-song.* Tokyo: Jiyu-sha, 1982.

Lüthi, Lorenz. *The Sino-Soviet Split: Cold War in the Communist World.* Princeton: Princeton University Press, 2008.

MacDonald, Callum A. *Korea, the War before Vietnam.* London: Macmillan, 1986.

Malcolm, Ben S., with Ron Martz. *White Tigers: My Secret War in North Korea.* Washington, DC: Brassey's, 1996.

Mansourv, Alexandre Y. "Communist War Coalition Formation and the Origins of the Korean War." Ph.D. diss., Columbia University, 1997.

May, Ernest R. ed. *American Cold War Strategy: Interpreting NSC 68*. Boston: Bedford Books, 1993.

Medvedev, Vadim A. *Raspad: kak on nazreval v "mirovoi sisteme sotzializma"* [Collapse: How it Happened in the "World Socialist System"]. Moscow: Mezhdunarodnye Otnosheniia, 1994.

Merrill, John. *Korea: The Peninsular Origins of the War*. Newark: University of Delaware Press, 1989.

Mommsen, Wolfgang J. *Theories of Imperialism*. Chicago: University of Chicago Press, 1982.

Morris-Suzuki, Tessa. *Exodus to North Korea: Shadows from Japan's Cold War*. Lanham, MD: Roman & Littlefield, 2007.

Muth, Ingrid. *Die DDR-Aussenpolitik, 1949–1972: Inhalte, Strukturen, Mechanismen*. Berlin: Ch. Links Verlag, 2001.

Myers, Brian. *Han Sŏrya and North Korean Literature: The Failure of Socialist Realism in the DPRK*. Ithaca: Cornell University, 1994.

Nam, Koon-Woo. *The North Korean Communist Leadership, 1945–65: A Study on Factionalization and Political Consolidation*. Tuscaloosa: University of Alabama Press, 1974.

Natsios, Andrew. *The Great North Korean Famine*. Washington, DC: Institute of Peace Press, 2001.

Nie Rongzhen. *Inside the Red Star: The Memoirs of Marshal Nie Rongzhen*. Beijing: New World Press, 1988.

Noland, Marcus. *Avoiding the Apocalypse: The Future of the Two Koreas*.Washington, DC: Institute for International Economics, 2000.

Oberdorfer, Don. *The Two Koreas: A Contemporary History*. Rev. ed. New York: Basic Books, 2001.

Oh, Kongdan, and Ralph C. Hassig. *North Korea through the Looking Glass*. Washington, DC: Brookings Institution Press, 2000.

O Tuathail, Gearoid. *Critical Geopolitics: The Politics of Writing Global Space*. Minneapolis: University of Minnesota Press, 1996.

Park, Han S. *North Korea: The Politics of Unconventional Wisdom*. Boulder, CO: Lynne Rienner, 2002.

Park, Phillip. *Self-reliance or Self-destruction? Success and Failure of the Democratic People's Republic of Korea's Development Strategy of Self-reliance "Juche."* New York: Routledge, 2002.

Peng Dehai. *Memoirs of a Chinese Marshall: The Autobiographical Notes of Peng Dehuai*. Trans. Zheng Longpu. Beijing: Foreign Languages Publishing House, 1984.

Radchenko, Sergey. *Two Suns in the Heavens: The Sino-Soviet Struggle for Supremacy, 1962–1967*. Stanford: Stanford University Press, 2009.

Riley, John W. Jr., and Wilbur Schramm. *The Reds Take a City: The Communist Occupation of Seoul*. New Brunswick, NJ: Rutgers University Press, 1951.

Rothstein, Robert L. *Alliances and Small Powers*. New York: Columbia University Press, 1968.

Sassen, Saskia. *Losing Control? Sovereignty in an Age of Globalization*. New York: Columbia University Press, 1996.

Scalapino, Robert, and Chong-Sik Lee. *Communism in Korea*. 2 vols. Berkeley: University of California Press, 1972.

Scharder, Charles R. *Communist Logistics in the Korean War*. Westport, CT: Greenwood Press, 1995.

Shen, Zhihua, and Danhui Li. *After Leaning to One Side: China and Its Allies in the Cold War*. Stanford: Stanford University Press, 2011.

Siebs, Benno-Eide. *Die Aussenpolitik der DDR 1976–1989: Strategien und Grenzen*. Paderborn, Germany: Ferdinand Schoeningh, 1999.

Snyder, Scott. *Negotiating on the Edge: North Korean Negotiating Behavior* Washington, DC: US Institute of Peace, 1999.

Spruyt, Hendrik. *The Sovereign State and Its Competitors*. Princeton: Princeton University Press, 1994.

SSSR i Koreia [USSR and Korea]. Moscow: USSR Academy of Sciences, 1988.

Stephanson, Anders. "Stalin's Hyper-Realism." *Diplomatic History* 25, no. 1 (winter 2001): 129–39.

Stueck, William. *The Korean War: An International History*. Princeton: Princeton University Press, 1995.

——. *Rethinking the Korean War: A New Diplomatic and Strategic History*. Princeton: Princeton University Press, 2002.

Suh, Dae-Sook. *Korean Communism, 1945–1980: A Reference Guide to the Political System*. Honolulu: University of Hawaii Press, 1981.

——. *Kim Il Sung: The North Korean Leader*. New York: Columbia University Press, 1988.

Szalontai, Balázs. *Kim Il Sung in the Khrushchev Era: Soviet-DPRK Relations and the Roots of North Korean Despotism, 1953–1964*. Stanford: Stanford University Press, 2005.

Taubman, William. *Khrushchev: The Man and His Era*. New York: W. W. Norton, 2003.

Torkunov, A. V. *Zagadochnaia Voina: Koreiskii konflikt 1950–1953 gg.* [Secret War: The Korean Conflict, 1950–1953]. Moscow: Rosspyen, 2000.

Underwood, Horace G. *Korea in War, Revolution, and Peace: The Recollections of Horace G. Underwood*. Seoul: Yonsei University Press, 2001.

The U.S. Imperialists Started the Korean War. Pyongyang: Foreign Languages Publishing House, 1977.

Vital, David. *The Survival of Small States: Studies in Small Power/Great Power Conflict*. London: Oxford, 1971.

Volkogonov, Dmitri. *Autopsy for an Empire: The Seven Leaders Who Built the Soviet Regime*. Ed. and trans. Harold Shukman. New York: Simon & Schuster, 1998.

Weathersby, Kathryn. "New Russian Documents on the Korean War: Introduction and Translations by Kathryn Weathersby." *Cold War International History Project Bulletin* 6–7 (winter 1995/96): 30–84.

——. "Deceiving the Deceivers: Moscow, Beijing, Pyongyang, and the Allegations of Bacteriological Weapons Use in Korea." *Cold War International History Project Bulletin* 11 (winter 1998): 176–85.

——. "'Should We Fear This?' Stalin and the Danger of War with America." *Cold War International History Project Working Paper* No. 39 (July 2002).

Westad, Odd Arne, ed. *Brothers in Arms: The Rise and Fall of the Sino-Soviet Alliance, 1945–1963*. Stanford: Stanford University Press, 1998.

Williams, William J., ed. *A Revolutionary War: Korea and the Transformation of the Postwar World*. Chicago: Imprint Publications, 1993.

Wolff, David. "'One Finger's Worth of Historical Events': New Russian and Chinese Evidence on the Sino-Soviet Alliance and Split, 1948–1959." Cold War International History Project Working Paper No. 30 (August 2000).

Zhai, Qiang. *China and the Vietnam Wars, 1950–1975*. Chapel Hill: University of North Carolina Press, 2000.

Zhang, Shu Guang. *Mao's Military Romanticism: China and the Korean War, 1950–1953*. Lawrence: University Press of Kansas, 1995.

Zhang, Xiaoming. *Red Wings over the Yalu: China, the Soviet Union, and the Air War in Korea.* College Station: Texas A&M University Press, 2002.

Zhao, Suisheng. *Power Competition in East Asia: From the Old Chinese World Order to Post–Cold War Regional Multipolarity.* New York: St. Martin's, 1997.

Zubok, Vladislav. "The Khrushchev-Mao Conversations, 31 July—3 August 1958 and 2 October 1959." *Cold War International History Project Bulletin* 12–13 (fall/winter 2001): 244–72.

——. *A Failed Empire: The Soviet Union in the Cold War from Stalin to Gorbachev.* Chapel Hill: University of North Carolina Press, 2007.

Zubok, Vladislav, and Constantine Pleshakov. *Inside the Kremlin's Cold War: From Stalin to Khrushchev.* Cambridge: Harvard University Press, 1996.

SECONDARY SOURCES IN KOREAN, CHINESE, AND JAPANESE

Academy of Military Science, Research Division for Military History. *Kang-Mei Yuan-Chao zhanzhengshi* [History of the Resist-America Aid-Korea War]. 3 vols. Beijing: Junshi kexue chubanshe, 2000.

Academy of Military Science, Research Division for Military History, ed. *Zhongguo renmin zhiyuanjun Kang-Mei Yuan-Chao zhanshi.* [History of the Chinese People's Volunteers Resist-American Aid-Korea War]. Beijing: Junshi kexue chubanshe, 1999.

An Ch'an-il. *Chuch'e sasang ŭi chongŏn: chŏnt'ong sasang ŭi suyon ŭl chungsim ŭro* [Juche Ideology and Traditional Thought]. Seoul: Uryu Munhwasa, 1997.

Bazhanova, Natalia. *Kiroe sŏn Puk Han kyŏngje* [North Korean Economy at the Crossroads]. Translation of *Vneschneekonomicheskie sviazi KNDR: v poiskah vyhoda iz tupika.* Trans. Yang Chu-yong. Seoul: Hanguk kyŏngje sinmunsa, 1992.

Chai Chengwen and Zhao Yongtian. *Banmendian Tanpan* [Panmunjŏm Negotiations]. Beijing: Jiefangjun chubanshe, 1989.

Chinese Military Affairs Museum, ed. *Kang-Mei Yuan-Chao zhanzheng jishi* [Account of the Resist-America Aid-Korea War]. Beijing: Jiefangjun chubanshe, 2000.

Chŏng Kyu-sŏp. *Puk Han oegyoŭi ŏjewa onŭl* [North Korean Foreign Relations Yesterday and Today]. Seoul: Ilsinsa, 1997.

Hong Xuezhi. *Kang-Mei Yuan-Chao zhanzheng huiyi* [Recollections of the Resist-America Aid-Korea War]. Beijing: Jiefangjun wenyi chubanshe, 1991.

Hwang Chang-yŏp. *Nanŭn yŏksaŭi chillirŭl poatta: Hwang Chang-yŏp hoegorok* [I Have Seen the Truth of History: Memoirs of Hwang Chang-yŏp]. Seoul: Hanul, 1999.

Kim Il-sŏng [Kim Il Sung]. *Kim Il-sŏng chŏnjip* [Complete Works of Kim Il Sung]. Pyongyang: Chosôn Nodongdang Ch'ylp'ansa, 1992.

Kim Sŏng-bo. *Nam-Puk Han kyŏngje kujoŭi kiwŏn kwa chŏngae: Puk Han Nongŏp ch'ejeŭi hyŏngsŏngŭl chungsimŭro* [Origins and Development of North and South Korean Economic Structures]. Seoul: Yŏksa pipyŏngsa, 2000.

Kim Yŏn-chŏl. *Puk Hanŭi sanophwawa kyŏngjejŏngch'aek* [Industrialization and Economic Policy in North Korea]. Seoul: Yŏksa pip'yŏngsa, 2001.

Kim Yong-ho. *Hyŏndae Puk Han oegyoron* [Contemporary North Korean Foreign Relations]. Seoul: Orum, 1996.

Ko Rim. *Chuch'e ch'ŏrhak immun* [Introduction to Juche Philosophy]. N.p., 1988.

Korea Institute of Military History. *Hanguk chŏnjaengsaŭi saeroun yŏngu* [New Research on Korean War History]. Seoul: Ministry of National Defense, Korea Institute of Military History, 2002.

Paek Sŭng-jong. *Tongdok top'yŏnsu Ressel ŭi Puk Han ch'uok* [East German Architect Ressel's North Korean Reminiscences]. Seoul: Hyohyŏng ch'ulp'ansa, 2000.

Pak Myŏng-nim. *Hanguk chŏnjaengŭi palbal kwa kiwŏn* [The Outbreak and Origins of the Korean War]. 2 vols. Seoul: Nanam, 1997.

———. *Hanguk 1950: Chŏnjaeng kwa p'yŏnghwa* [Korea 1950: War and Peace]. Seoul: Nanam, 2002.

Pak T'ae-ho. *Chosŏn Minjujuŭi inmin konghwaguk taewae kwangyesa* [History of the Foreign Relations of the Democratic People's Republic of Korea]. 2 vols. Pyongyang: Saehoe Kwahak Ch'ulp'ansa, 1985.

Pak Yong-gŏn. *Chuch'e sasang immun* [Introduction to Juche Ideology]. Tokyo: Kuwŏl Sŏbang, 1989.

Peng Dehui nianpu [Chronology of Peng Dehuai]. Beijing: Renmin chubanshe, 1998.

Shen Zhihua. *Zhong-Su tongmeng yu Chaoxian zhanzheng yanjiu* [The Sino-Soviet Alliance and the Korean War]. Guilin: Guangxi Normal University Press, 1999.

———. *Zhong-Su tongmeng de jingji beijing, 1948–1953* [Economic Background of the Sino-Soviet Alliance, 1948–1953]. Hong Kong: Hong Kong Institute of Asia-Pacific Studies, Chinese University of Hong Kong, 2000.

Sim Chi-yŏn. *Sanjongeparŭl maego: Nongch'on Yi Ku-yŏng sŏnsaengŭi saeroan iyagi* [Mooring the Ship to the Mountaintop: New Conversations with Yi Ku-yŏng]. Seoul: Kaemasŏwŏn, 1998.

Soryŏn kunsagomundanjang Razubayev ŭi 6.25 chŏnjaeng pogosŏ [The Korean War Memoirs of Soviet Military Advisory Group Commander Razubayev]. 4 vols. Seoul: Ministry of National Defense, Research Institute for Military History, 2001.

Wada Haruki. *Chōsen Sensō Zenshi* [Complete History of the Korean War]. Tokyo: Iwanami, 2002.

Yang Fengan and Wang Tiancheng. *Beiwei sanshibaduxian: Peng Dehuai yu Chaoxian zhanzheng* [North of the 38th Parallel: Peng Dehuai and the Korean War]. Beijing: Jiefangjun chubanshe, 2000.

Yang Sŏng-ch'ŏl and Kang Sŏng-hak, eds. *Puk Han oegyo chŏngch'aek* [The Foreign Policy of North Korea]. Seoul: Seoul Press, 1995.

Yang You. *Zai zhiyuanjun silingbu de wanyueli* [In the General Headquarters of the People's Volunteers]. Beijing: Jiefangjun chubanshe, 1998.

Yi Chong-sŏk. *Hyŏndae Puk Hanŭi ihae* [Understanding Contemporary North Korea]. Seoul: Yŏksa pip'yŏngsa, 2000.

———. *Puk Han-Chungguk kwanggye, 1945–2000* [North Korean-Chinese Relations, 1945–2000]. Seoul: Chungsim, 2000.

Zhou Enlai Nianpu [Chronology of Zhou Enlai]. 3 vols. Beijing: Zhongang wenpian chubanshe, 1997.

Zhu Ping. *Zai zhiyuanjun zongbu* [With the Volunteer Army]. Beijing: Jiefangjun chubanshe, 1989.

Index

Studies of the Weatherhead East Asian Institute
Columbia University

SELECTED TITLES

(Complete list at http://www.columbia.edu/cu/weai/weatherhead-studies.html)

The Nature of the Beasts: Empire and Exhibition at the Tokyo Imperial Zoo, by Ian J. Miller. University of California Press, 2012.

Redacted: The Archives of Censorship in Postwar Japan, by Jonathan E. Abel. University of California Press, 2012.

Asia for the Asians: China in the Lives of Five Meiji Japanese, by Paula Harrell. MerwinAsia, 2012.

The Art of Censorship in Postwar Japan, by Kirsten Cather. University of Hawai'i Press, 2012.

Occupying Power: Sex Workers and Servicemen in Postwar Japan, by Sarah Kovner. Stanford University Press, 2012.

Empire of Dogs: Canines, Japan, and the Making of the Modern Imperial World, by Aaron Herald Skabelund. Cornell University Press, 2011.

Russo-Japanese Relations, 1905–17: From Enemies to Allies, by Peter Berton. Routledge, 2011.

Realms of Literacy: Early Japan and the History of Writing, by David Lurie. Harvard University Asia Series, 2011.

Planning for Empire: Reform Bureaucrats and the Japanese Wartime State, by Janis Mimura. Cornell University Press, 2011.

Passage to Manhood: Youth Migration, Heroin, and AIDS in Southwest China, by Shao-hua Liu. Stanford University Press, 2010.

Imperial Japan at Its Zenith: The Wartime Celebration of the Empire's 2,600th Anniversary, by Kenneth J. Ruoff. Cornell University Press, 2010.

Behind the Gate: Inventing Students in Beijing, by Fabio Lanza. Columbia University Press, 2010.

Postwar History Education in Japan and the Germanys: Guilty Lessons, by Julian Dierkes. Routledge, 2010.

The Aesthetics of Japanese Fascism, by Alan Tansman. University of California Press, 2009.

The Growth Idea: Purpose and Prosperity in Postwar Japan, by Scott O'Bryan. University of Hawai'i Press, 2009.

National History and the World of Nations: Capital, State, and the Rhetoric of History in Japan, France, and the United States, by Christopher Hill. Duke University Press, 2008.

Leprosy in China: A History, by Angela Ki Che Leung. Columbia University Press, 2008.

Kingdom of Beauty: Mingei and the Politics of Folk Art in Imperial Japan, by Kim Brandt. Duke University Press, 2007.

Mediasphere Shanghai: The Aesthetics of Cultural Production, by Alexander Des Forges. University of Hawai'i Press, 2007.

Modern Passings: Death Rites, Politics, and Social Change in Imperial Japan, by Andrew Bernstein. University of Hawai'i Press, 2006.

The Making of the "Rape of Nanjing": The History and Memory of the Nanjing Massacre in Japan, China, and the United States, by Takashi Yoshida. Oxford University Press, 2006.